FINANCIAL INSTITUTIONS AND SERVICES

REGULATION AND COMPETITION IN THE TURKISH BANKING AND FINANCIAL MARKETS

FINANCIAL INSTITUTIONS AND SERVICES

Additional books in this series can be found on Nova's website
under the Series tab.

Additional E-books in this series can be found on Nova's website
under the E-book tab.

BANKING AND BANKING DEVELOPMENTS

Additional books in this series can be found on Nova's website
under the Series tab.

Additional E-books in this series can be found on Nova's website
under the E-book tab.

FINANCIAL INSTITUTIONS AND SERVICES

REGULATION AND COMPETITION IN THE TURKISH BANKING AND FINANCIAL MARKETS

TAMER ÇETIN
AND
FUAT OĞUZ
EDITORS

Nova Science Publishers, Inc.
New York

Copyright © 2012 by Nova Science Publishers, Inc.

All rights reserved. No part of this book may be reproduced, stored in a retrieval system or transmitted in any form or by any means: electronic, electrostatic, magnetic, tape, mechanical photocopying, recording or otherwise without the written permission of the Publisher.

For permission to use material from this book please contact us:
Telephone 631-231-7269; Fax 631-231-8175
Web Site: http://www.novapublishers.com

NOTICE TO THE READER

The Publisher has taken reasonable care in the preparation of this book, but makes no expressed or implied warranty of any kind and assumes no responsibility for any errors or omissions. No liability is assumed for incidental or consequential damages in connection with or arising out of information contained in this book. The Publisher shall not be liable for any special, consequential, or exemplary damages resulting, in whole or in part, from the readers' use of, or reliance upon, this material. Any parts of this book based on government reports are so indicated and copyright is claimed for those parts to the extent applicable to compilations of such works.

Independent verification should be sought for any data, advice or recommendations contained in this book. In addition, no responsibility is assumed by the publisher for any injury and/or damage to persons or property arising from any methods, products, instructions, ideas or otherwise contained in this publication.

This publication is designed to provide accurate and authoritative information with regard to the subject matter covered herein. It is sold with the clear understanding that the Publisher is not engaged in rendering legal or any other professional services. If legal or any other expert assistance is required, the services of a competent person should be sought. FROM A DECLARATION OF PARTICIPANTS JOINTLY ADOPTED BY A COMMITTEE OF THE AMERICAN BAR ASSOCIATION AND A COMMITTEE OF PUBLISHERS.

Additional color graphics may be available in the e-book version of this book.

Library of Congress Cataloging-in-Publication Data

Regulation and competition in the Turkish banking and financial markets / editors, Tamer Getin, Fuat Oguz.
    p. cm.
 Includes index.
 ISBN 978-1-61324-990-1 (hardcover)
 1. Banks and banking--Turkey. 2. Finance--Turkey. I. Getin, Tamer. II. Oguz, Fuat, 1969-
 HG3256.5.A6R44 2011
 332.109561--dc23
               2011018773

Published by Nova Science Publishers, Inc. † New York

CONTENTS

Preface		vii
Contributors		ix
Part I	**Introduction: The Political Economy of Turkey**	
Chapter 1	Introduction to the Turkish Banking and Financial Markets *Tamer Çetin and Fuat Oğuz*	3
Chapter 2	Transformation of the Turkish Economy: An Overview *Necmiddin Bağdadioğlu and Ergül Halisçelik*	15
Chapter 3	Property Rights Issue and Rent Seeking in Turkey: A Time Series Study with Cointegration and Error Correction Techniques for the Period of 1960-2002 *Dilek Demirbas and Safa Demirbas*	33
Part II	**Transition to Regulatory State in the Turkish Banking System**	
Chapter 4	The Structure and Regulation of Turkish Banking System: 2000-2010 *Gülsün Gürkan Yay and Turan Yay*	49
Chapter 5	Restructuring and Market Structure of the Turkish Banking Sector *Münür Yayla*	93
Chapter 6	Deregulation and Entry Performance in Turkish Banking *Ihsan Isik and Lokman Gunduz*	121
Chapter 7	Deposit Insurance and Bank Resolution in Turkey Regulation and Experience *Ridvan Cabukel and Sanem Frisch*	141
Chapter 8	Interaction between Payment Services and Credit Services in Credit Card Markets *G. Gulsun Akin, Ahmet Faruk Aysan, Gultekin Gollu and Levent Yildiran*	163

Part III	**Regulation of Financial Markets in Turkey**	
Chapter 9	Turkish Capital Market Regulation *Guray Kucukkocaoglu and Cemal Kucuksozen*	**179**
Chapter 10	Efficiency and Productivity of the Brokerage Houses in Turkey *Necmiddin Bağdadioğlu, Mehmet Reşit Dinçer* *and Ahmet Burçin Yereli*	**201**
Chapter 11	Institutional Investors in Turkey *Ayhan Algüner*	**225**
Name Index		**247**
Subject Index		**249**

PREFACE

This book presents a detailed analysis of the Turkish banking and financial markets. The emphasis of the book is on the interrelations between competition and regulation. The author's hope is to draw attention to the close relationship between the regulatory environment and the nature of the competition in the banking and financial markets in Turkey. Also, this book looks into various aspects of the banking and financial markets and the authors discuss the relationships between regulatory environment and competition in the industry.

Chapter 1 – In the banking industry, better institutions starts with the nature and performance of the independent regulatory authority. In Turkey, the Banking Regulatory and Supervisory Authority (BRSA) regulates and supervises the industry and is responsible over the efficient and healthy working of the industry. This introductory chapter looks into the relative position of the independent regulatory agency in the industry. The authors discuss whether the agency should have broad powers and regulate potential risks more aggressively, or act more passively by restraining itself. This chapter will also provide a ground for other chapters which are more empirical in nature and address specific issues.

Chapter 2 – The transformation process of the Turkish economy from an import substituting economy to export based economy initiated in 1980 was interrupted several times by either external (in 1997/1998 and 2008) or internal crisis (in 1994 and 2000/2001). In each case, the transformation plan was revised as required around its fundamentals, identified in the Washington Consensus, to face the challenges. The recent global financial crises of 2008 provided the last testing ground for the political and economic flexibility of not only the Turkish government but also other governments to face external as well as internal instabilities. The Turkish response so far regarded as quite successful. The continuity of this success, however, will largely be dependent on the Turkish government's adjustment of the structural transformation in line with the changes in the world economy.

Chapter 3 – The property rights issue is one of the most important institutional differences between democratically developed and developing countries. In most of the cases, the violation of the property rights results with rent-seeking activities. In this chapter, Katz and Rosenberg's budgetary variable model has been tested in a time series study for the period of 1960 to 2002 to measure rent-seeking activities in Turkey.

Chapter 4 – The aim of this study is to discuss the structure, problems and regulation of Turkish Banking System during the 2000s. In this context, this chapter first analyzes the structural and cyclical reasons behind the Turkish financial crisis experience in 2000-2001.

Secondly, the restructuring and regulation process of the Turkish Banking System in the post-crisis period is examined. The impact of the stand-by arrangement with IMF on this process and the degree of adaptation of the available legal framework to the international banking principles (Basel 1 and Basel 2) will be especially clarified. Lastly, it is argued that the decisive maintenance of this restructuring and regulation process up to 2010 is the main reason why the Turkish Banking system was relatively unaffected from the global financial crisis in 2008.

Chapter 5 – Banking sector has a complex and close interaction with other economic units. Recent global financial crisis has once again shown that troubles in this sector have repercussions on the whole economy. Between 1990 and 2000 there have been several episodes of financial turmoil in Turkey. In fact the most severe financial crisis occurred during November 2000 and February 2001 which clearly had profound effects on both regulatory environment and market structure of the sector. Following this crisis, the structure of the regulatory environment was altered in order to create an efficient and stable banking sector. As a result of this regulatory change, the sector experienced a sharp change from instability towards financial soundness. After the restructuring of the sector by means of relevant regulatory and institutional set up, the main characteristics of the Turkish banking system can be identified as rehabilitation, growth, foreign participation and financial stability.

Chapter 6 – The newly chartered domestic and foreign banks constituted about half of the Turkish banking industry at the turn of the past century. This record number of new entries is the by-products of deregulatory reforms launched in the 1980's and onward. In this chapter, the authors investigate the productivity performance of these new banks vis-à-vis that of old banks in an era of financial deregulation in Turkey. Employing a non-stochastic inter-temporal production frontier approach over a period of sixteen years, the authors found that new banks are significantly superior to old banks in resource utilization. Apparently, not hampered by a legacy of inefficiency from the past, new banks could operate nearer the efficiency frontier. Moreover, new banks register faster productivity, technology and efficiency growth than old banks. Equipped with better and newer technology, local partners for foreign entries and holding affiliation for domestic entries appear to have helped these young banks to overcome initial asymmetric information problems and demonstrate higher performance. The authors' overall results suggest that new entries, especially from more advanced markets, could be instrumental in boosting resource allocation and utilization in banking.

Chapter 7 – An examination of various financial crises experienced in different parts of the world shows that, among the measures taken in terms of post-crisis restructuring, establishing new deposit insurance schemes and empowering existing ones play a major part in maintaining confidence and stability in financial systems. For example, the financial crisis of the 1930s in the US was the catalyst that led to the establishment of Federal Deposit Insurance Corporation (FDIC), and the savings and loan crisis of 1980s led to increased authority vested in the FDIC to resolve the assets of failed institutions through the Resolution and Trust Corporation (RTC). The authors observe similar developments in countries including Japan, Korea and Russia after the Asian crisis of 1998. The recent global economic crisis triggered international organizations including the International Association of Deposit Insurers (IADI), the Bank for International Settlements (BIS) and the International Monetary Fund (IMF) to work collaboratively and set internationally accepted best practices for deposit insurance and bank resolution regimes. In Turkey, the Savings Deposit Insurance Fund

(SDIF) acquired new mandates such as receivership after the economic crisis of 1994 and became an independent agency with additional tools including the ones for the recovery of bank assets after the banking crisis of 2001. This chapter will provide information about the SDIF's deposit insurance and resolution practices and the legal grounds associated with it.

Chapter 8 – Credit card markets are complicated structures where two different services, payment services and credit services, are provided. The Turkish credit card market has recently undergone two important regulations: one on payment services in November 2005 and the other on credit services in June 2006. As these two service markets have externalities on each other, regulating one may have unintended consequences on the other. In this regard, their chapter aims to shed light on the link between these two service markets by investigating the revenues from each of them: the non-interest and interest revenues. Estimating the interest and non-interest revenues of banks simultaneously in a 3SLS framework, the authors examine the effects of the regulations on payment services and credit services. Their results indicate that the regulations on payment services had no significant impact on banks' revenues, whereas the regulations on credit services affected the interest and non-interest revenues in opposite directions. Reacting to stifled interest revenues, banks shifted their focus toward non-interest revenues. Looking at the results, they suggest careful consideration of the possible effects on all segments of a credit card market when a regulatory action is planned. Moreover, from the response of revenues to changing prices in these two service markets, the authors infer that the demand in the Turkish credit card market is inelastic.

Chapter 9 – The securities market in Turkey is supervised by the Capital Markets Board of Turkey (CMBT). The principal statute governing the securities market is the Capital Market Law No 2499. The subject of this law is to regulate and control the secure, transparent and stable functioning of the capital market and to protect the rights and benefits of investors with the purpose of ensuring an efficient and widespread participation by the public in the development of the economy through investing savings in the securities market. This law contains regulations with respect to company and shareholder disclosure obligations, admission to listing and trading of listed securities, public tender offers and insider dealing, among other things. CMBT monitors compliance with these regulations and aiming to achieve international best practices, and encourage market-integrity through clear and self-enforcing rules of the game while encouraging the game itself. Within the framework of investor protection and moving the capital market forward and to be a major source of medium and long term finance, laws and regulations assist the CMBT to perform its role in maintaining market integrity and meeting fairness and transparency principles. The objective of this chapter is to examine the current developments and their effect on changes in capital market regulations and to provide conceptual understanding and in-depth knowledge of securities laws and the regulatory framework concerning capital markets in Turkey.

Chapter 10 – This chapter calculates the efficiency and productivity of 63 Brokerage Houses operating in Turkey by applying the well known methodology of Data Envelopment Analysis to the most recent data available covering the period between 2000 and 2008. The findings clearly depict the adverse impacts of both the domestic financial crisis of 2001 and the global financial crisis of 2008 on the Turkish Brokerage Sector as very low efficiency scores and declining productivity. The main sources of inefficiency and poor productivity during the period, however, appear to be originated from managerial incompetency at individual brokerage houses level, and dominance of banks at the financial sector level.

Chapter 11 – Securities mutual funds, pension mutual funds, life insurance companies, real estate investment trusts, venture capital investment trusts, securities investment trusts are the types of institutional investors that have operations in Turkey. Mutual funds are established in the form of open-end investment companies in Turkey. They do not have any legal entity. They are operated in terms of the rules stated in the internal statute of the fund, which includes general terms about management of the fund, custody of the assets, valuation principles and conditions of investing in the fund. The ratio of the investment funds' portfolio size to GDP is an indicator of the development level of the institutional investor base in that country. Although the ratio of the investment funds to GDP in Turkey has increased through the years, it is considered to be low when compared with other countries. There are two major classes of mutual funds in Turkey; fixed income and equity. Fixed income funds are the leading group, constituting 2/3 of total assets. Equity mutual funds represent only 2.5% of total assets. On the other hand, the private pension system that was introduced towards the end of 2003 has been growing exponentially. It is required to make the investment fund legislation coherent with European Union Directives and to provide the integration of European fund market and Turkish funds. Investment trusts are closed-end investment companies managing portfolios composed of capital market instruments, gold and other precious metals. Three types of investment trusts operate in Turkey, namely; Securities Investment Trusts, Real Estate Investment Trusts and Venture Capital Investment Trusts. As of the end of 2009, 48% of Istanbul Stock Exchange companies' shares which are open to public are in the custody accounts of foreign institutional investors at The ISE Settlement and Custody Bank Inc.

CONTRIBUTORS

G. Gulsun Akin
Bogazici University, Turkey

Ayhan Algüner
Baskent University, Turkey

Ahmet Faruk Aysan
Bogazici University, Turkey

Necmiddin Bağdadioğlu
Hacettepe University, Turkey

Rıdvan Çabukel
Savings Deposit Insurance Fund of Turkey, Turkey

Tamer Çetin
Yildiz Technical University, Turkey

Dilek Demirbaş
New Castle Business School, England

Safa Demirbaş
TASIS, Turkey

Mehmet Reşit Dinçer
Turkish Court of Accounts, Turkey

Sanem Frisch
Savings Deposit Insurance Fund of Turkey, Turkey

Gultekin Gollu
University of Wisconsin, USA

Lokman Gunduz
Central Bank of Republic of Turkey, Turkey

Ergül Halisçelik
Republic of Turkey Prime Ministry Undersecretariat of Treasury, Turkey

Ihsan Isik
Rowan University, USA

Guray Kucukkocaoglu
Baskent University, Turkey

Cemal Kucuksozen
Capital Markets Board of Turkey, Turkey

Fuat Oğuz
Baskent University, Turkey

Gülsün Yay
Yildiz Technical University, Turkey

Turan Yay
Yildiz Technical University, Turkey

Munur Yayla
Banking Regulatory Supervision Agency, Turkey

Ahmet Burçin Yereli
Hacettepe University, Turkey

Levent Yildiran
Bogazici University, Turkey

PART I. INTRODUCTION: THE POLITICAL ECONOMY OF TURKEY

In: Regulation and Competition in the Turkish Banking…
Editors: Tamer Çetin and Fuat Oğuz

ISBN: 978-1-61324-990-1
© 2012 Nova Science Publishers, Inc.

Chapter 1

INTRODUCTION TO THE TURKISH BANKING AND FINANCIAL MARKETS

Tamer Çetin[1] and Fuat Oğuz[2]***

[1]Yildiz Technical University, Department of Economics, Istanbul, Turkey
[2]Baskent University, Department of Economics, Ankara, Turkey

ABSTRACT

This book presents a detailed analysis of the Turkish banking and financial markets. The emphasis of the book is on the interrelations between competition and regulation. We hope to draw attention to the close relationship between the regulatory environment and the nature of the competition in the banking and financial markets in Turkey.

Banking sector in Turkey has faced a radical transformation for the last decade. The 2001 financial crisis was an opportunity to reform the industry and increase the regulatory authority over banks in order to reduce possible banking crisis. Because of post-2001 efforts by the regulatory authority, the banking industry fared relatively well during the crisis of 2008. The sector was tightly regulated and watched by the regulator, there was not any new entry and banks were relatively well-positioned against the risks. Naturally, this safety net came with its own social costs. An oligopolistic market structure created monopoly rents for banks and wealth transfers from consumer. The regulator's attitude was decisive in this framework.

This book looks into various aspects of the banking and financial markets and discuss relationships between regulatory environment and competition in the industry. Economists widely believe that better institutions provide better performance. A better institutional framework ensures a credible commitment and reduces political transaction costs of regulatory processes. This discourages rent seeking and encourages wealth-enhancing profit seeking activity. The banking reform in Turkey aimed to establish a better regulatory environment to reduce moral hazard problems in the industry. It also intended to minimize the negative effects of another financial crisis. After the 2008 financial crisis, this policy seemed to be a prudent one. By reducing the level of

---

* tcetin@yildiz.edu.tr.

** foguz@baskent.edu.tr.

competition and transferring some of the risk to consumers, banks did well during and after the financial meltdown.

In the banking industry, better institutions starts with the nature and performance of the independent regulatory authority. In Turkey, the Banking Regulatory and Supervisory Authority (BRSA) regulates and supervises the industry and is responsible over the efficient and healthy working of the industry. This introductory chapter looks into the relative position of the independent regulatory agency in the industry. We discuss whether the agency should have broad powers and regulate potential risks more aggressively, or act more passively by restraining itself. This chapter will also provide a ground for other chapters which are more empirical in nature and address specific issues.

There are alternative methods of studying the relationship between banking performance and regulatory power. First, an interpretive analysis of regulations may be presented. Another is running empirical tests of key variables such as tightness of regulation and efficiency in banking. A survey is also usually used in investigating the link. In economies such as Turkey, institutional factors explain more than empirical testing of variables. Institutional analysis provides a theoretical model to systematically study the influence of regulatory governance, regulatory structure and banking performance.

The major determinant of the efficiency of restrictions is the institutional structure. In Turkey, for example, full deposit insurance through government ownership encouraged banks *and* costumers to take excessive risks. In these cases, a strict regulation and supervision of banks tend to improve overall performance. Alternatively, as an example of intra-market regulation, the level of deposit insurance may be reduced.

There are complex interrelations among institutional factor. For example, BRSA reacts to activities in the banking sector. Banking industry reacts to regulations. Regulation is a dynamic process in which both sides change their position taking the other side's actions and reactions. So, there is a simultaneity problem that plagues any empirical study. In a sense, it is a two-way street. Explanations can be made both ways: from regulations to banking performance and from performance to regulations.

Economic reasons for banking regulation are well-known. There is a close relationship between the effectiveness of regulation which may impose fewer restrictions or enforce them loosely and performance. For example, a complete deposit insurance which encourages greater risk-taking, forces regulators to control the market more strictly. It is our belief that this is a fundamental problem in the Turkish banking market. BRSA could not impose and/or enforce strict regulations even though there was full deposit insurance in the industry. Lack of enforcement created an ideal environment for banks to pass on risks to the state and eventually to the society. BRSA, being a risk-averse institution, tends to stay on the safe side and does not allow new banks to enter the industry. It strictly controls both entry and exit. Following the theory, we expect that this attitude of BRSA increases inefficiency in the industry.

1. SHOULD THE REGULATORS HAVE BROAD POWERS OVER THE INDUSTRY?

In the worldwide trend towards liberalization, it is usually assumed that less regulation is better for banking industry. While there is widespread consensus on the existence of a bank regulator, the limits of the regulatory power is debated extensively. Following Barth et al., 2004)[1] we summarize the advantages of broad power in the following way.

To begin with, monitoring banking industry effectively is very costly. The level of transaction costs gives much leeway to banks to ignore regulations to the extent of the magnitude of monitoring and information costs. In economics literature this can be related to market failure arguments, assuming that it is something market cannot supply at efficient levels. On the other hand, transaction costs are not some kind of failure from a new institutionalist view (Furubotn and Richter, 2005).

In case of market failure, a powerful regulator may control the industry tightly and implement widespread regulations to improve market environment. This view assumes that transaction costs of regulation are lower than the costs of market failure. However, there are not many studies that compare transaction costs of broad power and a narrowly defined regulator. So, this argument begs empirical testing on the comparable costs of powerful regulators.

Secondly, banking industry creates many informational asymmetries. For example, consumers cannot easily get information about the health of banks. Nor they can easily evaluate the information they obtain. The level of sophistication of information gives room for maneuvering to banks. A powerful regulator may force banks to declare most information by using efficient mechanisms.

Lastly, deposit insurance mechanisms allow banks to undertake more risk than they would otherwise take. In order to offset this situation, regulators can strictly control banking performance, to eliminate any risk. Alternatively, consumers may ignore the bank's relative strength and take more risk, under the assumption that deposit insurance will protect them in the end.

Assuming that the regulator can ameliorate inefficiencies originating from excess risk-taking on both sides, a powerful regulator may improve the efficiency of banking sector.[2]

However, there are also some disadvantages of strong regulation. First, strong regulators may use their power to extract and seek rents for themselves and their political allies. These rents may be pecuniary in some cases. However, most of the time rents are non-pecuniary and fits well with the public choice models of regulator as a middleman between the society and special interest groups. In a rent-seeking society, regulation will be negatively correlated with bank performance and efficiency. If there are not a well-defined parliamentary oversight or other kind of political control, regulators will have more room for maximizing their own goals rather than making decisions on the basis of efficiency.[3]

Secondly, powerful regulators need more information and better tools to monitor the industry. However, there are both epistemological and practical problems to obtaining

---

[1] Barth, J. R., G. Caprio and R. Levine, 2004, 'Bank regulation and supervision: what works best?', *Journal of Financial Intermediation*, 13 (2), 205-248.

[2] Recent Turkish experience shows that BRSA was not very successful to control this risk. Banks abused the system by defaulting and transferring their liabilities to the state.

[3] A fundamental problem in Turkey is the lack of oversight over BRSA's decisions. No institution checks whether its decisions increases social welfare or not. This aspect of regulation allows BRSA to ignore a detailed economic cost-benefit analysis of its decision. BRSA also does not consider full effects of its decisions. While the effect on banks is measured in a rough manner, the effects on consumers, and society in general are not quantitatively or qualitatively measured.

information and using it. Banks can manipulate information very easily and abuse data in many cases. It is very costly for the regulator to follow bank on many accounts.

Priorities of banks make the effects of regulatory power more complicated. BRSA may give more emphasis to:

- competition in the industry[4]
- consumer protection[5]
- reducing moral hazard problems because of misallocation of risks[6]
- strict monitoring of banking activity
- the extent of the market by widening or limiting bank activities.
- adapting to Basel-II requirements[7]
- or, following interest groups.[8]

Some of these objectives are legitimate and originates from the legal structure. Some others are political. They may follow political preferences. Still, others are rent-based. They provide for political support and/or economic benefit to regulator or industry. These goals usually conflict with each other. For example, competition and consumer protection are two basic objectives for any regulator. Turkish Banking Law gives BRSA the responsibility to institutionalize competition and protect consumers. Measures taken to increase competition not always protect consumers and vice versa.

A problem in the Turkish Banking system stems from the incentives that push supervisors (sworn bank auditors) to seek jobs in banks. They see banks as possible future career options.[9] This view influences their supervisory abilities. In Turkey, banks employ former supervisors in their boards or managerial positions. This trend also supports the thesis that interest group politics play some role in the process.

Barth et al. (2004: 235) find that increasing the level of restrictions move together with crises. Similarly, more restriction comes with lower level of bank development. However, they do not provide a clear-cut explanation on the nature of relationship. While, we expect that regulators are ill-equipped with crises for a number of reasons, the direction of causality requires more work. It is our expectation that causality works both ways. Powerful regulators

---

[4] In Turkey, competition does not take a high place in terms of priorities. BRSA prefers to limit the number of banks in the industry, rather than allowing more banks and let them undertake their own risks. In a sense, BRSA distributes risks from banks to consumers by making them pay higher prices.

[5] BRSA seems to be slow on imposing restrictions on banks to protect consumers. Regulations on credit cards, Internet banking and pricing on banking services justify this view.

[6] Empirical tests (e.g., Barth, 2004) tighter capital regulations and strict regulatory activity do not mitigate the risks of generous deposit insurance on bank fragility. Interestingly, stronger property rights, rule of law and political accountability play a substantial role.

[7] Currently, adopting Basel II takes a prominent role in BRSA. This provides a ground for a more active official supervision and regulates capital requirements more strictly. However, it is controversial whether Basel II will improve bank performance in Turkey, since the experience of developed countries with an established regulatory governance and Turkey differ to some extent.

[8] Banks usually lobby politicians in order to push the regulator in their direction (Shleifer and Vishny, 1998). Under these circumstances, regulators tend to see banks as their primary customers. They tend to introduce regulations principally to satisfy the needs of banks rather then consumers. Since, customers do not have any comparable lobbying power, they tend to be on the supplier side of wealth transfers.

[9] On this point see Wilson (1980). Sworn bank auditors can be seen as an example of careerists in Wilson's classification system.

may not correctly find problems and cures for them. On the other hand, expected crises provide more reasons to control.

Barth et al. (2004: 238) do not find a strong association between bank development and performance and official supervisory power, including the quality of regulatory power. This is understandable, because the stability of the rules of the game is more important than behaviors of players. In this vein, they find a positive relationship between supervisory tenure and bank performance, which reflects the effect of regulatory commitment on the industry.

Regulatory commitment affects banking performance more than whether BRSA has broad or narrow control over the industry. It works by reducing transaction costs for both banks and consumers and by closing doors to rent extraction activities. A measure of regulatory commitment would support our thesis that a committed regulatory authority encourages efficiency-enhancing policies in the market more than changing rules arbitrarily and/or often. This is true for independence and supervisory powers as well. However, we believe that accountability and commitment remain theoretically related to banking performance.

Turkish banking industry has an oligopolistic structure with strictly limited entry and exit. These restrictions make the banking sector more prone to crises. Banks fragility increases with a regulator that aims to control the industry more strictly in order to eliminate the negative consequences of recent crises. The Turkish experience is exemplary in this connection. BRSA limits entry into the market and impose very strict restrictions on banks in some respects.

In this respect, regulatory structure that increases commitment and sees regulations as a contract between the state and players (both banks and consumers) may contribute positively to banking performance and increase efficiency.

The regulator must bind itself by its laws and should not change them abruptly at its discretion. To this end, both the regulator and banks should provide accurate information about their activities. Regulatory commitment encourage player in the market to turn to market instead of the regulator in order to solve their problems. Opening the door to private litigation increases efficiency in the industry.

Before delving into an analysis of BRSA and Turkish Banking industry, it will be beneficial to discuss briefly the meaning and nature of regulatory commitment and its significance for banking industry.

2. CREDIBLE COMMITMENT IN REGULATORY PROCESS

Regulatory reforms are usually presented as ways to improve quality and reduce prices. This statement carries all the advantages of having a theoretical model, but none of the divergences between theory and reality. Empirical literature shows that these twin goals of high quality and low price may be rhetoric rather than reality. The institutional background, including political preferences, usually plays against the predictions of the neo-classical model. The interactions between politicians, regulators and market participants create a new environment where the high quality/low price rhetoric hides more than it reveals.

The credibility of a regulatory framework is closely correlated with arbitrary interventions to the system by the government, judiciary or bureaucracy. Three constraints limit the role of arbitrariness and increase the credibility of the reform: limited discretion of the regulator, continuity of the regulatory system, and the existence of institutional restraints.

The lack of regulatory commitment may easily turn a reform into a failure, whereas the success depends on the continuous perseverance on the commitment. Regulatory commitment does not work in the same way in all environments. Institutional structure determines the direction of the market. In most cases there may be a trade-off between flexibility and commitment. While the costs of inflexibility may overweigh the benefits of commitment in well-established markets, newly created market structures, as in the case of Turkey, may require more weight on credible commitment as opposed to the costs of rigidity.

The regulatory reform must include mechanisms to restrain the discretion of executive and legislation so that the legal structure remains intact. Establishing an independent regulatory authority is the usual remedy for credible commitment. Limited empirical work shows that having an independent regulator increases efficiency and output in the generation market.

Regulatory commitment plays a crucial role as a signal toward establishing a competitive structure in the market. In the absence of institutional restraints, and a continuous regulatory system, limits on the discretionary power become the pivotal market signal on the direction of the market. As in the case of the Turkish banking reform, negative signals on the discretion of regulator and government may institutionalize costs of transition. Short-term political preferences may transform into deficiencies of the institutional background of the industry.

Regulation imposes new rules of game and new incentives. It changes both the institutional setting and behavioral patterns. However, the rate of change depends on many factors, including market participants' resistance, judicial constraints and so on. In Turkey, the resistance to the reform was strong and forced the government to take the lead in the market, which promoted the spirit of the pre-reform times.

An important proposition of the institutional analysis of regulation is that regulatory incentives work only if regulatory governance is working. The recent administrative intervention aims to push for regulatory incentives without institutionalizing regulatory governance. The evidence from other countries shows that it is very hard to establish regulatory commitment by increasing executive discretion.

A fundamental problem in Turkey, which is also related to restricted entry, stems from the implicit bailout by the state for fragile banks.

3. POLITICS AND BANKING REGULATION

Politicians exert a powerful influence over regulatory institutions. Banking is no exception. Regulatory commitment can be seen as a tool to keep politicians away from the industry. In countries, regulatory commitment more or less established

a) Information is easily accessible and public. This increases trust in the industry.
b) Government banks cannot be used by politicians and special interest groups easily. Regulatory authorities have rules to restrict this clearly.
c) Bank entry and exit is relatively easy. Regulators do not protect incumbents at the cost of consumers and loss of efficiency in the industry.

d) Regulatory body does not increase transaction costs so it can reduce them for specific groups later. This may take the form of excessive regulation in some cases and exceptions for some banks. Or banks may use the regulators to act collectively. In most countries, banks cannot act together, which is against competition laws. Regulations are efficient means of collective action and reduce transaction costs of rent-seeking.

The influence of politics over regulation may bring non-governmental regulation to the fore. From our perspective, banking regulations can be seen as a contract between the state (including BRSA) and market participants. This increases regulatory commitment in the industry and restricts governmental opportunism.

4. TRANSITION TO REGULATORY STATE IN THE TURKISH BANKING AND FINANCIAL MARKETS

During the 1990s the main issues regarding economic conditions are structure of banks, which put them in a position to supply funds to meet public debt and excessive public spending. In addition to that, politic risk which was realized as a result of coalition government policies increased the cost of capital, influence direction of capital flow to developing countries and shortened the maturity of available capital.

On the other hand, when considering the political power on supervisory authority in privatization of public banks and issuing new banking licenses, it is noticed that the basic criteria, "fit and proper owner" has not been assessed properly[10]. As majority of bankers perform activities in the field of industry and commerce, bank funds were transferred to group companies and economically ineffective projects. Besides, by investing in to banking industry some of the media industry owners became a banker and created a pressure on politicians and bureaucrats.

While banking regulation and supervision power was given directly to a minister and bureaucrats appointed by him until 1999, this power and personal relationship was abolished by foundation of Banking Regulation and Supervision Agency (BRSA). During the period after this major change took place, regulation supervision power was executed by BRSA considering current economic conditions. Banking industry restructuring program was perceived as a transition period in disciplining banking industry.

Changes in regulatory environment, known as "fit and proper", corporate management, loan restrictions, activity field of banks, capital adequacy, financial responsibilities and penalties set for bank owners may be viewed as a restriction in savings deposit insurance. Such changes commenced especially after the foundation of BRSA and continued within the context of restructuring program. By the Bank Act 4389 introduced in 1999 and with secondary arrangements several changes were made. Bank Act 5411, dated November 2005 and regulations made with respect to the new law involves regulations which are suitable to

---

[10] Majority of banks failed before the period 1990-2001 are the banks which were privatized or issued licenses during the 1990s.

EU norms and international standards. Supervisory board of an independent organization plays a key role in introducing effective regulations in a short period of time[11].

In this regard, the book consists of 3 parts. Part I includes an introduction the political economy of Turkey in order to understand the general structure and the ongoing transformation process of the Turkish economy. The focus of Part II is on the Turkish banking system. The part is designed to scrutinize the effect of the first-term deregulation experience in the market, the market developments in the last decade, concentration and the current market structure, regulations and experience in the deposit insurance and resolution processes, and the effects of the credit card regulation on the market. Lastly, Part III analyzes regulation of the financial markets. In this context, the analysis includes efficiency and productivity of the brokerage houses, institutional investors, and regulation of the Turkish capital markets.

4.1. The Political Economy of Turkey

Part I consist of 3 chapters. Chapter 1 by Çetin and Oğuz constructs introduction of the book. In this chapter, Çetin and Oğuz mention the importance of transition to the regulatory state in the banking and financial markets during the process of economic change in Turkey, and the role and context of the book.

In Chapter 2, Bağdadioğlu and Halisçelik overview the transformation process of the Turkish economy from an import substituting economy to export based economy initiated in 1980 was interrupted several times by either external (in 1997/1998 and 2008) or internal crisis (in 1994 and 2000/2001). In each case, the transformation plan was revised as required around its fundamentals, identified in the Washington Consensus, to face the challenges. The recent global financial crises of 2008 provided the last testing ground for the political and economic flexibility of not only the Turkish government but also other governments to face external as well as internal instabilities. The Turkish response so far regarded as quite successful. The continuity of this success, however, will largely be dependent on the Turkish government's adjustment of the structural transformation in line with the changes in the world economy.

According to Bağdadioğlu and Halisçelik, considering Turkey's promising political and economic flexibility in response to the recent global economic challenge, the projected recovery of the Turkish economy is expected. The speed and depth of recovery, however, will largely be determined by not only the Turkish commitment to the transformation process, but also the improvements in the World economy.

In Chapter 3, Demirbas and Demirbas analyze the property rights issue is one of the most important institutional differences between democratically developed and developing countries. In most of the cases, the violation of the property rights results with rent-seeking activities. In this chapter, Katz and Rosenberg's budgetary variable model has been tested in a time series study for the period of 1960 to 2002 to measure rent-seeking activities in Turkey. Demirbas and Demirbas found that there is a cointegrating relationship exists between

---

[11] In this context, regulation arrangement quickness can be viewed as effectiveness of banking regulation. However, one must think about how to reflect this to an article. In particular, it is crucial to make a decision that will keep in pace with quick changes in banking industry and developments in international arena.

variables, by which mean that there is a long-run relationship between budgetary rent-seeking, GNP per capita and Government Size. They also found that independent variables help to explain rent-seeking activities in Turkey during the period 1960-2002. In addition to these cointegrated relationships, it is showed that adjustments are made towards restoring the long-run relationship between rent-seeking and other variables. Part I concludes this chapter.

4.2. Transition to Regulatory State in the Turkish Banking System

Part II consists of five chapters that focus on the general structure transition to regulatory state in the Turkish banking system. In chapter 4, Yay and Yay aim to discuss the structure, problems and regulation of Turkish Banking System during the 2000s. In this context, this chapter first analyzes the macroeconomic environment in the 1990s as the structural and cyclical reasons behind the Turkish financial crisis experience in 2000-2001. Secondly, Yay and Yay examine the restructuring and regulation process of the Turkish Banking System in the post-crisis period. The impact of the stand-by arrangement with IMF on this process and the degree of adaptation of the available legal framework to the international banking principles (Basel 1 and Basel 2) is especially clarified. Thirdly, they argued that the decisive maintenance of this restructuring and regulation process up to 2010 is the main reason why the Turkish Banking system was relatively unaffected from the global financial crisis in 2008. In the end, the chapter concludes a detailed analysis of the latest situation of the sector in the face of the crisis.

In Chapter 5 of Part II, Yayla analyzes the market structure of the last-term banking system by measuring concentration ratio of the market with a comparison between the pre-2000 term and the post-2000 term. In this chapter, the regulatory transformation in the Turkish banking system is summarized, and apart from the traditional approaches, concentration (market structure) in the banking sector is considered simultaneously in terms of assets, loans, and deposits. In order to analyze market structure more comprehensively, dominance, disparity and dynamic indexes are applied in addition to traditional static measures.

The chapter finds, parallel to the regulatory phase, concentration in the relevant markets shows decreasing trend in the period of 1995-1999 and increasing tendency between 2000 and 2010. However, net interest margins (intermediation costs) which can be seen as the relevant prices in the sector have declined through the analyzed periods. Thus, the chapter concludes that the new regulatory framework constitutes a strong ground for stability and fair competition.

In Chapter 6, Isik and Gunduz measure the performance of the first-term deregulation experience in the Turkish banking system. The newly chartered domestic and foreign banks constituted about half of the Turkish banking industry at the turn of the past century. This record number of new entries is the by-products of deregulatory reforms launched in the 1980's and onward. In this context, Isik and Gunduz investigate the productivity performance of these new banks vis-à-vis that of old banks in an era of financial deregulation in Turkey. Employing a non-stochastic inter-temporal production frontier approach over a period of sixteen years, they found that new banks are significantly superior to old banks in resource utilization. Apparently, not hampered by a legacy of inefficiency from the past, new banks could operate nearer the efficiency frontier. Moreover, new banks register faster productivity, technology and efficiency growth than old banks. Equipped with better and newer technology, local partners for foreign entries and holding affiliation for domestic entries appear to have helped these young banks to overcome initial asymmetric information problems and demonstrate higher performance. Their findings suggest that new entries, especially from more advanced markets, could be instrumental in boosting resource allocation and utilization in banking.

In Chapter 7, Çabukel and Frisch focus on regulation and experience in the deposit insurance and resolution processes in Turkey. This chapter provides information about the SDIF's (the Savings Deposit Insurance Fund) deposit insurance and resolution practices and the legal grounds associated with it. In Turkey, the SDIF acquired new mandates such as receivership after the economic crisis of 1994 and became an independent agency with additional tools including the ones for the recovery of bank assets after the banking crisis of 2001. Çabukel and Frisch observe similar developments in countries including Japan, Korea and Russia after the Asian crisis of 1998. The recent global economic crisis triggered international organizations including the International Association of Deposit Insurers (IADI), the Bank for International Settlements (BIS) and the International Monetary Fund (IMF) to work collaboratively and set internationally accepted best practices for deposit insurance and bank resolution regimes.

The chapter concludes that the SDIF played a particularly important role by restructuring the banking system and resolving non-performing assets of failed banks during the 2001 crisis. During this period, banks that had franchise value and could be effective in terms of their credit channels were brought back into the system by PandAs and bank sales. During the institutional development of SDIF, experienced personnel who worked in failed banks and worked effectively during resolutions became its permanent employees.

In chapter 8, Akin, Aysan, Gollu, and Yıldıran analyze the effects of regulation in the Turkish credit card market on payment services and credit services. The Turkish credit card market has recently undergone two important regulations: one on payment services in November 2005 and the other on credit services in June 2006. They aim to shed light on the link between these two service markets by investigating the revenues from each of them: the non-interest and interest revenues. The chapter begins with a brief account of the Turkish credit card market. The next section explains the data and methodology used in the analysis. The chapter presents the results and concludes with comments of the findings.

They find that the regulations on payment services had no significant impact on banks' revenues, whereas the regulations on credit services affected the interest and non-interest revenues in opposite directions. Reacting to stifled interest revenues, banks shifted their focus toward non-interest revenues. The chapter suggests careful consideration of the possible effects on all segments of a credit card market when a regulatory action is planned. Moreover, from the response of revenues to changing prices in these two service markets, it infers that the demand in the Turkish credit card market is inelastic.

4.3. Regulation of Financial Markets in Turkey

Part III focuses on regulation of financial markets in Turkey and consists of three chapters. The first chapter of Part III, Chapter 9 by Kucukkocaoglu and Kucuksozen discusses the institutional structure of regulation in the Turkish capital markets. The chapter purposes to examine the current developments and their effect on changes in capital market regulations and to provide conceptual understanding and in-depth knowledge of securities laws and the regulatory framework concerning capital markets in Turkey. The securities market in Turkey is supervised by the Capital Markets Board of Turkey (CMBT). The principal statute governing the securities market is the Capital Market Law No 2499. The subject of this law is to regulate and control the secure, transparent and stable functioning of the capital market and to protect the rights and benefits of investors with the purpose of ensuring an efficient and widespread participation by the public in the development of the economy through investing savings in the securities market. This law contains regulations with respect to company and shareholder disclosure obligations, admission to listing and trading of listed securities, public tender offers and insider dealing, among other things. CMBT monitors compliance with these regulations and aiming to achieve international best practices, and encourage market-integrity through clear and self-enforcing rules of the game while encouraging the game itself.

Within the framework of investor protection and moving the capital market forward and to be a major source of medium and long term finance, laws and regulations assist the CMBT to perform its role in maintaining market integrity and meeting fairness and transparency principles. According to Kucukkocaoglu and Kucuksozen, all of these increasing efforts by these regulators and agencies aiming to enhance the existing corporate governance and investor relations practices in a risk-focused effort to achieve further transparency and supervision in the markets make Turkish capital markets more appealing for further investments while supporting Turkey's endeavor to realize its full potential as a significant capital markets player in the world.

In Chapter 10, Bağdadioğlu, Dinçer, and Yereli measure efficiency and productivity of the brokerage houses in Turkey. This chapter measures the efficiency and productivity of 63 Brokerage Houses operating in Turkey by applying the well known methodology of Data Envelopment Analysis to the most recent data available covering the period between 2000 and 2008. With such as analysis, the chapter aims to provide a valuable opportunity to observe the state of BHs after one of the worst internal financial crisis hit the Turkish economy in 2001 and just before the global financial crisis of 2008 started to show its full impact on the Turkish economy.

The findings of the chapter clearly depict the adverse impacts of both the domestic financial crisis of 2001 and the global financial crisis of 2008 on the Turkish Brokerage Sector as very low efficiency scores and declining productivity. The main sources of inefficiency and poor productivity during the period, however, appear to be originated from managerial incompetency at individual brokerage houses level, and dominance of banks at the financial sector level.

In the end, in Chapter 11, Algüner considers institutional investors in Turkey. The types of institutional investors that have operations in Turkey are securities mutual funds, pension mutual funds, life insurance companies, real estate investment trusts, venture capital investment trusts, securities investment trusts. Mutual funds are established in the form of open-end investment companies in Turkey. They do not have any legal entity. They are operated in terms of the rules stated in the internal statute of the fund, which includes general terms about management of the fund, custody of the assets, valuation principles and conditions of investing in the fund. The ratio of the investment funds' portfolio size to GDP is an indicator of the development level of the institutional investor base in that country.

Although the ratio of the investment funds to GDP in Turkey has increased through the years, it is considered to be low when compared with other countries. There are two major classes of mutual funds in Turkey; fixed income and equity. Fixed income funds are the leading group, constituting 2/3 of total assets. Equity mutual funds represent only 2.5% of total assets. On the other hand, the private pension system that was introduced towards the end of 2003 has been growing exponentially. It is required to make the investment fund legislation coherent with European Union Directives and to provide the integration of European fund market and Turkish funds. Investment trusts are closed-end investment companies managing portfolios composed of capital market instruments, gold and other precious metals. Three types of investment trusts operate in Turkey, namely; Securities Investment Trusts, Real Estate Investment Trusts and Venture Capital Investment Trusts. As of the end of 2009, 48% of Istanbul Stock Exchange companies' shares which are open to public are in the custody accounts of foreign institutional investors at The ISE Settlement and Custody Bank Inc.

REFERENCES

Barth, J. R., G. Caprio and R. Levine, 2004, 'Bank regulation and supervision: what works best?', *Journal of Financial Intermediation*, 13 (2), 205-248.

Furubotn and Richter, 2005, *Institutions and Economic Theory*, University of Michigan Press.

Shleifer, A. and R. W. Vishny, 1998. "The Quality of Government," *Harvard Institute of Economic Research Working Papers,* 1847, Harvard - Institute of Economic Research.

Wilson, J. Q, 1980, *The Politics of Regulation*, New York: Basic Books.

In: Regulation and Competition in the Turkish Banking... ISBN: 978-1-61324-990-1
Editors: Tamer Çetin and Fuat Oğuz © 2012 Nova Science Publishers, Inc.

Chapter 2

TRANSFORMATION OF THE TURKISH ECONOMY: AN OVERVIEW

Necmiddin Bağdadioğlu[1] and Ergül Halisçelik[2]
[1]Hacettepe University, Department of Public Finance, Ankara, Turkey
[2]Republic of Turkey Prime Ministry Undersecretariat of Treasury,
Ankara, Turkey

ABSTRACT

The transformation process of the Turkish economy from an import substituting economy to export based economy initiated in 1980 was interrupted several times by either external (in 1997/1998 and 2008) or internal crisis (in 1994 and 2000/2001). In each case, the transformation plan was revised as required around its fundamentals, identified in the Washington Consensus, to face the challenges. The recent global financial crises of 2008 provided the last testing ground for the political and economic flexibility of not only the Turkish government but also other governments to face external as well as internal instabilities. The Turkish response so far regarded as quite successful. The continuity of this success, however, will largely be dependent on the Turkish government's adjustment of the structural transformation in line with the changes in the world economy.

INTRODUCTION

This chapter overviews the ongoing transformation process of the Turkish economy from import substituting to market based economy initiated with the announcement of the Stabilization Program in 24 January 1980. The Stabilization Program was designed, and revised as needed, in line with the Washington Consensus supported by major international financial institutions, such as, the World Bank (WB) and the International Monetary Fund (IMF).

The Washington Consensus recommended market guided solutions to the external government deficits of developing countries caused largely by excessive rise in price of imported oil and accelerating international interest rates during the 1970s. To attract foreign financial resources many countries, including Turkey, introduced comprehensive economic reforms involving various blends of ten policy measures intended for trade liberalization, competitive exchange rates, market based interest rates, stimulus of inward foreign direct investment, deregulation, fiscal discipline, tax reform, redirection of public spending from indiscriminate subsidies to growth enhancing areas (education, health and infrastructure), privatization of state economic enterprises, and security of property rights (Williamson, 1989).

These measures, though implemented at different levels and paces by many countries, globalized economic relations, and made countries more vulnerable to the spillover effects of economic crises (Kaul and Conceição, 2006). Notably the impacts of the Asian and the Russian financial crises of the late 1990s (Radelet, et al., 1998, Chiodo and Owyang, 2002), and more recently the United States's (US) financial crisis of 2008 quickly spread over trading blocks (IMF, 2009). The exposure of many countries to economic crises regardless of their development stages however led many to question the validity of the Washington Consensus, which was subsequently replaced by the Seoul Development Consensus agreed by the G20 group of nations in November 2010. Based on similar fundamentals, the new Consensus aimed at adjustment of the deficiencies of the Washington Consensus.

The economic transformation process pursued in line with the fundamentals of the Washington Consensus produced mixed results in Turkey. In the early 1980s, Turkey experienced relatively high growth levels, low inflation rates and healthy balance of payments. However, particularly after the switch from closed foreign exchange regime to open foreign exchange regime in 1989, growth performance deteriorated, inflation rates risen, and high public sector deficit started to characterize the Turkish economy, which then became more dependent on short-term capital inflows called "hot money" to balance the consequent current account deficit. As becoming more open to external forces accompanying with insufficient economic policies implemented, Turkey faced four major economic crises, two internal in 1994 and November 2000/February 2001 and two external in 1997/1998 and 2008, respectively. The former crises, particularly the one in February 2001, had devastating impacts on the Turkish economy, led to the announcement of the Transition Program to the Strong Economy in May 2001. Owing to the economic measures taken as part this program and the economic adjustments implemented for the accession process to the European Union (EU) initiated in 2005, unlike many countries, Turkey managed the external crisis of 2008 reasonably well. These measures strengthened the financial sector, but the real sector stayed problematic since the exports of the Turkish economy based on imported raw and intermediate goods and materials.

In the light of these developments, the transformation process of the Turkish economy is reviewed in two main sections. The following section evaluates the progress of the transformation process until the global financial crisis of 2008 spread from the US. The second section extends the evaluation to cover the Turkish response to the recent US led financial crisis. The chapter ends with an overall assessment of the transformation process and the envisaged prospect of Turkish economy.

1. Progress until the 2008 Global Financial Crisis

The price shocks of two major oil crises and inconsistent monetary and fiscal policies pursued to cope with these shocks during the 1970s created significant problems in balance of payments, production, inflation and external debt in Turkey (Krueger, 1995). The stabilization program of 1980, financially and technically supported by the IMF and the WB, aimed to cure these problems by transforming the Turkish economy from import substituting economy into export oriented economy. Five successive structural adjustment loans were extended to Turkey to ease the economic transformation during the first years of the Stabilization Program (Onis and Kirkpatrick, 1985), and as shown later, the stand-by agreements were available whenever needed.[12]

The support of the IMF and the WB was conditional on steps taken on liberalization of Turkish product, exchange, capital and labor markets. These conditions were met at various degrees due to the internal resistance to the shift to the expert oriented growth strategy and the negative consequences of aforementioned financial crises. Accordingly until now the Stabilization Program of 1980 has been revised as needed to complete the process of opening the Turkish markets to foreign competition by abolishing barriers on imports and introducing regulatory processes in financial and real sectors. The structural reforms undertaken by Turkey in line with the Washington Consensus and the key achievements are summarized in Table 1.

The early results of macroeconomic performance of the transformation process were not satisfactory due to dominance of inefficient public sector and serious structural problems in many sectors, particularly in banking. As can be seen from Table 2, compared with large deficits in balance of payments, insufficient production levels, accelerating inflation and mounting levels of external debt experienced during the 1970s (Krueger, 1995), Turkey showed a promising macroeconomic performance only with growth rate and balance of payment. Nevertheless, the growth performance was unstable, and the current account and budget deficits, the high and unsustainable public sector debt, and the high and volatile inflation rates remained as problematic areas of the Turkish economy leading to the internal financial crises of 1994 and 2000/2001, respectively.

The political uncertainties also contributed to the occurrence of internal financial crises. The frequently changing coalition governments until 2002, and corresponding lack of transparency and accountability in public sector activities produced adverse economic consequences and interrupted the implementation of the Stabilization Programs. Evidently, towards the end of the 1980s, the growth performance declined and the inflation rate started to increase, affecting both the real sector in the form of decrease in growth and employment, and the financial sector in the form of unreliable banking and other financial sectors, foreign exchange and stock markets.

---

[12] Since became a member in 1947, Turkey signed 19 stand-by agreements (first in 1961 and last in 2005) with the IMF, of those four were after 1990.

Table 1. Principles of the Washington Consensus, Structural Reforms and Key Achievements of Turkey

Principles of the Washington Consensus[*]	Structural Reforms[**]	Key Achievements of Turkey[**]
• Fiscal discipline • Redirection of public spending priorities from subsidies to education, health and infrastructure • Tax reform – broadening the tax base and cutting marginal tax rates • Unified and competitive exchange rates • Secure property rights • Deregulation – abolition of regulations that impede market entry or restrict competition • Trade liberalization – liberalization of imports and any trade protection • Privatization of state enterprises; • Elimination of barriers to direct foreign investment • Financial liberalization- interest rates that are market determined and positive in real terms	1. Public Sector Reforms • Public Financial Management and Control Law • Public Procurement Law • Code of Ethical Conduct for Civil Servants • Law on Freedom and Information for Citizens 2. Structural Fiscal Reforms • Administrative Social Security Reform • Tax Reforms 3. Financial Sector Reform • A new Banking Law • A new Insurance Law • A new Mortgage Law and development of Mortgage market • Strengthening the Private Banks • State Bank Reform 4. Increasing the Role of Private Sector in the Economy • Opening the Keys Markets to Competition and Regulation by Independent Agencies • Improving Investment Environment • Accelerating Privatization.	• High, less volatile, private sector led, and productivity driven growth • Progress in real income convergence • Substantial disinflation • Transformation in the employment structure • Remarkable fiscal consolidation • More resilient public debt composition • Strong financial sector • Competitive investment environment • Boosted privatization implementations • Strong foreign direct investment inflows • Enhanced trade and financial integration • Implementation of comprehensive structural reforms

Source: [*]Todaro and Smith (2009: 551-552), [**]Undersecretary of Treasury (2008: 3, 29).

Transformation of the Turkish Economy: An Overview

Table 2. Main Macroeconomic Indicators, 1980-2001

	1980	1985	1990	1993	1994	1999	2000	2001
GNP (Billion $)	73,1	68,0	152,4	181,0	130,5	186,3	201,4	144,0
GNP Per Capital (Current $)	1.589	1.353	2.714	3.042	2.153	2.811	2.987	2.102
Growth Rate (%)	-2,8	4,3	9,4	8,1	-6,1	-6,1	6,3	-9,5
Unemployment Rate (%)	8,3	7,3	8,2	7,7	8,1	7,6	6,6	8,4
Inflation Rate (%, CPI)	115,6	45,0	60,3	66,1	106,3	64,9	54,9	54,4
A) Domestic Debt Stock (% of GNP)	13,60	19,70	14,40	17,90	20,60	29,30	29,00	69,20
B) External Debt Stock (% of GNP)	19,34	38,09	32,59	37,45	48,29	41,66	44,69	57,74
Public Sector Debt (% of GNP, A+B)	32,94	57,79	46,99	55,35	68,89	70,96	73,69	126,94
Budget Balance (% of GNP)	-3,1	-2,3	-3,0	-6,7	-3,9	-11,7	-10,6	-16,5
Primary Deficit (Surplus) (% GNP)	-2,5	-0,3	0,5	-0,8	3,8	2,0	5,7	6,8
Current Account Balance (% GNP)	-4,7	-2,4	-1,7	-3,6	2,0	-0,7	-4,9	2,4
Current Account Balance (Billion $)	-3,4	-1,4	-2,6	-6,4	2,6	-1,3	-9,8	3,4
FDI Inflows (Billion $)	0,035	0,099	0,684	0,746	0,636	0,813	1,71	3.29
Central Bank Foreign Exchange Reserves (End of the Year-Billion $)	1,1	1,0	6,07	6,28	7,07	23,18	19,63	18,74

Sources: Compiled from various tables published by the Undersecreteriat of Treasury, the Central Bank, the State Planning Organization, the Undersecreteriat of Foreign Trade, the Turkstat, and the Ministry of Finance.

The instability of economic growth was, and still is, largely caused by the requirement of imported raw and intermediate goods and materials for the new export led growth strategy, which necessitated constant inflow of foreign capital. The removal of selective credit policies, free determination of interest rates on deposits and credits, and liberalization of foreign exchange transactions, higher interest rate on domestic assets and lower depreciation rates attracted the required foreign capital inflow, but usually in the form of short term "hot money" (BRSA, 2002). However, the rapid increases in short-term foreign capital inflows and outflows accompanied with high public sector deficits, high domestic interest rates, and low exchange rate prepared the base for the first major internal financial crisis of Turkey occurred in April 1994 (TÜSİAD, 1995).

To ease the difficulties arised as a result of the financial crisis of 1994, Turkey immediately renewed the Stabilization Program on 05 April 1994. This program was supported by the IMF with the 16th stand-by agreement applied during the period of 08 July 1994-26 September 1995. The program aimed to complete the ongoing structural reforms, and thus, stabilize the Turkish economy at a lower inflation rate, higher export level and lesser budget deficit. However, the success of this program stayed limited due to lack of political commitment and economic slowdown occurred in the second half of 1998, this time caused by the external financial crises of Asia and Russia (Kantarcı and Karacan, 2008). Consequently, the Turkish economy experienced a period of contraction in the form of negative economic growth (-6.1%), high inflation rate (65%) and budget deficit (-11,7%) at the end of the 1999 (see Table 2).

To stabilize the economy, Turkey set off another three-year program covering the period between 1999 and 2002 supported by the 17th stand-by agreement signed with the IMF. Yet, this program was interrupted as well, due to two interrelated internal financial crises the Turkish economy experienced in November 2000 and February 2001, respectively. The crises were ignited largely by liquidity, interest rate and foreign exchange problems in banking sector. As was the case in the financial crisis of 1994, before the crisis a large amount of short-term foreign capital inflow and during the crises large-scale capital outflow occurred resulting in decline in output and growth of Turkish economy (Celasun, 2002, Ercel, 2006). During the financial crises of November 2000 and February 2001, as a result of the exchange rate, interest rate and liquidity risks, the banking sector faced significant losses leading the transfer of as many as 22 private and public banks to the Savings Deposit Insurance Fund (SDIF).

The Banking Regulation and Supervision Agency (BRSA) prepared the "Banking Sector Restructuring Program" in May 2001. The program was mainly based on restructuring of public banks, resolution of banks taken over by the SDIF, rehabilitation and strengthening of private banking system by increasing capital adequacy criteria, adding their profit to capital, strengthening of surveillance and supervision frame and the increase of competition and efficiency in the banking sector and other measures to strengthen the financial sector as a whole (BRSA, 2002).

Accordingly, the capital structure of public banks was strengthened during the implementation period of the program. The state banks were restructured on operational scale by bringing professional management style and by reducing number of branches and employees to more rational levels. Moreover, the Treasury issued government securities to compensate the accumulated duty losses which deteriorated the financial structure of public banks. The Treasury also made new regulations to improve the financial status of banks by preventing the public banks from making new duty losses. The banks transferred to the SDIF were resolved by various ways like merger, sales or direct liquidation in quite short time period. The re-structuring of 22 banks costed $53.6 billion, but at the expense of increasing the public debt (BRSA, 2010).

These crises made the structural fragilities of the Turkish economy more apparent, making the design of another extensive restructuring program inevitable. Hence, the Transition Program to the Strong Economy was announced. The program was supported by the 18th stand-by agreement signed with the IMF. The approved amount was SDR12,82 billion (about US$16 billion) covering the period between 04 February 2002 and 03 February 2005 (Uygur, 2010, IMF, 2010a). The aim of the 18th stand-by arrangement was not only to decrease high public debt burden, but also to strengthen the fragile structure of banks against any potential future economic crisis (Toprak, 2010). This was to be done by fiscal adjustment, disinflation under the planned inflation targeting framework, and structural reforms such as completing banking sector restructuring, intensifying public sector reform, and strengthening the private sector's role in the economy. The key elements of the program involved the continuation of the floating exchange rate regime to limit the potential for speculative attacks, the reform and strengthening of the financial system to make banks less vulnerable to withdrawal of funds, and to boost confidence in domestic financial assets, and the expenditure and tax reforms to help sustain the fiscal adjustment needed in the medium term to ensure debt sustainability (IMF, 2010b).

Meanwhile, as mentioned before, the measures taken with the prospect of membership to the EU also helped the improvement of Turkish economy. Turkey prepared the Pre-Accession Economic Program in line with the EU procedures following the acquirement of candidate statute at the Helsinki summit in December 1999. The negotiations with the EU were officially started after the European Council announced that Turkey sufficiently fulfilled the Copenhagen Criteria on 3 October 2005. While the Copenhagen criteria described the EU full membership principles, the Maastricht criteria defined the economic performance criteria and the necessary conditions that the EU member states must meet to qualify for the Economic and Monetary Union. To ensure economic and social transformation during the EU membership process, as well, Turkey adjusted the length of its Ninth Development Plan, extending it from five-year period to seven-year period covering 2007-2013 period to coincide with the period of EU financial programming (Halisçelik, 2009).

Table 3. The Strategy of the Ninth Development Plan (2007-2013)

Economic and Social Development Axes	Targets of the Ninth Development Plan (2007-2013)
Increasing Competitiveness	1) Making Macroeconomic Stability Permanent 2) Improving the Business Environment 3) Reducing the Informal Economy 4) Improving the Financial System 5) Improving the Energy and Transportation Infrastructure 6) Protecting the Environment and Improving the Urban Infrastructure 7) Improving R&D and Innovativeness 8) Disseminating Information and Communication Technologies 9) Improving Efficiency of the Agricultural Structure 10) Ensuring the Shift to High Value-Added Production Structure in Industry and Services
Increasing Employment	1) Improving the Labor Market 2) Increasing the Sensitivity of Education to Labor Demand 3) Developing Active Labor Policies
Strengthening Human Development and Social Solidarity	1) Enhancing the Educational System 2) Making the Health System Effective 3) Improving Income Distribution, Social Inclusion and Fight Against Poverty 4) Increasing Effectiveness of the Social Security System 5) Protecting and Improving Culture and Strengthening Social Dialogue
Ensuring Regional Development	1) Making Regional Development Policy Effective at the Central Level 2) Ensuring Development Based on Local Dynamics and Internal Potential 3) Increasing Institutional Capacity at the Local Level 4) Ensuring Development in the Rural Areas
Increasing Quality and Effectiveness in Public Services	1) Rationalizing Powers and Responsibilities Between Institutions 2) Increasing Policy Making and Implementation Capacity 3) Developing Human Resources in Public Sector 4) Ensuring the Dissemination and Effectiveness of e-Government Applications 5) Improving the Justice System 6) Making Security Services Effective

Source: SPO (2006: 13).

Table 4. Main Macro Economic Indicators, 2002-2010

Macro Economic Indicator	2002	2003	2004	2005	2006	2007	2008	2009	2010
GDP (Billion $)	230,49	304,90	390,39	481,50	526,43	648,63	742,09	616,75	-
GDP Per Capital (Current $)	3,492	4,559	5,764	7,021	7,583	9,234	10,440	8,578	10,043[3]
Growth Rate %	6,2	5,3	9,4	8,4	6,9	4,7	0,7	-4,7	6,8[3]
Unemployment Rate %	10,3	10,5	10,8	10,6	10,2	10,3	11,0	14,0	11,2[2]
Inflation Rate % (CPI)	45,0	25,3	10,6	8,2	9,6	8,8	10,4	6,3	6,4[1]
A) Domestic Debt Stock % of GDP	42,8	42,7	40,2	37,7	33,2	30,3	28,9	34,6	-
B) External Debt Stock % of GDP	26,5	19,4	16,5	13,4	12,3	9,3	11,1	11,7	-
Public Sector Debt % of GDP (A+B)	69,2	62,2	56,6	51,1	45,5	39,6	40,0	46,3	-
Budget Deficit % of GDP	11,47	8,84	5,21	1,06	0,61	1,63	1,83	5,54	3,60[4]
Primary Deficit (Surplus) % GDP	3,2	4,8	5,5	5,0	4,6	3,1	1,7	-1,1[3]	-
Current Account Balance % GDP	-0,3	-2,5	-3,7	-4.6	-6.1	-5.9	-5.7	-2.3	5,4[3]
Current Account Balance (Billion $)	-0,6	-7,5	-14,4	-22,1	-32,1	-38,2	-41,9	-14,3	-41,6[4]
Total Capital Inflows (Billion $)	6,9	6,4	20,1	37,6	48,5	48,3	44,3	3,8	38,1[4]
-FDI Inflows (Billion $)	1,1	1,7	2,8	10,0	20,2	22,0	18,3	8,3	6,3
-External Borrowing of NonBank Private Sector (net)	1,9	2,3	7,7	12,5	17,1	28,7	27,0	-12,3	-4,7
-Other (net)	3,9	3,1	9,7	15,1	11,2	-2,5	-0,9	7,8	36,5
Central Bank Foreign Exchange Reserves (End of the Year-Billion $)	26,73	33,64	36,01	50,52	60,85	71,26	70,08	69,63	80,70[1]

Sources: Undersecreteriat of Treasury, Central Bank, State Planning Organization, Undersecreteriat of Foreign Trade, Turkstat, Ministry of Finance. 1-As of 31-12-2010, 2- As of October 2010, 3- Estimation , 4- 2010 Jan-November.

The Ninth Development Plan was prepared within the framework of the Long Term Strategy (2001-2023) by the Government of that time with the vision of Turkey becoming "… a country of information society, growing in stability, sharing more equitably, globally competitive and fully completed her coherence with the European Union" (SPO, 2006). The necessary documents in the EU accession process, such as the Pre-Accession Economic Program and the Strategic Coherence Framework as well as other national and regional plans and programs, primarily the Medium Term Program and sectoral and institutional strategy documents were defined accordingly to the Ninth Development Plan. Table 3 shows the development axes and targets identified to achieve the Plan's vision.

Despite that there was not any sign of a new economic crisis at that time, Turkey developed another comprehensive three-year macroeconomic and financial program supported by the IMF with the 19th stand-by arrangement in May 2005, totaling SDR6.66 billion (approximately US$10 billion). The three-year program aimed to establish the conditions for sustainable growth, facilitating union towards the EU economies and an orderly exit from the IMF support. The sustainable growth was expected to be attained by reducing the current account deficit to more sustainable levels so that the economy become more resistant to short-term macroeconomic challenges; retaining the floating exchange rate, preserving central bank independence, and adopting formal inflation targeting to bring inflation closer to the EU levels; making the government debt position more sustainable through continued sizable primary surpluses; lowering Turkey's vulnerability to balance of payment shocks by restoring its net foreign exchange reserve position; maintaining financial sector stability by further improving the supervisory and regulatory framework, accelerating asset recovery and restructuring state banks; and finally, implementing a structural reform agenda that enhances Turkey's growth prospects, lowers unemployment, and improves the investment climate (IMF, 2005).

The considerable improvements the Turkish economy displayed after the crisis of 2001 can be seen from Table 4. The Turkish economy grew by 4.5% annually during the period of 2002-2009, while high unemployment rate and current account deficit remained as major problems. During this period, the Turkish economy significantly improved as a result of successful structural reforms in critical sectors, particularly in banking, telecommunication and energy; public sector reform such as privatization to minimize state involvement in the economy; financial sector reform such as establishment of regulatory and supervisory authorities and policies to improve the functions and independence of Central Bank together with fiscal and monetary policy measures. The accession process to the EU provided an anchor for the continuation of the reform process (Halisçelik, 2009).

This successful implementation of stabilization policies and economic programs accompanied with the political stability obtained since 2002 subsequently resulted in one of the longest-uninterrupted growth in the Turkish economic history (BRSA, 2010). As illustrated in Table 2, Table 4, and Figure 1, despite the severe financial crises experienced in the years of 1994, 2000 and 2001 costing as much as one third of national income, the Turkish economy had a relatively sound growth performance. Furthermore, after a long period with high inflation rates, Turkey experienced significantly low inflation rates. The average inflation was 62.7% between 1983-1994 and 71.6% between 1994-2001, to reduce nearly to single digits of inflation since 2004. Unfortunately, this positive trend was interrupted by the global financial crisis originated from the US housing market crash in the second half of 2007, to which the Turkish response is accounted for in the following section.

2. TURKISH RESPONSE TO THE GLOBAL FINANCIAL CRISIS

The global financial crisis of 2008, spread from the US because of the decline in asset prices and domestic demand in developed markets, led the world economies to enter a period of contraction in 2009. The public debt and budget deficit figures of many countries became one of the major concerns creating severe sources of risks against fiscal balances. As the effects of financial crisis deepened both domestic and foreign demand diminished making these problems more severe and risky for not only developed countries but also developing countries. Consequently, the financial crisis turned very quickly into an economic crisis and affected the whole world in a very short period of time (UT, 2010).

Having strong trade and financial ties with the world economy, Turkey was affected by the global economic crisis negatively, as well. The impact of the crisis spread over through three main channels: the finance channel owing to deteriorating external financing position of private companies, the trade channel due to declining export, and finally, the expectations channel because of decreasing consumer and real sector confidence (RT, 2010). However, as a result of the measures taken for the financial sector in terms of restructuring and strengthening banks after 2001 crisis, the impacts of global crisis on the Turkish banking sector was quite limited. Turkey did not even need to transfer resource to the banking sector. Therefore, contrary to many countries, in Turkey the global financial crisis showed its first impacts on the reel sector instead of financial sector, as decline in growth rate and increase in unemployment.

Turkey introduced various economic policies, programs and stimulus packages including various monetary and fiscal policy measures to mitigate the adverse impacts of the global financial crisis and to accelerate the exit from the crisis particularly through promoting internal demand (CBRT, 2009). These initiatives were organized under eight main headings, namely, measures and incentives for increasing domestic demand, tax and other incentives for increasing employment, tax and premium support and other incentives for increasing capital inflow and investments, credit and guarantee support for production and export, financial supports and other measures such as regulation for using credit and credit cards, liquidity support for the banking sector, and incentives for research and development (UT, 2009).

The recent outcomes of the economic policies, programs and fiscal stimulus packages implemented during 2008-2009 and recovery period of 2010 in Turkey are summarized below using the set of indicators prepared by the Undersecretariat of Treasury about different areas of the Turkish Economy (UT, 2011).

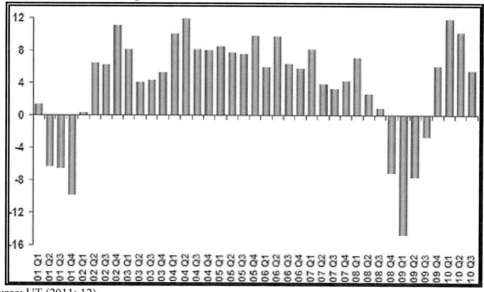

Source: UT (2011: 12).

Figure 1. GDP Growth Rates (%, YoY).

As seen from Figure 1, the Turkish economy grew impressively with an annual rate of 5.9% between 2002 and 2008. However, its export-oriented economy and high rate of unemployment accompanied with diminishing external demand made Turkey to feel the impacts of the current economic crisis on the real sector considerably. The crisis caused a sharp decrease in the fourth quarter growth rate of GDP in 2008 (-7,0%) after an increase in 27 quarters in row since 2001.

The decline continued until the last quarter of 2009, but, the first and second quarterly growth rates in 2009 were much worse than the previous quarter. The growth rate of GDP in 2009 decreased to -14,6% in the first quarter, -7,6% in the second quarter and -2,7% in the third quarter, respectively, while the economy started to grow again by 6% in the last quarter of 2009. As a result, the yearly average growth rate at the end of 2009 become negative (-4,7%) for the first time since the financial crises of 2001. The growth continued during 2010 due to favorable expectations about the Turkish economy and improvement in the external demand and internal demand. The first quarter growth rate of GDP in 2010 increased to 11,7%, which then started to decline in the second quarter to 10,3%, and in the third quarter to 5,5%. As a result of this trend, the growth rate increased to 8,9% in the first 9 months of 2010 and expected to continue to increase in the last quarter of 2010 (UT, 2010).

High unemployment level characterizes the Turkish economy, where almost half of the labor force employed in the service sector while a quarter in the agriculture sector, since even during the periods in which the Turkish economy experienced growth (see Figure 1), the unemployment rate stayed over 10% (see Figure 2). As a result of the crisis of 2008 the unemployment rate increased to 13.6% in 2008. However as the recovery of the Turkish economy picked up in 2010, the unemployment rate started to decrease to became 11,2% as of October 2010.

Another characteristic of the Turkish economy the high inflation rate was on average 62,7% and 71,6% during 1983-1994 and 1995-2001, respectively. However after a long period with these high inflation rates, Turkey experienced outstandingly low inflation rates during the last decade (12,5%), and achieved almost single digit inflation since 2004. The downward trend of inflation continued, however, it has become harder for the Turkish authorities to get further lower inflation rates.

Although the crisis of 2008 affected the Turkish economy adversely, it had some positive consequences on current account balance and foreign debt stock. As seen in Figure 4 both imports and export figures declined during the crises. The trade figures in 2009 and 2010 were still below the pre-crisis year of 2008.

Since imports declined faster than exports, the current account deficit decreased significantly and thus facilitated the finance of deficit during the years of crisis. However, the large current account deficits become problem again in 2010 as the growth increased. The aforementioned high rates of growth increased the demand for imports considerably and led to deterioration in the current account balance of Turkey. This ascertains the positive correlation between growth rate and import, so correlation with current account. Today the current account deficit and its financing with "hot money" seems to be one of the most important structural problems for the Turkish economy (see Figure 5).

Evidently, as seen in the Table 4 above, the share of foreign direct investment and external borrowing of non-bank private sector increased during the 2004-2008 period to finance current account deficit. This capital inflow was financing trade and investment activities. As seen in Figure 6, the share of these in total capital inflows decreased during the 2009-2010 period.

Meanwhile in terms of the prospect of EU membership, although many of member states of EU did not meet the Maastricht criteria for along time, Turkey succeeded to meet the requirements before the global crisis thanks to the recent fiscal policy implementations reflected themselves on the balances of the general government sector and declining debt figures. The general government deficit/GDP ratio was less than 3% during the period of 2005-2008.

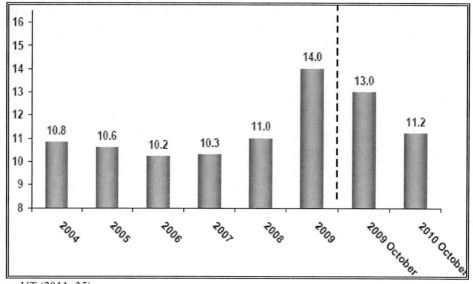

Source: UT (2011: 35).

Figure 2. Unemployment Rates (%).

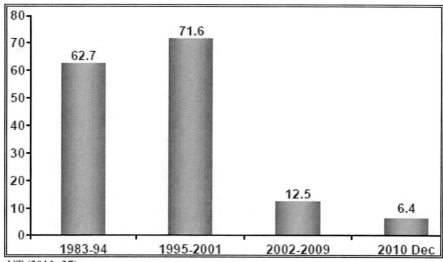

Source: UT (2011: 37).

Figure 3. Average Inflation in Periods (%).

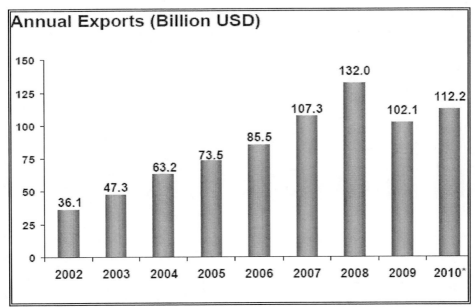
* Annualized as of November 2010.

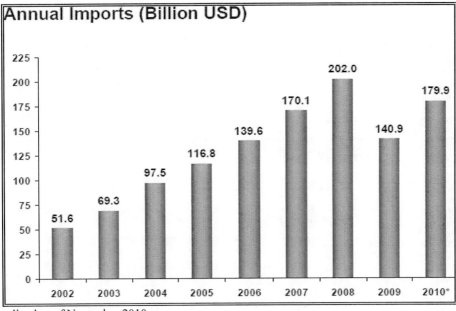
* Annualized as of November 2010.
Source: UT (2011: 51-52).

Figure 4. Foreign Trade, in billions of US dollars.

However, with the global crisis the public finance performance in Turkey deteriorated (see Figure 7). While the tax revenues were realized well below the projected budget forecasts because of the contraction in growth and tax cuts to support the real sector, the expenditures increased due to the fiscal stimulus measures introduced to mitigate the negative effects of the global financial crisis by increasing domestic demand. So, the budget deficit, debt burden and the Treasury debt rolling ratio increased more than projected. As a result of the effects of current crisis in 2009, the general government deficit/GDP ratio realized as %6,7, which was above the requirement of the Maastricht criteria of 3% (SPO, 2009, and UT, 2010)

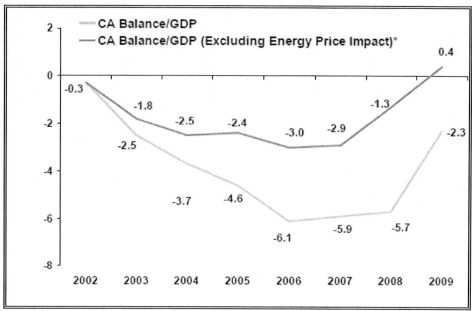

* With 2002 energy prices.
Source: UT (2011: 62).

Figure 5. Current Account Deficit/GDP Ratio (%).

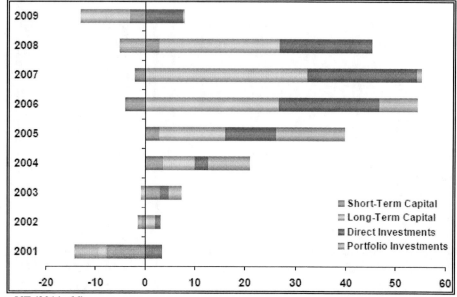

Source: UT (2011: 66).

Figure 6. Capital Inflows (Billion USD).

On the other hand, despite the adverse impacts of the global crisis of 2008 on the public finance performance and the debt figure, Turkey managed to keep the EU-defined public sector gross debt stock to GDP ratio below the level stated in the Maastricht Criteria. As seen in Figure 8, this ratio was decreasing during the 2001-2008 period and it was below the 60% threshold since 2004. The developments in the budget balance, decrease in the tax revenue, and the contraction in the economy caused an increase in the EU-defined general government nominal debt stock to GDP ratio. Although this ratio increased to 39.5% in 2008, and 45.5% in 2009, the public debt stock/GDP ratio stayed below the 60% threshold, better than in many EU member states.

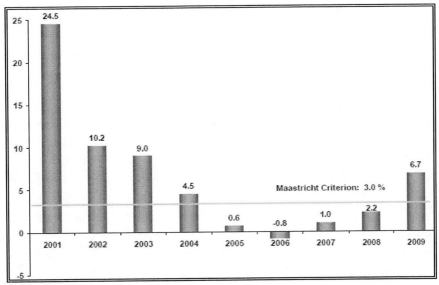

Source: UT (2011: 73).

Figure 7. EU Defined Government Budget Deficit (% of GDP).

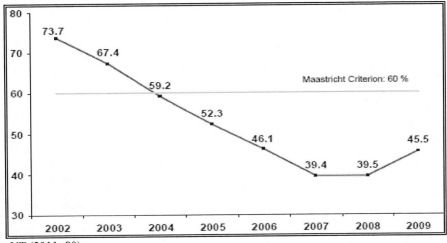

Source: UT (2011: 80).

Figure 8. Public Sector Gross Debt Stock (EU Defined, % of GDP).

CONCLUSION

During the transformation process initiated in 1980, the dimensions of macroeconomic indicators and the size of the Turkish economy changed remarkably. Turkey became a more diversified economy, integrated with European and World markets through trade and financial channels. As expected, accompanied with political uncertainties derived from frequently changing coalition governments and applied inappropriate economic policies, these channels made the Turkish economy more vulnerable to the impact of external influences. As illustrated in the previous section, Turkey seems to be facing the first shock waves of the last external test of economic transformation reasonably well.

Accordingly, as seen in Figure 9, in the Medium Term Program (2011-2013), the envisaged growth of Turkish economy (6,8%) worth $730 billion in 2010, making Turkey one of the fastest growing states in Europe and World. This economic growth is expected to continue, though at a lower rate, at 4,5%, 5,0% and 5,5% in these three years, respectively, reaching approximately $913 billion at the end of 2013. Meanwhile, the decline in the inflation rate is also expected to carry on, diminishing to 4,9% at the end of 2013.

Nevertheless, the unemployment rate and current account deficit are likely to remain as major structural problems of the Turkish economy in the foreseeable future. The unemployment rate is estimated to remain high around 14% until the end of 2012 (EC, 2010). Besides, the high risk derived from large current account deficits of foreign trade transactions is anticipated to continue as the growth rate increases (5,2%, estimate for 2013). The government deficit/GDP ratio is also projected to have similar trend as current account deficit. The estimate for 2010 (-4%) is higher than the Maastricht criteria of -3%, but it is projected to decline in the following three years, settling at -1,1% at the end of 2013.

As a result, considering Turkey's promising political and economic flexibility in response to the recent global economic challenge, the projected recovery of the Turkish economy is expected. The speed and depth of recovery, however, will largely be determined by not only the Turkish commitment to the transformation process, but also the improvements in the World economy.

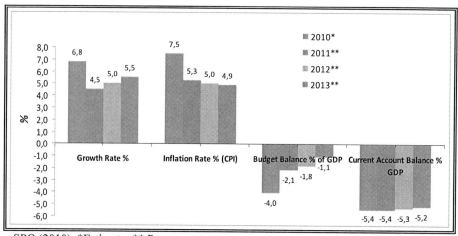

Source: SPO (2010), *Estimate, ** Programme.

Figure 9. Main Macroeconomic and Fiscal Targets of Medium Term Program (2011-2013).

REFERENCES

BRSA (2002), *Banking Sector Restructuring Program Progress Report*-(V), Banking Regulation and Supervision Agency, November 2002.

BRSA (2010), From Crisis to Financial Stability (Turkey Experience), Banking Regulation and Supervision Agency, Working Paper, Revised Third Edition, September 3, 2010.

CBRT (2009), Financial Stability Report, Central Bank of Republic of Turkey, May 2009.

Celasun, M. (2002), 2001 Krizi, Öncesi ve Sonrasi: Makroekonomik ve Mali Bir Değerlendirme, Retrieved December 23, 2010 from http://www.econ.utah.edu/~ehrbar /erc2002/pdf/i053.pdf, Page:1-42.

Chiodo, A. J. and M. T. Owyang (2002), A Case Study of a Currency Crisis: The Russian Default of 1998, The Federal Reserve Bank of St. Louis, November-December, page:7-17.

EC (2010), 2010 Pre-accession Economic Programmes of candidate countries: EU Commission assessment", Directorate-General for Economic and Financial Affair, Occasional Papers 69, European Commission, September 2010.

Ercel, G. (2006), Globalization and the Turkish Economy. Vanderbilt University, November 2006, Page:2-10.

Halisçelik, E. (2009), Cooperation of the International Funding Organizations for Developing Countries - The Case of Turkey, Carnegie Mellon University, Heinz College, May 2009.

IMF (2005), Turkey: IMF Executive Board Approves US$10 Billion Stand-By Arrangement for Turkey, International Monetary Fund, Press Release No. 05/104, May 11, 2005, Page: 1-3

IMF (2009), World Economic Outlook: Crisis and Recovery, Retrieved December 22, 2010, from, http://www.imf.org/external/pubs/ft/weo/2009/01/pdf/text.pdf, International Monetary Fund, 10 April 2009.

IMF (2010a), Turkey: Financial Position in the Fund as of November 30, 2010, Retrieved December 26, 2010, from http://www.imf.org/external/np/fin/tad/exfin2. aspx? memberkey1=980anddate1Key=2010-11-30.

IMF (2010b), IMF Managing Director Sees Impressive Commitment by Turkey to Economic Reforms; Executive Board Approves US$16 Billion Stand-By Credit, Press Release No. 02/7, February 4, 2002, Retrieved December 28, 2010, from http://imf.org /external/np/sec/ pr/2002/pr0207.htm.

Kantarcı, H.B. and Karacan, R. (2008), Mali Disiplinin Sağlanması Açısından Türkiye IMF İlişkilerinin Değerlendirilmesi, Maliye Dergisi Sayı 155 Temmuz-Aralık 2008, Page:149-150.

Kaul, I. and P. Conceição (2006), *The New Public Finance: Responding to Global Challenges*, Oxford University Press.

Krueger, A. O. (1995), Partial Adjustment and Growth in the 1980s in Turkey, in: Dornbusch, R. and S. Edwards (ed.), Reform, Recovery, and Growth: Latin America and the Middle East, p. 343 – 368. http://www.nber.org/books/dorn95-1.

Onis, Z. And C. Kirkpatrick (1985), "Industrialization as a Structural Determinant of Inflation Performance in IMF Stabilization Programmes in Less Developed Countries", Journal of Development Studies, Vol. 21, No. 3.

Radelet, S., Sachs, J.D., Cooper, R.N., Bosworth, B.P. (1998). The East Asian Financial Crisis: Diagnosis, Remedies, Prospects. Brookings Papers on Economic Activity.

RT (2010), Ministerial Dialogue between the Economic And Finance Ministers of the EU and the Candidate Countries, Speech of Minister Of State And Deputy Prime Minister Ali Babacan, Republic of Turkey, 18 May 2010.

SPO (2006), Turkey Ninth Development Plan (2007-2013), Retrieved December 19, 2010, from http://ekutup.dpt.gov.tr/plan/ix/9developmentplan.pdf, State Planning Organization

SPO, 2009, Medium Term Programme (2010-2012), State Planning Organization, September 2009.

SPO (2010), Medium Term Program (2011-2013), Main Macroeconomic and Fiscal Targets, State Planning Organization, 11 October 2010.

Todaro, M.P. and S.G. Smith (2009), *Economic Development*, Addison Wesley, Tenth Edition.

Toprak, D. (2010), The Trend of the Debts in Times of Crisis in Turkey: 1994 and 2001 crises, Suleyman Demirel University, *The Journal of Visionary*, Y.2010, Vol.2, No.2. Page:1-14

TÜSİAD (1995), Türkiye İçin Yeni Bir Orta Vadeli Istikrar Programına Doğru, Haziran 1995, (Yayın No: TÜSİAD.T/95.6.180).

UT, 2008, Turkish Economy: Key Achievements and Medium Term Outlook, Retrieved December 21, 2010, from http://www.treasury.gov.tr/iro_files/Reports-Presentations/Turkish%20Economy_Roadshow2008.pdf, Undersecretary of Treasury, January 2008.

UT (2009), Kuresel Mali Krize Karsi Politika Tedbirleri, Retrieved December 15, 2010, from. http://www.hazine.gov.tr/doc/Guncel/Politika_Tedbirleri.pdf, Undersecretariat of Treasury, 10 August 2009.

UT (2010), Public Debt Management Report 2010, Retrieved December 26, 2010, from http://www.hazine.gov.tr/irj/go/km/docs/documents/Treasury%20Web/Research%26Data /Public%20Debt%20Management%20Report/pdmr_2010_eng_06.07_v4.pdf, Undersecretariat of Treasury.

UT (2011), Turkish Economy, Indicator Set About Different Areas of Turkish Economy, Retrieved January 19, 2011, from http://www.treasury.gov.tr/irj/go/km/docs/ documents/ Treasury%20Web/Statistics/Economic%20Indicators/egosterge/Sunumlar/Ekonomi_Sun umu_ENG.pdf, Undersecretariat of Treasury (Last update: January 17, 2011).

Uygur, E. (2010), The Global Crisis and the Turkish Economy, Working Papers 2010/3, Turkish Economic Association, Page:1-2.

Williamson, J. (1989), What Washington Means by Policy Reform, in: Williamson, J. (ed.): Latin American Readjustment: How Much has Happened, Washington: *Institute for International Economics*.

In: Regulation and Competition in the Turkish Banking… ISBN: 978-1-61324-990-1
Editors: Tamer Çetin and Fuat Oğuz © 2012 Nova Science Publishers, Inc.

Chapter 3

PROPERTY RIGHTS ISSUE AND RENT SEEKING IN TURKEY: A TIME SERIES STUDY WITH COINTEGRATION AND ERROR CORRECTION TECHNIQUES FOR THE PERIOD OF 1960-2002

Dilek Demirbas[1] and Safa Demirbas[2]***

[1]Reader in Economics and International Business Northumbria
University, Newcastle Business School, Newcastle Business School,
CCE1 442, Newcastle upon Tyne, NE1 8ST, UK
[2]Freelance Economist and Deputy General Manager
at TASIS, Ankara, Kizilay, Turkey

ABSTRACT

The property rights issue is one of the most important institutional differences between democratically developed and developing countries. In most of the cases, the violation of the property rights results with rent-seeking activities. In this chapter, Katz and Rosenberg's budgetary variable model has been tested in a time series study for the period of 1960 to 2002 to measure rent-seeking activities in Turkey. It is found that there is a cointegrating relationship exists between variables, by which mean that there is a long-run relationship between budgetary rent-seeking (R_t), GNP per capita ($GNPC_t$) and Government Size (GY_t). It is also found that independent variables help to explain rent-seeking activities in Turkey during the period 1960-2002. In addition to these cointegrated relationships, it is showed that adjustments are made towards restoring the long-run relationship between rent-seeking and other variables.

Keywords: Property Rights, Rent-Seeking, Budgetary Allocation, and Time Series Study

---

* E-mail: Dilek.Demirbas@unn.ac.uk; Tel: 00 44 (0)191 227 4972.

** Tel: 00 90 (0)312 3069020; safademirbas@yahoo.com.

1. INTRODUCTION

In the Keynesian view of the economy it was accepted that governments generally play an important role in stimulating economic activity by operating their functions appropriately and effectively. In particular, the main functions of government in both developed and developing countries are expected to be maintaining public services, influencing attitudes, shaping economic institutions, influencing the distribution of income, influencing the use of resources, controlling the quantity of money, controlling economic fluctuations, ensuring full employment and influencing the level of investment.

Many developing countries are in a vicious circle of low living standards (low per capita national income, unequal distribution of national income, poverty, poor health and education opportunities); low levels of productivity; high population growth rates; high unemployment; high foreign debts; underdeveloped industries; high dependency on agriculture etc. (Thirwall, 1989). In addition to these common characteristics, developing countries also suffer because of weak economic and political institutions; such as unprotected property rights, absence of a constitutional framework and undeveloped government that cannot carry out its functions properly.

It is widely accepted that governments, in general, play an important role in stimulating economic activity by operating their functions appropriately and effectively. In particular, the main functions of government in both developed and developing countries are expected to be; maintaining public services, influencing attitudes, shaping economic institutions, influencing the distribution of income, influencing the use of resources, controlling the quantity of money, controlling economic fluctuations, ensuring full employment and influencing the level of investment.

There are no doubt we all need government to protect us, to secure my rights from violation and to provide public goods that cannot be well provided through ordinary market processes. The ability of governments to use their monopoly of legitimate forces is central to the fulfillment of those tasks. However, this monopoly power may be used for other purposes. Governments in developing countries may do things for bad reasons that are essentially corrupt, e.g. giving favors to their supporters. Therefore, governments may fail either because they do too little, or because they do too much. In many developing countries, the degree of economic power of governments dominates their political power, since they find it difficulty to isolate the economic role of the state from its political, social and military roles.

If governments do the right things economic growth and political stability might be achieved. Nevertheless, if they do too little or too much or the wrong things, growth and stability are retarded. For instance, protectionism in trade in many developing countries is still seen as one of the main functions of a dominant state[13]. This point led Hayek (1944) and many other liberal economists to argue that an extension of state ownership or the forms of the state involvement in the economy necessarily gave rise to a totalitarian, repressive political system.

Indeed, in many developing countries, governments fail to maintain equality, promote the exploitation of one class by another and neglect public services. At the same time, they may put in place excessive controls (by regulations) and end up with over spending. More importantly, rather than protecting rights from violation, governments use their power as an

---

[13] Economically, politically and socially dominant state.

instrument of violation of property rights as much of the literature on rent-seeking notes. As it is known, if capital formation is one of the conditions of economic growth, the existence of a law of property is one of the conditions of capital formation. With the concept of property it is meant that the legal right to exclude other people from using a particular resource. In order to secure property rights it is necessary for governments to protect public property from private abuse and it is necessary to protect private property from public abuse and private abuse. Nevertheless, governments in developing countries often use their authority and their confiscatory power to provide privileges desired by particular politically-influential people at public expense (Tullock, 1993). In other words, if governments cannot or do not want to protect the property rights of the public for the favor of some privileged groups, rent-seeking increases.

According to Tullock (1967), undesirable rent-seeking occurs in the case of unwilling uncompensated transfers. On the same line, McNutt (1996:164) emphasized that "when I interpret rent-seeking activity as an abridgement of property rights, then traditional rent-seeking is undesirable if the individual or society is inadequately compensated for the transfer of resources that takes place". If these uncompensated groups are investors whose property rights are not protected and whose welfare losses are uncovered, capital is discouraged and this deepens the vicious circle of poverty of developing countries.

Although these unprotected property rights issues seem to be mainly a problem of developing countries, it actually affects both groups of countries but to a different degree. It is certainly true that rent-seeking is everywhere, but at different levels. In the public choice approach, it is considered that a theory of property rights is a very important issue and requires a complete theory of 'the state'. As an extension of this idea it is also considered that property rights, the state structure and rent-seeking activities are closely interrelated with each other. For this reason, in order to reduce rent-seeking, Tullock (1993) suggests several political reforms that might improve violated property rights. These are; qualified majority voting, greater use of referenda, a balanced budget, limits on the size and the extent of government, and better constitutional enforcement. In the light of the property rights issue, it is considered that if rent-seeking is the violation of property rights, it can be interesting to associate and compare rent-seeking with different institutional settings in a country.

According to Katz and Rosenberg (1989:140), "developed economies with established hierarchies tend to be less wasteful than less developed economies, which are typically still trying to find their political and social identity by shifts in the relative power of pressure groups". Katz and Rosenberg (1989: 140) stated that, "strong property rights reduce rent-seeking activities". It is important to mention here that understanding rent-seeking activities in many developing countries and especially in Turkey is the key to deal with property rights problems.

In order to examine the institutional issue in Turkey in the context of rent-seeking, we undertook a time series study. When we carry out a time series study we should consider cointegration analysis to deal with the long term relationships between variables. Cointegration analysis confronts spurious regression, attempting to identify conditions under which the regression relationship is not spurious. The problem of spurious regression occurs because most economic time series are non-stationary. A stochastic process is said to be stationary, if the mean, variance and covariance of a series remain constant over time. If one or more of the conditions are not satisfied, the process is non-stationary (Charemza and Deadman, 1997).

This chapter is organized as follows. In section 2 rent-seeking in developing countries will be examined. In section 3, rent-seeking variable and key assumptions will be looked at and in section 4 the methodology and the estimation techniques will be explained. Then, in section 5 the findings will be presented and the study will be concluded in section 6.

2. RENT-SEEKING IN DEVELOPING COUNTRIES

After World War II many colonized countries began to achieve their independence and chose statism as their development path. This approach to economic development emphasized the role of state control. However, economic planning became highly politicized and, therefore, rent-seeking intensified. Unfortunately, many of the new constitutions in these newly independent countries were not designed to respond effectively to demand by the people for greater levels of economic and political participation and for structures which reflected domestic realities, needs, customs etc. In addition, since their institutional frameworks were also developed on the basis on state coercion and not on the institutions of popular participation, the choice of statism put significant amounts of resources into the hands of the bureaucrats and the military, allowing them to manipulate policy outcomes to benefit themselves. On many occasions such as trade protection, control of the economy by the state has encouraged and facilitated bureaucratic corruption, nepotism, political violence and increased the level and the extent of rent-seeking in these countries (Mbaku, 1992).

Increasing political violence and high rent-seeking in many developing countries took the attention of some public choice scholars to understand their political structure and to seek solutions to stop such extreme rent-seeking activities. For that reason, in the mid-1970s, a new political economy started to be applied to politics in developing countries. Public policy is examined from the new political economy perspective with particular reference to the state's role in resource allocation in those countries, on the basis of the behaviour of state regulators and interest groups seeking government favours. Such favors include access to import and other licenses, commodities sold at government-controlled prices, subsidized housing, government scholarships for advanced training abroad, etc. As is known, the type of behavior most often associated with interest groups in these heavily regulated economies is rent-seeking (Mbaku, 1994).

Initial applications of rent-seeking to the developing countries were carried out by Krueger (1974) and Bhagwati (1982)[14]. According to Meier (1991), in applying the new political economy to developing countries, the economic role of the state has to be specified very carefully to know whether the state is autonomous (having its own objectives), or merely passive (responding to the demands of various interests or classes in society).

Findlay (1991) grouped the types of states in the developing countries as traditional monarchies (Saudi Arabia, Morocco, Jordan etc.), traditional dictatorships (Cuba, Paraguay, Haiti etc.), authoritarian states with on the right wing: (Turkey, Egypt, Brazil, Argentina etc.), and on the left: (China, Vietnam, North Korea etc.); the democratic states of Sri Lanka, Venezuela, Costa Rica, Jamaica etc. Findlay stated that most under developed countries today are ruled by military juntas or are one-party dictatorships, and the state tends to dominate civil

---

[14] Although some of the early rent-seeking studies were considered without political content the quantitative restriction or tariff was simply imposed exogenously.

society. He believes that if the new political economy is applied to developing countries, we can highlight some of the most important problems such as corruption, trade restrictions, import substitution policies, resource allocation, and dependence on foreign capital.

Tullock also stated that the majority of the world's population is ruled by autocracies. Moreover, he predicted that "since 1914, on the whole, democracy has become a less significant form of government and dictatorship more important" (Tullock, 1987:1). Since most autocratic systems are in developing countries, the property rights issue in those countries gain in importance.

Grindle (1991: 42) researched "the applicability of new political economy to conditions in developing countries". He suggested that "new political economy is not applicable to the dynamics of policy making in developing countries when it takes a society-centered approach"[15]. However, "it might be more applicable when this society-centered approach is replaced with a more state-centered perspective"[16]. In this way, Grindle analyzed lobbying by interest groups, the actions of policy makers and the activities of bureaucrats. He considered that although the interaction of individualistic rent-seeking bureaucrats and individualistic rent-seeking citizens does not explain the most critical aspects of the politics of policy implementation in developing countries, it still provides crucial information on corruption, nepotism, bribery between bureaucrats and private businessmen.

On the applicability of the new political economy to conditions in developing countries, Ranis (1991) also analyzed and concluded that he is quite skeptical of the relevance of the new political economy to developing countries on the existence of autonomous states. For him, the new political economy will not be enough to explain the whole structure in developing countries since it also consists of customs, traditional institutions, religion etc.

Bagchi (1993: 1729) claimed that "we have to redefine the concept of rent-seeking and its application in order to denigrate all government intervention and virtually to abolish the domain of politics in the developing countries". According to him, in most developing countries, the biggest groups of rent-earners are still landlords and rich farmers. The effect of landlordism has to be taken into account, and incentives under this system in developing countries have to be examined.

Brough and Kimenyi 1986, Kimenyi 1989, 1987, Mbaku 1991a, 1991b, 1992, 1994, Mbaku and Paul 1989, Anderson 1988 and others have concentrated mainly on African countries, in which dictatorships and military coups are both the most common types of rent-seeking. By examining these non-democratic countries either historically or analytically, these writers intended to analyze interest groups and their rent-seeking creation from the public choice perspective. They concluded that the civil and military bureaucrats are the most dominant rent-seeking interest groups in those countries, and bureaucratic corruption and political violence are also the most common rent-seeking activities.

---

[15] It is based on assumptions about interest mobilisation and government response to lobbying activities.

[16] It is based on political elites who are actively engaged in maximising their political power or on rent-seeking bureaucrats.

3. Rent-Seeking Variable and Assumptions

For our estimation, we use a variable for rent-seeking the way Katz and Rosenberg considered. According to Katz and Rosenberg (1989), government transfers generate waste and lower actual national income[17], whilst not necessarily changing the accounting of national income[18]. Thus, they offered a method for measuring the waste due to rent-seeking which results from the government's budget. Their measure of rent-seeking was related to changes in government *spending* rather than only changes in government *transfers* alone. Katz and Rosenberg (1989:138) claimed that "to the extent government spending uses up some real resources, any rent-seeking in that category is unlikely to be equal to 100 percent of spending. Yet that is what we are forced to assume by the data available" Therefore, Katz and Rosenberg stressed that they may have overestimated rent-seeking when the changes in government *spending* are considered. In order to capture the total change in the proportional allocation of government spending for different purposes, they use a measure, R_{ij}, which is the measure of total budget related rent-seeking and equals the sum of marginal changes in property rights. To do that, Katz and Rosenberg divided the budget into nine categories including; Health, Defense, Education, Social Security and Welfare, Housing, Other Community and Services, Economic Services, Other Purposes. In addition, they took the *changes* in each of the nine categories between period (t-1) and (t) as a proxy for rent-seeking. With this study they intended to fill a gap in the literature by examining the macroeconomic effects of rent-seeking, since many studies have dealt mostly with rent-seeking effects of microeconomic government intervention such as government's microeconomic policy or regulation.

Katz and Rosenberg's estimates of rent-seeking induced by the government budget were based on two assumptions. *First*, it is assumed that every inter-period change in government budget shares arose from rent-seeking activities by special interest groups. This assumption stems from the idea that interest groups lobby government officials. Since government officials would like to stay in the office, they increase their budget to transfer more to interest groups in order to satisfy their demands. Rent-seeking battles take place at the margin in order to alter the structure of property rights over the budget and governments are lobbied in return of benefits. Hence, any change in the proportional composition of total government spending was assumed to be indicative of a waste of resources resulting from rent-seeking. In other words it is assumed that these changes occur from transfers for special interest groups to maximum their benefits. This assumption views government spending as self-serving by the government rather than as an altruistic response to the needs of the public.

Katz and Rosenberg's *second assumption* was that the aggregate net benefit from this special rent-seeking is zero; that is resources are expended until the marginal benefit from budgetary allocations is equal to marginal cost. Thus, the activities of special interest groups in pursuit of rents are a pure waste of national resources.

---

[17] It is considered that scarce resources are wasted, since they are used by economic acents to obtain monopoly power and not used in productivity increasing activities.

[18] Indeed, even the composition of accounting national income might remain unchanged.

4. Methodology: Cointegration Test and Error Correction

The concept of cointegration was first used by Granger in 1981. Cointegration is the statistical implication of the existence of a long-run relationship between economic variables (Thomas, 1993). The main idea behind cointegration is that if, in the long-run, two or more series move closely together, even though the series themselves are trended, the difference between them is constant. It is possible to regard these series as defining a long-run equilibrium relationship, for the difference between them is stationary (Hall and Henry, 1989).

Charemza and Deadman (1997: 144) defined cointegration as:

Time series x_t and y_t are said to be cointegrated of order d, b where $d \geq b \geq 0$, written as;

$$x_t, y_t \sim CI(d,b), \tag{1}$$

If:

1. both series are integrated [19] of order d,

2. There exists a linear combination of these variables, say $\alpha_1 x_t + \alpha_2 y_t$, which is integrated of order d-b

According to this definition, $[\alpha_1, \alpha_2]$ is called a cointegrating vector. Cointegrating coefficients, which constitute the cointegrating vector, can be identified with parameters in the long-run relationship between the variables. In the case of cointegration, if these variables are cointegrated, they cannot move too far away from each other. In contrast, a lack of cointegration suggests that such variables have no long-run relationship (Dickey et al., 1991, Eagle and Boo, 1987).

The order of integration of the variables is one very important topic related to cointegration. In the literature, much of the theory of cointegration has been developed for the cases where all series are integrated of order one, that is I(1). It must be stressed that if variables in a long run relationship are of different orders of integration and the order of integration of a dependent variable is lower than the highest order of integration of the explanatory variables, there must be at least two explanatory variables integrated of this highest order if the necessary conditions for stationary of the error term are to be met.

There are three notions behind cointegration to be mentioned here: spurious correlation, stationary [20] time series and error correction modeling (ECM). According to Granger and Newbold (1974), spurious regressions are typically characterized by a very low Durbin-

---

[19] Integration is the representation of a process as a sum of past shocks. A process is said to be integrated of order d ((I(d)) if after differencing d times the resulting process is stationary (denoted I(0)).

[20] Stationarity of a series implies that graphs of a realisation of a time series over two equal-length time intervals should exhibit similar statistical characteristics. Stationary series have a tendency to return to their original value after a random shock; the mean and the variance of such a series do not change with the passage of time.

Watson statistic.[21] If there is a high degree of correlation between two variables, it does not automatically imply the existence of a casual relationship between the variables concerned (Holden and Thomson, 1992). For example, a high R^2 may only indicate correlated trends and a not true economic relationship (Miller, 1991). To remedy this problem, the cointegration technique and error correction modeling are recommended (Bahmani-Oskooee and Alse, 1993).

The most common used cointegration technique is the Engle-Granger's cointegration and error correction modeling which involves two stages. *The first stage* determines the orders of integration for each of the variables; that is, differences each series successively until stationary series emerge, then attempts to estimate cointegrating regressions by ordinary least squares, by using variables with the same order of integration. *The second stage* if there is a cointegrating relationship between the variables, constructs the error correction representation of the model.

Since standard regression analysis requires that data series be stationary, the first step is to identify the order of integration of each of the variables. Therefore, the unit root test will be applied. Although there are several tests for the presence of unit roots in time series data, the standard testing procedure for determining the order of integration of a time series is the Augmented Dickey-Fuller (ADF) test (Dickey and Fuller, 1979, 1981, Maddala,).

5. TIME SERIES MODELS AND TEST RESULTS FOR THE PERIOD OF 1960-2002

5.1. Time Series Models and Data

In order to analyze Turkey's case in more detail, we carried out a time series analysis in which government size and a few dummy variables are added to the equation. Our main hypothesis is that the smaller the government size and the higher GNP per capita are (it means that resources are directed to productive areas rather than employing more staff or interest group activities), then the less rent-seeking there will be in the economy, since smaller government will waste of resources less and invest resources for welfare enhancing activities. Turkey is very interesting country from the viewpoint of institutional economy. The Turkish state can be classified as a 'strong state', which is "those simultaneously capable of resisting pressures and generating public policy initiatives on their own" (Caporaso and Levine, 1992: 183). On the other hand, the interest groups are weak unorganized and seek for protection. The government budget will represent the policy initiatives of the state (the civil and military bureaucrats).

The size of government and its relationship with rent-seeking has been explored by Tullock (1967), Downs (1957) and Niskanen (1971). In the mainstream public choice literature, while Buchanan and Tullock (1962) advanced the central idea that strong interest groups determine the size of the government. Niskanen (1971), using an oversupply hypothesis, has argued that the bureaucracy contributes to the size of government. When rent-

---

[21] "Spurious regression problems may exist when the adjusted R^2 is higher than the DW statistic; under such circumstances the coefficient estimates are problematic"(Miller, 1988: 31-32).

seeking costs arise from politico-economic models based on the size and the growth of government, the size of government variable as an explanatory variable will be employed to explain rent-seeking activities. It is true that both "bureaucracy growth and rent-seeking reflect government failure; while bureaucrats as agent provocateurs may induce rent-seeking politicians aware of their re-election constraint" (McNutt, 1996:136). Therefore we expect a positive relationship between rent-seeking (R_t) and government size (GY_t).

On the other hand, the higher the per capita income the lower the emphasis on the need for government transfers. Simply at higher income levels, the margin of interest group competition is likely to be exercised in the market place. However, when the income is low, political allocation yields higher income benefits through transfers relative to the income derived from the market. In other words, it is more profitable for interest groups to invest their scarce resources to influence government policy than it is for them to invest in the market where the returns are low. The competition to control the instruments of wealth transfer is therefore likely to be more vigorous in low income than in high income countries.

In sum, the lower the per capita income (GNPC), the higher the political instability and the lower degree of political competition because the ruling coalition always seeks to monopolize the supply of legislation and to dissipate its transfers to the members of the supporting coalition. We, therefore, expect a negative relationship between the level of per capita income and rent-seeking. In order to capture this relationship we estimate two models. In the first model we excluded dummy variables and in the second we added dummies, and *Ln* stands for natural logarithm. Dummy variables are added to model to capture Turkey's special times.

Model 1

$$LnR_t = \alpha + \beta LnGNPC_t + \varphi LnGY_t + \varepsilon_t \tag{2}$$

Model 2

$$LnR_t = \alpha + \beta LnGNPC_t + \varphi LnGY_t + \chi Dum80 + \delta Dum71 + \gamma Dum74 + \varepsilon_t \tag{3}$$

In where;

LnR_t :The Logarithm of Budgetary Rent-Seeking (Data related with budget 1960-2002 in constant prices (1986=100)) from the Government Finance Statistic Yearbook, 1960-2002)

$LnGNPC_t$:The Logarithm of GNP per capita (1960-2002 in constant prices, from the Government Finance Statistic Yearbook, 1960-2002)

$LnGY_t$:The Logarithm of The Government Size (G) in where G stands for Government Expenditure from the Government Finance Statistic Yearbook, 1960-2002)

Dum80: Dummy variable for the 1980 Military Intervention
Dum74: Dummy variable for the 1974 Cyprus Conflict
Dum71: Dummy variable for the 1971 Military Intervention

The ADF test for order of Integration is shown in Table 1.

5.2. Unit Root Test for Order of Integration

Table 1. The ADF Test for Order of Integration

Variables.	Levels		1st Differences		Order of Integration
	ADF	CV	ADF	CV	
LnR_t	-0.60(0)	-2.95	-7.32(0)	-2.95	I(1)
$LnGNPC_t$	-0.68(0)	-2.95	-6.66(0)	-2.95	I(1)
$LnGY_t$	-0.10(1)	-3.56	-6.73(0)	-3.56	I(1)

The results in TABLE 1 suggest that all the variables appear to be stationary in their first differences. On the basis of this information, we can now estimate the Engle-Granger cointegration test first stage estimation.

5.2.1. The Engle-Granger First Stage Estimation for Turkey

In this section we estimated two Models in order to find out the long-run relationship between variables. TABLE 2 presents these results.

Table 2. Cointegration Regressions (Dependent Variable is LnR_t)

Regress	Model 1	Model 2
α	-1.60(-2.50)	-0.76(-1.86)
$LnGNPC_t$	-1.29(-2.02)	-0.47(-2.19)
$LnGY_t$	0.88(10.01)	0.77(8.67)
Dum80	--------	1.22(1.74)
Dum74	--------	1.21(1.72)
Dum71	--------	1.95(2.91)
R^2	0.91	0.94
$\overline{R}^2$	0.90	0.93
DW	1.43	1.72
F	162.82	92.08
SC	1.68	0.04
FF	2.96	2.19
N	1.01	0.27
H	0.00	0.16
ADF	-4.83	-5.59
ADF C.V. 95%	-4.00	-5.22

Notes: t-statistics are in parentheses. Asterisks donate significant at 5% . $\overline{R}^2$ is the adjusted coefficient of multiple determinations. DW is the Durbin-Watson statistic, F is the F statistic-ratio, SC is the serial correlation, FF is the functional form, N is the normality and H is the heteroskadasticity. *ADF c.v. has been taken from Charemza and Deadman (1997) at 5 % significance level.

As can be seen from TABLE 2, Model 2 with dummy variables have more explanatory power than Model 1, since, with dummy variables, DW, R^2 and $\overline{R}^2$ are much higher and the signs of all variables are as expected.

Since the calculated ADF values are more negative than the critical values we can now claim that a cointegrating relationship exists between variables, by which mean that there is a long-run relationship between budgetary rent-seeking (R_t), GNP per capita ($GNPC_t$) and Government Size (GY_t). Now we proceed to its second stage of the Engle-Granger estimation, which is the ECM model.

5.2.2. Error Correction Mechanism (ECM)

According to Engle and Granger (1987), if there is a cointegrating relationship between variables, there is a long-run relationship between them. Furthermore, the short-run dynamics can be described by the (ECM). This is known as the Granger representation theorem.

Below we present an equation in order to estimate whether short run adjustments are guided by, and consistent with, the long-run equilibrium or not for the case of rent-seeking, government size, income per capita, and some dummy variables to measure the effects of 1980 and 1971 Military Interventions and 1974 Cyprus Conflict.

This model is as follows:

Model 1

$$\Delta LnR_t = \beta \ ECM_{t-1} + \delta \ Ln\Delta GNPC_t + \varphi \ Ln\Delta GY_t + \varepsilon_t \tag{4}$$

Model 2

$$\Delta LnR_t = \beta \ ECM_{t-1} + \delta \ Ln\Delta GNPC_t + \varphi \ Ln\Delta GY_t + \chi\Delta Dum80$$
$$+ \delta\Delta Dum74 + \gamma\Delta Dum71 + \varepsilon_t \tag{5}$$

The ECM results can be seen from TABLE 3 and TABLE 4:

Table 3. ECM (Error Correction Mechanism) for Model 1

Dependent Variable is ΔLnR_t		
31 observations used for estimation from 1961 to 2002		
Regress	Coefficient	*T-Ratio*
$\Delta LnGNPC_t$	-1.16	-1.79
$\Delta LnGY_t$	0.28	1.87
ECM(-1)	-0.80	*-4.02*
$R^2 = 0.36$ $\overline{R}^2 = 0.30$ DW= 1.71 F -Stat. = 5.60 SC= 3.92 FF= 1.32 N= 0.76 H= 0.08		

Table 4. ECM (Error Correction Mechanism) for Model 2

Dependent Variable is ΔLnR_t		
31 observations used for estimation from 1961 to 2002		
Regress	Coefficient	T-Ratio
$\Delta LnGNPC_t$	-1.02	-1.95
$\Delta LnGY_t$	0.16	1.79
ECM(-1)	-0.91	-4.25
$\Delta Dum80$	0.75	1.79
$\Delta Dum74$	1.52	3.68
$\Delta Dum71$	1.33	3.05
R^2 =0.60 $\overline{R}^2$ = 0.50 DW= 1.60 F -Stat. = 6.57 C= 3.76 FF= 0.69 N=0.67 H=0.65		

It can be interpreted as ECM is less than one, minus and statistically significant. Not only error correction term but government size and GNP per capita also statistically significant. In that case only intercept has insignificant value. It shows that one unit increase in the change of GNP per capita causes 1.16 unit decreases and one unit increase the change in government size results with 0.28 unit increase in the change of budgetary rent-seeking in Turkey.

The coefficient on the ECM for the second model is also negative and significant. This means that adjustment is made towards the long-run relationship. In addition, all variables are statistically significant. In this model, one unit change in GNP per capita income causes 1.02 unit negative change in rent-seeking. Moreover, one unit increase in the change of government size results 0.16 increases in the change of rent-seeking.

CONCLUSION

In this chapter, Turkish budgetary rent-seeking activities are examined in a time series framework in order to understand developing countries better. To do so, we use a variable for rent-seeking the way Katz and Rosenberg (1989) considered. As they offered a method for measuring the waste due to rent-seeking which results from the government's budget, we used the same method and measured rent-seeking in relation to changes in government *spending* rather than only changes in government *transfers* alone, which is the measure of total budget related rent-seeking and equals the sum of marginal changes in property rights. To do that, we also divided the budget into nine categories including; Health, Defense, Education, Social Security and Welfare, Housing, Other Community and Services, Economic Services, Other Purposes, and took the *changes* in each of the nine categories between period (t-1) and (t) as a proxy for rent-seeking. Once we had the rent seeking data we looked the long run relationship between budgetary rent-seeking and government size as an indicator of property rights issue.

Secondly, it is found that there is a cointegrating relationship between rent-seeking as a percentage of the budget, government size and GNP per capita income in Model 1 and with dummies in Model 2. We found that independent variables help to explain rent-seeking activities in Turkey during the period 1960-2002. In addition to these cointegrated relationships, it is showed that adjustments are made towards restoring the long-run relationship between rent-seeking and other variables.

REFERENCES

Anderson, T. L. (1988). Public Finance in Autocratic Process: An Empirical Note. *Public Choice*, 57, 25-37.

Bagchi, A. K. (1993). Rent-Seeking, New Political Economy and Negation of Politics. *Economic and Political Weekly*, 28(34), 1729-35.

Bahmani-Oskooee, M. and Alse, S. (1993). Export Growth and Economic Growth: An Application of Cointegration and Error Correction Modeling. *The Journal of Development Areas*, 27, 535-42.

Bhagwati, J. N (1982). Directly Unproductive Profit-Seeking (DUP) Activities", *Journal of Political Economy*, 90, 988-1002.

Brough, W. T. and N. S. Kimenyi (1986). On the Inefficient Extraction of Rents by Dictators. *Public Choice*, 48, 37-48.

Buchanan, J.M. and G. Tullock (1962*). The Calculus of Consent. Logical Foundations of Constitutional Democracy*, Ann Arbor: University of Michigan Press.

Caporaso, J.A. and Levine, D.P. (1992). *Theories of Political Economy*, USA: Cambridge Univ. Press

Cheramza, W.W. and D. F. Deadman (1992; 1997*). New Directions in Econometric Practice*, Second Edition, Edward Elgar.

Dickey, D.A., Jansen, D.W. and Thornton, D.C. (1991). A Primer on Cointegration with an Application to Money and Income. *Review Federal Reserve Bank of ST. Luis*, 73(2), 58-78.

Dickey, D. A. and Fuller, W. A. (1979). Distribution of the Estimators for Autoregressive Time Series With a Unit Root. *Journal of the American Statistical Association*, 74, 427-431.

Dickey, D. A. and Fuller, W. A. (1981). Likelihood Ratio Statistics for Autoregressive Time Series With a Unit Root. *Econometrica*, 49, 1057-1072.

Downs, A. (1957). *An Economic Theory of Democracy,* New York: Harper and Row.

Engle, R.F. and Yoo, B.S. (1987). Forecasting and Testing in Co-integrated Systems. *Journal of Econometrics*, 35, 143-59.

Engle, R.F. and Granger, C.W.J. (1987). Cointegration and Error Correction: Regression, Estimation, and Testing. *Econometrica*, 55 (2), 251-276.

Findlay, R. D. (1991). The New Political Economy: Its Explanatory Power for LDCs, in G. M. Meier, (1991). *Politics and Policy Making in Developing Countries: Perspectives on the New Political Economy*, USA: ICS Press, 13-41.

Granger , C.W. J.and Newbold, P. (1974). Spurious Regressions in Econometrics. *Journal of Econometrics*, 35,143-159.

Grindle, M. S. (1991). The New Political Economy: Positive Economics and Negative Politics. in G. M. Meier (edit), *Politics and Policy Making in Developing Countries: Perspective on the New Political Economy,* 1991, ICS Press: US., pp.41-69.

Hall, S.G. and Henry, S.S.B. (1989). *Macroeconomic Modelling,* Amsterdam,: Elsevier Science Publishers.

Hayek, F.A. von (1944/1962). *To Road to Serfdom*, London: Routladge and Kegan Paul.

Holden, K. and Thomson, J. (1992). Co-integration: An Introductory Survey. *British Review of Economic Issues*, 14(33), 1-55.

Katz, E. and Rosenberg, J. (1989). Rent-seeking for Budgetary Allocation: Preliminary Results for 20 countries. *Public Choice*, 60, 133-144.

Kimenyi, M. S. (1987). Bureaucratic Rents and Political Institutions. *Journal of Public Finance and Public Choice*, 3, 189-199.

Kimenyi, M. S. (1989). Interest Groups, Transfer Seeking and Democratization: Competition for the Benefits of Governmental Power May Explain African Political Instability. *American Journal of Economics and Sociology*, 48(3), 339-349.

Krueger, A. (1974). The Political Economy of the Rent-Seeking Society. *American Economic Review* 64, 291-303.

Maddala, G.S.(1992). Introduction to Econometrics, 2nd. Edition, Prentice Hall, USA

Mbaku, J. (1991a). Military Expenditures and Bureaucratic Competition for Rents. *Public Choice*, 71, 19-31.

Mbaku, J. (1991b). State Control, Economic Planning and Competition Among Interest Groups for Government Transfers in Africa. *Journal of Social, Political and Economic Studies*, 16(2), 181-194.

Mbaku, J. (1992). Bureaucratic Corruption as Rent-Seeking Behavior. *Konjunkturpolitic*, 38, 247-265.

Mbaku, J. (1994). Military Coups as Rent-Seeking Behavior. *Journal of Political and Military Sociology*, 22, 241-284.

Mbaku, J. and C. Paul (1989). Political Instability in Afrika: A Rent-Seeking Approach. *Public Choice*, 63, 63-72.

McNutt, P. A.(1996). *The Economics of Public Choice,* UK: Edward Elgar.

Meier, G. M. (1991). *Politics and Policy Making in Developing Countries: Perspectives on the New Political Economy*, USA: ICS Press.

Miller, S.M. (1988). Are Saving and Investment cointegrated?. *Economic Letters*, 27, 31-34.

Niskanen, W.A.(1971). *Bureaucracy and Representative Government*, Chicago: Aldine-Atherton.

Ranis, G. (1991). The Political Economy of Development Policy Change. in G. Meier (edit), *Politics and Policy Making in Developing Countries: Perspective on the New Political Economy,* 1991, ICS Press, 69-123.

Thirwall, A.P. (1989). *Growth and Development*, 4th ed., London:Macmillan.

Thomas, R.L. (1993). *Introductory Econometrics: Theory and Applications*. 2nd ed, Logman.

Tullock, G. (1967). The Welfare Cost of Tariffs, Monopolies and Theft. *Western Economic Journal*, 5, 224-32.

Tullock, G. (1987). *Autocracy*, Boston: Kluwer Academic Publisher.

Tullock, G. (1993). *Rent-Seeking,* Cambridge: Edward Elgar.

PART II. TRANSITION TO REGULATORY STATE IN THE TURKISH BANKING SYSTEM

In: Regulation and Competition in the Turkish Banking...   ISBN: 978-1-61324-990-1
Editors: Tamer Çetin and Fuat Oğuz   © 2012 Nova Science Publishers, Inc.

Chapter 4

THE STRUCTURE AND REGULATION OF TURKISH BANKING SYSTEM: 2000-2010

Gülsün Gürkan Yay and Turan Yay
Yildiz Technical University, Department of Economics,
Istanbul, Turkey

ABSTRACT

The aim of this study is to discuss the structure, problems and regulation of Turkish Banking System during the 2000s. In this context, this chapter first analyzes the structural and cyclical reasons behind the Turkish financial crisis experience in 2000-2001. Secondly, the restructuring and regulation process of the Turkish Banking System in the post-crisis period is examined. The impact of the stand-by arrangement with IMF on this process and the degree of adaptation of the available legal framework to the international banking principles (Basel 1 and Basel 2) will be especially clarified. Lastly, it is argued that the decisive maintenance of this restructuring and regulation process up to 2010 is the main reason why the Turkish Banking system was relatively unaffected from the global financial crisis in 2008.

1. INTRODUCTION

A country's financial system is the backbone of that country's economy. The financial system fulfills significant functions if it is "efficient" and "perfect". Those functions are; providing savings and liquidity between different parties of the system (fund suppliers /savers and fund demanders/ investors), mitigating and sharing risk and supplying information. The financial system is a whole comprised of many financial markets, financial intermediaries and financial instruments. Moreover, banks constitute the centerpiece of the financial system although their weight may change from country to country.

Financial system in general and banks in particular are institutions that are based on trust. Although they are risk-averse, they are also innovative and creative. Tides and fluctuations among those few characteristics (being reliable and being creative) sometimes result in imbalances and system vulnerabilities. The internal and micro problems of the system (low profitability, time and currency mismatches, non-performing loans, shortcomings in risk-management, information asymmetry, corruption, etc.) as well as macroeconomic problems play a role in the emergence of those vulnerabilities. In this respect, the problems of the financial system stem both from market failures and government failures. Another characteristic of the system is that vulnerabilities or a loss in confidence that emerge in an institution/in a bank spreads quickly to the whole system or the economy (contagion and domino effect). One should also add to those characteristics national financial systems gaining an international dimension along with the rapidly developing financial and technological globalization in the last quarter of the 20th century. International positive and negative effects have also started to have a rapid contagion effect.

Due to all those characteristics, there is a necessity to regulate the financial sector (banks in particular). In a more detailed manner, we may name setting up the rules concerning banks' behaviors as *regulation*, controlling whether those rules are obeyed as *monitoring* and the general control of the banks' operations as *supervision* (Yay, Yay and Yılmaz, 2004: 102). The fact that regulations have an economic rationale of mitigating financial vulnerabilities, building up confidence in the system and eliminating market failures have been approved by most academics and institutions. However, the question of -how to- and -to what extent-regulate is always valid. Too much regulation and intervention, just as in the case of deregulation and problems caused by a limitless financial sector, have also consequences such as suffocating and disabling the financial sector and limiting innovations. For all those reasons, an optimal regulation-supervision framework should be created that takes into account the cost-benefit issues of regulation, which is a double-edged sword.

With the wave of deregulation that became widespread after the 1980s, stringent interventions to the financial sector (interest rate caps, required reserves, etc.), though loosened to a certain extent, have not been completely eliminated. An optimal regulation should avoid imposing costs on the sector, be market-friendly, harmonize the interests of the financial agents with the targets of the regulation authority, be oriented to the target not to the process and have a flexibility that does not hinder financial innovations. There are eight basic areas in banking regulations. These can be listed as government safety net, restrictions on bank asset holdings, capital requirements, chartering and bank examinations, assessment of risk management, disclosure requirements, consumer protection and restrictions on competition (Mishkin and Eakins, 2009). All of those regulations excluding the first one are regulation tools that prevent a financial vulnerability (or a crisis). On the other hand, the first one, that is government safety net, is a protective regulation tool that aims to protect the deposit owners, banks and the whole financial system in case of a bank failure. Other than the well-known deposit insurance applications that belong to this context, there are protective applications such as the state becoming a partner of the bank in trouble, the purchase of problematic assets by a fund created by the state, the Central Bank giving special loans to the troubled bank as a lender of last resort or financial consolidations. The presence of those protective tools that are expected to step in in case of a crisis enables a structure that prevents the spread of systemic crises by creating an environment of trust. However, this presence also increases the possibility of becoming a moral hazard by itself (Van Hoose, 2008: 133). Economic agents (depositors and banks) who expect that these measures are to be taken may tend not to avoid taking risks. For this reason, measures that prevent crises from happening are highly recommended over others. These protective measures, however, do not always have a power to eliminate crises completely. In the Basel I and Basel II Accords that were specifically created for this purpose in the international context, preventive measures are taken as a basis and a great deal of importance is attributed to implementing market discipline.

The financial system is usually the most regulated/monitored sector of all economies. Moreover, in times of financial crises regulations may become inevitable measures. Therefore, financial regulation and financial crisis are discussed in an intertwined manner.

Financial crises are as old as the history of capitalism. After the Great Depression in 1929, banking/financial crises broke out in many countries. Likewise, emerging markets went through debt crises in the 1970s and 1980s. However, twin crises of banking and balance of payments in 1990s that emerged mostly in the emerging markets, on grounds of their frequency and contagion effect, led to the impression that globalization had differentiated familiar crises in terms of their impact and shape. Consequently, new crisis theories were formulated to explain those twin crises of regional, if not of global, dimension (Yay and Yay, 2007: 345). The latest 2008 global crisis, on the other hand, started in the developed countries, mainly in the USA, the center of capitalism and gained a global character by spreading in waves. Although those crises have been explained every time by various factors; financial vulnerabilities, incomplete regulation and poor governance have come to the fore as the main ones. It is quite often emphasized in crises that insufficient/incomplete regulation is one of the reasons. Moreover, it is claimed after every crisis that increasing, diversifying and extending regulations are, so to speak, solutions to the existing problems.

Turkey, too, had a crisis at the end of 2000/beginning of 2001 similar to the twin crises (Kaminsky, Reinhart, 1999) that happened in many emerging markets (Mexico, Asia, Russia, Brazil, Argentine) in the 1990s. This crisis happened due to a lot of internal and external factors. Besides, its impacts and costs were greater than their counterparts in the past. However, the effort, determination and courage that was demonstrated was also more intensive and sustainable than before. Therefore, Turkey went through, as one might say, a structural and mental transformation on its way out of this crisis and learned important lessons accordingly. Although Turkey had felt the impact of the global crisis of 2008 only in 2009, it saw its immunity and perseverance against crises rise with the help of the lessons it had learned and the implementations it introduced. Moreover, Turkey also saw its resistance increase thanks to the improvements in its macro-fundamentals and structural reforms.

In this chapter, we will first examine the macroeconomic environment in the 1990s and the reasons for financial vulnerability along with the structural problems of the banks that set the ground for 2000-2001 crises. In the following section, the contribution of the Standby Agreement with the IMF, which started at the end of 1999, to the crisis of 2000 will be discussed. Secondly, post-crisis measures and the restructuring of the banking sector will be addressed. The section will also cover to what extent Basel I and Basel II Criteria have been met in this restructuring process. Thirdly, macroeconomic and banking measures that were taken against the global financial crisis of 2008 will be discussed. Furthermore, the latest situation of the sector in the face of the crisis will be explained based on figures.

2. MACROECONOMIC PROBLEMS AND THE STRUCTURE OF THE BANKING SECTOR IN THE 1990s

Turkish financial system is a bank-based financial system in which fund requirements are met mainly through the banking system. By the year 2010, the banking sector constitutes the most significant portion of the financial sector with a share of 88% thanks to the size of its assets. With those characteristics, it resembles the financial sector of continental Europe more than that of Anglo-Saxon countries.

In the 1980s, the financial sector improved significantly thanks to a series of decisions and implementations that were made for the purpose of encouraging private sector investments to the financial sector as well as developing and strengthening the market mechanism. Legal and institutional structure was formed with the introduction of the Capital Market Law in 1982. Istanbul Stock Exchange started its operations in 1986. The securities in commercial banks' balance sheets rose considerably in 1986 when the Treasury started issuing bonds and bills. In 1987, open market operations began to be used as a monetary policy tool within the scope of the Central Bank to control liquidity in the market. In 1989, the Turkish Lira became convertible and the limits on capital movements were abolished. Although those novelties that the 1980s saw triggered improvements in the sector, the general failure to cope with macroeconomic imbalances (to decrease inflation and to establish budget discipline) and the capital mobility that came too early produced upward fluctuations on the interest rates. The public sector continued to have a direct and an indirect impact on the financial sector.

In the 1990s, on the other hand, the macroeconomic environment got even worse and the structural problems of the economy accelerated and deepened. These macroeconomic problems had serious negative consequences on the banking sector:

- During the 1990s, an unstable economic growth prevailed, fluctuating between 9% to - 9% .
- Between the years 1990-1999 the average inflation rate was 80%. Between 1990-2001 Budget Deficit/GNP ratio was 7,5%, Government Deficit/GNP ratio was 10,2%. Inflation rates fluctuated between 60% and 106% with an average of 80% during the whole period. In that period of high inflation, the real interest rates manifested an increase due to the rising domestic borrowing requirements since the government debt was being financed through domestic borrowing (Real interest rate averaged 15% between 1990-2001 and reached its highest at 30% during 1995-96). High yields of government securities caused domestic government bonds to have a continuously increasing share in the security portfolios of banks. Along with their high yield, their low risk also made government bonds attractive for banks. Moreover, loans decreased due to the presence of high inflation that made loans riskier. Accordingly, balance sheets of banks could not grow healthily and the banks became unable to fulfill their real banking functions. However, banks made high profits despite the state of their total assets and shareholder's equity (Babuşçu and Koksal, 2000:41). Besides, high inflation hindered creation of long term financial resources, reduced the supply of savings, increased the need for foreign resources,

speeded up currency substitution, increased the risk premium and created unfavorable expectations.

- The financial liberalization process after 1989 made foreign borrowing easier and the process mentioned above caused short positions of banks to widen by fostering borrowing. Banks raised their short positions further by increasing their borrowing in foreign currency in the form of syndication loans and by using their foreign reserves in the form of TL in the treasury auctions for bidding in high sums. (The short position of banks amounted to 19 billion USD in June 2000. This means a banking system with a capital base of 11-12 billion USD had a short position of about twice its capital (Keyder, 2001:40). The increase in the discrepancy between exchange rate changes and the interest rates has a significant role in this rise in short positions. As this discrepancy increases in favor of auction interest rates, banks increase their short positions and multiply their profits. This situation is also favored by the state in that the mechanism allows foreign exchange reserves to increase and a greater number of treasury bonds are traded with lower interest rates.

- The high share of state banks in the banking system and the inefficient and nontransparent functioning of those banks have also been significant problems. State banks had long been intermediaries and implementers of support policies to certain sectors. Besides, inefficient employment policies and political interventions distanced those banks from rational banking principles. Interventions of state banks that contradicted with economic activities, their poor administration and duty losses had a negative impact on the system. One of the reasons for "duty losses" was low-interest, long term loans and subsidies given to farmers and tradesmen in areas such as agriculture, real estate and small scale trade. The other reason was that the Treasury sold treasury bonds to those banks under the name of "no cash equivalents" with an interest rate lower and a term longer than what prevailed in the market. Public debt and budget deficit may be seen much lower on paper than their actual amount due to this practice (Çakman ve Çakmak, 2001: 50). In 1996, the total Duty Losses/GNP ratio of the two large state banks, Ziraat and Halk, was 3% and this ratio rose to 12% in 2000 (BDDK/BRSA, 2010/b).

- It is recognized that the banking sector has a poor and multi-headed regulation and supervision. The number of banks increased rapidly in the 1990s due to the extreme loosening of conditions to found a bank. The total number of banks that used to be 66 in 1990 rose to 81 in 1999. Most of these were small banks that were founded with inadequate capital and usually for the purpose of financing its founder's affiliates and production. It was also a fact that in this unsupervised environment (where entry was easy but license revocations were difficult); banks mostly gave loans to their subsidiaries and in certain circumstances deliberately emptied out their banks. Some of them carried large amounts of government bonds that were multiples of their capital amounts. Actually, the small scale banking crisis in 1994 gave the early signal about the weaknesses of the banking sector. Four banks were handed over to TMSF (Savings Deposit Insurance Fund) and the 100% deposit insurance was a decision that was taken at that time. However, concrete steps forward in terms of the supervision and regulation of banks were not really taken. The Banking Law was enacted in 1999. Only in August 2000 did the BDDK (Banking Regulation and

Supervision Agency), which was necessary for the Banking Reform, start its operations. Continuation of deposit insurance also constituted a ground for moral hazard and was influential in carrying the problems of the system to 2000s. Deposit insurance became limited to 50.000 TL in 2004.

- The administrative problems and the presence of elements that threaten competition also constituted another group of problems. Administrative problems stem from the public authority's approach to the legislation, application and supervision concerning the banking sector as well as the administration mentality of the banks themselves. The most basic problems are: the presence of competition-distorting elements in the legislation, high intermediary costs due to high taxes, ineffective supervision and monitoring, the haphazard giveaway of banking licenses, loans given to banks' own partners, poor risk management in banks and deposit interest rates above market averages offered by some banks.
- Foreign factors also contributed to domestic factors mentioned above. Starting from the 1990s the emerging markets saw rapid capital entries with the improvements in technology and the increase in capital mobility. Turkey was also one of the countries that were immediately affected by this trend. Apart from their positive effects these capital entries also cause problems. The rapid exit of capital that entered the country had negative consequences on the sector due to the presence of a poorly-regulated financial sector that had only a little depth.

We see that in the first half of 1990s the financing of budget deficits heavily relied on the short-term loan usage of the Treasury from the Central Bank (10% of total budget expenditure). In the second half of 1990s, on the other hand, domestic borrowing gained more importance over the former. Therefore, a dynamic of high inflation, low growth rate and unsustainable domestic debt was created incorrect and inconsistent economic policies. In addition to this, current account deficit remained high during the whole period. Eventually, signing of a Stand-by Agreement with the IMF at the end of 1999 became inevitable due to distorted macro foundations and a vulnerable financial structure. (Macroeconomic indicators of the period 1990-2000 are given in the Appendix, Tables 1 and 2. Indicators concerning banks are demonstrated in Table 5.)

3. NOVEMBER 2000-FEBRUARY 2001 CRISES IN TURKEY

As given in a detailed manner above, Turkey signed the Standby Agreement with the IMF and started a serious and challenging disinflation/stabilization process to solve its accumulated macroeconomic problems that became unsustainable at the end of 1999. The foremost aim of this three-year stabilization program was to decrease the inflation rate that reached 63% in 1999 to a level as low as 7% in 2002. Further goals of the program were pulling real interest rates down to a reasonable level, to increase public sector primary surplus that was -2.8% of GNP in 1999 to 3.7% of GNP in 2000 and to increase the overall economic growth potential. The program was based on four basic principles:

1. A tight public policy that cuts down government expenditures and is supported by taxes in order to keep public sector primary surplus as high as possible.
2. A semi-fixed exchange rate system that involves an exchange rate basket that was declared to be (1$ + 0.77€) in the first half of the three-year period and a continuously and symmetrically widening band around the central parity in the second 18-month term of the period along with a tight monetary policy that puts a limit to the Central Bank's Net Domestic Assets. (This system is similar to the Currency-Board System.)
3. An income policy that supports Monetary, exchange rate and public policies and that is compatible with them.
4. Structural reforms, which were the most significant of all as well as being the most challenging to implement (Yay, 2001:77). These reforms included the restructuring/ regulation of agriculture and social security reforms, a comprehensive privatization program, tax reform and transparency in the public finance system.

Throughout the process until November 2000, economic growth rate and consumer expenditures were above target levels. However, the inflation rate stayed high (38%) exceeding its target level by 25% and the TL became overvalued due to the inflation rate that did not fall as targeted, combined with the fixed exchange rate. Besides, there were delays in structural reforms. Other than these implementation problems of the program, there were also well-known risks specific to the stabilization programs based on fixed exchange rates that all countries implementing this program experienced without exception: The overvaluation of the country's currency, current account deficits, recession due to the inability to sustain the initial growth rate and weaknesses of the financial sector due to the fixed exchange rate system.

Before the end of the first year of the stabilization program, in November 2000, the ground was set for the start of the banking crisis with the hand-over of a middle-scale bank, Demirbank, to the Savings Deposit Insurance Fund due to the liquidity and interest risk created by its poor risk management. A second wave of crisis came in February 2001. It became clear with these crises that the stabilization program that was based on a fixed exchange rate added new vulnerabilities to the existing weaknesses of the banking sector and aggravated its already-existing problems:

- In a banking system that was based on financing the public sector; banks, which relied on stabilization policies and expected interest rates to fall, tended to hold large amounts of government bonds to increase their capital gains, thereby making incorrect portfolio choices.
- Fixed exchange rate system encouraged all economic agents (and banks) to borrow in foreign currency. Banks frequently resorted to syndication loans. Thus, as stated before, time and currency mismatches prevailed. This, in turn, aggravated banks' already-existing short positions. The [Total Foreign Assets/Total Foreign Liabilities] ratio of the banking system continuously fell until November. Besides, one should not ignore the restlessness in the sector caused by the tight supervision/regulation measures taken by the BDDK, which started its operations in September and the agency obliging banks to cover their short positions by the end of the year (Yay, Yay and Yılmaz, 2001/a: 48).

- Fixed exchange rate policy increased consumption in favor of savings since it resulted in an overvaluation of the domestic currency. Throughout the 8-9 month period in which the program was carried out, loan/deposit ratios rose, consumer credits quadrupled and banks started to get used to normal banking activities such as giving loans and taking on loan risk. However, this proved to be a significant risk for banks with poor risk management.
- With a practice similar to the Currency Board, when the foreign capital inflow increased, Central Bank foreign exchange reserves increased and the monetary base was enlarged. Thus, the interest rates were dragged down. However, this process was reversed after September-October of 2000 because of increasing risk when the foreign capital inflow fell rapidly. Accordingly, liquidity problems emerged and the interest rates rose. This, in turn, caused capital losses for those banks that held government bonds and aggravated their liquidity problems.
- After the November crisis monetary and exchange rate policies that were the strongest leg of the stabilization program became messy, interest rates were not able to fall to their pre-crisis levels and the domestic debt market could not recover after the crisis. Financial situations of the state banks that were desperately in need of overnight borrowing and the banks within the TMSF (Savings Deposit Insurance Fund) that held large amounts of government bonds in their portfolios deteriorated due to the devaluation risk on the one hand and high interest rates on the other. Foreign currency demand of especially the State Banks increased rapidly in February. The efforts made by the Central Bank to control liquidity resulted in a deadlock of payment systems due to the extreme daily liquidity need of the State Banks. The Central Bank's choice of not funding the market evoked criticism in both crises. The Central Bank's abandoning its flexibility to protect its credibility (credibility/flexibility trade-off) for the purpose of fulfilling its commitments to the IMF abolished its characteristic of being the lender of last resort. The Central Bank's dilemma was the following: There would have been a rush to the foreign currency if the Central Bank increased liquidity and if it did not, then the rising interest rates would have multiplied banks' debt. Consequently, the banking sector incurred significant losses due to interest risk in the November crisis and due to both interest and exchange risks in the February crisis. With the introduction of the floating exchange rate system the currency and liquidity crisis turned into a banking crisis.

4. RESTRUCTURING PHASE (2002-2007)

In this period, two three-year Stand-by agreements were made with the IMF (The 18th and 19th Stand-by Agreements). The first program was signed in February 4, 2002 under the name "Program for Transition to a Strong Economy". A continuation of the first program with duration of three years that implied the same philosophy and targets was signed in May 11, 2005. The 18th Stand-By Agreement was a period during which the first and the most significant steps of the restructuring process were taken and most of them were completed. 19th Stand-By (2005-2008), on the other hand, aimed at finalizing the incomplete issues in the restructuring of the economy. Within this context, creating necessary conditions for the sustainability of growth, improving standards of living, reducing unemployment and approaching the standards of EU countries were the main targets. Parallel targets to the ones in the 18th Stand-By were set in terms of inflation, creating financial discipline, pulling current account deficit down to 3% and sustaining stable growth (averaging 5%). Besides; Tax, Local Administrations and Social Security Reforms as well as privatization targets were determined.

4.1. Crisis Management Process (2001) and the "Program for Transition to a Strong Economy" (2002-2004)

Following the February crisis, a serious uncertainty prevailed in the Turkish economy in the period between the decision to adopt floating exchange rate as a result of the negotiations with the IMF and the gradual announcement of a new program that started in April and lasted until mid-May. A three-stage strategy was followed in the crisis management process (BDDK/BRSA, 2010/b). In the first stage, the floating rate was adopted. Besides, securing an uninterrupted functioning of the payment systems for the Central Bank immediately and reestablishment of stability in the securities and money markets gained priority. The Central Bank directly funded state banks and the banks within TMSF by overnight repurchase agreements (Repo). Money market interest rates were not allowed outside of the interest rate band. In the second stage, in April 2001, faced with duty losses of the state banks and capital deficits of the banks within the TMSF (Savings Deposit Insurance Fund), the Treasury in coordination with the Central Bank, supplied treasury bonds. Those bonds were then bought by the Central Bank from the banks and their liquidity needs were fulfilled. TMSF's covering the international liabilities of the banks within it limited the contagion risk of the crisis. The third stage of the crisis management process was the Domestic Debt Exchange (Swap) Operations of the Treasury. In June 2001, it exchanged short-term TL bills for long-term US dollar indexed or long-term TL indexed bills to extend the maturity of domestic borrowing and to reduce risk. Existing government bonds within the banks were returned to the public sector. In return for this, a government bond stock worth 6,6 billion dollars (1/3 TL , 2/3 foreign exchange indexed) was renewed by extending their maturities. The maturity of domestic borrowing was extended from 5,3 months to 37,2 months.

Foreign financing opportunities were also considered besides domestic resources. Loans from the IMF began to be used to finance payment of domestic debt. In December 2000, after the first crisis, additional reserves of 7,5 billion dollars were provided. Besides, a new agreement worth 15 billion dollars was concluded in the framework of the three-year Stand-by that is valid for the period 2002-2004. In the framework of the 19th Stand-by that covers the period 2005-2008, the amount of resources that was projected to be used was 10 billion dollars. Basic targets of the program, which was called the Program for Transition to a Strong Economy, are the following:

- Applying a monetary policy that enables price stability and an effective fight with inflation
- Making the necessary reforms to solve the problem of public finance permanently (strengthening public finance, increasing public transparency, achieving budgetary discipline, privatization, increasing competition and effectiveness in the economy)

- Restructuring of the banking sector to enable a healthy relationship with the real sector
- Creating a legal framework that would pave the way for structural reforms and bringing about the necessary regulations without deviating from schedule (Yay, 2002)

As stated before, the first step of the fight against inflation was adopting the floating rate system. The system that was, throughout the 1990s, implicitly and was then in the 1999 Program explicitly based on exchange rate commitment did not bring any success in pulling inflation down. In that sense, the transition to a flexible exchange rate system was believed to provide an opportunity to pursue a more independent monetary policy. The most significant transformation to increase the persuasiveness of the fight against inflation was enabling the Central Bank to gain a more autonomous structure and instrument independence. For this purpose, by making a change in the Central Bank Law, a strong commitment was made by citing *price stability* as the main target of the Central Bank. Moreover, Monetary Policy Board (PPK) was founded for the establishment of a more autonomous monetary policy. Between 2002 and 2005, an implicit inflation targeting was carried out. According to this system, short-term interest rates were being used as the main instrument of monetary policy while a monetary base that is compatible with the inflation target and the expected growth rate served the function of a nominal anchor. Cap related to net domestic assets and the cap related to net international reserves also served as performance criteria. (TBB/BAT, 2008:36-37)

Explicit inflation targeting began after 2006. Another significant reform concerning monetary policy was the transition to the New Turkish Lira (YTL) for the purpose of building up trust in the national currency. According to a law that was enacted in January 2004, six zeros were dropped from the old TL and New Turkish Lira (YTL) banknotes and coins were put into circulation starting from 2005. In January 2006, TL banknotes and coins were withdrawn from circulation. The transition to TL was completed in January 2009 when the phrase "new" in the name of the currency was abolished. The fact that no trouble was encountered throughout this process increased trust in the national currency.

Reforms that were directed towards maintaining financial discipline started with determining the primary surplus/GNP ratio as 6,5%.This ratio was 0,3% on average during 1993-2002. In the new program period between 2002 and 2005, it was 5%. Emphasis was put on financial discipline; one-time tax increases were made in certain taxes and a new payment plan was set through tax peace for the payment of tax debt.

Significant betterments were recorded in tax policies during the period 2002-2005. Indeed, significant changes that simplified the tax structure, enlarged the tax base and brought the tax policies closer to the European Union standards were realized.

After 2002 the debt burden was mitigated and the sensitivity of debt to risks was decreased for the purpose of establishing *financial discipline*. The Maastricht Criterion regarding the ratio of public sector budget deficit to GNP was met in 2004 thanks to the success of financial reforms.

To rationalize labor in the public sector; employment was restricted and idle personnel was abolished in the PEEs(Public Economic Enterprises). Efforts were directed towards the betterment of the investment atmosphere. The law regarding Public Finance and the Regulation on Debt Management was issued in March 28, 2002. The goal of this law was the effective management and monitoring of domestic and foreign debt of the public sector. A *market maker* mechanism was put in practice in September 2002. That mechanism enabled specialization in the government bond market while ensuring that the participating banks fulfilled their obligations. Besides, an official statement was issued regarding the coordination of debt and risk management with the aim of developing a debt management strategy based on risk. Moreover, with the Public Procurement Law that came into effect on January 1, 2003 fight with corruption and increasing transparency on public sector accounts was aimed. With the Public Finance Management and Control Law that had a reformative characteristic, public finance management and supervision was re-regulated and the categorizations of budget institutions were amended and new practices were introduced; analytical budgeting method and performance supervision mentality for supervisors being the most important among them. Law regarding Moral Duty and Application Principles for Civil Servants and Public Administrators came into effect on May 25, 2004 (BDDK/BRSA, 2010/b:35-36). (Basic macroeconomic indicators of 2000s are given in the Appendix Tables 3 and 4.)

Furthermore, in this period, many *Autonomous Regulation and Supervision Agencies and Boards* were established. Banking Regulation and Supervision Agency (BRSA), Competition Authority, Energy Market Regulatory Authority (EMRA), Information and Communication Technologies Authority (ICTA) are some of these. Secretariat General for EU Affairs was established in 2000 in order to coordinate public institutions and organizations related to the preparation for an EU membership. Law on Obtaining Information and Public Finance Management and Control Law were issued in 2003. Electronic Signature Law was issued in 2004 and Public Servants Ethical Board was established in the same year.

4.2. Banking Sector Restructuring Program

In addition to the macroeconomic measures taken in the context of the Stand-by agreements with the IMF, the need for a serious banking sector reform arose. In fact, the ideal strategy in the restructuring of the banking sector is determining the system's need for reform beforehand and putting the necessary reforms into practice when the financial markets are relatively calm. However, generally the political authorities make important reform decisions only after the crises. The management of this type of banking crises has usually been carried out as a three-stage process (Fischer, 2001). First stage is stopping panic and providing stability in payment systems in the short term. Second stage is preparing a reliable short-term strategy that would restructure financial institutions and the financial system rapidly. Finally, third stage is supervising the implementation of the financial strategy and normalizing the system (Yay, Yay and Yılmaz, 2001/a: 141). In the first panic instance, tools such as deposit insurance, blanket guarantee and lender of last resort are used. The restructuring strategy, on the other hand, is composed of three-dimensional tools:

(i) Financial Restructuring Process that ensures improving banks' balance sheets and overcoming insolvency;
(ii) Operational Restructuring Process that encompasses measures directed towards increasing profitability of banks, reducing operational costs, renewing administrative and accounting registration systems and improvements in the loan and risk evaluation methods;

(iii) Prudential Regulation, Supervision and Monitoring System that supports these two dimensions.

In the framework that was explained, Turkey aimed, with the Banking Restructuring Program that was declared on May 15, 2001, at correcting the damage in the sector done by the 2000-2001 crises and constructing a strong base by getting rid of the weak banks in the system. The regulation and supervision duties and authorities that were used to be shared between the Central Bank and the Undersecretariat of Treasury up to that time were then transferred to the Banking Regulation and Supervision Agency (BDDK). BDDK explained its restructuring program based on five main fundamentals (TBB/BAT,2008: 41):

- The financial and operational restructuring of the State Banks
- Providing solvency for the banks within the Savings Deposit Insurance Fund (TMSF) in the shortest time possible
- Providing the private banks with a healthy structure
- Bringing about legal and institutional regulations that would increase the effectiveness of supervision and monitoring in the Banking Sector and give the sector a more effective and competitive structure
- The restructuring of the debt of real sector that owes credit debt to the banks: The Istanbul Approach

4.2.1. Restructuring of State Banks

The state banks that started the restructuring process are Ziraat Bankası, which has focused on agricultural loans and supports agriculture; Halk Bankası, which serves small and middle-sized producers and Emlak Bankası, which is active in financing trade and housing construction. BDDK completed the financial restructuring of the state banks within the year 2001 and ensured their operational restructuring to a large extent by the end of 2002. In the context of financial restructuring; duty losses, which were 17,5 billion dollars by the end of 2001, had been liquidated and by applying interest to duty losses, special floating rate government bonds of 23 billion TL were issued. In addition, the law and the cabinet decrees that resulted in duty losses were abolished with a legal arrangement made on July 3, 2001.

The 8,5 billion dollars worth short-term liabilities of the state banks to the private banks and the non-banking sector were nullified in March 2001.

In order to strengthen the capital structure of the state banks, 4,7 billion TL (approx. 3,5 billion dollars) capital support came from the Treasury by the end of 2001, of which 3 billion TL was cash and 1,7 billion TL was through issuing special government bonds. By the end of 2001, the total resources that were transferred to state banks in order to to index duty losses to marketable securities and to provide capital support, reached 28,7 billion TL (21,9 billion dollars). (TBB/BAT, 2008: 42).

Within the framework of operational restructuring, Ziraat Bankası, Halk Bankası and Emlak Bankası gained the status of joint-stock companies with the Banking Law. As the first step of restructuring, a "State Banks' Common Board of Directors" was appointed to these banks. The administration of state banks was handed over to this board. Moreover, the task of restructuring and preparing banks for the privatization process was also given to the same board.

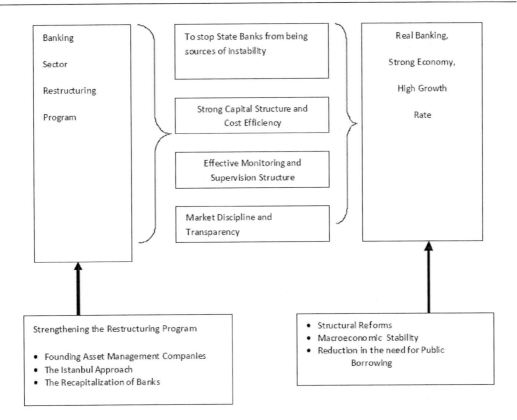

Source: BDDK/BRSA (2010/b: 39).

Scheme 1. The Restructuring Program.

The license of Emlak Bankası to engage in banking activities and to collect deposits was revoked. The bank was integrated to the body of Ziraat Bankası. Besides, Pamukbank, one of the banks that were transferred to the Savings Deposit Insurance Fund (SDIF) (TMSF in Turkish), was transferred to Halk Bankası in 2004.

The number of branches of the state banks was reduced, 27% of their personnel retired. By 2003, 32% of the branches were closed down, and 50% of the personnel were transferred to other state institutions. As a result of these efforts, state banks made a profit of 1,2 billion TL by September 2002 (BDDK/BRSA, 2002; TBB, 2008).

4.2.2. The Liquidation of the Banks that were Transferred to SDIF (Savings Deposit Insurance Fund)

SDIF (TMSF), which was established in 1983 and was carrying out its activities within the body of the Central Bank, was transferred to BRSA (BDDK) in August 2000. From 2004 on, it obtained an autonomous structure after having been detached from BRSA (BDDK). Between 1997 and 2002, 20 banks were transferred to SDIF (TMSF). Later, this number increased to 22. By this period, the total liabilities of the 20 banks was 25,8 billion dollars, and their total loss was 13,6 billion dollars. The losses of the fund banks were caused by foreign exchange losses, capital market operations losses and non-performing loans. Especially, losses from non-performing loans were comprised of the resources that the prevailing partners used from their own banks and from other fund banks and these losses amounted to a significant sum (7,9 billion dollars).

The funds necessary for strengthening the financial structure of the banks within SDIF (TMSF), for their restructuring and for the transfer of their liabilities were raised through special bonds issued by the Undersecretariat of Treasury as a loan to the Fund, advance loans given by the Central Bank and the Fund's own resources. The value of the bonds issued by the Treasury amounted to 16,9 billion dollars. Besides, SDIF (TMSF) transferred 2,2 billion dollars to the fund banks from its own resources. The fund banks, in turn, used these resources and nullified their short-term liabilities of 5,2 billion TL in March 2001 and their short-term liabilities of 2,6 billion TL to the TCMB (the Central Bank of the Republic of Turkey)in 2002. The foreign currency short positions of these banks dropped from 4,5 billion dollars in May 2001 to 561 million dollars in June 2001 thanks to the effect of the injection of the foreign currency government bonds. With the integration of Pamukbank into the fund, this figure increased a little bit but in October 2002 it fell back to 306 million dollars. 10 of the 22 banks within the SDIF (TMSF)'s body were sold in a short while and reintegrated into the sector. 8 banks were liquidated by way of mergers and acquisitions. There are still two banks in the process of insolvency and liquidation as well as one bank in the process of transition within the Fund (see Table 2)

The resources transferred to the banks within TMSF by December 2009 can be seen on Table 1 below:

Table 1. The resources transferred to the banks within SDIF (TMSF)

31 December 2009	USD (millions)
• Resources transferred to the banks	29,641
• Share of capital	2,182
• Precautionary Reserves	19,173
• Loan, Affiliates, Movable- Real Estate Property Transfer (Government Bonds + Cash + Fund Deposit)	1,612
• Transferred amount to take over loans, affiliates and movable-real estate property	116
• Resources transferred due to the banks in liquidation process/ Depositor's payment (including Imar Bankasi)	6,557
Other liquidation expenses	590
TOTAL	30,231

Source: BDDK/BRSA(2010/b).

4.2.3. Providing Private Banks with a Healthy Structure

In this period of crisis, private banks were exposed to liquidity and interest risk because of their very-short-term resource structure. By November 2000, they were faced with exchange risk because of the foreign currency short positions in their balance sheets that reached 8,5 billion dollars.

Table 2. Liquidation Strategies of the Banks Transferred to the TMSF

	Name of the bank	Date of Transfer	Liquidation strategy
1	Türk Ticaret Bankası	06.01.1997	Still in the process of liquidation.
2	Bank Ekspres	12.12.1998	Sold to the Tefken Group on 30.06 2001
3	İnterbank	07.01.1999	Merged with Etibank on 15.06.2001
4	Egebank	21.12.1999	Merged with Sümerbank on 26.01.2001
5	Yurtbank	21.12.1999	Merged with Sümerbank on 26.01.2001
6	Yaşarbank	21.12.1999	Merged with Sümerbank on 26.01.2001
7	Esbank	21.12.1999	Merged with Etibank on 15.06.2001
8	Sümerbank	21.12.1999	Sold to the Oyak Group on 09.08.2001
9	Kıbrıs Kredi Bankası	28.09.2000	Still in the process of liquidation.
10	Etibank	27.10. 2000	Merged with Bayındırbank on 04.04.2002
11	Bank Kapital	27.10. 2000	Merged with Sümerbank on 26.01.2001
12	Demirbank	06.12.2000	Sold to HSBC Bank PLC on 20.09.2001
13	Ulusal Bank	28.02.2001	Merged with Sümerbank on 17.04.2001
14	İktisat Bankası	15.03.2001	Merged with Bayındırbank on 04.04.2002
15	Kentbank	09.07.2001	Merged with Bayındırbank on 04.04.2002
16	EGS Bank	09.07.2001	Merged with Bayındırbank on 18.01.2002
17	Sitebank	09.07.2001	Sold to Novabank A.Ş.. on 20.12.2001
18	Tarişbank	09.07.2001	Sold to Denizbank A.Ş. on 21.10.2002
19	Bayındırbank	09.07.2001	Has been structured as a transition bank
20	Toprak Bank	30.11.2001	Merged with Bayındırbank on 30.09.2002
21	Pamukbank	19.06.2002	Merged with Halk Bankası on 12.11.2004
22	İmar Bankası	03.07.2003	Still in the process of liquidation.

Source: BDDK/BRSA(2010/b).

Since November and February crises came one after the other, it became impossible for the banks with already malfunctioning financial structures to pursue their activities, and the ones that were financially well-off suffered significant capital losses. After the crisis; in the process of meeting the capital requirements and restructuring of the state banks; the fact that state banks allocated reserves equal to their non-performing loans and limited the loan supply aggravated the problems of other banks.

A series of measures were taken for the restructuring of the private banks (Yay, Yay and Yılmaz, 2004:126)

- Private Banks submitted scheduled letters of commitment that they would strengthen their capitals with their own resources. These commitment issues covered topics such as increasing capital, mergers, rationalizing the number of branches and personnel, cost reduction, disposal of the affiliates and real estate as well as selling of shares to domestic and foreign partners. In this context, private banks achieved a capital increase of around 2,7 billion dollars in the period between 2001-2003. In 2004, this amount exceeded 4 billion dollars.
- With the domestic debt exchange operation that took place in June 2001, short positions in banks' balance sheets, which reached 8,5 billion dollars, were covered to a considerable extent. This amount dropped back to 1,5 billion dollars by the end of 2001 and decreased to 764 million dollars in October 2003. By this means, interest and currency risk were reduced.

- The persistence of recession after the crisis and the increase in uncertainty in the global economy after 9/11 limited possibilities of turning fixed assets into cash and restricted the opportunities of increasing capital. With the law that came into force on January 31, 2002, both the strengthening of the eroded capital structures of private banks -with public support if necessary- and solving the bad assets problem in the banking sector by way of Istanbul approach plus asset management companies were adopted. This way, non-performing loans would be liquidated and assets of the banks would gain liquidity.
- In 26 private banks, three-stage audits were carried out by independent auditing firms and reports regarding the banks' financial situations were prepared. The three-stage audit is composed of two auditing stages of banks' financial bodies by two different independent auditing firms and a final auditing stage by banks' sworn auditors. In the audit of financial statements of banks in 2001, the inflation accounting method was taken as a basis for the first time by (BRSA) BDDK. One bank with capital deficit was provided with capital support from the SDIF (TMSF) sufficient to increase its capital adequacy ratio to 9%. Moreover, the capital deficit of another bank was covered by the partners in cash. The cost for the restructuring of the private banks was covered up to 2,7 billion dollars by private banks and up to 5,2 billion dollars by SDIF (TMSF) and it reached 7,9 billion dollars in total.
- Tax barriers were removed in order to foster the expansion opportunities, through mergers and acquisitions, of banks, whose shareholder's equity eroded with the economic crisis and whose survival became more challenging under reduced inflation. In 2001 and 2002, significant developments happened regarding mergers and acquisitions. The total assets of all banks that were subject to mergers and acquisitions were about 26,5 billion dollars. The mergers in question were made on a voluntary basis and increased the effectiveness as well as the competitive power of the sector (BDDK/BRSA; 2010/b). (One can track the progress of mergers in the sector on Table 3, and the total cost of the restructuring of the banking sector on Table 4.)

4.2.4. Improving the Regulatory Framework

In the period following the crisis, a series of regulations were made in order to make the Turkish banking system firm and stable and to improve the regulatory framework. Although the regulations made within the short period following the crisis were intensely concentrated on issues with priority, such as deposit insurance, requirements, capital and loan limits, they also covered accounting standards, competition, effectiveness and institutional regulations, which contribute to the long-term stability of the sector. The implementation of regulation, monitoring and supervision was to a great extent brought to the line of EU directives as well as of international regulations and recommendations.

The Regulations Strengthening the Institutional Framework

The autonomy of the Central Bank was strengthened with the amendments to the law no. 4651 made on April 25, 2001.

In March 2002, the Turkish Accounting Standards Board started its operations.

In December 2003, SDIF (TMSF), which had been working dependently on BRSA (BDDK), acquired the identity of an autonomous institution.

In 2003, the Act of Enforcement and Bankruptcy was amended.

On 17th June 2003, the Act of Foreign Direct Investments was passed.

Table 3. Mergers in the Banking Sector

Merged institutions	The title after the merger	Date	Explanation
Tefken Yat. And Finansman Bank AŞ ve Bank Ekspres Aş	Tekfenbank Aş.	18.01.01	Tefken Bank was transferred to Bankekspres and acquired the title of Tekfenbank A.Ş.
Morgan Guaranty Trust Co. and The Chase Manhattan Bank	The Chase Manhattan Bank	10.11.01	Morgan Guaranty Trust Co. was merged with the "The Chase Manhattan Bank" branch.
Birleşik Türk Körfez Bankası AŞ and Osmanlı Bankası	Osmanlı Abnkası AŞ	29.08.01	Birleşik Türk Körfez Bankası was transferred to Osmanlı Bankası A.Ş.
Osmanlı Bankası AŞ. and T. Garanti Bankası AŞ	T. Garanti Bankası AŞ	11.12.01	Osmanlı Bankası A.Ş. was transferred to T. Garanti Bankası A.Ş.
Demirbank and HSBC	HSBC Bank Plc.	14.12.01	Demirbank was transferred to HSBC Bank A.Ş.
Oyak Bank and Sümerbank	Oyak Bank	11.01.02	Sale of Sümerbank was completed and the bank carried out its activities under the name of Oyak Bank.
Türkiye Sınai Kalkınma Bankası AŞ and Sınai Yat. Bankası Aş.	TSKB AŞ.	27.03.02	The decision regarding the transfer of general boards of TSKB A.Ş. and Sınai Yat. Ban. A.Ş. was registered.
Benkar Tük. Fins.- Kart Hiz. and HSBC	HSBC	25.12.02	Benkar Consumer Finance and Card Services Company was transferred to HSBC Bank.
Milli Aydın Bankası and Denizbank	Denizbank	27.12.02	MAB was transferred to Denizbank..
Finansbank Aş and Fiba Bank Aş	FinansBank Aş	03.03.03	The decisions of the two banks regarding the transfer of their general boards were registered.
Credit Lyonnais SA and Credit Agricole Indosuez TAŞ	Credit Agricole Indosuez TAŞ	03.03.04	Credit Lyonnais SA and Credit Agricole were transferred to Indosuez TAŞ.
Ak Uluslararası Abankası Aş and Akbank	Akbank	09.09.05	Ak International Bank A.Ş. was transferred to Akbank TAŞ.
Koç Bank and Yapı Kredi Bank AŞ	Yapı Kredi Bank AŞ	28.09.06	Koç Bank was transferred to Yapı Kredi Bank A.Ş.

Source: BDDK/BRSA(2010/b).

The Regulations that Bring Capital Standards, Capital Measurement and Risk Management Closer to EU Directives

With the amendment made on the Banking Law in June 2001, the definition of shareholder's equity was brought closer to the EU directives and the definition of "Consolidated Shareholder's Equity" was introduced. A transition period was allotted until 2009.

On February 10, 2001, "Regulation Concerning the Measurement and Evaluation Banks' Capital Adequacy" was issued.

Table 4. Costs of Restructuring of the Banking Sector (Billion USD)

Resources Transferred to State Banks	21.9
• Debt from Duty Losses	19.2
• Cash Capital Support	2.5
• Non-cash Capital Support	0.2
Resources Reserved for SDIF (TMSF) Banks	22.5
• Resources Transferred from the Public Sector	17.3
• Deposits made by and Resources Transferred from SDIF (TMSF) Income	5.2
Resources Transferred from the Private Sector	7.9
• Resources Transferred from the Private Sector Banks	2.7
• Resources transferred from SDIF (TMSF)	5.2
İmar Bank	6.5
Total	53.7

Source: BDDK/BRSA(2010/b) and TBB/BAT(2008).

This regulation determined the basis and procedures concerning the calculation of banks' standard capital adequacy ratios on a consolidated and non-consolidated basis taking into account market risk that is composed of interest rate risk, exchange rate risk and equity risk.

In February 2001, procedures and principles needed to build an efficient internal auditing system were defined with the "Regulation Concerning the Internal Auditing and Risk Management of Banks". Starting from July 2001, banks have been delivering reports every three months on their activities and organizational preparations within the framework of the Regulation and these reports have been evaluated and monitored regularly.

In order to track banks' foreign exchange position risks effectively, calculating their foreign exchange positions on a consolidated basis became obligatory.

Loan and Affiliate Limitations Concerning Non-Performing Loans and Required Reserves

With the Regulation Concerning Founding and Activities of Banks dated June 27, 2001, direct and indirect loans were considered collectively in the calculation of the loan limits to be given to a certain group, for the purpose of avoiding risk concentration in loans. Besides, the definition for the risk group was made. The concentration of the banks' resources on certain groups was prohibited with this regulation, in which bank shareholders and affiliates were considered within the same risk group. The loan a bank can give to a real or a legal person directly or indirectly is limited to 25% of its shareholder's equity. The loans exceeding 10% of the bank's shareholder's equity are considered as large loans. Moreover, the total sum of these loans cannot exceed eightfold of the bank's shareholder's equity.

A transition period was allotted until 2009 and the participation of banks in non-financial institutions was limited by 15% of their shareholder's equity; and the total worth of these affiliates was limited by 60% of the bank's shareholder's equity.

From January 1st 2002 onwards, futures, option contracts and other similar derivative instruments were integrated into the definition of loan.

The classification of the loan receivables in five different categories according to their features of redeem-ability and collaterals was introduced.

Accounting Standards and Independent Audit Regulations

Amendments, to be valid as of 2002, were made to the banks' accounting standards, uniform accounting system and Registration statement for the harmonization of repo and inverse repo transactions' accounting principles with international regulations and for risks to be monitored more safely.

The Regulation concerning Principles of Independent Audit Principles was published on January 31, 2002 for the independent audit process to be carried out in a more transparent and reliable way in the sector.

As per Provisional Article 4 of Banking Law, promulgated on February 1, 2002, with the Regulation on Principles and Procedures of Independent Audit, regulation of financial statements in accordance with inflation calculation was foreseen.

In November 2004, the Announcement of Uniform Accounting Plan and Registration System, which was to be implemented by private financial institutions, was published.

Regulations Increasing Competition and Effectiveness in the Sector

BRSA has determined the criteria on bank ownership with its resolution published in November 2002. These conditions are to be also looked for in investors placing a bid to buy shares of the banks within the Saving Deposit Insurance Fund (SDIF).

With the announcement published on May 5, 2000, the cash ratio, calculated based on excess amount in excess positions, was increased from 8% to 100%, so as to control the open position of the banks more strictly (BDDK/BRSA, 2010/b: 67).

After 2001, interest payment on required reserves for TL deposits started to implemented.

In 2001, withholding rates, applied to interest income on Repo as well as TL and foreign currency deposits, were differentiated by maturity. Withholding rates over TL deposits were reduced to 14% for short-term deposits, 10% for medium-term deposits, and 6% for long-term deposits. The withholding rate was increased to 18% for foreign exchange deposit accounts and 20% for repo.

The Central Bank amended required reserves and disposable cash reserves implementations in March 2002 for financial brokerage fees to decrease and liquidity management to become more flexible; also, interest started to be paid to foreign currency required reserves. As of November 2005, implementation of disposable cash reserves was terminated.

4.2.5. Real Sector Debt Restructuring: Istanbul Approach

Following the crises, rising inflation, increasing interest rates, increases in exchange rates caused by transition to floating rate, resulted in losses in real sector as well as financial sector. The reflection of the crisis on the real sector realized very quickly; on the one hand, rises in the interest and exchange rates increased the production costs; on the other hand, shrinking demand resulting from losses in wealth and income put a downward pressure on production activities of the real sector. The companies whose financial state deteriorated in consequence of these developments could no longer pay their debts and there was an increase in the banks' non-performing loans. Because of these reasons, to ensure the continuity of the companies' activities in the private sector and to ensure that these companies, by recovering their insolvency, pay their debts to the financial sector, a regulation known as "Istanbul Approach" was enacted with the Law No. 4743 "Restructuring the Debts to the Financial Sector" that was put into effect on January 30, 2002. Accordingly, within the scope of the Financial Restructuring framework agreements, these agreements were made legally binding within 3 years after their approval by BRSA; and restructuring of banks' receivables or binding them to a new repayment schedule was made possible, under the condition that when necessary, supplementary finance support would be provided to the borrower. Within the framework of the same law, establishment of the Asset Management Companies was encouraged, granting various tax concessions on non-performing receivables. With the regulation published by BRSA in October, 2002 concerning this issue, the legal infrastructure of the asset management companies to be established was completed.

The Istanbul approach was implemented between June 2002 and June 2005. Belonging to 322 firms in total, of which 221 were large-scale and 101 were small-scale, USD 6.021 million worth of debt was restructured. As of 2002 year end, share of restructured debt in the banking sector's total credit volume was approximately 20%. An approach similar to Istanbul approach was also implemented to small and medium sized enterprises as of 2007. Within the framework of this approach (named as Anatolian approach), debts of 120 small and medium sized enterprises were restructured. Within the framework of the restructuring, credit debt maturities of the companies were extended; the companies' credits were renewed or new credits were provided; interest rate cuts took place. The share of 200 million TL worth of restructured debt in total non-performing SME credits was 7,5%.

Progress and Improvements in the Sector

At the end of the Restructuring Process of the Banking Sector explained above in detail, there have been substantial improvements in the sector (See, Supplementary Table 6 and 7):

-   -Capital of private banks was strengthened.
-   -The ratio of the banks' total assets to GNP increased; credits increased and became diversified. The credits/GNP ratio, increasing by 23 points, went up to 43%; and the share of credits in total assets increased up to 50 %.(2002-2007)
-   -Credit risk, market risk, and exchange rate risk decreased; the share of fixed assets in total assets decreased; shareholder's equity increased. Shareholder's equity increased from 9,7 billion TL in 2002 to 73,5 billion TL in 2007; free shareholder's equity increased from 4,1 billion TL in 2002 to 50,7 billion TL in 2007. Capital adequacy ratio was realized at a level of 19,1% (2007).
-   -The banks' private banking services were not limited to an increase in retail loans, but also they integrated with high technology and product range diversified. Service quality was improved to international standards.
-   -After the restructuring, mergers and acquisitions and strategic investments in the sector increased. Developments such as competition environment, organic growth, financial innovations, technological infrastructure, access to financial system,

corporate capacity, diffusion of risk management culture, and change in culture of business conduct came into prominence.

- -There was an increase in the number of branches, employees, POS-terminals, and ATMs above the European Union average.
- -An important change in the banking sector's structure was realized in the ownership structure. In the sector, the share of global (foreign) capital increased. From May 2001, in which the "Banking Sector Restructuring Programme" started, to 2007 year end, a total of 20 bank sales agreements were signed. The total amount of these agreements was approximately USD 17,5 billion. The share of assets of banks with foreign capital in sector's total assets was 3% in 2002, whereas it increased to 24% in 2007. Three out of 20 bank sales agreements were signed between 2001 and 2002 and the others were signed after 2004. After 2004, improvements in the macroeconomic data (inflation rate reduced to a single digit figure, high and continuous growth) as well as improvements in relation to the sector (steady growth in bank assets, increases in credit volume, high liquidity, falling interest rates, increasing shareholder's equity, effective risk management), accession negotiations with EU and increasing confidence encouraged foreign investors to invest in the Turkish banking sector. 11 of the foreign investors that invested in these banks were of EU origin; 5 were of Middle East origin; 3 were of USA origin; and one was of Far-East origin. Another issue was that Turkey-based banks increased their overseas activities by opening branches (especially in EU countries), establishing banks, and becoming affiliated with other financial subsidiaries (TBB/BAT, 2008).
- -Banking Sector carries out quite an effective risk management implementation. After 2001, important works and studies have been undertaken on management scale and technical sufficiency of banks' risk management implementations. There was a transition from conventional supervision approach to risk-based approach. Besides the supervision based on regulations, market supervision also gained importance. For banking activities to be monitored more easily by investors and public opinion, implementations regarding accounting standards, reporting, and informing the public were made much more effective. We will give more detailed information regarding improvements in risk management and Basel Standards in the following section.

4.3. Basel I and Basel-II and Risk Management Implementations in Turkey

Basel Committee on Banking Supervision was established within The Bank for International Settlement (BIS) by governors of G-10 central banks at the end of year 1974 in which fluctuations in international money and banking markets took place. The committee was established as a discussion platform providing continuous cooperation between member countries with regard to banking supervision. As a result of decrease in major international banks' capital ratios at the beginning of 1980s and increase in international risk especially due to Latin American countries with high levels of debt, the Committee concentrated on "capital adequacy" concept of banks. As a consequence of this, in 1988, a measuring system for capital adequacy ratio, named as Basel Capital Accord, was approved by governors of G-10 central banks and put into effect. The 1988 Accord, applied to set out a minimum measure for banks' capitals, concentrated especially on capital assessment concerning credit risk. In the first part of the Accord, which consists of 4 parts, principal capital and supplementary capital items of capital as well as assets deducted from capital are defined. In the second part, in which risk weighting is discussed, weighted risk ratio method, according to which assets are weighted in accordance with their degree of risk, is adopted for the determination of capital adequacy. In this part, concentration is mainly on credit risk and one of its dimensions, country transfer risk, although other risks are also discussed. In the third part, target standard capital ratio (seed-principal capital being at least %4) is adopted as 8% for assets weighted according to risk. The last part consists of regulations with regard to transition period. This system, in addition to having been implemented in all G-10 countries until 1993, is adopted in more than one hundred countries, member or non-member (BIS, Basel Committee, 1988, 1999). This measurement method that was established with Basel I started to be implemented also in Turkey with the regulation published in 1989 and including a 3 year transition period. However, Basel I framework did not remain static and, being criticized in various ways, was improved in due course. In 1996, an amendment took place, also covering risks other than credit risk which is the focus of Basel I (especially market risks) and this amendment started to be implemented in 1997. Another important point of this insertion is that it allows use of Value-at-risk methods as an alternative to standard measurement methods in calculating capital requirement (Yay, Yay and Yılmaz, 2001/a). This framework started to be first implemented in Turkey in 2002 with the Regulation on Measurement of Banks Capital Adequacy and Assessment that was put into force in February 2001 and market risks were included in measurement of capital adequacy.

In 1999, Basel Committee, taking into account the developments in financial markets and shortcomings with regard to capital adequacy measurement of Basel I, prepared a new capital adequacy framework proposal to substitute for 1988 Accord. This first draft (consultative paper-1) was followed by an improvised second draft published in 2001 as a package open to criticism and views of relevant institutions within international banking and financial sectors. In 2003, third text was released. Final versions of these texts, revised within the scope of various criticism and comments, were released in June 2004. This new frame established by Basel II is based on three pillars:

1) The fundamental pillar is the new minimum capital adequacy regime that revised standard principals of the 1988 Accord.
2) The second pillar is the monitoring-supervision of banks' capital adequacy and internal assessment processes by audit authority and strengthening transparency-openness.
3) Third pillar is the use of market discipline in an effective way for encouragement of safe and robust banking implementations (BIS, Basel Committee, 1999).

In Basel I, there was a capital obligation only for credit and market risks, whereas in Basel II, in addition to these risks, operational risk capital has been also imposed. Accordingly, minimum capital adequacy ratio is indicated as follows:

Total Capital/(Credit Risk+Market Risk+Operational Risk) $\geq$ 8 (Capital Adequacy Ratio)

In Turkey, necessary actions started to be undertaken in 2002 for establishment of infrastructural elements with regard to issues brought by Basel II (such as risk management, corporate governance system, accounting, information systems) in the Turkish Banking System in parallel with international developments.

In March 2003, with the participation of BDDK/BRSA authorities and top management of various banks in charge of risk management, Basel II Steering Committee was established within the Banks Association of Turkey(TBB) for the purposes of informing the banking system about Basel II, consulting the banking system's opinions regarding the relevant regulations, and determining a common Strategy. Studies concerning various topics on transition to Basel II were carried out with the Committee. On the other hand, with the participation of authorities of BRSA, Treasury, Capital Markets Board, The Banks Association of Turkey, Basel II Coordination Committee was established for the purposes of forming an effective discussion platform in the preparing for Basel II process and carrying out works on various technical issues with regard to Basel II. The Committee prepared a road map regarding the preparations for transition to Basel II and this report was published by BRSA in May 2005.

Turkey participated in 3. Quantitative Impact Study (QIS-3) with 6 large banks that was undertaken by Basel Committee on a global scale. Benefitting from this experience, in July 2003, with the participation of 23 banks whose assets constituted 95% of the total assets in the banking sector, a local quantitative impact analysis (QIS-TR) was completed. Following this analysis, based on September 2006 data, QIS-TR2 analysis was carried out with the participation of 31 banks whose assets constituted 97% of the total assets in the banking sector. The analysis was undertaken between October 2006 and June 2007.

Basel II compliance process is carried out by BRSA. In June 2007, operational risk item was included in calculations of capital adequacy. Hence, the calculation of capital adequacy has become partly in harmony with EU Directives on Basel II.

The document of international harmonization of capital measurement and capital standards, established by the Basel Committee, was included in the European Union acquisition with directives 2006/48/EC and 2006/49/EC (CRD) and the relevant directives were put into effect in EU countries during a specific transition period (BDDK, 2010/c).

In Turkey, Capital Requirement Directive for Basel II and regulating drafts in harmony with Basel II were presented to the sector and public for their opinions as of April 2010. In order to keep track of the activities undertaken by banks regarding their compliance with CRD/Basel II, "Progress Survey in relation to the transition of banks to CRD/Basel II" is demanded from the banks for half-yearly periods and the answers given are assessed for the purposes of informing the public.

Table 5. The Effect of Operational Risk on Capital Requirement

	Capital Adequacy Standard Ratio (%)		
	(Without Oper. Risk)	(Including Oper. Risk)	Difference
Deposit Banks	20.4	17.8	2.6
Public Banks	25.9	20.8	5.1
Private Banks	19.2	17.2	2.0
Banks with Foreign Capital	17.5	15.6	1.8
Development and Investment Banks	77.2	66.4	10.8
Total	22.4	19.5	2.9

Source: TBB/BAT, 2000:48.

As of June 2010, the answers given in the survey were put into a report form (BDDK/BRSA, 2010/c). The report was prepared using answers of 46 banks. We can summarize the report's results as follows:

- Banks, whose assets constituted 48% of the total assets in the Turkish Banking Sector, on an individual basis submitted their strategy and policies regarding transition to CRD/Basel II to their board of directors or after submitting their strategy and policies to their board of directors implemented them on an individual basis, whereas banks, whose assets constituted 35,5% of the total assets in the sector, did this on a consolidated basis. It is observed that 99% of the banking sector determined the top management that will carry out the works regarding CRD/Basel II; 88% determined the top management units that will carry out the harmonization works; 83% determined the employees that will work in this context; and 70% determined the committees.
- In *credit risk* measurement, it is observed that 99% of banks reached 50-100% compliance with Standard Approach and 53% of banks reached 50-100% compliance with the approach based on Internal Rating. Most of the banks planning to move onto progressive methods in credit risk calculation defers this transition to 2013 and afterwards. Among the methods used to decrease credit risk are collateral (with 87%) and guarantee and security (with 84%) the most-used ones. In 40% of the sector, more than 5 years worth of data was compiled on default ratios. 70% of the sector accumulated more than 5 years worth of data on default ratios and internal rating scores. Banks performing stress test regarding credit risk consist of 85% of the sector. In *market risk*, all banks were compliant with Standard methods, whereas shares of banks that were majorly (75%-100%) compliant with internal measurement methods and issues regarding assessment are respectively 86% and 83%. The share of banks indicating that they were majorly compliant with issues regarding specific risks remains at the level of 38%. A major part of banks implements the stress test using scenarios in which only one parameter is changed. In *operational risk*, all of the banks comply with basic indicator approach currently in use, whereas share of banks that were 75%-100% compliant with Standard approach remains at the level of 31%. 44% of banks indicated that their compliance levels are above 50% in progressive measurement methods. In operational risk calculation, 57% of the sector plans to move onto progressive measurement methods within 2 years period.
- Among problems and restraints faced with regard to CRD/Basel II, the most primary obstacle banks face is lack of data; this is followed by uncertainties in regulations and technological problems.
- There are important expectations of the sector from BRSA: (i) determination of dates and road map regarding Basel II transition period; (ii) Issuance of regulations needed for compliance at the proper time; (iii) Effective working of Basel II Committee embodied in the Banks Association of Turkey so as to handle regulations and implementations in risk management; (iv) Assessment of Basel II compliance in accordance with banks' scales; (v) In the upcoming period, gathering of questions asked by banks to BRSA and answers given by BRSA in a document and issuance of that document on BRSA web-site, as was the case for QIS-TR3 analysis.

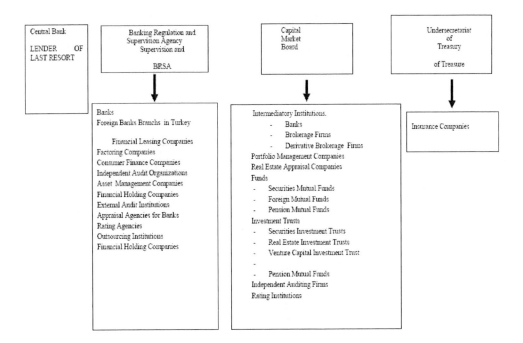

Scheme 2. The Regulation Structure of Turkish Financial Markets.

The positive improvement is the issuance of Basel II Regulation drafts and opening them to discussion within the last six months.

5. 2008 GLOBAL CRISIS AND TURKISH BANKING SYSTEM

Global crisis, arising more apparently in the second half of 2007, at first affected other developed countries and thereafter the emerging markets. The crisis is known to have emerged due to weaknesses in financial markets of USA. After the beginning of 2000s excessive global liquidity and falling interest rates started to increase the risk appetite in financial sector, causing creation of many complicated/complex financial instruments and securitization and an increase in high-leveraged transactions. Falling interest rates increased debts of the households where especially housing loans rose at a very fast pace. Many derivative instruments based on mortgage loans emerged in this way. Within this structure, in which banks, firms and households are borrowers, an upward movement in interest rates in 2006 led to a decrease in wealth of security owners and also caused subprime owners with little ability to pay to return the houses of which they could pay the debts. This caused housing prices to decrease and share prices of real estate companies to lose value at the stock exchange. At this point commercial banks as well as investment banks using extremely high leverages started to experience liquidity problems. As a result of high securitization volumes, use of high leverages, creation of many complicated financial instruments, pricing and risk evaluation of these assets became uncertain. Another issue brought out by the crisis was the issue of too much risk borne by instruments and institutions with low regulations. Besides the issue of lack of financial regulations in some areas, the failure of current regulations in mitigating the cyclical movements of leverages, loan expansions and housing prices was also brought into attention. The first phase of the crisis was the huge loss in financial sector; the second phase was its reflection on the real sector despite many liquidity measures taken. The only reason of the global financial crisis is not the weaknesses of financial sector. More fundamental-macroeconomic structural problems lie behind it. The problem of foreign trade-current account deficit imbalance between a consuming USA economy and a producing Far East (especially China), named as Global imbalance problem, is behind it. In order to maintain this imbalance, USA struggled to create so many financial assets which triggered the crisis.

The impact of the global crisis started to be felt in Turkey in the last quarter of 2008. In 2009, the impact of the crisis started to be observed in many macroeconomic indicators. However, despite the deteriorating indicators, the financial sector in Turkey has not been seriously affected from the crisis. It has maintained its profitability and activities in a healthy way. The crisis has affected the real sector more deeply. The first channel of the reflection of the crisis is the contraction in capital inflows. The second channel is the foreign trade channel. Decreasing foreign demand put a break on exports and shrinking domestic demand decreased the imports. A third channel is the effects created by pessimistic expectations of global economy. The recession in prices of commodities, raw material, and oil is another effect channel.

5.1. Macroeconomic Indicators in the Crisis

- The GDP growth rate, was maintained at a high level between 2003 and 2007, was 0,7% in 2008 and in 2009 economy contracted by 4,7% with fixed prices. In 2010, growth rate increased again and the estimation is that it will be 6,8% by the end of the year.
- Unemployment rates are as high as 14,4%. Some measures taken have not been sufficient to decrease structural unemployment.
- Due to the decrease in domestic demand, raw material prices, and oil price, inflation rate was 6,5% in 2009. This rate has been the lowest rate since 1968. In 2010, due to the increase in domestic demand, improvements in consumption loan market, and increase in government consumption, a rise in inflation rate is observed. It is forecasted that this rate will fluctuate within 8,5-10% bandwidth. The policy interest rate which had increased up to 16,5% in 2008 decreased to 6,5% in November 2009. In 2010, this level is maintained (BDDK/BRSA, 2010/a).
- The most important impact of the crisis on public fiscal stability has been the necessity of turning towards expansionary fiscal policy. Public deficit increased due to the rise in public expenditures as well as tax cuts imposed as a result of contraction in economic activities and financial measures taken. Ratio of public deficit to GDP was 1,6% in 2008, whereas it increased to 6,4% in 2009. Ratio of outstanding domestic public debt to GDP, increasing by 6 points, rose to 35% in 2009; ratio of outstanding external debt, increasing by 2 points, rose to 12%. However, in the first

six months of 2010, with the increase in budget incomes, budget deficit decreased along with a small increase in primary surplus.

- In 2009, the ratio of foreign trade volume to GDP, decreasing by 6 points, came down to 39% and the ratio of current account deficit to GDP, with the impact of domestic demand contraction, decreased swiftly to 2,3%. However, as of the first quarter of 2010, compared to the same period of the previous year, exports increased by 11% whereas imports increased by 36%. Hence, ratios of foreign trade and current account deficits to GDP started to increase again.
- Foreign direct investment (FDI) which was USD 19 million in 2007 decreased to USD 6 million in 2009. In the first quarter of 2010, compared to the previous year's same period, FDI decreased by %50. Net portfolio investment was worth USD 717 million in 2007, whereas it was USD 196 million in 2009. In 2010, portfolio investments started to increase.

Turkey's credit rating was upgraded four times in 2009 by various rating agencies. As of December 2009, Turkey's sovereign credit rating was announced as BB- by SandP, as Ba3 by Moody's and as BB+ by FITCH (TBB/BAT, 2010/a).

5.2. Measures taken by Turkey in the Crisis

To prevent the negative reflections of the crisis on Turkey, many measures were taken by the government and relevant institutions starting from the last quarter of 2008 which also continued in 2009.

Measures taken by the Government

- The Turkish Ministry of Finance introduced tax concessions for the real sector. Accordingly, it was decided that tax debts accrued before September 1, 2008 would be started to be paid as of December 2008 and the payment would be split into 18 installments.
- With the Law on Repatriation of Capital accepted in the Grand National Assembly of Turkey and ratified on November 21, 2008, in case money, gold and other securities owned by natural and corporate legal persons as of October 1, 2008 are brought to Turkey, it is ensured that these items are taxed at 2% level and registered. Implementation of repatriation of capital, whose scope was later broadened, was first extended until July 2009 and later until the end of 2009.
- With measures package announced in March 2009, tax rates on white goods, automotive, and housing sectors were reduced. Supplementary allowance was provided to SMEs; Resource Utilization Support Fund (RUSF) was decreased; and Turk Eximbank's capital was increased. The use of reduced tariff for industrial electricity was generalized.
- With the second package announced in March 2009, VAT on furniture, heavy construction equipment, IT and office furniture was reduced. In April 2009, broadening the scope of this implementation, sectors such as automotive sub-industry and telephone were added. Tax cuts were extended until October 2009.

- In March 2009, maturity of agricultural loans provided by Ziraat Bank was extended.
- In June 2009, with the amendment in Law on Public Finance and Debt Management, a resource allocation of 2,6 billion TL to Turkish Grain Board and government bond issuance by the Treasury were ensured.
- In June 2009, new incentive system was announced. The aim of the new incentive system, which will be valid until 2010 year end, is to support large investments in 12 sectors and by separating Turkey into 4 regions, to provide sectoral and regional incentives. Incentive instruments are corporate and income tax cuts, interest support, VAT exemption, investment place allocation, and customs exemption.
- Restructuring of credit card debts was put into effect in July 2009.
- With the employment package, 120.000 unemployed people were provided jobs.
- In December 2009, with the Medium-Term Programme, it tried to tackle with the ambiguity problem and to have a positive impact on expectations and behaviors by announcing the targets in relation to basic economic indicators for the 3 year period 2010-2012.

Measures taken by the Central Bank

- The Central Bank took a decision to start its brokerage transactions in Foreign Exchange and Banknotes market FX deposit market as of October 2008 until the uncertainty in international markets is swept away.
- In FX deposit markets, it doubled the transaction limits as of October 2008 and it announced the limits as USD 10,8 billion.
- After March 2009, foreign exchange sale bids were started due to the increase in foreign exchange demand and the month March experienced sales worth USD 900 million in a total of 18 bids. Net foreign exchange purchase of Central Bank in 2009 was USD 3,3 billion.
- In 2008, the Central Bank extended the maturity of foreign exchange deposits that could be received by banks from 1 week to 1 month and in February 2009 extended this time period to 3 months. Lending interest rate on Dollar was reduced from 7% to 5,5%; lending interest rate on Euro was reduced from 9% to 6,5%.
- In order to reduce the impact of the crisis experienced since March-April 2009 on the real sector, the Central Bank, raised the export rediscounting credit limit by USD 500 million, thereby increasing it to USD 1 billion.
- At the end of 2008, required foreign currency reserve ratios of banks were decreased from 11% to 9% and in October 2009, required TL reserve ratios were decreased from 6% to 5%. In October 2010, this ratio was again increased to 5,5% and in November 2010, it was raised to 6%.
- Funding was provided in order to meet liquidity need of the market and as of June 2009, three-month long-term repo bids have been added to the funding resources.

Measures taken by the Banking Regulation and Supervision Agency (BRSA)

- In 2008, for one time only, the banks were permitted to reclassify their securities.

- BRSA asked the banks to withhold their profits and not to distribute them as a dividend payment and made the profit distribution subject to the Board's consent.
- BRSA, with a new regulation made on January 23, 2009, made it also possible for loans that appear to be non-problematic to be restructured.

5.3. Indicators of the Banking Sector in the Crisis

After the last quarter of 2008, the Global Crisis has also affected the banking sector in Turkey. Foreign borrowing resources declined; loan demand decreased; balance sheet risk increased; liquidity need mounted up in the sector. However, despite these contractions, banking sector still performed quite well in the crisis. It did not need any financial support from the government and in fact borrowing requirements of the government were substantially met by banks. No change has been needed in existing government guarantee on deposits in Turkey, whereas in many countries, 100% guarantee were given to deposits. The underlying factor behind this achievement in the sector is that restructuring of Banking Sector after 2001 Crisis has been quite successful. An effective supervision of government, a successful risk management, a healthy balance sheet structure, strong and growing shareholder's equity, decreases in interest rates, and increasing confidence in TL are the effective factors behind this success.

Based on the known indicators of the sector, it is possible to give the following information (See, Supplementary Table 6 and 7):

1. The sector's asset size is gradually increasing in the third quarter of 2010, total assets size, increasing by 11% compared to 2009 yearend level, reached to 927,4 billion TL. Total loans amounted to 392,6 billion TL in 2009 and 475,4 billion TL as of September 2010. In 2009, the share of loans in total assets, decreasing by 4 points compared to its level in 2008, was 48%; and the share of securities portfolio in total assets, increasing by 6 points, rose to 35%. However, in 2010 with this effect reversing, the share of loans in assets in the last quarter of 2010 rose to 51,3%, i.e. increasing by 4,2 points compared to its level in 2009. The share of security portfolio decreased to 29,6%. As of September 2010, of the total loans, corporate/commercial loans accounted for 43,8%; retail loans accounted for 33,%; and loans provided to SMEs accounted for 22,9%. In 2010, the share of retail loans and SME loans increased while the share of corporate loans decreased. Loans and securities portfolio include conventional banking products. There is no "toxic assets" in banks (TBB/BAT, 2010/b).

2. Increases in non-performing loans and non-performing loans (NPL) ratio in 2009 experienced a falling tendency in 2010. Gross non-performing loans, decreasing by 3,3% compared to 2009, decreased to 21,1 billion TL in 2010. NPL ratio which was 3,7% in 2008 increased to 5,4% in November 2009, decreased to 5,3% as of 2009 year end and to 4,3% as of September 2010.

3. As of September 2010, 61,8% of banking sector's liabilities was deposits; 11,3% was foreign debt; and 6% was repo. Deposits, increasing by 58,4 billion TL (11,3%) compared to 2009, rose to 573 billion TL. In the last quarter of 2010, TL deposits

decreased and foreign currency deposits increased. As of September 2010, 91,5% of deposits consisted of demand deposits and up to three months term deposits. This is the basic reason of time mismatch in Assets/Liabilities (BDDK, 2010/d).

4. The rate at which deposits are turned into loans started to increase after 2002 (from 35,5%), rose up to 80,8% in 2008 and decreased to 76% in 2009. In September 2010, this ratio increased to 86,7%.

5. After 2002, with the restructuring of Turkish Banking Sector, foreign borrowing resources have increased and the sector has started to utilize more of the global funds. Foreign borrowings which amounted to USD 2,8 billion in 2001 reached to USD 62 billion at the end of 2008 and USD 70 billion in 2009. Nevertheless, the share of the relevant figure in total liabilities has been below 10%. However, as of September 2010, foreign borrowings consisted 11,3% of liabilities. There has been a decrease in repos and an increase in debts to foreign countries.

6. The sector's syndication and securitization loans, increasing by USD 1,8 billion in the first nine months of 2010, reached to a level of USD 19,9 billion as of September 2010.

7. The sector's shareholder's equity level increased to 126,9 billion TL in September 2010. 12 banks increased their shareholder's equity amounts by 4 billion TL. Since the beginning of 2010, the sector, which had started to make profits after 2002, has been experiencing a decrease in the growth rate of its net profit income of the period. Nevertheless, the net income for the period, increasing by 1,165 million TL compared to 2009, reached to 16,876 million TL in September 2010. 31 banks out of 49 experienced a loss in their profits in the recent year. The basic reason of the rise in the sector's profit in 2009 was the increase in net interest margins as a result of time mismatch upon decreasing policy interest rates. In 2010, with the end of policy interest rate cut process, increase in net interest margins halted and this affected profitability in a negative way. In 2007, return on equity (Net income of the period/Average shareholders' equity) reached to its maximum level (24,8%). At the end of 2008, with the impact of the crisis, return on equity decreased to %18; this ratio was 24,7% in September 2009 and 21,1% in September 2010. Return on equity decreased by 3,6 points compared to the same period of 2009.

8. Capital adequacy/requirement ratio (CAR), which is calculated based on Basel criteria and indicates the share of shareholder's equity in total risks (credit risk, market risk, and operational risk), is the basic indicator for banks' riskiness. This ratio which is supposed to at least 8% was determined as 12% "Target ratio" with BRSA's decision. Banks with a lower ratio than this are not permitted to open branches. This resulted in banks' achieving a capital adequacy ratio above 12%. BRSA, by ensuring the addition of a substantial part of banks' profits to the capital since 2005, ensured that CAR reached 21,9%. CAR was 17,9% in 2008, 19,3% in 2009, and also 19,3% in September 2009.

9. Since 2003, Foreign Exchange Net General Position (FEXNGP) is calculated to monitor and control exchange rate risk. Thanks to the regulation of this position's not exceeding 20% of shareholder's equity, exchange risk borne by banks is limited.

As per the data of the banking sector as of September 2010, expectations with regard to 2010 year end are deceleration in the growth rate of the sector, decrease in profit margins, deceleration in the growth rate of shareholder's equity, a slow increase in non-performing loans and also continuation of these developments. Foreign borrowing is more desirable and foreign capital inflows continue. The expectation is that borrowing demand of the government will persist and will be higher and that risk sensitivity will gain importance in line with messages and advices of the Central Bank and BRSA (TBB/BAT, 2010/b). The sector, taking into consideration the increase in loans, should pay attention to harmonization with safety and liquidity principles as well as risk-return balance in extension of loans and every stage of credit process should be carried out rationally.

Within the framework of Exit Strategy, announced by the Central Bank in April 2010, means provided in relation to TL and foreign currency liquidity will revert to their pre-crisis levels. Based on this, decision to increase required reserve ratios of Turkish and foreign currency deposits and decision to terminate interest payments on TL required reserves are expected to result in a loss of more than 1 billion TL in the sector's annual income. Moreover, the Central Bank, after observing exit strategies of developed countries' central banks, will terminate its brokerage service in FX deposit market; lowering of the Central Bank's limit for foreign currency loans to banks and lowering of foreign exchange reserves from 3 months to 1 week will also take place within the Exit strategy (TCMB/CBRT, 2010).

5.4. Basel III Discussions

Basel II text, published in June 2004, was included in the European Union acquisition in 2006 with directives no. 49. However, after the 2008 global financial crisis, Basel Committee developed Basel III criteria as a new regulations set to remedy the deficiencies observed in Basel II. Basel III is a not a revolution amending all of Basel II, but is a complimentary amendments set, updating and enriching Basel II's three structural blocks with regard to the crisis. Philosophy and methodology of Basel II have not been amended. Although Basel III is an important part of international financial regulations, coordination regarding the regulations is provided by Financial Stability Board (FBS) and also is discussed in IMF and G-20 Platforms.

In Basel III, it is targeted that banking system's endurance to financial and economic shocks increases under all circumstances (all cycles). Secondly, Basel III aims to increase the system's endurance to shocks with regulations at macro level as much as to increase banks' endurance to shocks individually at micro level (Macroprudential Approach). The third target is improvement of corporate management, risk management implementation, transparency and information provision.

For these targets, many change proposals primarily in relation to *capital adequacy* have been suggested and ratios with regard to these have been determined:

- Increasing minimum capital quantity: seed capital ratio(common equity ratio), Tier 1 ratio, and total legal capital ratio have been all increased. In Turkey, Tier 1 represents principal capital and Tier 2 represents supplementary capital. It has been determined that supplementary capital cannot surpass 100% of principal capital. Common Equity/Risk-Weighted Assets ratio has been increased.

- Amending quality of capital/Higher quality capital: The highest quality capital within principal and seed capital is common equity. Common equity is a higher quality capital compared to preferred equity/stock (Hanson, Kashyap, Stein, 2010).
- Time-varying capital requirements that are in harmonization with cycles: Establishing capital conservation buffer for this. Capital level that should be determined according to economic conjuncture will be subject to 0%-2,5% addition (BIS, 2010; Hanson, Kashyap, Stein, 2010).
- Determining risk weight for securitization and resecuritization transactions.
- Higher risk weights on credit risks (increasing the conversion to loans ratio from 20% to 50%)
- Revision studies continue in calculation of capital adequacy with regard to counterparty credit risk and trade accounts.
- Marginal risk modeling in risk calculation for options and other non-linear instruments (mortgage-backed securities) (Candan, 2009)

Leverage Ratios that Are Not Risk-based

As an enhancer and compliment of risk-based capital adequacy measurements, simple leverage ratios that are not risk-based have been determined to ensure that banks maintain their activities in a healthy way (Shin, 2009). (Principal Capital/Assets+Off balance sheet times) ratio is targeted to be 3% or it is targeted that assets size of approximately 33 times the size of Principal capital (Tier 1) will be incrementally (until 2017) tested and then realized.

Liquidity Regulations

Two ratios named as Liquidity Coverage Ratio and net stable funding ratio with 100% minimum levels are planned to be included in the regulations and a compliance period is designated until 2018. The first ratio is the ratio of banks' liquidity assets to net cash outflows that will be realized within 30 days. This ratio should be at least 100%. The second ratio is obtained by dividing current stable funding amount to stable funding amount needed and should be at least 100% (BIS, 2009).

Moreover, with regard to 2. structural block, the following issues were brought to the agenda (Candan, 2009):

- -Need for long-term utilization of capital requirement rather than short-term
- -Approval mechanisms that will provide insight into the new financial instruments as well as their implementations considering the risks borne by these instruments which are passed onto the Board of Directors through a chain
- -Policy determination for identification and measurement of reputation risk.
- With regard to 3. structural block, securitization and re-securitization risks and valuation methods as well as information on the ways and evaluations by which assets subject to securitization risks are classified are laid emphasis on.

Basel III has a quite extensive and complex structure and the transition/harmonization period is designated as 2013-2019. Concepts such as seed capital that are not yet implemented in Turkish regulations are included. However, in Turkey, leverage ratios are low compared to many other countries and level of capital is quite satisfactory in terms of quantity and quality.

CONCLUSION

Turkish Banking System constitutes a major part of the country's financial system. However, compared to the world and EU, it is small in terms of volume. The ratio of Turkish Banking sector's balance sheet size to GDP was 77,1% in 2008 and 87,4% in 2009. This ratio is higher compared to Poland and Romania, but lower compared to other EU countries. Credit/GDP and Deposit/GDP ratios, measures of sector's depth, have been increasing in Turkey. However, also these ratios are lower than those in the EU.(See Table 6)

Looking at the concentration in the banking sector, it is possible to observe that the shares of the first 5 and 10 banks in total assets have shown an important change between 2002 and 2009. The same change is observed in the concentration of loans and deposits (See, Supplementary Table 9). There were 4 banks in 2009 with asset share above %10 and the largest bank's asset share was %14,9. Convergence of asset shares of large-scale banks shows that competition structure in the sector has strengthened.

After the 2000-2001 Financial Crisis, the system was restructured within the framework of Stand-by agreements signed with IMF; important efforts were made to meet International banking rules and Basel criteria. With the lessons learned from this very serious and bad experience, in the sector, a stronger supervision and regulation infrastructure and a more healthy competition structure were established. Coordination between the banks and BRSA was established in order to ensure risk management effectiveness; the infrastructure of laws and regulations in internal audit, internal control, and risk management was formed. Transparency in the system was increased.

As much as the banking sector tried to meet Basel criteria with regard to risk measurement, it also established its own risk control mechanisms. Special measurement/management standards regarding exchange rate and liquidity risk, "target CRR" implementation with respect to capital adequacy ratio, and creation of quick ratio were cautious implementations that BRSA carried out on its own initiative. At the end of this restructuring process, the financial position of the sector strengthened. Also, general macroeconomic stability had a positive impact on the sector. The role of decreasing borrowing need of the government and lowering of inflation in interest rate decrease is unquestionable. Hence, with these positive developments, real banking activities became to be performed. These developments and changes also attracted the attention of foreign investors; after 2004, foreign banks became important actors in the sector. In the banking sector, as of 2008 year end, foreign share was 26%. This ratio was 19% for EU region and 26% for EU-27.

The sector that faced the 2008 Global Crisis with these circumstances benefited from the advantage of its "excess prudently" and "very-regulated" look; also, with the measures taken throughout the crisis, the crisis did not damage the sector. We had mentioned that after the 2008 Global Crisis, there were new regulation standards introduced under the name Basel III.

With these standards, taking also into account the more quality capital and low leverage ratios that are especially put emphasis on, it seems that the Turkish banking sector has a head start and will not have difficulty in abiding with this new process. The shareholder's equity of the banking sector, unlike in many other countries, consists of income reserves and paid-up capital whose loss remedy capacity is higher.

Table 6. Comparison of Selected EU Countries[1,2,3]

Countries	Deposit/ GDP (%)	Loan/ GDP (%)	Loan/ Deposit (%)	Total Assets/ Number of Credit Agencies (Million Euros)	Sector Share of the Top 5 Credit Agencies (%)	Number of Credit Agencies	Share of Foreign Stockholders in the Banking Sector (%)
Germany	123	129	105	3,959	23	1,989	11,5
Austria	112	149	134	1,330	39	803	23,4
Belgium	157	117	74	12,116	81	105	26,9
Bulgaria	63	74	118	1,228	57	30	83,4
Czech Rep.	67	52	78	2,871	62	54	90,8
Denmark	82	238	290	6,385	66	171	17,5
Estonia	60	105	175	1,296	95	17	97,3
Finland	61	90	146	1,075	83	357	69,5
France	86	117	137	9,925	51	728	13,3
Holland	168	185	110	7,401	87	302	5,7
UK	285	282	99	22,609	37	391	50,9
Ireland	165	259	157	2,819	56	501	56,6
Spain	160	181	114	9,340	42	362	10,6
Sweden	56	130	231	4,944	62	182	9,4
Italy	76	115	152	4,436	33	818	12,1
Latvia	58	99	172	949	70	34	67,8
Lithuania	35	65	186	316	81	84	84,8
Luxembourg	718	553	77	6,129	27	152	95,2
Hungary	52	72	139	633	55	197	60,4
Poland	42	44	103	370	44	712	71,7
Portugal	127	170	133	2,756	69	175	22,1
Rumania	29	37	126	1,966	54	43	79,4
Slovakia	62	47	76	2,520	72	26	92,8
Slovenia	57	93	76	2,520	72	26	92,8
Greece	116	91	78	7,000	70	66	22,2
Euro Area Avrg.	117	138	118	4,653	45	438	18,7
EU 27 Avrg.	134	154	115	4,960	44	315	26,4
Turkey 2008	48	40	84	7,008	60	49	25,6
Turkey 2009	54	43	81	7,944	60	49	23,9

[1] The table includes 2008 data of the EU countries. The meaning of the term "Credit institution" varies by the EU countries and some include non-credit institutions as well. As for Turkey, data pertaining to banks are considered.

[2] Regarding Turkey, participation funds are included in deposit data and funds extended by participation banks in credit data.

[3] Parallel to the data for the EU, NPLs and financial leasing receivables are also included in the data for the credits in Turkey.

Source: BRSA-CBRT, Eurostat, ECB Report – 2009

Looking at the leverage ratios, we observe that in Turkish banking system this ratio is (units of asset per each share of equity shares) 7-8 units. In EU countries, banks function with

30 units of assets per each share of equity shares, whereas in US, they function with approximately 10 units of assets (TCMB/CBRT, 2010).

However, for this course of events to continue well, correction of existing deficiencies, keeping up with international innovations in supervision and risk management, continuation of coordination between banks and other relevant institutions (CBT, BRSA, SDIF, The Banks Association of Turkey, and Treasury) should be ensured. In the last period, within the framework of Exiting from the Crisis Strategy, there has been a reflection that while a decision was being made regarding an increase in required reserves, Central Bank and BRSA did not coordinate. Also, tension between the banking sector, whose profits decreased in 2010 compared to 2009, and government as well as Central Bank increased. Banks are uncomfortable with excessive regulation, funds transferred to the public sector (RUSF), and an early increase in required reserve ratios (as a final situation, it is 6% for TL and 11% for foreign currency) and are concerned that the growth of the sector is hindered with these implementations. Government and Central Bank, on the other hand, do not approve especially the increase in consumer loans, believe that it will heat up the economy too much, and assert that a moderate and manageable growth in the sector will be appropriate for financial stability. Head of BRSA asserts that despite the very tight and strict regulations that Turkish Banking still faces (as compared to Western banks), the sector reached an asset size of 927 billion TL in the first nine months of 2010, provided loans of amount 83 billion TL, and lowered non-performing loan(NPL) ratio to 4,3%; however that profit margins decreased, and emphasizing the high competition between the banks, indicates that a clear picture of the banks will appear in 2011. He attributes the sector's weathering the crisis without getting damaged to the supervision carried out by BRSA.

The most basic problem with risk management is the deficiencies in data quality and data provision; secondly the deficiencies in technical information and risk modeling at IT systems. The third problem is the ambiguity regarding transition to Basel II process. A road map has not yet been determined as to how to carry out the postponed transition process.

APPENDIX

Supplementary Table 1. Main Economic Indicators of Turkish Economy I (1991 – 2000)

		1991	1992	1993	1994	1995	1996	1997	1998	1999	2000
GNP Growth (%)		0.4	6.4	8.1	-6.1	7.9	7.1	8.9	3.9	-6.1	6.1
GDP (USD) (billion)		153	160	183	131	174	182	192	207	185	195
GNP per capita (USD)		2.657	2.752	3.056	2.159	2.784	2.936	3.032	3.159	2.827	2.987
Inflation	Producer	66	70	66	106	93	79	85	83	64	54
(Twelve month change)	Consumer	69	30	18	9	8	10	8	10	7	9.2
	DGBB	81	88	88	164	122	135	127	123	110	38
Interest rates	(3months deposit)	70	69	64	77	84	80	83	83	60	106
Exchange rates	USD	60.2	64.7	60.5	169.9	54	78	86.8	71.7	60.9	48.5
Budget Deficit	(Billion)TRL	-33.5	-47.4	134	-152	-317	-1238	-2246	-3803	-9072	12
BD / GNP		5	4	7	4	4	8	8	7	11	
PSBR /GNP		12	11	12	8	5	9	8	9	15	12

Source: SPO, CBRT.

Supplementary Table 2. Main Economic Indicators of Turkish Economy II (1991-2000)

		1991	1992	1993	1994	1995	1996	1997	1998	1999	2000
Balance of Payment											
Foreign Trade	Export	14	15	16	18	22	32	33	31	29	32
(USD billion)	Import	-21	-23	-30	-23	-35	-43	-48	-45	-40	-54
	Trade Deficit	-7	-8	-14	-4	-13	-11	-15	-14	-10	-22
Current Account Balance/GDP(%)		0.3	-1	-6.4	2.6	-2.3	-2.4	-2.6	2	-1.4	-9.8
Outstanding domestic debt	Total	98	194	357	799	1.361	3.149	6.238	11.613	22.920	36.421
	Outstanding Domestic G. securities/GDP (%)	15.4	17.6	17.9	20.6	17.3	21.0	21.4	21.9	29.3	29.0
Outstanding external debt (USD million)	Total	50.5	55.6	67.4	65.6	73.3	79.6	84.9	96.9	103.3	116.1
	Short Term	9.1	12.7	18.5	11.3	15.7	17.4	18.1	21.2	23.5	28.9

Source: SPO, CBRT.

Supplementary Table 3. Main Economic Indicators of Turkish Economy III (2001-2010)

		2001	2002	2003	2004	2005	2006	2007	2008	2009	2010 Sep.
GDP Growth (%)		-7.5	7.9	5.3	9.4	8.4	6.9	4.7	0.7	- 4.7	5.2
GDP (USD) (billion)		143	182	303	392	483	529	649	730	615	711
Income per capita (USD)		2200	2,746	4,602	5.862	7,108	7,767	9,422	10,484	8,723	9,950
Inflation (Twelve month change)	Producer	89	31	14	14	3	12	6	8	6	8.9
	Consumer	60	30	18	9	8	10	8	10	7	9.2
Interest rates (Annual,compound, average)	O/n	59	44	26	19	14	19	17	16	7	
	G-Securities	74	53	28	23	14	22	17	19	9	
Exchange rates (Twelve month chg)	USD (Year-end) (Twelve month chg)	1.4466 99	1.6397 13	1.3933 - 15	1.3363 -4	1.3418 0	1.4056 5	1.1593 -18	1.5218 31	1.4873 - 2.3	1.4434- 3.0
	Euro (year-end) (Twelve month chg)		1.7189	1.75752.2	1.82334	1.5875- 13	1.851517	1.7060- 8	2.143525	2.14270.4	1.9693- 8,1
	PSPR/GDP	16	13	9	5	0	-2	0	1	0	0

Source: SPO, CBRT.

Supplementary Table 4. Main Economic Indicators of Turkish Economy IV (2001-2010)

		2001	2002	2003	2004	2005	2006	2007	2008	2009	2010Sep.
Balance of Payment											
Foreign Trade (USD billion)	Export	34	40	51	63	73	85	107	132	102	112
	Import	38	47	65	97	116	137	170	202	141	178
	Trade Deficit	4	7	14	34	43	52	63	70	39	66
Current Account Balance/GDP (%)		2	-1	-3	-4	-5	-6	-6	-6	-2	-5
Central Government Budget	Budget Deficit (TL billion)	-29	-40	-40	-30	-10	-5	-14	-19	-56	-50
	Primary Balance (TL billion)	12	12	18	26	36	41	35	33	1 7	
	BD/GDP	17	15	11	7	2	1	2	2	6	5
	PSPR/GDP	16	13	9	5	0	-2	0.07	1.6	5.5	3.7
Outstanding domestic debt	Total	122	150	194	225	245	252	255	275	330	
	Outstanding Domestic G. Securities/GDP (%)	16.4	12.7	9.4	40	38	33	30	29	35	
Outstanding external debt (USD million)	Total	114	130	146	161	169	207	249	278	268	266
	Short Term	16	16	23	32	37	43	43	50	49	62

Source: SPO, CBRT.

Supplementary Table 5. Main Operational Indicators of Turkish Banking Sector (1990-2000)

	1990	1991	1992	1993	1994	1995	1996	1997	1998	1999	2000
Numbers of Banks	66	65	69	70	67	68	69	72	75	81	79
Numbers of Branches	6560	6477	6206	6241	6104	6240	6442	6819	7370	7691	7837
Number of Personnel	*154,089*	*152,901*	*146,823*	*143,983*	*139,046*	*144,793*	*148,153*	*154,864*	166,492	173,998	170,401
Number of ATMs	3.209				4.023			6.735	8.363	9.939	11.991
Number of POS Machines (Thousand)					16.135			58.636	113.816	188.957	299.950

Source: BRSA, TBAT.

Supplementary Table 6. Main Operational Indicators of Turkish Banking Sector (2001-2010)

	2001	2002	2003	2004	2005	2006	2007	2008	2009	2010
Numbers of Banks	63	54	50	53	51	50	50	49	49	49
Public Deposit Banks	3	3	3	3	3	3	3	3	3	3
Private Deposit Banks	22	20	18	18	17	14	12	11	11	11
Banks within SDIF	6	2	2	1	1	1	1	1	1	1
Foreign Deposit Banks	15	15	13	13	13	15	17	17	17	17
Dev. And Inv. Banks	15	14	14	13	13	13	13	13	13	13
Participation Banks	6	5	5	5	4	4	4	4	4	4
Numbers of Branches	6477	6206	6241	6104	6240	6442	6819	7370	9581	9935
Number of Personnel	152,901	146,823	143,983	139,046	144,793	148,153	154,864	166,492	173,998	184,205
Number of ATMs		12.035	12.726	13.556	14.836	16.513	18.795	21.953	23.952	24.593
Number of POS Machines (Thousand)				912	1.141	1.283	1.629	1.886	2.048	2.067
Nr. Of Intern. Bank Active Customers					3.177	3.368	4.274	5.169	5.974	6.006

Source: BRSA, T BAT.

Supplementary Table 7. Turkish Banking Sector Financial Soundness Indicators (2001-2010)

	2001	2002	2003	2004	2005	2006	2007	2008	2009	2010
Capital Adequacy Standard Ratio	20,8	25,3	30,9	28,8	23,7	22,3	18,9	18,0	20,6	19,3
Free Capital / Total Own Funds		36	3 51	0 56	65,7	72,6	75,3	77,0	79,6	80,5
Total Own Funds / Total For. Resources (1)	6,2	13,7	16,6	17,6	15,5	13,5	15,0	13,4	15,3	15,7
Total Own Funds /Total Assets	7,2	12,1	14,2	15	13,4	11,9	13,0	11,8	13,2	13,7
Loans / Total Own Funds	421,2	219,4	196,9	224,6	284,8	376,1	381,6	425,7	354,1	374,6
Liquidity Indicators (2)					51,8	50,3	47,0	34,4	43,0	43,0
FX Net General Position / Own Funds	-	-	1,1	- 0,5	-0,2	0,5	-0,3	0,0	0,1	-0,6
Non-Balanced Sheet Transactions/ Total Assets					55,5	66,3	66,3	64,9	69,5	73,8
NPLs /Gross Loans	25,2	17,6	11,5	6,0	4,8	3,8	3,5	3,6	5,3	4,3

	2001	2002	2003	2004	2005	2006	2007	2008	2009	2010
NPLs Provisions / NPLs					88,7	89,7	86,8	79,9	83,5	82,9
Individual Loans / Total Loans		13	8 19	9 27	31,1	32,3	33,2	32,1	33,3	33,0
Nr. Of Profiting Banks/Total Nr. Of Banks		37	39	40	45/51	41/50	46/50	45/49	46/49	46/49
Assets of Profiting Banks/Total Assets		92	8 97	6 91	93,9	99,4	99,3	99,9	99,8	99,6
After-Tax Return on Assets (ROA)	-6,1	1,4	2,5	2,3	1,7	2,5	2,8	2,0	2,6	2,6
After-Tax Return on Equities (ROE)	-57,5	11,2	18,1	15,8	10,9	19,2	21,7	16,8	22,9	21,1
Interest Expenses / Total Expenses					55,8	65,3	67,1	67,3	60,9	
Interest Incomes / Interest Expenses	145,2	147,4	147,9	189,1	184,4	160,9	159,20	156,5	19,1	199,7
Non- Interest Incomes / Non-Interest Expenses	-47,9	73,1	114,0	78,4	52,0	79,3	72,3	65,5	68,7	83,8
Total Foreign Liabilities=Total Liabilities–Total Own Funds										
Liquidity Indicator= (Cash Values+ Receivables from Banks (including receivables from Central Bank and Monetary Markets +Marketable Securities +Securities Ready to Sale +Required Reserves)/(Deposit+ Debts to Banks (including debts to Central Bank and Monetary Markets)										
Total Gross Incomes = Interest Incomes +Non-Interest Incomes										

Source: BRSA.

Supplementary Table 8. The Main Financial Indicator of Turkish Banking System (TL Billion)

	2001	20002	2003	2004	2005	2006	2007	2008	2009	
Total Assets	173,4	212,7	249,7	306,4	406,9	499,7	581,6	732,5	834,0	
Total Loans	38,0	49,0	66,2	99,3	156,4	219,0	285,6	367,4	392,6	
Total Deposits	110,4	138,0	155,3	191,1	251,5	307,6	356,9	454,6	514,6	
Securities	17,5	86,1	106,8	123,7	143,0	158,9	164,7	194,0	262,9	
Own Funds	18,3	25,7	35,5	46,0	54,7	59,5	75,8	86,4	110,9	
Asset /GDP (%)	72,2	60,7	54,9	54,8	62,7	65,9	69,0	77,6	87,5	
Loans/GDP (%)	15,8	14,0	14.6	17,8	24,1	28,9	33,9	38,7	41,2	
Deposit/GDP (%)	45,7	39,3	34,1	34,2	38,8	40,6	42,3	47,8	54,0	
Securities/GDP (%)	7,3	24,6	23,5	22,1	22,0	21,0	19,5	20,4	27,6	
Own Fund /GDP (%)	7,6	7,3	7,8	8,2	8,4	7,8	9,0	9,1	11,6	

Source: BRSA.

Supplementary Table 9. Concentration in Turkish Banking Sector

		1980	1990	1999	2000	2002	2007	2009
Top Five Banks	Assets	63	54	46	48	58	62	63
	Deposits	69	59	50	51	61	64	66
	Loans	71	57	42	42	55	57	55
Top Ten Banks	Assets	82	75	68	69	81	85	87
	Deposits	88	85	69	72	86	89	91
	Loans	90	78	73	71	74	83	85

Source: BRSA, TBAT.

REFERENCES

Babuşçu,Ş., M.O.Köksal (2000): "Yüksek Enflasyondan Düşük Enflasyona Geçiş Sürecinde Türk Bankacılık Sektörü: Sorunlar ve Çözüm Önerileri", *İktisat, İşletme ve Finans*, 15 (174),Eylül.

BIS, Basel Committee on Banking Supervision (1988): "International Convergence of Capital Measurement and Capital Standards", July, Basel, www.bis.org.

BIS, Basel Committee on Banking Supervision (1999): "A New Capital Adequasy Framework", Consultative Paper, June, Basel, www.bis.org.

BIS, Basel Committee on Banking Supervision(2009): "International Framework for Liquidity risk measurement, Standards and Monitoring" Consultative Document, December, Basel, www.bis.org.

BIS, Basel Committee on Banking Supervision (2010): "Countercyclical Capital Buffer Proposal" Consultative Paper, July, Basel, www.bis.org.

BDDK/BRSA (2001): Towards a Sound Turkish Banking Sector, May 15, (http://www.bddk.org.tr).

BDDK/BRSA(2002*): Banking Sector Restructuring Program:Progress Report*, November, http://www.bddk.org.tr).

BDDK/BRSA(2007): *Sermaye Ölçümü ve Sermaye Standartlarının Uluslararası Düzeyde Uyumlulaştırılması (Yeni Basel Sermaye Uzlaşısı) Gözden Geçirilmiş Düzenleme Çerçevesi- Kapsamlı Versiyon*, (Translated to Turkish of the International Convergence of Capital Measurement and Capital Standarts)(http://www.bddk.org.tr).

BDDK/BRSA (2009): Structural Developments in Banking, Issue:4, December, (http://www.bddk.org.tr).

BDDK/BRSA(2010/a): Financial Markets Reports, Issue:18, June, (http://www.bddk.org.tr).

BDDK/BRSA (2010/b): From Crisis to Financial Stability:Turkish Experience, September, (http://www.bddk.org.tr).

BDDK (2010/c): *Bankacılık Sektörü Basel II İlerleme Raporu,* Eylül, (http://www.bddk.org.tr).

BDDK (2010/d): *Türk Bankacılık Sektörü Genel Görünümü*, Kasım, (http://www.bddk.org.tr)

Candan, H.(2009): " Kriz Sürecinde Basel II'de Öngörülen Değişiklikler", *Bankacılar Dergisi,* Mart, 68.

Çakman, K., U. Çakmak(2001): "Krizin Oluşumu Üzerine Yorumlar ve Prognoz", *İktisat, İşletme ve Finans*, 16(185), Ağustos.

Erdönmez, P.A.(2009): "Küresel kriz ve Ülkeler Tarafından Alınan Önlemler Kronolojisi", *Bankacılar Dergisi,* Mart, 68.

Fischer,S.(2001): "Financial Sector Crisis Management, IMF Speeches, file://A: Financial Sector Crisis Management, Remarks by Stanley Fischer.htm.

Hanson,S., A.K. Kashyap, J. Stein (2010): "A Macroprudential Approach to Financial Regulation" July http://www.signallake.com/innovation/JEP-macroprudential-072210. pdf.

Kaminsky, G. L., C. M. Reinhart (1999): "The Twin Crises: The Causes of Banking and Balance of Payment Problems", *American Economic Review,* 89(3), June, pp.473-500.

Keyder, N.(2001): "Türkiye'de 2000-2001 Krizleri ve İstikrar Programları", *İktisat, İşletme ve Finans*, 16(183), Haziran, pp.37-53.

Mishkin,F.S. and Stanley G. Eakins (2009): Financial Markets and Institutions, Sixth Edition, Pearson International Edition. .

Prasad,E.S.(2010): "Financial Sector Regulation and Reforms in Emerging Markets: An Overview" NBER, Working Paper 16428. http://www.nber.org/papers/w16428.

Schooner,H.M., M. Taylor(2010): *Global Bank Regulation: Principles and Policies*, Academic Press, Elsevier Inc.

Shin,H.S.(2009): "Reflections on Northern Rock: The bank Run that Heralded the Global Financial Crises", *Journal of Economic Perspective*, 23(1), pp.101-119.

TBB/BAT(2008): *50th Anniversary of the Bank Association of Turkey and Banking System 1958-2007*, No: 262 (http://www.tbb.org.tr).

TBB/BAT (2010/a): *Banks in Turkey 2009*, No.267, May, (http://www.tbb.org.tr).

TBB/BAT (2010/b): Bankacılık Sektörü 2010 Ocak-Eylül Dönemindeki Gelişmeler, Ekim, (http://www.tbb.org.tr).

TCMB/CBRT(2010): *Financial Stability Report*, May, (http://www.tbb.org.tr).

Van Hoose, D. (2010): *The Industrial Organization of Banking- Bank behavior, Market Structure and Regulation*, Springer Verlag Berlin Heidelberg.

Yay, G.G.(2001): "Enflasyonu Düşürme Politikalarının Maliyetleri: Teori, Uygulama ve Türkiye", *İktisat, İşletme ve Finans,*16(184), Temmuz, pp.66-83.

Yay, G. G.(2002): "Türkiye ve Meksika'da İstikrar Programlarının Karşılaştırılması", in A.A.Dikmen (ed.): *Küreselleşme, Emek Süreçleri ve Yapısal Uyum* (7. Ulusal Sosyal Bilimler Kongresi), Türk Sosyal Bilimler Derneği, Ankara 2002, pp.167-215

Yay, G. G. (2007): "1990'lı Yıllardaki Finansal Krizler ve Türkiye Krizi", in T. Yay and G.G. Yay(2007): *İktisat Yazıları-Metodoloji, Düşünce, Politika* , Nobel Yayınları, Ankara.

Yay,T. and G.G. Yay, E. Yılmaz (2001/a): *Küreselleşme Sürecinde Finansal Krizler ve Finansal Düzenlemeler,* İTO, İstanbul.

Yay,T. and G.G. Yay, E. Yılmaz (2001/b): "Financial Regulation and Financial Crises", *Yapı Kredi Economic Review*, 12(2), December, pp.3-21.

Yay,T. and G.G. Yay, E. Yılmaz (2004): "Finansal Krizler, Finansal Regülasyon ve Türkiye", *İ.Ü. Siyasal Bilgiler Fakülte Dergisi,* 30, Mart, pp. 101-133.

In: Regulation and Competition in the Turkish Banking...   ISBN: 978-1-61324-990-1
Editors: Tamer Çetin and Fuat Oğuz   © 2012 Nova Science Publishers, Inc.

Chapter 5

RESTRUCTURING AND MARKET STRUCTURE OF THE TURKISH BANKING SECTOR

Münür Yayla[*]

Strategy Development Department of Banking Regulation and Supervision
Agency of Turkey (BRSA), Ankara, Turkey

ABSTRACT

Banking sector has a complex and close interaction with other economic units. Recent global financial crisis has once again shown that troubles in this sector have repercussions on the whole economy. Between 1990 and 2000 there have been several episodes of financial turmoil in Turkey. In fact the most severe financial crisis occurred during November 2000 and February 2001 which clearly had profound effects on both regulatory environment and market structure of the sector. Following this crisis, the structure of the regulatory environment was altered in order to create an efficient and stable banking sector. As a result of this regulatory change, the sector experienced a sharp change from instability towards financial soundness. After the restructuring of the sector by means of relevant regulatory and institutional set up, the main characteristics of the Turkish banking system can be identified as rehabilitation, growth, foreign participation and financial stability. Meanwhile, a significant change in the market structure has been also observed. As it is known, regulatory authorities of the USA and the European Union have incorporated concentration measures in their regulations to understand market structure. In this chapter, the aforementioned regulatory transformation in the Turkish banking system has been summarized, and apart from the traditional approaches, concentration (market structure) in the banking sector has been considered simultaneously in terms of assets, loans, and deposits. On the other hand, to analyze market structure more comprehensively, dominance, disparity and dynamic indexes have been applied in addition to traditional static measures. Although static measures are commonly used in the existing literature, disparity and dynamic indexes are not frequently utilized with banking data. According to the findings of this study, parallel to the regulatory phase, concentration in the relevant markets shows decreasing trend in the period of 1995-1999 and increasing tendency between 2000 and 2010. However, net interest margins (intermediation costs) which can be seen as the relevant prices in the

---

[*] The views expressed in this chapter are the author's alone, and *do not reflect* the views of the BRSA.

sector have declined through the analyzed periods. Thus, we conclude that the new regulatory framework constitutes a strong ground for stability and fair competition.

Keywords: Banking, Regulation, Concentration, Competition
JEL Classification: D40, G21, G28, L11

1. INTRODUCTION

Recent global financial crisis of 2008 has shown the crucial role of the financial sector, in particular the banking system. The global financial crisis created devastating problems for the world economy. Policymakers from both developed and developing economies are still struggling to strengthen the confidence in financial markets. All efforts shown by G-20 countries and relevant regulators of financial system are towards restructuring the global financial system. Contagion and systemic nature of the recent crisis forced policymakers to develop extra ordinary policy measures. Especially in the USA and in the EU region, restructuring the financial system via fiscal support was the main response to the financial distress which resulted in enormous cost on tax payers. So far, it is not very clear whether these efforts will be sufficient for rehabilitating the financial system. In fact, as pointed out by Sakarya (2007), the global financial system has entered a cycle of recurrent financial turbulences.

While recent global crisis is a focus of interest for the international institutions and academia, the Turkish financial crisis of 2000/2001 has not been sufficiently stressed in the literature. Partly this is understandable, since the roots of the crisis were mainly in the weak domestic fundamentals and the crisis remained largely within domestic borders without any spillover effects. Nevertheless, to our knowledge, it was one of the largest financial crises that a particular country experienced during the past decades.

Restructuring of the Turkish banking sector resulted in major structural changes. And market structure is at the centre of these developments. In fact, market structure is both important for the players of the sector as well as for consumers of the banking system. Institutional set up, regulations, supervision and legal enforcement are factors which shape the market structure of the banking system. The main elements of the market structure are the number of players, concentration or the distribution of banking activities among these players and competition level. This chapter highlights the main ingredients of the restructuring of Turkish banking system with an emphasis on the change of market structure.

This chapter is organized as follows. In section two, an overview and stylized facts of the Turkish banking system are given together with the change in institutional set up and the restructuring following the financial crisis of 2000/2001. Section three provides a literature survey on market structure and competition issues in the banking sector, both on theoretical and empirical grounds. This section also provides a detailed survey on static, dominance, disparity and dynamic concentration measures. In section four, by using the Turkish banking data, different class of market structure indicators are calculated. Section five comments on competition issues in the sector based upon findings of the previous part. Section six concludes this chapter.

2. STYLIZED FACTS AND RESTRUCTURING OF THE TURKISH BANKING SECTOR

2.1. Overview and Stylized Facts

The emergence of a widespread "modern" banking sector in Turkey dates from 1920s with the foundation of the Republic of Turkey. Following this period, number of public and private banks has been increased to meet the growing demands of the economy. There are three different types of banking institutions active in the banking sector. Deposit banks, investment and development banks that work on traditional banking principles, and participation banks which work on a non-interest basis[22]. The Turkish financial system is dominated by the banking industry. As of September 2010, banks' assets constitute 80% of the total assets of the financial system. On the other hand, deposit banking institutions are the major players in the banking sector both in terms of number and asset size. It also worth to note that the financial system is small scaled compared to major European countries. Prior to the year 2000 the total asset of the banking sector was only 155 billion USD.

Up to 1980 the Turkish economy was inward oriented and the banking sector was regulated through state intervention policies. Major structural change in the Turkish economy and Turkish banking sector occurred after the introduction of financial liberalization policies in 1980s. During this decade, ceilings on deposit and interest rates were abolished, interbank money market was set up, and Capital Marked Board (CMB) and Istanbul Stock Exchange (ISE) were established to enhance efficiency and competition in the financial markets.

Consequently, financial and non financial institutions started to implement initial public offerings on ISE to collect new funds. Besides, the government changed its borrowing policy and subsequently domestic borrowing instruments became increasingly important. While these reforms took place, entry in the banking sector was eased, too. Hence, the number of deposit banks which was 52 in 1988 increased to 62 in 1999. Relatively high and risk free real interest rates of government debt instruments motivated the entry to the sector, which played an important role in the acceleration of the number of banks especially in the early 1990s.

1990s, however, were the initial era of structural problems in the banking sector. The macroeconomic environment of Turkey was instable due to the weak domestic fundamentals and long lasting structural problems. Volatile growth, high inflation, unsustainable current account deficit, high and persistent budget deficit and loose monetary policy were surrounding the banking environment.

In this period, banks shifted their portfolios from traditional banking activities towards low risk bearing government debt instruments. High borrowing requirement of the government supported by loose monetary policies produced a high inflationary environment, leading eventually to very high real interest rates in the economy. Borrowing requirement and interest rate policies of the government created a "crowding out" effect for the private sector by demanding the bulk of the savings in the economy. High inflation and increasing risks in the financial system lowered the average maturity of savings, which caused loan rates to be very high even in the long run.

---

[22] Before the introduction of new banking law of 2005 (law number 5411), these banks were known as Special Finance Institutions. In the Turkish banking literature these banks are called non-interest banks. In the global banking literature such institutions are referred as Islamic Banking Institutions.

Table 1. Selected Indicators
of the Turkish Banking Sector (before 2001)

	1988	1990	1995	1998	1999	2000
Total Number of Banks	60	66	68	75	81	79
Number of Deposit Banks	52	56	55	60	62	61
Number of Banks Taken Over by SDIF	-	-	-	-	8	11
Loans (Billion USD)	15,3	27,3	28,6	45,2	40,2	50,9
Deposit (Billion USD)	42,3	32,6	43,6	77,4	89,4	101,9
Total Assets (Billion USD)	37,6	58,2	67,2	117,9	133,6	154,9
Loans/Deposit (%)	36.1	84.0	65.4	38.3	30.1	50.0
Return on Equity (ROE), %	-	36.0	55.7	44.9	-14.9	-72.8
Return on Asset (ROA), %	-	2.8	3.4	2.7	-0.6	-3.1
Share of Foreign Banks, (%)	3,6	3,5	2,9	4,4	5,2	3,4

Source: Banks Association of Turkey (BAT).

Especially, some banks with industrial and non industrial subsidiaries financed their long term projects with the very short termed and high interest rates. Such an environment in Turkish economy was further worsened by political instabilities. Also international borrowing conditions deteriorated for emerging markets in the late 1990s due to crises in East Asia and Russia over the years 1997-1999.

Moreover, inadequate level of own funds, maturity mismatch as mentioned above, amount of nonperforming loans, overvalued domestic currency, high level of "open FX" positions (being short in FX), systemic distortions on competition caused by state banks, insufficient risk management practices, and bad governance contributed to the structural problems of the Turkish banking sector.

To sum up, the banking sector was insufficient in its traditional intermediation function and therefore inadequate in providing funds to non financial sector. Under these circumstances, economic slowdown in late 1990s and the Turkish financial crisis of 2000/2001 aggravated the weak financial stance of some banks operating in the sector. As a result, a total of 11 banks were transferred to Saving Deposits Insurance Fund (SDIF) between the years of 1997 and 2000 as they were not able to meet their liabilities.

2.2. Restructuring of Institutional and Legal Framework

The first step toward rehabilitation of the sector was the change in institutional set up. The most important structural change was the shift in the regulatory framework of the sector. Prior to this change, the two main regulatory and supervisory bodies in the banking sector were Undersecretariat of Treasury and the Central Bank of Turkey (CBRT). With the Banks Act No. 4389 (issued on June 23, 1999), the Banking Regulation and Supervision Agency (BRSA) was formed. On the top of the agency, a seven member Board[23] operates as a decision making body and the chairman of the agency is also the chairman of the Board. By the mentioned law, this new institution was equipped with financial and administrative

---

[23] The Banking Regulation and Supervision Board (BRSB).

autonomy with the mission to safeguard the rights and benefits of depositors and create the proper environment in which, banks and financial institutions can operate within market discipline, in a healthy, efficient and globally competitive manner. BRSA commenced its operations as of August 31, 2000. Furthermore, the Turkish deposit insurance fund, namely the Saving Deposit Insurance Fund (SDIF) which was under the administration of Central Bank of Turkey (CBRT) became a part of the BRSA. The management and administration of SDIF was conducted by BRSA, until SDIF was transformed to an independent structure in late 2005.

In addition to establishing new authorities for banking sector, existing institutions were either reinforced or supported by relevant legislative changes. For instance, the law of central bank was amended. With this amendment, the Central Bank of Republic of Turkey (CBRT) now focuses on price stability and implements monetary policy that is independent from government interventions. There have been considerable improvements in accounting and financial reporting standards which were a serious source of reliability problem especially during the high inflationary period. Additionally, the close collaboration between the Treasury, BRSA, SDIF and CBRT that was deficient before the crisis period has been strengthened. Moreover, in 2005 a new banking law (act No. 5411) has been enacted to further enhance the soundness and stability of the sector.

Complementary to institutional change and regulatory achievements, the banking sector was rehabilitated through various actions of which the restructuring program played the most important role. In the aftermath of the financial crisis of 2000/2001, the sector was restructured by means of a program that consisted of (i) restructuring of public (state) banks, (ii) prompt resolution of SDIF banks, (iii) strengthening of private banks, and (iv) strengthening the regulatory and supervisory framework.

In the past, public (state) banks were used by governments as channel of distributing subsidized loans that caused massive amounts of so called "duty losses". The restructuring of state banks consisted of removing past losses and hindering the possibility of new duty losses. Moreover, removal of the license of a public bank, capital injection and the downsizing the number of employees in state banks were other measures. The resolution process of SDIF banks was the second stage of the aforementioned program. These banks were sold, merged or liquidated within the framework of the Banking Sector Restructuring Program. A total of 20 banks were transferred to the Saving Deposits Insurance Fund (SDIF) between the years of 1997 and 2003[24]. Consequently, the number of deposit taking banks declined to 46 in 2001 and 40 in 2002. The third component, strengthening of private banks was done through a three stage audit program. Several banks were found to be in need of additional capital and through this stage balance sheet of banks were evaluated more realistically. The total cost of restructuring amounted to one third of the gross domestic product as of 2002[25].

The fourth stage, perhaps the most important one in terms of market structure developments, has been the changes in regulatory and supervisory framework.

Regulations on accounting standards, risk management process, provisions related to non performing loans, regulations on enhancement of efficiency and competition were milestones in the changing banking environment.

---

[24] Moreover two banks were liquidated directly without taking over by the SDIF.

[25] The details of the restructuring program can be found on the web site of BRSA (www.bddk.org.tr).

Table 2. Selected Indicators
of the Turkish Banking Sector (After 2000)

	2001	2002	2003	2004	2005	2006	2007	2008	2009	2010
Total Number of Banks	66	59	55	53	51	50	50	49	49	49
Number of Deposit Banks	46	40	36	35	33	33	33	33	32	32
Number of SDIF Banks	6	2	2	1	1	1	1	1	1	1
Loans (Billion USD)	28,5	29,7	47,3	74,0	116,0	155,0	245,2	240,3	262,7	352,7
Deposit (Billion USD)	81,4	83,7	110,9	142,3	186,5	217,8	306,3	297,3	344,3	431,9
Total Assets (Billion USD)	115,6	129,1	178,3	228,2	301,8	353,8	499,3	479,1	558,1	648,5
Loans/Deposit (%)	35,0	35,5	42,6	52,0	62,2	71,2	80,0	80,8	76,3	81,7
Share of Foreign Banks (%)	3,0	3,3	3,0	3,5	6,3	13,1	14,0	17,0	15,8	16,2

Source: BAT and BRSA. Figures for 2010 are as of September.

The rehabilitation procedure with the aforementioned restructuring program and the legislative changes to present produced very positive outcomes. The strengthening of public (state) and private banks together with the improvement of the regulatory and supervisory framework contributed to the stability of the banking sector. As of September 2010, there are 32 deposit banks, 13 development and investment banks and 4 participation banks[26] operating in the sector. Compared to the year 2003, additional decline in the number of deposit banks was due to voluntary mergers and acquisitions as a result of the consolidation in the sector and also because of the increasing competition concerns. Besides, both high economic growth rates following the recent crises and Turkey's accession towards European Union membership boosted foreign capital interest towards the banking sector which in turn increased considerably the franchise value of banks operating in Turkey.

It is widely argued that, BRSA's continuous proactive supervision capabilities increased the soundness of the Turkish banking sector. As a matter of fact, credit card law and liquidity regulation are peculiar to the Turkish banking authority that attracts the attention of other authorities all over the world. Not surprisingly, banking sector resisted strongly to the global shock despite its adverse effect on overall economy. Unlike banking sectors in EU countries, The Turkish banking sector maintained its capital adequacy and profitability along with a sustainable asset growth pattern. Many stakeholders of the financial system interpreted this period as a test of the Turkish banking sector and argued that important benefits must have been achieved via the strengthening efforts of the sector. After the year 2002, the banking sector can be best described by high growth performance, increasing foreign participation, resilience to external shocks and stability.

---

[26] Participation banks (previously named as special finance institutions) operate on a non-interest basis and hence are slightly different than traditional commercial banks and are complementary institutions in the sector.

3. REVIEW OF LITERATURE
AND THE MEASUREMENT OF MARKET STRUCTURE

3.1. Literature Review

Market structure is best understood simultaneously with concepts like relevant market, market dominance, market shares or market concentration. To speak of a "relevant market", we need a set of homogenous and substitutable products that is available in the market both for buyers and sellers. A set of rules for the conduct of the market (regulations), geographical and time limitations are also required for the definition of the market. Market dominance occurs when a single bank or several banks can determine the price and quantity of the product independent from the rivals. Market power concept intersects with market dominance, but they are not always the same. Market power is necessary for market dominance but it is not sufficient. Market power can be described as quantitative (patents, franchise agreements) or qualitative (market share, turnover). The distribution of market shares is called concentration which can be measured by various indices.

In addition to this, market structure is related to competition which is another important topic in the banking literature. Apart from pure theoretical models as suggested by Monti-Klein (1971), Salop (1979) and Frexias and Rochet (1998), the investigation of competition is usually done by the structural approach which is based on the relationship between structure, conduct and performance (SCP). Structure is represented by the concentration of the banking sector. Conduct of the banks can be represented by research and development efforts and performance by their market power. Alternatively, competition is analyzed by direct approaches without using explicit information about the market structure. In this context, Panzar and Rosse approach is applied for various countries. There are a number of applied studies on this field. We are going to summarize several of them in comply with the scope of this chapter.

In the seminal paper on this field, Shaffer (1993) has found that the Canadian banking sector is in line with perfect competition in the period of 1968–1989 and monopolistic competition hypothesis for this country was rejected. Contrary to the Canadian case, Suominen (1994) predicted a monopolistic competition for deposit and loan market of Finland at the end of 1980s. By applying Panzar and Rosse approach for 23 European countries, Bikker and Haaf (2002a) have concluded that, in aggregate, there is monopolistic competition in banking sectors of these countries. However, individual analysis implied that perfect competition for some of these countries could not be rejected. In this paper, competition in European markets was found to be stronger than banking sectors of US, Canada and Japan.

Deposit and loan markets of EU countries are classified as highly competitive in Bikker (2003) with the application of Bresnahan's Model. In aggregate, perfect competition in all EU countries was rejected, but competition in deposit and loan markets of Germany, Spain, Portugal, Sweden and UK were found to be relatively high. In this context, the abuse of market power in these countries was considered to be limited.

As an example of developing countries, Yeyati (2003) investigated competition issues in the Latin American countries.

Table 3. Examples on the Theoretical and Empirical Studies on Market Power/Structure

Author	Approach	Coverage/Country
Monti-Klein (1971)	Pure Theoretical	Monopolistic and oligopoly models
Salop (1979)	Pure Theoretical	Monopolistic competition
Frexias and Rochet (1998)	Pure Theoretical	Perfect competition
Shaffer (1993)	Theoretical and Empirical	Econometric study on Canadian banking
Bikker and Haaf (2002a)	Theoretical and Empirical	Panzar-Rosse approach on 23 countries
Hannan (1997)	Empirical	Applied on US banking data
Suominen (1994)	Theoretical and Empirical	Finland banking is analyzed with Cournot model
Appelbaum (1981)	Theoretical and Empirical	Oligopoly market power is tested
Bikker (2003)	Theoretical and Empirical	Market power of EU deposit and loan market are tested by means of Bresnahan model.
Yeyati (2003)	Theoretical and Empirical	Latin America banking system is analyzed by Panzar and Rosse model
Bos (2003)	Theoretical and Empirical	Dutch banking sector.
Gunalp and Celik (2006)	Theoretical and Empirical	Turkish banking sector
Kasman (2001)	Theoretical and Empirical	Turkish banking sector
Ruthenford (2006)	Theoretical and Empirical	Banking sector of Israel
Bikker and Haaf (2002b)	Descriptive and Empirical	Dutch banking sector by means of concentration measures
Stich (1995b)	Descriptive and Empirical	Insurance sectors of Sweden and Finland are analyzed by means of static and dynamic indices

According to the findings of this research, concentration and foreign entry has increased considerably in Latin American banking markets, however it is argued that the level of competition in these countries has not been diminished. Moreover, due to increasing merger and acquisitions in these countries, it is suggested that the supervisory and competition authorities should find a balance between prudential banking principles and competition policies.

US banking sector, on a state basis, was investigated by Dick (2005) with a view to analyze the relations between market size, quality of services and competition. In this research, it was stated that even though US states had banking markets at different sizes, their concentration levels were similar. According to this study, banking markets with large scales supply increased quality of banking services and dominant banks provide better service. Although increased concentration might be seen as a disadvantage for the consumer welfare, large scaled and dominant banks invest a lot to serve their customers with more qualitative products. This, in return, creates a barrier to entry implying higher cost for the consumers who are oriented to large scale banks because of the better service quality.

The relationship between financial stability and market power is evaluated by Northcott (2004) in a survey about the concentration and competition in banking sectors. This chapter states the importance of competitive environment for efficiency and the allocation of resources. At time same time it is accepted that, in a market with a certain level of market power, loans are monitored carefully, risk appetite is lower, credit quality of banks are higher and thus financial stability can be achieved easier.

As regards the Turkish banking sector, there are several studies. For instance, Kasman (2001) has found that market concentration did not affect profitability in the period of 1988-1996. Similarly in Okumuş (2002), no significant statistical evidence was found between market power and profitability concerning the period of 1989–1995. Parallel to these researches, Günalp and Çelik (2004) could not find any evidence for profitability as a result of market concentration. For this reason they suggested that the authorities should focus on regulations which would enhance efficiency rather than trying to decrease concentration. Furthermore, Panzar and Rosse approach applied by Aydınlı (1996) and Günalp and Çelik (2006) shows similar findings for different time periods. In the first study, monopoly market was determined with the fact that this structure was weakening towards monopolistic competition. The latter study by Günalp and Çelik (2006), revealed that the revenue obtained by banks between the years 1990-2000 were in accordance with monopolistic competition. In a relatively recent study on Turkish banking sector applied with Panzar and Rosse approach by Abbasoğlu et al (2007), no robust relation was found between concentration and competition. Çelik and Ürünveren (2009) claim that, except the year 2006, the Turkish banking sector operates in compliance with monopolistic competition conditions. On the other hand, Korkmaz (2010) applied Bresnahan-Lau model for the deposit banks and concluded that the sector is perfectly competitive. This result is clearly a digression from existing empirical findings of other studies on Turkish banking sector.

Finally, there are also methods for determining market structure which do not depend on any economic theory. Such descriptive methods rely on parameters that are depending on information theory and/or mathematical statistics. In this framework, an extensive survey on static measures of concentration is provided by Bikker ve Haaf (2002b). In addition to these, dominance and dynamic indices are elaborated in Stich (1995a, 1995b).

3.2. Consentration Measures[27]

The measurement of concentration is done by means of mathematical indices. For this reason, various indices have been developed in order to have comparable indicators on concentration. These indices show an "inequality state" and change within a given interval which is a common property for all of concentration indices. Indices' lower and upper boundaries or the distance to a certain number give a clue on the current state of inequality. In this context, all concentration measures have a common mathematical representation.

Concentration can be defined as a function on the set of real numbers. However, an inequality index is needed in order to have a measurable concentration indicator. Once the inequality index is defined, concentration can be thought as a function of number of banks (n) and the inequality index (I). As the number of banks increases, concentration will decrease

---

[27] In this part, we benefit from the excellent survey of Bikker and Haaf (2002b). We will use the relevant indicators from this study and also we will add other type of concentration measures that will be useful for the purpose of this chapter. Other useful resources are Hall and Tideman (1967), Hart (1971, 1975), Stich (1995a, 1995b), Bajo and Salas (1998) and Shannon (1948). Details, proofs or the derivation of the indices are provided in these papers.

and as the inequality index inclines, concentration will go up. This property can be summarized mathematically with the following equation.

$$C = f(n, I) \quad, where \quad f_n < 0 \quad and \quad f_I > 0$$

(1)

The Equation above indicates that a new entrant in the sector will lower the level of concentration. However, at the same time the new entrant may alter the inequality state of the sector. If the new entrant is "sufficiently" big enough relative to the incumbent banks, then the degree of concentration may increase. In general, an entry to the market would lower concentration since n will increase and the relative share of each bank would be diminished. But, in cases where the new entrant's effect on inequality is larger (i.e. the new entrant has a great amount of output relative to the existing banks) than the effect on concentration through the number effect, overall concentration will increase.

In the context of this chapter, if number of banks is shown by n and bank output (asset, deposit or loans) by x, then total output of the banking sector would be ($\sum_{i=1}^{n} x_i$). Moreover, the proportional share of output of each bank ($i=1,2,.....n$) within the whole sector can be formulated easily by $s_i = x_i / \sum_{i=1}^{n} x_i \geq 0$, and the vector $s=(s_1, s_2, s_3,....,s_n)$ represents the bank's shares among total output.

There are a number of concentration measures which satisfies the aforementioned properties. Accordingly, we will summarize those ones which are most frequently used in the existing literature.

The Concentration Ratio (CR$_k$)

First, an arbitrary number (k) is chosen and the index is calculated according to this number k. This index is greater than 0 (zero) and less than 1 (unity). In practice, number of banks (k) is usually chosen as 3, 4, 5 or 10 and by assuming that each bank has the same importance, CR_3, CR_4, CR_5 and CR_{10} ratios are calculated. As expected, as k increases concentration ratio converges to unity. For any k, the concentration ratio is the sum of proportional shares.

$$CR_k = \sum_{i=1}^{k} s_i \qquad s_1 \geq ..... \geq s_k \geq .... \geq s_n$$

(2)

As the value of this index approaches to one, it is assumed that market power of k bank in the sector increases.

The Herfindahl- Hirschman Index (HHI)[28]

HHI is used extensively for the reason that it is calculated easily and it is relatively simple to comment on it. The index takes directly sector shares (s_i) into account and is a basis for other types of concentration indicators. The most basic form of HHI is formulated as follows.

$$HHI = \sum_{i=1}^{n} s_i^2$$
(3)

While calculating this index, sector shares are frequently expressed as percentage points and the calculation is done also as $HHI = \sum_{i=1}^{n} s_i^2 * 100^2$. For instance, we may assume that a sector consists of 4 different banks and each of these banks has a market share (in terms of total asset) of %40, %35, %15 and %10, respectively. In this case, HHI would be found as the sum of $40^2 + 35^2 + 15^2 + 10^2 = 3.150$ points. Furthermore, if we assume that there is only one (single) bank in the sector which controls all the 100% of the market, then HHI will approach to its upper bound of 10 thousand ($=100^2$) points[29]. Equation (3) is not the only mathematical form of HHI. By taking the statistical distribution properties (average and standard deviation) of bank shares, HH index can be revised to obtain the following form.

$$HHI = (1/n) + n\sigma^2$$
(4)

In empirical research on this field, HH index is calculated alternatively as,

$$HHI = (V^2 + 1)/n$$
(5)

where the coefficient of variation, $V^2 = \sigma^2 / \mu^2$, is used in this formula (Hart,1975).

The Comprehensive Concentration Index CCI[30]

CCI is a derivative of HH index. It is developed with a view to consider the effect of larger banks. In this way, contrary to HH or other similar indices, both dispersion and absolute value are taken into account when calculating CCI.

---

[28] This index was proposed for the first time by Hirschman (1945). However, the index is known after the paper by Herfindahl (1950). For this reason, in the literature the index is commonly referred as the Herfindahl index (Hart, 1975). In this study, the abbreviations Herfindahl (H) or Herfindahl-Hirschman (HH) refers to equation number (3) and means the same index.

[29] It is apparent form equation 3 that HHI is the sum of shares (si) of n bank. If market shares are adjusted as to be 100 in total, then HHI would take a upper value of 10,000 (monopolistic case). If there are many banks with equal shares, then HHI approaches to zero (atomistic market), but never equals to zero. If shares are not adjusted to 100 then the lower and upper bounds of HHI is going to be (1/n, 1].

[30] Comprehensive Concentration Index (CCI) was first proposed by Horvath (1970). For the details see Hart (1975).

$$CCI = s_1 + \sum_{i=2}^{n} s_i^2 \left(1 + (1 - s_i)\right)$$

$$(6)$$

Summation of squares of shares of each bank weighted by the shares is added to the leader bank's share to find the value of CCI. The index varies between zero and unity. Values close to unity indicates the case of monopoly.

The Rosenbluth-Hall-Tideman Index (RHTI)[31]

According to the basic principle of RTH, the ranking of each bank in the sector plays an important role similar to their shares. Accordingly, the index value is both affected by the share and the ranking of each bank within the sector. The bank with the largest output is considered to be the first bank ($i=1$).

$$RHTI = 1/(2\sum_{i=1}^{n} is_i - 1)$$

$$(7)$$

The interval for this index is $(0,1]$. In cases when there are many banks (lowest concentration) the index approaches to zero and it goes to unity in case of monopoly.

The Hannah and Kay Index (HKI)

In addition to its standard application for concentration calculation, the Hannah and Kay Index (HKI) is also useful for analyzing the effect of a new entry, exit or output transfer between banks. The elasticity parameter (α) which reflects these effects can be chosen arbitrarily. Thus the HKI is sensitive to market shares and the elasticity parameter. HKI attains its minimum value that is equivalent to the reciprocal of the market share of the largest bank (as α converges to infinity). The maximum value of HKI is the number of banks in the market (when α approaches to zero).

$$HKI = \begin{cases} (\sum_{i=1}^{n} s_i^{\alpha})^{1/(1-\alpha)} \, , \, \alpha > 0 \, , \, \alpha \neq 1 \\ e^{\sum_{i=1}^{n} s_i \ln s_i} \, , \quad \alpha = 1 \end{cases}$$

$$(8)$$

When the market structure is given, and if the new entrant bank's size is equivalent to the average size of the market then the decrease in concentration would be the largest. Contrary to this, if the new entrant bank's size is greater than the average size of the market, the

---

[31] This index is known also as Rosenbluth Index or Hall-Tideman Index. For derivation of this index see Hall and Tideman (1967).

decrease in concentration is smaller. Moreover, concentration may even incline in cases where size effect overweighs the number effect[32]. HKI is a decreasing function of α, in other words, as α goes up, the index value declines. For constant elasticity parameters, an increase in the index value is interpreted as decline in concentration and vice versa.

The Hause Index

$$H(\alpha, s_i) = \sum_{i=1}^{n} s_i^{2 - (s_i(HHI - s_i^2))^{\alpha}}, \qquad \alpha \geq 0.15 \tag{9}$$

As it is clear from the above equation, Hause index is based up on market shares, HHI and collusion parameter α. Therefore, this index is a Cournot measure. Similar to the above mentioned indices, the collusion parameter α can be chosen by the researcher and the value of the Hause index is determined accordingly. Monopolistic case occurs when the index takes the value of unity. If there are many banks with the same size, then the index converges to zero. The Hause index is a decreasing function of α which means that when α converges to infinity, the value of Hause index approaches to HHI.

The Entropy[33] Index (Ent)

In information theory, entropy is a measure for an uncertainty that is represented by a probability distribution (p_i). Let E_i ($i=1,...,n$) to be the set of n different events each with a probability of occurrence p_i. In this case probability theory tells us that $\sum_{i=1}^{n} p_i = 1$. Therefore, the event and the corresponding probability of occurrence is the only information that is available. Shannon (1948) tried to find an answer to the question as how much uncertainty is inherent in choosing an event. In this regard, if the information value of an event is assumed to be a decreasing function of ex-ante probability of that event, i.e. $h(p_i) = log (1/p_i) = - log (p_i)$, then the total information value of set E will be the product of the probability of each event and the corresponding information value. In other words,

$$H(p) = \sum_{i=1}^{n} p_i h(p_i) = -\sum_{i=1}^{n} p_i \log p_i \tag{10}$$

By assuming equal probabilities ($p_i=1/n$), Shannon (1948) has proven that the general form of the information measure can be represented by the following equation[34].

---

[32] In terms of equation (1), the effect of fl exceeds the effect of fn.

[33] In Information theory and statistics it is also known as Theil Index or Shannon (or Shannon-Wiener) Index. For details see Shannon (1948), Hart (1971), Stich (1995) and Bikker and Haaf (2002b).

[34] Shannon (1948, p.29).

$$H(p) = -K \sum_{i=1}^{n} p_i \log p_i \quad , K > 0 \tag{11}$$

The parameter K is a constant and can be chosen arbitrarily. The above equation is an entropy measure and depending on K it can be expressed in different forms. It is not difficult to adapt this inequality (entropy) measure to an analysis in banking sector. In harmony with the previous notations, if we take market share (s_i) instead of probability (p_i) and do the calculations as suggested by Bikker and Haaf (2002b) according to logarithmic base 2, and transform it to natural logarithm, then we obtain the Entropy Index as,

$$E = -\sum_{i=1}^{n} s_i \log_2 s_i = -(1/\ln 2) \sum_{i=1}^{n} s_i \ln s_i \tag{12}$$

The transformation applied in this case is $log_2\ s_i = ln\ s_i / ln\ 2$. Consequently the index is not limited to [0,1] interval. The value of the entropy varies reciprocally with the degree of concentration. The entropy indicator above takes values between in the interval of [0, log n]. As the index goes to zero monopolistic case occurs, and as the index diverges from zero towards log n, there will be minimum concentration with equal market shares[35].

3.3. Dominance Measures

Static concentration measures as outlined in the previous section shows us how unequal the total output is distributed in the market. Despite the fact that these measures provide valuable information about the market structure they are not sufficient for the scope of this study. It is possible to enhance the market structure analysis through additional measures which are capable of understanding oligopolistic market structure. Within this framework, it possible to understand the effect of large scaled banks on the market. Is the market controlled by a monopolist? or does there exist an oligopolistic group that controls the market? are relevant questions to be answered. To address these issues Stich (1995b) proposes two different dominance measures one based upon Herfindahl and the other based upon Entropy (Ent).

Similar to our previous notations, x is for output, CR_k is for k-bank concentration ratio, n is number of total banks and H is for Herfindahl index and entropy index is abbreviated by Ent. Given these notations the dominance measures (D) suggested by Stich (1995b) takes the form

$$D_k^H(x) = \frac{CR_k^2}{k} + \frac{(1-CR_k)^2}{n-k} \tag{13}$$

---

[35] An appropriate choice of K would result with an entropy index with lower and upper boundaries [0,1]. However for the sake of illustration we prefer the transformation as suggested by Bikker and Haaf (2002b).

$$D_k^{Ent}(x) = \frac{CR_k \ln(\frac{k}{CR_k}) + (1 - CR_k) \ln(\frac{n-k}{1-CR_k})}{\ln n} \qquad (14)$$

In order to determine the oligopoly group in the market dominance index is calculated for $k=1, ..., n$.

$$D_{k^*}^{H}(x) = \max_{k=1,.....n} D_k^{H}(x) \qquad (15)$$

$$D_{k^*}^{Ent}(x) = \min_{k=1,.....n} D_k^{Ent}(x) \qquad (16)$$

The parameter k^* which satisfies the above equations gives us the number that distinguishes the oligopoly group from pursuer group. Subsequently, the k^* largest banks constitute the oligopoly group and the remaining banks are the pursuer group.

Furthermore, the disparity in the oligopoly group, pursuer group and a weighted average of these groups are also measurable. Stich (1995b) provides disparity[36] measures for oligopoly and pursuer group as follows (where o is abbreviation for oligopoly and p for pursuer and $V^2 = \sigma^2 / \mu^2$)

$$I_o^H = V_o^2 / (V_o^2 + 1) \qquad (17)$$

$$I_p^H = V_p^2 / (V_p^2 + 1) \qquad (18)$$

The weighted average disparity for both groups is

$$\bar{I}^H = wI_o^H + (1-w)I_p^H \qquad (19)$$

which is obtained by means of the following weights.

$$w = \sum_{i=1}^{k^*} x_i^2 / \sum_{i=1}^{n} x_i^2 \quad , k^* < n \qquad (20)$$

The value interval for disparity indexes is [0, 1]. As the index approximates to 1, disparity within the group increases.

---

[36] Disparity measures in Equation 17 and 18, are based upon Herfindahl index. These equations can be modified and can be based upon Entropy. In this chapter we prefer Herfindahl that is sufficient for the purpose of this study.

3.4. Dynamic Indices

Indices mentioned so far are calculated for a given period and are of static nature. Change of concentration with respect to time can be done by means of dynamic indices. There are certain conditions for an index which must be met in order to be a dynamic one. These properties are outlined in various studies. For instance, in Stich (1995a and 1995b) these properties are elaborated extensively.

At maximum level of concentration increase, the value of dynamic index attains unity. If the decrease in concentration is the smallest then the dynamic index takes the value of minus one. When there is no change in concentration then the index remains at zero. Moreover the dynamic index needs to be decomposable. In other words, if x, y, z are output vectors then $\Delta(x,y)=\Delta(x,z)+\Delta(z,y)$. The total change in dynamic index is the sum of changes is sub periods. In fact it is proven that dynamic indices satisfy the following equality (Stich, 1995b).

$$\Delta(x, y) = \frac{C(y) - C(x)}{\sup C(z) - \inf C(z)}_{37} \tag{21}$$

where C is the concentration function. Static indices like CR_k and RBTI that falls within the interval of $(0,1)$ satisfy the above conditions when their first difference is taken with respect to time (Stich, 1995a).

As a final issue for this section, following table summarizes the indices with their properties. Static indices are important for determining the concentration and market structure. These indices can be also used for policy purposes. Dominance, disparity and dynamic indices on the other hand are helpful in analyzing the market structure more comprehensively.

4. DATA AND APPLICATION

Assets, total loans and deposits of Turkish banking sector are used for the calculation of concentration ratios. The use of asset size for determining concentration in banking sector is quite common. Calculations with deposits or loans are less frequent. In this context, we assume that asset is an indicator for the banking market itself, whereas deposit and loan market can be thought two different markets in the banking sector.

Obviously, it would be preferable to use specific markets such as mortgage loans, consumer loans, credit card receivables, etc. Unfortunately, on a bank basis the lack publicly[38] available data limits such an approach. We start with results of static concentration measures. According to CR_k, the asset and loan concentrations are near to each other. Deposit concentration is higher compared to the asset and loan concentration. In Figure 1, k is chosen as 7. Subsequently, CR_7 indicates significantly higher deposit concentration[39]. The decreasing

---

[37] Supremum (sup), is the least upperbound of a set, and infimum is the greatest lower bound.

[38] Thus we employ the data that is published on the web site of The Banks Association of Turkey.

[39] In Figure 1, we choose k intentionally as 7 since the dominance index (IH) based on Herfindahl indicates the oligopoly group size (k*) as 7 over the past few years.

trend in concentration between the years 1995-2000 and the rising trend afterwards is confirmed by the HHI (Figure 2).

Table 4. Static, Dominance-Difference and Dynamic Indices

Index	Value Interval	Parameters	Characteristic
I. Static Concentration Measures			
CR_k	$0 < CR_k \leq 1$	k=1,3,5,7,10 (arbitrary choice)	Large scaled banks are more important.
HHI	$1/n < HHI \leq 1$ or $0 < HHI \leq 10.000$	-	All banks are covered and it is sensitive to new entry.
CCI	$0 < CCI \leq 1$	-	Relative difference and absolute magnitude is important and can produce suitable results for cartel markets.
RHTI	$0 < RHTI \leq 1$	-	It is sensitive to number of banks in the market. It is also sensitive to the change of scale of small sized banks.
HKI	$1/s_1 < HKI \leq n$	$\alpha = 0,005$	It is sensitive to scale, small sized banks are more important.
		$\alpha = 0,25$	.
		$\alpha = 5$	.
			.
		$\alpha = 10$	.
			It is sensitive to scale, large sized banks are more important.
Hause	$0 < H_m \leq 1$	$\alpha = 0,25$	Suitable for collusive markets.
		$\alpha = 1$	
		$\alpha = 2$	
		$\alpha = 3$	Suitable for non collusive markets.
Entropy	$0 \leq Ent \leq \log n$		Expected information value of the distribution is important.
II. Dominance and Disparity Indices			
D_{k*}^{H}	(0,1)	k*	By using Herfindahl index oligopoly group and pursuer group is determined (k*).
D_{k*}^{Ent}	(0,1)	k*	By using entropy index oligopoly group and pursuer group is determined (k*).
I_o	(0,1)	k*	Disparity within the oligopoly group is determined.
I_t	(0,1)	k*	Disparity within the pursuer group is determined.
$\bar{I}^{H}$	(0,1)	w	By using Herfindahl index weighted average disparity of both groups an be found.
III. Dynamic Indices			
Dyn. (CR_k)	(-1,1)	-	As the index approaches to 1, the change in concentration is at maximum and as it approaches to (-1) the change is minimum.
Dyn. (RBTI)	(-1,1)	-	

Note: Compiled from various sources including Bikker and Haaf (2002b) and Stich (1995a, 1995b).

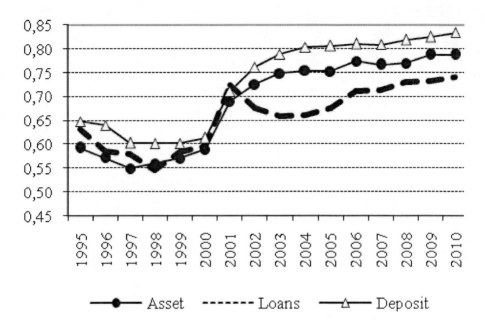

Figure 1. CR$_7$

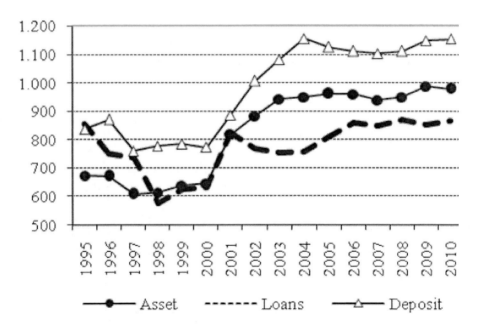

Figure 2. HHI.

In terms of asset and loans, HHI attained its minimum value in 1997 and for the deposit market in 1998. At the beginning of 2000s, due to the financial crisis many banks had to exit the sector, transfers of market shares have occurred between banks, merger and acquisitions and consolidation were also observed. Subsequently, HHI reached to maximum value in

2004. US and EU regulations on market concentration assumes a threshold value for HHI of 1,000 points or grater for a market to be considered as concentrated. Therefore, according to HHI, one may argue that in terms of asset and loans the Turkish banking sector is not concentrated. However, deposit market has been concentrated following the year 2002 (Figure 2).

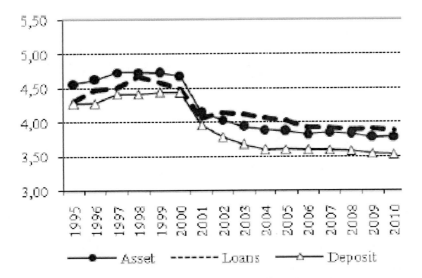

Figure 1. Entropy.

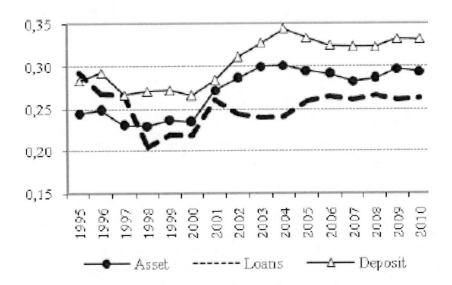

Figure 2. CCI.

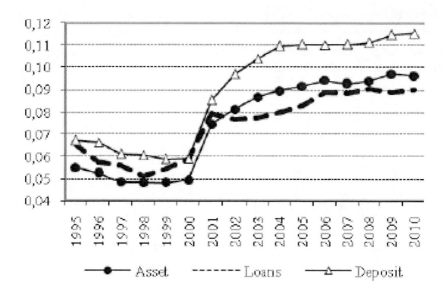

Figure 3. RHTI.

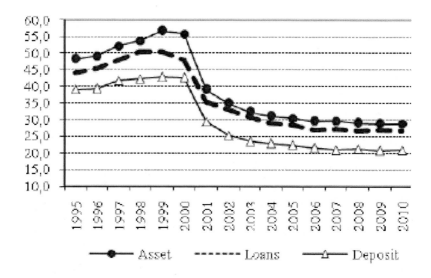

Figure 4. HKI ($\alpha=0.25$).

Even though it doesn't entirely overlap with the first two concentration measures, the Entropy and CCI indicators provide similar results. According to the Entropy, the highest concentrations seems to be in deposit market in 2010 with a value of 3.6 (Figure 3). On the other side, the CCI which is derived from the HHI provides results similar to other static indicators (Figure 4). Furthermore, the RTHI is almost identical to CR_7 measure (Figure 5 and Figure 1).

HKI shows that the concentration in the sector has been diminished in the period 1995-1999 as a result of *de novo* entries. On the other side, *de novo* entries and exits that happened during the 2000-2005 period are small scaled when compared to the average sized bank in the sector[40]. For this reason we choose the parameter of elasticity as 0.25 (Figure 6). The rate of change of HKI implies a gradual decline in concentration for the period of 1995-1999. New entries in that period caused concentration to decrease at a mild rate which is indicated by the change of HKI. To put it differently, the number effect of new entries on concentration (f_n) has outweighed the size effect (f_l). Contrary to this, due to the reconstruction of the sector and market developments number of banks decreased significantly. Subsequently, asset, loan and deposit concentration inclined sharply after the year 2000. This decline in concentration and the change in market share is more obvious in deposit market (Figure 6)[41].

In addition to the findings above, more comprehensive statistical inference can be made via dominance/disparity and dynamic indices. Dominance indices provide a clue about dominant bank or a group of banks (leader banks) and pursuer banks in terms of market shares. Disparity indices, on the other hand, show how much disparity exists within the dominant and pursuer group. Table 5 is Herfindahl based calculations using equation 13.

Values of the dominance indices imply that the largest dominance exists in deposit market followed by asset dominance, and the smallest dominance is in the loan market. The relationship between the value of the dominance index and the size of the oligopoly group (k*(H) in the above table as implied by equation 13) tells us that after the year 2000, on the average, the size of the oligopoly group is determined as 7. In other words, 7 banks in the sector are the leaders and constitute the oligopoly group. The remaining banks can be seen as the pursuer group.

In terms of assets, the disparity index of the oligopoly group (I_o) was around 20% in the period of 1995-1999 when the concentration was in a declining period. This value is realized as low as 7% during the period of raising concentration that is observed after the year 2000. Therefore, as concentration decreases (increases) the disparity of the oligopoly group grows (shrinks). The growth of this index can be interpreted as the disparity of conduct within the group. On the other side, the disparity of the pursuer group (I_p) is on the average between 55% and 70%. The disparity of the pursuer group is larger compared to the disparity of the oligopoly group. This means that pursuer banks which have smaller market shares behave more disconnected from each other than the oligopoly group.

When compared with respect to total asset, in "loan market" I_o is smaller (4% in 2001), I_p is bigger (as much as 81% in 2008) and $k*$ becomes as small as 6. For that reason, the disparity of leader banks in loan market is considerably lower compared to total asset.

As stressed in the discussion on static indicators, deposit market was the most concentrated one. The disparity index in this market declined to 6% in the year 2000 and $k*$ to 2, confirming the fact that the value of the dominance index is the largest among the three variables. Thus, during the turmoil period of 1999-2000, depositors may have oriented themselves towards large scaled banks.

The dynamic index RBTH illustrates that the maximum decrease in concentration in asset and deposit occurred in 1997 and in loan market in 1996. On the other hand, this index has shown that the largest increase in concentration in all data variables was observed in 2001.

---

[40] Small-scaled deposit and investment and development banks entered the system and at the same time relative changes in market shares occurred. The elasticity parameter α is chosen to be 0.25 to reflect the effect of small scaled banks on HK index.

[41] The results of Hause index are not shown since they are almost identical to HHI and CCI.

Table 5. Dominance, Disparity and Dynamic Indices (Turkish Banking Sector)

	1995	1996	1997	1998	1999	2000	2001	2002	2003	2004	2005	2006	2007	2008	2009	2010
I. Assets																
D_{k*}^{H}	0.0528	0.0499	0.0477	0.0490	0.0494	0.0521	0.0704	0.0769	0.0816	0.0828	0.0824	0.0868	0.0852	0.0861	0.0897	0.0897
I_o	0.1766	0.2445	0.2070	0.1924	0.2121	0.1748	0.1289	0.1147	0.1269	0.1156	0.1303	0.0797	0.0718	0.0730	0.0789	0.0679
I_t	0.6644	0.6132	0.5628	0.5594	0.6270	0.6256	0.6730	0.6608	0.6471	0.6746	0.6862	0.6884	0.6904	0.6890	0.6901	0.6910
k* (H)	7	8	9	9	8	8	8	7	7	7	7	7	7	7	7	7
D(RHTI)	-	-0.003	-0.004	0.000	0.000	0.002	0.025	0.007	0.006	0.003	0.002	0.003	-0.002	0.001	0.003	-0.001
II. Loans																
D_{k*}^{H}	0.0597	0.0534	0.0531	0.0519	0.0545	0.0553	0.0764	0.0676	0.0648	0.0662	0.0689	0.0753	0.0749	0.0781	0.0788	0.0803
I_o	0.3046	0.2887	0.2889	0.0789	0.0954	0.0578	0.0358	0.0751	0.0831	0.0311	0.0793	0.0485	0.0684	0.0570	0.0271	0.0246
I_t	0.6875	0.6254	0.5840	0.5732	0.6814	0.7527	0.7164	0.6792	0.6807	0.7028	0.6679	0.7094	0.7110	0.8111	0.7049	0.7139
k* (H)	8	9	10	10	10	7	7	7	7	6	6	7	7	7	7	7
D(RHTI)	-	-0.007	-0.002	-0.005	0.003	0.004	0.021	-0.003	0.001	0.002	0.003	0.006	0.000	0.002	-0.002	0.001
III: Deposits																
D_{k*}^{H}	0.0629	0.0611	0.0558	0.0572	0.0574	0.0572	0.0759	0.0845	0.0904	0.0936	0.0942	0.0952	0.0949	0.0971	0.0985	0.1005
I_o	0.2393	0.2888	0.2496	0.2627	0.1239	0.0645	0.1184	0.1340	0.1450	0.1761	0.1451	0.1057	0.0997	0.0869	0.1049	0.0927
I_t	0.5990	0.6293	0.6137	0.5453	0.6749	0.6813	0.6581	0.6532	0.6301	0.6593	0.6422	0.6518	0.6599	0.6523	0.6806	0.6726
k* (H)	8	7	8	9	2	2	8	7	7	7	7	7	7	7	7	7
D(RHTI)	-	-0.001	-0.005	-0.001	-0.002	0.000	0.026	0.012	0.007	0.006	0.001	0.000	0.000	0.001	0.004	0.001

5. EMPIRICAL FINDINGS ON CONCENTRATION AND COMPETITION

Empirical findings of the previous section can help us to comment on the competition issues of the sector. One may expect decreasing prices for customers of the banking sector if the degree of competition gets sharper. Customers may face different types of prices for different banking products. From the loan customer's point of view, interest rate for a loan can be seen as the price of the financial product. Typical financial services are credit card services, money transfer and payment services. And each of them may be provided with different prices. In this context, it is hard to speak of a single price. For this reason the derivation of an average price would be beneficial. On the other hand, banks pay interest to customers (depositors) for their savings. The difference between loan rate and deposit rate, which is defined as net interest margin (NIM), can be assumed as an average price in the sector. The CBRT publishes monthly data on weighted loan interest rate and deposit interest rate starting from end 2001. Net interest margin based on this data is shown in Figure 7. To investigate the relationship between "price" and concentration we can use alternative implicit forms for net interest margin[42]. These are;

NIM_1=[(total interest income – total interest expenses)/total asset]*100
NIM_2=[(interest from loans/loans)-(interest paid to deposit/deposit)]*100
NIM_3=[(int. from loans/loan.)-(interest paid to deposit and other funds/deposit + other funds)]*100
NIM_4=[(interest from loans and securities portfolio/ loans + securities portfolio)-(interest paid to deposit and other funds/ deposit + other funds)]*100

Figure 8 shows the evolution of loan and deposit concentration versus an implicit net interest margin (NIM_3).

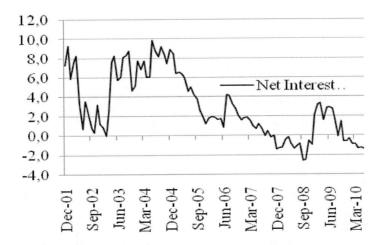

Figure 7. NIM (Monthly Data).

---

[42] Similar margins are used by Bhattacharya and Das (2003).

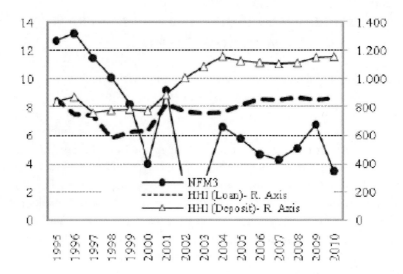

Figure 8. Annual NIM and HHI.

Moreover, net interest margins defined as above are summarized in the following table.

Table 6. Net Interest Margins of the Turkish Banking Sector

%	1995	1996	1997	1998	1999	2000	2001	2002	2003	2004	2005	2006	2007	2008	2009	2010
NFM_1	6.3	7.6	7.7	9.4	6.6	4.3	7.8	6.0	4.5	5.8	4.6	4.2	4.5	4.2	5.0	3.1
NFM_2	11.8	11.1	8.6	7.5	5.3	2.4	7.7	1.7	0.5	5.3	5.1	4.1	3.8	4.5	6.5	3.3
NFM_3	12.7	13.2	11.5	10.1	8.2	4.0	9.2	2.8	1.7	6.0	5.8	4.7	4.3	5.1	6.8	3.5
NFM_4	16.1	14.4	13.2	12.9	10.4	6.7	28.2	10.1	5.7	7.3	5.8	4.8	4.7	5.1	5.7	3.4

Note: Data from BAT and BRSA. Ratios are own calculations. Figures for 2010 are as of September 2010.

Table 7. Correlation Matrix of Net Interest Margin and Concentration

	H-Asset	H-Deposit	H-Loan	NFM_1	NFM_2	NFM_3	NFM_4
H-Asset	1.000						
H-Deposit	0.980	1.000					
H-Loan	0.711	0.692	1.000				
NFM_1	-0.680	-0.679	-0.538	1.000			
NFM_2	-0.545	-0.486	0.019	0.651	1.000		
NFM_3	-0.686	-0.627	-0.166	0.735	0.972	1.000	
NFM_4	-0.512	-0.599	-0.141	0.749	0.634	0.638	1.000

H: Herfindahl Index.

As it seen from the above Table 6 and Figure 8, net interest margin was in a downward trend before 1999 and volatile afterwards. And in financial crises years, including the global crisis year 2008, net interest margins showed upward trend. On the other side, concentration of the sector behaves differently before 1999 and after. Concentration is decreasing before 1999 and rising after this year. We may speak of a negative correlation between net interest margin and concentration. But this relationship is not very strong and does not hold for each year. In fact this issue can be observed from the following correlation matrix below (Table 7).

To sum up, between the years of 1995-1999, the decrease in net interest margins could be as a result of increased competition that was due to the new entries into the sector. Falling margins due to competition are for the advantage for the consumers. However, before 1999, the sector was shaped by weak fundamentals, insufficient capital, bad governance and inefficient regulatory environment due to several different and disconnected behaving supervisory establishments. Moreover, full blanket guarantee for deposit were the main source of moral hazard. High level competition under these circumstances did not provide the desired outcomes. The cost was a deep financial crisis. Contrary to this, we observe an increase in concentration during 2000-2010 and a decreasing trend in net interest margin (except the global crisis period of 2008 and 2009). This implies that banks did not exercise their market power during this period. According to dominance indices, 7 banks lead the sector and disparity indexes of pursuer banks shows that the remaining (pursuer) banks are in search of greater market share which serves as a ground for increased competition.

CONCLUSION

In this chapter we have reviewed the institutional change in the Turkish banking sector with an emphasis on the market structure. According to the findings of this study, between 1995 and 1999, number of banks operating in the increased and concentration level went down due to lax entry requirements. And in the same period net interest margin showed volatile and declining trend. After the restructuring, many banks exited the market. Besides, mergers and acquisitions, transfer of market shares, foreign *de novo* entries caused number of active banks to decline and concentration to increase. But net interest margins continued to be downwards. The leader banks in the sector increased available funds to real sector and households whereas less government financing is preferred. Turkey's enhanced integration to global financial markets and accession process to EU stimulated foreign entry. Small and medium scaled banks (the pursuer group within the context of this study) implemented competitive banking activities in order to increase their franchise value.

But most importantly, better institutional and regulatory set up that is provided through the restructuring of the sector created a level of playing field for the banks. Abolishment of full blanket guarantee, strengthening the regulatory environment, new banking law, increased market discipline and higher efficiency led to a better allocation of resources despite the raising concentration level. Under these circumstances, declining net interest margin is an indication that banks do not exercise their increasing market power. The restructuring and stable market structure coupled with relevant regulations and enforcement, created a sound banking environment in Turkey. By this way, it was possible for the Turkish banking sector to avoid the spillover effects of the recent global financial crisis.

REFERENCES

Abbasoğlu O.F., Aysan, A. F. and Güneş, A. (2007). Concentration, Competition, Efficiency and Profitability of the Turkish Banking Sector in the Post-Crises Period. *Bogazici University Research Papers*, ISS/EC 2007-16.

Appelbaum, E. (1982). The Estimation of the Degree of Oligopoly Power. *Journal of Econometrics*, 19, 287-299.

Aydınlı, I. (1996). *Turk Bankacilik Sistemi Piyasa Yapisi*. Sermaye Piyasasi Kurulu Yayini No: 40, Ankara.

Bajo, O. and Salas, R. (1998). Inequality Foundations of Concentration Measures: An Application to the Hannah-Kay Indices. *Universidad Complutense de Madrid*, P.T. No: 2/98.

Bhattacharya, K. and Das, A. (2003). Dynamics of Market Structure and Competitiveness of the Banking Sector in India and its Impact on Output and Prices of Banking Service. *Reserve Bank of India Occasional Papers,* 24(3).

Bikker, J.A. and K. Haaf (2002a). Competition, Concentration and Their Relationship: An Empirical Analysis of the Banking Industry. *Journal of Banking and Finance*, (26), 2191-2214.

Bikker, J.A. and K. Haaf (2002b). Measures of Competition and Concentration in the Banking Industry: a Review of the Literature. *Economic and Financial Modelling*, (9), 53-98.

Bikker, J.A. (2003). Testing for Imperfect Competition on EU Deposit and Loan Markets with Bresnehan's Market Power Model. *De Nederlandsche Bank Research Series Supervision*, No 52.

Bos, J.W.B. (2003). Improving Market Power Tests: Does it Matter for the Dutch Banking Market ?". *De Nederlandsche Bank Research Series Supervision,* No 56.

Çelik, T. and Ürünveren, Ç. (2009). Yabanci Banka Girişlerinin Turk Bankacilik Sektorune Rekabet Etkisi:2002-2007, *Nigde Universitesi, İ.İ.B.F. Dergisi*, Cilt: 2, Sayi 2, 42-59.

Cotorelli, N. (1999). Competitive Analysis in Banking: Appraisal of the Methodologies. *Federal Reserve Bank of Chicago, Economic Perspectives*, Q1 (99), 2-15.

Dick, A.A. (2005). Market Size, Service Quality and Competition in Banking. *Federal Reserve Bank of New York*, NY.

Frexias, X. and Rochet, J.C. (1998). *Microeconomics of Banking*. Cambridge, MA: MIT Press.

Günalp, B. and Çelik, T. (2004). Turk Bankacilik Sektorunde Piyasa Yapisi ve Performans Ilişkilerinin Etkinlik Icin Dogrudan Bir Olcut Kullanilarak Test Edilmesi. *Gazi Universitesi Iktisadi ve Idari Bilimler Fakültesi Dergisi*, 6(3), 31–57.

Günalp, B. and Çelik, T. (2006). Competition in the Turkish Banking Industry. *Applied Economics*, 38(11), 1335–1342.

Hall, M. and Tideman, N. (1967). Measures of Concentration. *Journal of the Royal Statistical Society*, 62 (317), 162-168.

Hannan, H.T. (1997). Market Share Inequality, the Number of Competitors, and the HHI: An Examination of Bank Pricing. *Review of Industrial Organization*, 12, 23-25.

Hart, P.E. (1971). Entropy and Other Measures of Concentration. *Journal of the Royal Statistical Society*, 134 (1), 73-85.

Hart, P.E. (1975). Moment Distributions in Economics: An Exposition. *Journal of the Royal Statistical Society*, 138 (3), 423-434.

Horvarth, J. (1970). Suggestion for a Comprehensive Measure of Concentration. *Southern Econ. Journal*, 36, 446-452.

Kasman, A. (2001). The Profit-Structure Relationship in the Turkish Banking Industry Using Direct Measures of Efficiency. *Ege Akademik Bakış Dergisi*, 1(1), 141-164.

Klein, M. (1971). A Theory of the Banking Firm. *Journal of Money, Credit and Banking*, 3, 205-218.

Korkmaz A. (2010). Turk Mevduat Bankaciligi Sektorunde Rekabet Derecesi: Bresnahan-Lau Modelinden Kanitlar, Bankacilar Dergisi, Sayı 74, TBB.

Monti, M. (1971). A Theoretical Model of Bank Behavior and its Implications for Monetary Policy", *L'industria*, 2, 165-191.

Northcott, C.A. (2004). Competition in Banking: A Review of the Literature. *Bank of Canada Working Paper*, No: 2004-24.

Okumuş, H. Ş. (2002). Market Structure and Efficiency as Determinants of Profitability in the Turkish Banking Industry. *Yapı Kredi Economic Review*, 13(1), 65-88.

Ruthenford D. (2006). Competition in the Banking Industry: Theoretical Aspects and Empirical Evidence from Israel in an International Perspective. *The Banking Supervision Department, Bank of Israel.*

Sakarya, B. (2007). Degisen Kuresel Finansal Yapi ve 2007 Dalgalanmalari. Bankacilik Duzenleme ve Denetleme Kurumu Calisma Tebligi, 2007/No:2.

Salop, S. (1979). Monopolistic Competition with Outside Goods. *Bell Journal of Economics*, 10(1), 141-156.

Shaffer, S (1993). A Test of Competition in Canadian Banking. *Journal of Money, Credit and Banking*, 25 (1), 49-61.

Shannon, E. C. (1948). A Mathematical Theory of Communication. *The Bell System Technical Journal*, (27), 379-423.

Stich, A. (1995a). Die axiomatische Herleitung einer Klasse von dynamischen Ungleichheitsmassen. *University of Cologne Discussion Papers in Statistics and Econometrics*, No: 02/95.

Stich, A. (1995b). Insurance and Concentration: The Change of Concentration in the Swedish and Finnish Insurance Market 1989-1993. *University of Cologne Discussion Papers in Statistics and Econometrics*, No:10/95.

Suominen, M. (1994). Measuring Competition in Banking: A Two-Product Model. *Scandinavian Journal of Economics*, 96 (1), 95-110.

Yeyati Levy, E. (2003). Banking Competition in Latin America. *Inter-American Development Bank and OECD.*

In: Regulation and Competition in the Turkish Banking... ISBN: 978-1-61324-990-1
Editors: Tamer Çetin and Fuat Oğuz © 2012 Nova Science Publishers, Inc.

Chapter 6

DEREGULATION AND ENTRY PERFORMANCE IN TURKISH BANKING

Ihsan Isik[1] and Lokman Gunduz[2]

[1]Professor of Finance, Rohrer College of Business, Rowan University,
New Jersey, USA
and Research Fellow, Economic Research Forum (ERF), Cairo, Egypt
and Chairman and CEO of the American Turkish
Chamber of Commerce (ATCOM), New Jersey, U. S.
[2]Associate Professor of Finance, Board of Governors,
Central Bank of Turkey, Ankara, Turkey

ABSTRACT

The newly chartered domestic and foreign banks constituted about half of the Turkish banking industry at the turn of the past century. This record number of new entries is the by-products of deregulatory reforms launched in the 1980's and onward. In this chapter, we investigate the productivity performance of these new banks vis-à-vis that of old banks in an era of financial deregulation in Turkey. Employing a non-stochastic inter-temporal production frontier approach over a period of sixteen years, we found that new banks are significantly superior to old banks in resource utilization. Apparently, not hampered by a legacy of inefficiency from the past, new banks could operate nearer the efficiency frontier. Moreover, new banks register faster productivity, technology and efficiency growth than old banks. Equipped with better and newer technology, local partners for foreign entries and holding affiliation for domestic entries appear to have helped these young banks to overcome initial asymmetric information problems and demonstrate higher performance. Our overall results suggest that new entries, especially from more advanced markets, could be instrumental in boosting resource allocation and utilization in banking.

Keywords: Turkish banks; learning; bank entry; productivity; efficiency
JEL classification: D21; G21

INTRODUCTION

Before the initial deregulation of the financial system in 1980, bank regulators in Turkey believed that in order to have financial stability and soundness, there must be strong and profitable banks. To ensure this, the regulators tightened the entry barriers for a prolonged period of time.[43] Evidently, within two decades until 1980, there were only 3 commercial bank entries. The regulatory stance, however, has changed significantly since 1980 in favor of more competition and efficiency in the banking sector. Policy makers intended to achieve these goals through liberalization and promotion of entry into the system.

As a result of loosening restrictions on bank entries, there were 31 new entries into the industry during the period 1980-1996, of which 19 were from foreign markets and 12 from domestic markets.[44] This means that by 1996, half of the Turkish banking industry was made up of the newly chartered banks. Obviously, the liberalization policies introduced were instrumental in attracting new entries into the sector.[45] The common view among bankers and researchers is that new bank entry, especially by foreign ones, has made tremendous contributions toward improving the quality of human capital and financial technology of the Turkish banking sector (Atiyas and Ersel, 1994; Akcaoglu, 1998; Isik and Hassan, 2002). For instance, Isik and Hassan (2002) report that the average compensation for bankers working for these new institutions is significantly higher than the industry average (about three times). However, whether these new entries have intensified banking competition and efficiency in Turkey is still debated.

Rather than fighting with old banks for market share in retail banking, new banks in Turkey opted to focus on certain profitable market niches such as trade and wholesale corporate financing. New banks face substantial adverse selection problems because their initial loan customers are usually those denied by the existent banks. Regardless of origin, new banks appear to specialize in a certain financial product or service in response to such information problems.[46] Such strategy may require less expertise and help a new bank find its market niche. However, such specialization may also result in low diversification, which increases portfolio risk for new banks. Alternatively, because of high credit risk associated with loans, new banks may also purposefully concentrate on investment securities to eliminate asymmetric information problems.

---

[43] The regulators asked the prospective applicants to clearly demonstrate the need and benefits of new entry. New applications were also expected to show the compatibility of the new entry with the announced economic plans of the government.

[44] The number of banks increased from 43 in 1980 to 66 in 1990 and to 79 by the end of 2000. 5 banks under the management of the Saving Deposit Insurance Fund (SDIF) were merged under Sumerbank bringing the number of banks to 74 by mid-May 2001 (BRSA web-site: http://www.bddk.gov.tr).

[45] Like in many countries, no one can start a bank in Turkey without the express approval of regulatory authorities. The 1999 Banking Law (No. 4398) delegates a new regulatory body, the Banking Regulation and Supervision Agency (BRSA), as the independent authority to regulate and supervise bank entries and exits in Turkey. Under the BRSA regulations, any bank to be opened in Turkey must be founded as a joint-stock company, have founders who have not been declared bankrupt or enter into a composition with creditors and have a capital, paid in cash and free of any collusion, which shall not be less than TL 20 trillion (in 2003 currency rates, the initial capital requirement is about $US 1.5 millions). The bank, permitted to be founded, shall not start operation unless it possesses adequate management, personnel and technical equipment to carry out banking operations (Banks Act, Article 7).

[46] None of the new Turkish banks, domestic or foreign, has offices beyond the three largest cities despite the fact that there are no restrictions on the scope of their operations. Brislin and Santomero (1991) report that the U.S. new banks also adopted specialized lending strategies.

Old banks have a decided advantage over new banks in their greater experience, greater size, and well-established reputations (Rose, 1977). New banks may not adequately reap returns on their investments in their early times due to insufficient transaction volume that minimizes production costs and inefficiencies. As Mester (1996) suggests, high set-up costs for new banks result especially from the time needed to establish customer relationships. It may take several years for a new bank to form its "optimal" customer portfolio as a result of asymmetric information problems associated with a new market (Rose, 1977; Brislin and Santomero, 1991). Therefore, it is possible that banking technology inherits *learning by doing*, suggesting that as banks age, they could manage their operations better and become more efficient. As a matter of fact, the best practice banks are more likely to survive than inefficient banks. Evidently, majorities of failures are usually observed among newly established banks (DeYoung, 2003a). Hence, as compared to old banks, new banks are expected to demonstrate lower efficiency upon inception due to scale and experience problems. However, one should note that the pace of learning should be faster for new banks. As new banks move along the learning curve, they become able to produce more output per input since they experience a gigantic improvement in their outputs without their inputs changing much (DeYoung, 2001).[47] This could happen as a result of consuming possible economies of scale and eliminating asymmetric information problems related to the new market.[48]

In recent years, especially after 2001-2002 economic crises, a substantial number of banks have failed in Turkey (Isik and Uysal, 2009). As documented, new enterprises generally have higher failure rates than old banks (Geroski, 1995; DeYoung 2003a,b). It may be that learning to handle exogenous economic shocks is a very long process that requires a bank to be exposed to several business cycles (DeYoung and Hasan, 1998). There is no guarantee that a new bank will survive and prosper. For this reason, state agencies that grant charters to new banks pay a great deal of attention to the likely survival of the proposed bank in making their decisions. Therefore, the fates of new banks are of heightened policy concern and research interest for the Turkish regulators that are responsible for the safety and soundness of the financial system.

Empirical evidence indicates that the initial performance of a new bank is strongly related to its experience, financial strength, relations and contacts of its founders, and quality of its managers (Selby, 1981). Like any business start-ups in other sectors, most new banks incur initial losses as a result of substantial asymmetric information problems and high operational costs. The purpose of this chapter is to investigate the operational performance of new Turkish banks to see whether these institutions were able to compete effectively with old banks in terms of efficiency and productivity. These investigations are beneficial for the regulatory agencies that charter new banks, as they must allocate their limited resources to assess the conditions that have the most effect on the future performance of proposed banks.

---

[47] DeYoung (2001) mentions three separate and simultaneous experience processes that may be operating at start-up banks with innovative business plans: a maturity experience effect that transforms accumulated general banking experience into improved financial performance; a technology experience effect that transforms accumulated experience using the technology into improved fiancial performance; and a technology-specific scale effect that transforms increased bank size into scale efficiencies that will improve financial performance.

[48] However, fast growing new banks may encounter performance problems. Cyree and Wansley (2004) report that the US banks that choose to grow have lower profit efficiency.

Our results may also help bank regulators when deciding whether de novo entry should be made easier or more difficult.

Post-entry performance of young banks concerns both policy makers and investors. Following the main stream in recent literature, such as Aly et al. (1990), Wheelock and Wilson (1999), Mukherjee et al. (2001) and Isik and Hassan (2002, 2003a,b) among others, this study adopts a non-parametric approach, Data Envelopment Analysis (DEA), while measuring technical efficiency and productivity growth measures.[49] The range of our data spans a period of 16 years (1981-1996). We have purposely excluded the time period after 1996. The Turkish banking industry has experienced severe financial shocks in the post 1996 period. As a reflection of the severity of this period, over 20 (about one third) of Turkish banks have failed and were taken into the custody of the insurance fund after 1996. Even, the Banks Association of Turkey (BAT) was unable to provide bank level data for a number of years. Thus, the post 1996 period is mainly characterized by bank exits rather than bank entries. A crisis period has also the potential to contaminate the results and obscure the sought relationships between the financial variables of new and old banks. We have also excluded those new entries that made loans but did not collect deposits (development and investment bank entries) to ensure homogeneity among the sample banks in terms of production technology.

We refer to the banks that are 10 years old or younger as *new banks*; otherwise *old banks*. Early studies on new banks suggest that these banks are more sensitive to internal bank factors than to exogenous (market or regulatory) factors. Containment of operating costs and inputs, achievement of sufficient bank size, and pricing and operating policies set by management are important internal factors that impact bank performance conditions (Arshadi and Lawrence, 1987; Hunter and Srinivasan, 1990). Thus, in this chapter, we focus on the input efficiency aspect of bank performance, which is called technical efficiency. Technical efficiency is under the direct control of bank managers and measures how well they utilize their expensive factors of production as compared to a set of comparable other banks (Evanoff and Israilevich, 1991). Therefore, this type of efficiency is widely used in finance literature as the proxy of management quality in banks (Barr et al., 1994).[50]

Our results indicate that new banks are superior to old banks in resource utilization. Furthermore, new banks register faster productivity, technology, and efficiency growth. New banks in Turkey are the by-products of financial reforms launched in the 1980's that encouraged both domestic and foreign entries. It seems that the combined effects of substantial liberalization and granting of new banking charters have contributed to the improved efficiency of the Turkish banking industry, indicating that the extension of new

---

[49] Parametric approaches attribute deviations from the frontier to both purely random shocks and inefficiency, whereas non-parametric approaches attribute all deviations from the frontier to inefficiency. Berger and Humphrey (1997) report that in the financial institutions literature, efficiency studies employing non-parametric approaches outnumber efficiency studies using parametric approaches. Potential mistakes in the specification of a cost or revenue function as well as distributional assumptions about the error term in parametric approaches could confound the inefficiency scores with specification errors. The DEA uses exclusively quantity information and thus demands neither problematic price information nor a restrictive behavioral assumption in its calculation. For further comparison, please refer to Berger and Humphrey (1997).

[50] Ideally, it would be more informative if we measured both technical and allocative inefficiency. Fare et al. (1994) define overall inefficiency as the product of technical and allocative inefficiency. Lacking price data, we are unable to estimate allocative inefficiency. Clearly, our measure of technical efficiency will tend to understate overall efficiency. However, it is documented in the literature that technical inefficiency dominates allocative inefficiency in banking.

bank charters is likely to accelerate the efficiency gains expected from a period of deregulation. Not hampered by the past, new banks can choose the best production techniques, increase competition, and put restructuring pressures on incumbents. Evidently, the operational performance of old banks, although lower as compared to that of new ones, has also improved considerably in the new, more open and competitive business environment.

This chapter is organized as follows. The next section discusses the non-parametric procedures to measure the static technical efficiency indexes and dynamic productivity growth indexes. Section 3 covers the data and empirical design. Section 4 analyzes the results. Section 5 provides the summary.

1. METHODOLOGY AND LITERATURE REVIEW

Instead of relying on simple accounting ratios, we measure the performance of banks using an efficient production frontier approach that takes into consideration differences in input and output mixes of banks. In fact, the multidimensional nature of bank performance cannot be fully represented by a single variable or index (Arshadi and Lawrance, 1987, DeYoung and Hasan, 1998). Thus, we study the performance of new banks by multiple performance (efficiency and productivity) measures. It is also useful to break down these performance measures into their key components to track the causes of sub-performance and to suggest where bank regulators and managers need to look for remedies for any operational problems that do surface.

By means of Figure 1, the measurement of non-parametric Malmquist indexes and technical efficiency scores are discussed below. First, consider that N_t banks employ p inputs to produce q outputs for each time period $t = 1, 2,..., T$. Transformation of the vector of inputs, $x_t \in \Re_+^p$, into the vector of outputs, $y_t \in \Re_+^q$ during the production process is represented by the function: F_t: $F_t = \{(x, y): x \text{ can produce } y \text{ at time } t\}$, which is simply the production possibilities set, the set of all feasible combinations of inputs and outputs, at time t.[51] By forming the upper boundary (frontier) of F_t, the best-practices in the sample define the efficient production technology (frontier) at time t. Assume that x_t and y_t represent the observed input and output vectors of a bank at time t, respectively. The Shephard (1970) output distance function relative to the technology existing at time t is defined as: $d_t (x_t, y_t) = inf \{\phi: (x_t, y_t/\phi) \in F_t\}$, which gives a normalized measure of the distance from the location of a bank in the input/output space to the production frontier at time t in the hyper-plane, where inputs are held fixed. Thus, the distance of a combination of x_t and y_t to the frontier can be as low as zero and as high as one if measured relative to the contemporaneous technology (i.e., $0 \le d_t (x_t, y_t) \le 1$), but it can be higher than one if measured relative to the technology of another period (i.e., $0 \le d_{t+1} (x_t, y_t) [\le \text{ or } >] 1$).

The X-efficiency calculated under the constant returns to scale (CRS) assumption is called technical efficiency (henceforth, TE), while the X-efficiency calculated under the variable returns to scale (VRS) assumption is named pure technical efficiency (henceforth, PTE). If the bank under consideration operates at the optimum scale, where average input

---

[51] F_t is assumed to satisfy certain conditions which make it possible to obtain meaningful output distance functions (see Shephard, 1970).

usage (production cost) is minimized, the TE and PTE scores attain the same value (unity). In other words, TE=PTE because there is no production waste due to scale X-inefficiency. Thus, if there is a difference between these scores, it is because of problems in scale efficiency (henceforth, SE), which indicates that the bank operates either at the increasing returns to scale (IRS) or decreasing returns to scale (DRS) portion of the production (or cost) curve. These scores take a value between 0 and 1 for the worst-practice and best-practice banks, respectively, in the sample.

Assume that our bank is observed at point b in Figure 1 at time period t. Under both assumptions, CRS and VRS, the firm that operates at point b is technically X-*in*efficient. Under *CRS*, technical inefficiency of the bank at point b is the distance bh, while under VRS technical inefficiency would only be bg. The difference between these two measures, hg, is attributed to scale inefficiency, which simply indicates that the bank at point b can produce its current level of output with fewer inputs if it attains CRS. In the figure, the CRS frontier is represented by F_t (CRS$_t$), and it simply depicts the optimal level of output that can be obtained for the given input levels. In other words, CRS frontier shows what is attainable and what is unattainable with the given technology, and thus the banks either lie on or below it. The PTE and SE for the bank at point b can be expressed in ratio form: PTE = **(y_t g / y_t b)** and SE = **(y_t h / y_t g)**. The TE of the bank at point b is thus simply the product of PTE and SE: TE = PTE × SE = **(y_t g / y_t b)** × **(y_t h / y_t g)** = **(y_t h / y_t b)**.

If technology is changing over time, there will be shifts in the best practice technical frontier. To account for such shifts, we use the Malmquist index approach that allows separation between the shifts in the frontier and improvements in the efficiency relative to the frontier. In this context, *technological growth (TG)* and *efficiency growth (EG)* become the two mutually exclusive and exhaustive sources of *productivity growth (PG)*. It is also possible to divide efficiency growth (EG) into its distinct components with the Malmquist index: changes in management practices (*pure efficiency growth, PEG*) and changes in production scales (*scale efficiency growth, SEG*).

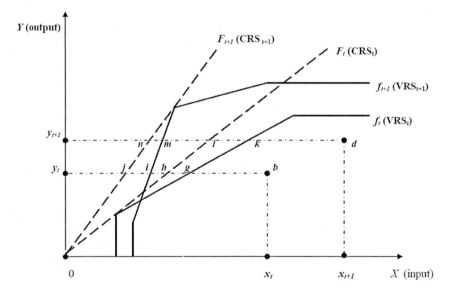

Figure 1. Measurement of efficiency and productivity growth indexes.

To understand the above productivity separations, return to Figure 1. Assume again a simple case with single-input/single-output and a constant returns to scale (CRS) technology, which shifted upward from F_t (CRS$_t$) to F_{t+1} (CRS$_{t+1}$) between two periods due to innovation. Assume that in year t, a bank was observed at point b, whereas in year $t+1$, it was observed at point d. In this multi-period setting, there are two corresponding benchmark banks for both observations. The first year observation, b, can be compared with either the efficient point, h, on its contemporaneous frontier F_t or the efficient point, j, on the next year frontier F_{t+1}. Likewise, the second year observation, d, can be assessed with respect to either the efficient point, n, on its contemporaneous frontier F_{t+1} or the efficient point, l, on the previous year frontier F_t. When measured relative to their contemporaneous frontiers, both observations represent feasible but technically inefficient production points because they are interior to the frontiers.

Rather than arbitrary selection of the technology of period t or $t+1$ as the benchmark, like Berg et al. (1991), Fare *et al.* (1994), Wheelock and Wilson (1999), and Mukherjee et al. (2001), we calculate the Malmquist index, PG, as the geometric mean of two Malmquist productivity indexes, $(PG_1 \times PG_2)^{0.5}$.

$$PG = \left[\underbrace{\left(\frac{d_t^c(x_t, y_t)}{d_t^c(x_{t+1}, y_{t+1})} \right)}_{(PG_1)} \times \underbrace{\left(\frac{d_{t+1}^c(x_t, y_t)}{d_{t+1}^c(x_{t+1}, y_{t+1})} \right)}_{(PG_2)} \right]^{0.5} \qquad (1)$$

Here, PG_1 represents the Malmquist index obtained relative to F_t frontier whereas PG_2 represents the Malmquist index calculated relative to F_{t+1} frontier. Equation 1 computes PG with reference to the CRS frontiers (c denotes a CRS technology). In terms of input distances on the x-axis in Figure 1, PG is equal to the following:

$$PG = \{[(|y_t b|/|y_t h|)/(|y_{t+1} d|/|y_{t+1} l|)][(|y_t b|/|y j|)/(|y_{t+1} d|/|y_{t+1} n|)]\}^{0.5} \qquad (2)$$

Assuming that technology is one of CRS, Fare et al. (1994) rewrites Equation 1 in such a way that one could determine the sources of the productivity growth,

$$PG = \underbrace{\frac{d_t^c(x_t, y_t)}{d_{t+1}^c(x_{t+1}, y_{t+1})}}_{EG} \times \underbrace{\left[\frac{d_{t+1}^c(x_{t+1}, y_{t+1})}{d_t^c(x_{t+1}, y_{t+1})} \times \frac{d_{t+1}^c(x_t, y_t)}{d_t^c(x_t, y_t)} \right]^{0.5}}_{TG} \qquad (3)$$

In Equation 3, PG = (EG×TG), i.e., PG is simply the product of efficiency growth (*EG*), how much closer a bank gets to the efficient frontier (*catching up* or *falling behind*), and technological growth (*TG*), how much the benchmark production frontier shifts at each bank's observed input mix (*innovation or shock*).

When we relax the CRS assumption and adopt the variable returns to scale (VRS) assumption, we get f_t (VRS$_t$) and f_{t+1} (VRS$_{t+1}$) frontiers for t and $t+1$ periods, respectively, in Figure 2. Through these VRS frontiers, we can divide the CRS efficiency change index in Equation 2 further into its *pure efficiency growth (PEG)* and *scale efficiency growth (SEG)* components. In sum, PG = (TG × EG) and EG = (PEG × SEG). Thus, the Malmquist index takes the following generalized form: PG = (TG × PEG × SEG):

$$PG = \underbrace{\frac{d_t^v(x_t,y_t)}{d_{t+1}^v(x_{t+1},y_{t+1})}}_{PEG} \times \underbrace{\left[\frac{d_{t+1}^v(x_{t+1},y_{t+1})}{d_t^v(x_{t+1},y_{t+1})} \times \frac{d_{t+1}^v(x_t,y_t)}{d_t^v(x_t,y_t)}\right]^{0.5}}_{TG} \times \underbrace{\left[\frac{d_{t+1}^c(x_t,y_t)d_{t+1}^v(x_{t+1},y_{t+1})d_t^c(x_t,y_t)d_{t+1}^v(x_{t+1},y_{t+1})}{d_{t+1}^v(x_t,y_t)d_{t+1}^c(x_{t+1},y_{t+1})d_t^v(x_t,y_t)d_t^c(x_{t+1},y_{t+1})}\right]^{-0.5}}_{SEG}$$

(4)

The superscripts c and v in Equation 4 denote that distance functions are measured with reference to the CRS and VRS frontiers, respectively. Obviously, the demarcation line for the above growth performance indices is unity. In other words, the Malmquist index, PG, and its subcomponents, TG, EG, PEG, and SEG, take a value greater than one in case of improvement, one in case of stagnation, and less than one in case of deterioration.[52]

There are a few studies on the operational performance of new banks. DeYoung and Hasan (1998) dwells particularly on the *profit efficiency* of the U.S. chartered new banks. They found that during the first three years of operation, de novo banks improve their profit efficiency rapidly, but on average it takes them about nine years to catch up with established banks. They also reported that the low profit efficiency at de novo banks is associated with their excess branch capacity, reliance on large deposits, and affiliation with a multi-bank holding company. In their correlation of cost or profit efficiency analyses on the U.S. banks, Mester (1996) and Berger and Mester (1997) used a dummy variable for bank age. The results from these indirect studies are inconclusive. For instance, consistent with a *learning by doing hypothesis*, Mester (1996) found that inefficient banks tend to be younger even after excluding new banks from the study due to their likely high start-up costs. Berger and Mester (1997) reported an insignificant *positive* relationship between age and cost efficiency, and a significant *negative* relationship between age and profit efficiency.

This investigation differs from the earlier ones in a number of ways. First, unlike them, it uses an inter-temporal non-parametric frontier approach, which takes into account both shifts in the frontier (technological progress) and changes in the proximity to the frontier (efficiency change). This is a critical issue especially for the industries that are passing through important structural and regulatory changes, as are the case of Turkey's (Wheelock and Wilson, 1999; Isik, 2007). Second, it uses a longer period of time, 16 years, to observe the performance differential between new and old banks, which may balance the measurement and idiosyncratic issues related to an emerging market data set. Third, it uses three indexes of technical efficiency, TE, PTE and SE, and five measures of productivity growth, PE, TG, EG, PEG, and SEG, to detect the sources of performance differential between new and old bank groups. Fourth, the results we provide are from an emerging market setting, which may enrich our understanding of the behavior of new and old banks in different market and regulatory regimes. Finally, our methodology avoids the problematic price data and relies exclusively on

---

[52] For further discussion, please see Wheelock and Wilson (1999) and Mukherjee et al. (2001).

the quantity data for bank inputs and outputs. The measurement of input and output prices have always been problematic for advanced markets, let alone developing markets (Berger and Mester, 1997; Berger and Humphrey, 1997).

2. DATA AND EMPIRICAL SETTING

We have gathered our bank data from the *Banks in Turkey* issues of the Banks Association of Turkey (BAT), which provide a rich source of information about all forms of Turkish banks including their balance sheet, income statement, off-balance sheet items, ownership and corporate structure, branch offices, bank personnel, etc. Because the data was not in electronic format for the entire study period (1981-1996), the required variables were entered manually. In selecting bank inputs and outputs, we adopted the so-called *intermediation approach*, which defines banks as multi-product firms that employ the inputs of labor and capital in order to transform bank deposits to an array of financial outputs such as bank loans and investment services. Thus three outputs, *short-term loans*, *long-term loans*, and *other earning assets*, constitute our output vector and three inputs, *labor*, *capital*, and *loanable funds*, make up our input vector. The specification of bank inputs and outputs used in this chapter are given in Table 1 along with their summary statistics. We denote all variables in $US million to control for inflation over the study period as well as to enhance the international comparison of the data. Overall, our unbalanced panel data encompass 794 observations, of which 271 belong to new banks and 523 belong to old banks.

Table 1. Specification and summary statistics of bank inputs and outputs[1]

Variables	Definition	New Banks (Age ≤10)		Old Banks (Age>10)	
		Mean	Standard Error	Mean	Standard Error
Outputs					
Short-term loans	Loans with less than a year to maturity	37.75	60.54	312.21	440.91
Long-term loans	Loans with more than a year to maturity	2.93	10.31	48.67	113.79
Other earning assets	Sum of investment securities, interbank funds sold and loans to special sectors (directed lending)	19.79	51.81	292.43	864.96
Inputs					
Labor	Number of full time employees on the payroll	134	197	4,210	7,440
Capital	Book value of premises and fixed assets	1.72	2.64	56.34	168.23
Funds	Core deposits (demand and time) from individuals and nonbank firms plus purchased funds from interbank, central bank, domestic and foreign banks, and others	93.53	170.10	957.39	1,603.02

[1] New banks are defined as the banks that are 10 years old or less while old banks are defined as the banks that are older than 10 years old.

There appears to be some significant differences in the asset (output) and liability (input) composition of new and old banks. The relative magnitudes of the variables in Table 1 indicate that new banks are starkly smaller than old banks. This is not surprising as most new banks start out as small institutions, as they generally face severe limitation on capital, management, and personnel until they can grow and attract additional resources. Another interesting observation is that the volume of short-term loans exceeds the volume of long-term loans in both forms of organizations. In the inflationary environment of Turkey, most of banks' deposits concentrate on short-term maturity class, and interest-sensitive liabilities of banks exceed their interest-sensitive assets. Apparently, due to inflation and interest rate risk, all Turkish banks prefer to extend short-term and working capital loans.

3. EMPIRICAL RESULTS AND ANALSYIS

Our investigation period corresponds to the time of financial liberalization and deregulation in the Turkish banking industry. In order to investigate the impact of these fundamental, environmental changes on the performance of new and old banks, we calculated the averages of efficiency scores and productivity growth measures of these banks for each year between 1981-96. It may be that new bank performance is also a function of time, i.e., there may be a positive association between time and performance in a deregulated environment, making aging banks look like better performers. In order to observe the effect of time on the results, we look at the performance of banks in each time period.

Table 2 summarizes means of TE, PTE and SE scores between 1981 and 1996. As can be seen, the total number of new banks per year in our sample ranges from 3 in 1981 to 26 in 1990. This number demonstrates fluctuation over time because of new entries and conversion of some new banks to the class of old banks during this time interval. The TE results in the table indicate that even after controlling for time, new banks invariably dominate old banks in each year, except for 1981.

When we disentangle the effects of scale problems and calculate the pure technical efficiency score PTE, we see that new banks are again superior to old banks in every year, including 1981.

On the other hand, the SE results of new banks do not look as impressive. In terms of scale efficiency, new banks cannot catch up with old banks until 1986. However, afterwards, new banks demonstrate better scale performance than old banks do. Apparently, as time passes, some of the earlier new banks grow in size and approach the optimum scale in terms of output maximization (or input minimization).[53]

Apparently, higher efficiencies are mostly observed in the later years of the study period than in the earlier part for both groups. In their analyses, Denizer (1997), Yulek (1998) and Isik and Hassan (2003b) took 1986 as the basis year for the launch of financial liberalization in Turkey, although financial liberalization started as early as 1980.

---

[53] Over the study period, average new bank TE ranges between 0.39 (in 1981) and 0.87 (in 1996), while average established bank TE ranges between 0.49 (in 1986 and 1991) and 0.78 (in 1996). The mean PTE ranges between 0.75 (in 1991) and 0.96 (in 1996) for new banks and between 0.66 (in 1984) and 0.86 (in 1996) for established banks. Whereas, the mean SE ranges between 0.40 (in 1981) and 0.97 (in 1992) for new banks and between 0.58 (in 1991) and 0.94 (in 1982) for established banks.

Deregulation and Entry Performance in Turkish Banking

Table 2. Technical efficiency of new and old banks over time[1]

YEAR	New Banks (Age ≤10)				Old Banks (Age>10)			
	#	TE	PTE	SE	#	TE	PTE	SE
81	3	0.39	0.80	0.40	35	0.69	0.75	0.93
82	5	0.76	0.93	0.82	33	0.66	0.70	0.94
83	7	0.61	0.91	0.64	31	0.65	0.75	0.89
84	10	0.62	0.93	0.65	30	0.57	0.66	0.87
85	14	0.65	0.85	0.76	30	0.58	0.74	0.82
81-85	39	0.60	0.88	0.65	159	0.63	0.72	0.89
86	19	0.71	0.80	0.88	30	0.49	0.77	0.68
87	19	0.77	0.83	0.92	31	0.50	0.81	0.63
88	23	0.83	0.88	0.92	29	0.60	0.77	0.77
89	24	0.82	0.85	0.96	29	0.66	0.85	0.77
90	26	0.81	0.87	0.93	30	0.68	0.85	0.80
86-90	111	0.79	0.85	0.92	149	0.58	0.81	0.73
91	23	0.66	0.75	0.84	31	0.49	0.84	0.58
92	25	0.87	0.90	0.97	32	0.68	0.84	0.81
93	25	0.78	0.83	0.93	33	0.66	0.82	0.82
94	19	0.78	0.85	0.92	36	0.65	0.80	0.83
95	17	0.66	0.79	0.84	39	0.59	0.78	0.78
96	12	0.87	0.96	0.90	44	0.78	0.86	0.91
91-96	121	0.77	0.85	0.90	215	0.64	0.82	0.79
All	271	0.76	0.85	0.88	523	0.63	0.79	0.81

[1] TE: Technical efficiency; PTE: Pure technical efficiency; SE: Scale efficiency.

The main reason proposed in these studies is that most of the important financial reforms were undertaken after this date, among which include: revitalization of capital markets, establishment of money and foreign exchange markets, liberalization of interest and currency rates, adoption of international accounting standards, and introduction of modern financial products and services, etc. (please refer to these studies for further discussion). Given these observations, we divide the entire study period into three time periods in order to capture the effects of macroeconomic changes on the performance of these two types of banks. Accordingly, we call the period 1981-85 as the *preparation period*, 1986-1990 as the *development period*, and 1991-1996 as the *maturity period* of liberalization. The results indicate that average new bank TE after 1986 improved remarkably, by 19% in the development period and 17% in the maturity period with respect to that of the preparation period. It appears that most of the improvement in new bank technical efficiency stemmed from positive developments in their scale efficiency (SE), as their PTE practically remained stagnant. As for old banks, they demonstrate declining TE throughout the preparation period, which picks up after 1986 in the development period. It may be that old banks faced a hard time adapting to the new environment and experienced a fall in their efficiency initially.

Table 3. Productivity growth in new and old banks over time[1]

	New Banks (Age ≤10)						Old Banks (Age>10)					
YEAR	#	PG	TG	EG	PEG	SEG	#	PG	TG	EG	PEG	SEG
81	-	-	-	-	-	-	-	-	-	-	-	-
82	3	9.66	1.07	9.03	7.36	2.73	32	1.06	1.12	0.99	0.98	1.02
83	5	1.09	1.04	1.02	0.98	1.36	31	0.97	1.01	1.06	1.18	0.91
84	7	1.50	0.92	1.55	1.67	1.01	30	0.86	1.03	0.91	0.87	1.05
85	10	4.40	1.11	3.60	1.70	1.40	30	1.08	0.99	1.14	1.27	0.90
81-85	25	3.56	1.04	3.16	2.23	1.44	123	1.00	1.04	1.03	1.07	0.97
86	14	1.66	0.77	2.19	1.63	1.31	30	0.95	0.73	1.31	1.14	1.17
87	18	1.41	1.18	1.15	1.12	1.04	31	1.19	1.18	1.06	1.13	0.93
88	19	1.08	0.94	1.22	1.16	1.01	29	0.95	0.80	1.23	1.00	1.24
89	23	1.12	1.07	1.04	1.01	1.03	29	1.20	1.01	1.21	1.12	1.09
90	24	1.06	0.93	1.13	1.09	1.03	29	1.06	0.93	1.14	1.00	1.15
86-90	98	1.23	0.99	1.28	1.17	1.07	148	1.07	0.93	1.19	1.08	1.11
91	23	1.19	1.73	0.84	0.92	0.89	31	0.97	1.61	0.66	0.96	0.71
92	21	0.93	0.66	1.74	1.39	1.21	32	0.98	0.61	1.76	1.16	1.56
93	24	1.02	1.08	0.93	0.95	0.98	33	1.02	1.01	1.02	1.00	1.07
94	19	1.07	0.86	1.34	1.28	1.01	36	1.06	0.98	1.06	1.06	1.00
95	16	1.00	1.36	0.75	0.82	0.92	39	1.28	1.20	1.21	1.11	1.15
96	12	1.16	0.83	1.46	1.30	1.17	44	1.24	0.88	1.43	1.21	1.21
91-96	115	1.06	1.11	1.16	1.10	1.02	215	1.11	1.04	1.20	1.09	1.12
All	238	1.39	1.05	1.42	1.25	1.08	486	1.07	1.01	1.15	1.08	1.08

[1] PG: Total factor productivity growth; TG: Technological growth; EG: Efficiency growth; PEG: Pure efficiency growth; SEG: Scale efficiency growth.

It should be noted that although fluctuating in between, the old bank TE reaches its peak at the end of maturity period. It appears that most of the decline in TE of old banks can be attributed to scale problems, as their SE demonstrates lower performance than their PTE over time.Table 3 displays the means of productivity growth measure (PG) and its subcomponents over time. These measures take into account the changes in the production frontier by time. It appears that on average, productivity grew stunningly for new banks in the preparation period, while it literally stagnated for old banks. However, in the development and maturity periods, both forms of banks recorded marked productivity growth on average: 23% and 6% for new banks, 7% and 11% for old banks, respectively. The superiority of old banks to new banks in the 1990s can be attributed to the increased business risk during this period due to macroeconomic instabilities, resulting in soaring inflation and concentration of deposits in very short maturities. In a risky environment, bank customers tend to switch to larger and older banks from small, inexperienced new banks.

Productivity growth (PG) is 39% versus 7%; technological growth (TG) is 5% versus 1%; efficiency growth (EG) is 42% versus 15%, per year between 1981 and 1996 for new and old banks, respectively. It appears that most of the productivity growth in both forms of banks originates from improvements in efficiency rather than technology. Over the same period for both groups, respectively, average pure efficiency growth (PEG) is 25% versus 8% and scale efficiency growth (SEG) 8% versus 8%. It appears that learning better management practices instead of improving scales is the dominant source of efficiency growth in new Turkish banks. This result is also consistent with the phenomenon referred to as technology experience effect by DeYoung (2001). The new banks with innovative business plans transformed their experience using a new and non-standard technology such as new management techniques into improved financial performance. If only maturity effect or general banking experience was operative, then financial performance at new banks would improve over time at the same rate as old banks, preserving any pre-existing performance gap.

The above assessments imply that the efficiency and productivity differences between new and old banks probably depend on some characteristics other than bank age. When we made horizontal (cross-sectional) or vertical (time-series) comparison between the performance of new and old banks earlier, we have not assessed whether these differences are significant in a statistical sense. In a multivariate setting, in this section, we test the significance of performance difference between new and old banks after controlling for some important bank factors.

Table 4 shows the results of the Generalized Least Square (GLS) multivariate regressions for the efficiency scores TE, PTE and SE. In contrast to the ordinary least square regressions (OLS), the GLS regressions take into account heterogeneities of sample units in size (Isik and Hassan, 2002). We first look at the impact of a number of independent variables on the performance of the pooled sample banks, which include all new and old banks. The number of total observations in TE, PTE and SE models in the pooled sample is 794, 790 and 777, respectively. In order to control for possible outliers, we ran preliminary regressions with the same set of independent variables discussed below, calculated standard errors, and then excluded those observations whose standard errors were 3 standard deviations away from the mean in the secondary regressions. This treatment resulted in variations in the number of observations in each model. For the model coefficients, *, **, and *** indicate statistical significance at 10, 5, and 1% levels, respectively.

Table 4. Multivariate GLS regressions of technical efficiency indexes[1]

	TE	PTE	SE
Constant	0.601***	0.521***	1.211***
DENOVO	0.138***	0.125***	0.013
PER86-90	0.012	0.062***	-0.107***
PER91-96	0.051**	0.081***	-0.076***
STATE	0.091***	0.047**	0.062***
FOREIGN	0.016	0.037*	-0.012
SIZE	-0.003	0.029***	-0.049***
Model			
#	794	790	777
R^2	0.081	0.088	0.274
DW	1.765	1.953	1.582

[1] *Significance at 10% confidence level; **Significance at 5% confidence level; ***Significance at 1% confidence level. TE: Technical efficiency; PTE: Pure technical efficiency; SE: Scale efficiency.

To be parsimonious in our model, we chose the following four factors as control variables, among other external or internal factors, which can play an independent and important role in determining bank performance: 1) changes in the marketplace and regulatory conditions, 2) bank ownership, 3) bank origin, and 4) bank size. We use three dummy variables to account for the changes in the business environment: PER1981-85, for the preparation period of liberalization (excluded from the regressions as the base case), PER1986-90, for the development period of liberalization, and PER1991-96, for the maturity period of liberalization.[54] Because of agency conflicts and differences in operational goals, state banks can demonstrate different performance than private banks (Altunbas et al., 2001; Isik and Hassan, 2003a,b; Isik and Uysal, 2009). In order to control for bank ownership, we formed the STATE dummy variable, which takes a value of 1 for publicly owned banks and 0 for privately owned banks. Banks of different origins may also display variations in performance because they may be coming from more advanced markets and may be equipped with better technology and management. To control for bank nationality, we use the FOREIGN dummy, which takes a value of 1 for foreign owned banks and 0 for domestic banks. In addition, bank size can also be a source of variation in bank performance due to economies of scale and reputation of large banks, among other things. We measure size by the log of total assets (SIZE). Variations especially in productivity growth and its subcomponents may be driven by differences in size, because new banks start relatively from a low base as compared to large old banks.

Table 4 results indicate that the coefficient of DENOVO dummy is positive in our multivariate model. With respect to old banks, new banks record about 14% more TE and about 13% more PTE, which are both statistically significant at the 1% level. In terms of scale efficiency (SE), new and old banks do not reveal any significant performance difference, although the relationship is also positive. These results overall indicate that new banks dominate old banks, especially in terms of managerial efficiency, after controlling for a variety of other bank factors.

As liberalization accelerates in the development and maturity phases, the Turkish banking industry experiences better efficiency performance on average. The average TE between 1991 and 1996 is significantly larger than between the 1981-1985 period at the 5% level. Even, the PTE performance looks much brighter over time. With respect to the basis period 1981-85, the average PTE is greater by 6.2% in the development period (1986-90) and by 8.1% in the maturity period (1991-96). These differences over time are also statistically significant at the 1% level. However, the SE results suggest that scale inefficiency has been significantly exacerbated in the deregulated environment. Altogether, the above results indicate that inter-temporal managerial performance for an average Turkish bank was impressive but has slowed down considerably due to scale inefficiencies.

We have two ownership variables, one for public ownership (STATE) and one for foreign ownership (FOREIGN). The coefficients of STATE dummy in the pooled and old banks regressions are all significant at the 1% level, indicating that publicly owned banks strongly outperform privately held banks in terms of efficiency. This result prevails whether new private entries from domestic and foreign markets are included or excluded in the regressions. On average, in the pooled sample, TE is greater by 9.1%, PTE by 4.7%, SE by

---

[54] In order to maintain sufficient degrees of freedom, instead of constructing a dummy for each year, we divided the whole period into three main segments.

6.2 % for state banks than private banks, when other factors are controlled. Although these results support the findings of Bhattacharya et al. (1997) for the Indian banks, Altunbas et al. (2001) for the German banks and Isik and Hassan (2003c) for the Turkish banks, it is contrary to conventional view held among the public and politicians. Public enterprises are often blamed for over-employment and inefficient operations, which is the premise of privatization programs implemented in many countries. However, empirical results indicate that state banks are at least as efficient as private banks. Banking largely depends on the credibility and trust of the public, as these institutions are one of the most leveraged firms. In contrast to private banks, state banks enjoy implicit or explicit guarantees from government against failure and financial distress. Thus, state banks are expected to be less susceptible to economic shocks, which have become part of the Turkish financial scene in recent years. Financial strength and reputation of state banks attract more funds and customers to these large institutions. Moreover, because of their social and political goals, state banks also generate relatively more loans and services, expanding their outputs and enhancing their efficiency.

As the coefficient of FOREIGN dummy variable in the pooled regression indicates, foreign banks reveal superiority over domestic banks in terms of PTE. On the other hand, both forms of banks literally demonstrate similar performance in terms of TE and SE. The coefficient of SIZE variable suggests that larger banks are significantly superior to smaller banks in PTE and significantly inferior to them in SE. These results support policies against consolidation in Turkish banking, as there are no significant economies of scale opportunities from extending bank scales, especially for old, large banks.

Table 5 presents the GLS regressions results for the productivity growth scores and its components for the pooled sample. Among other interesting results, it is apparent that DENOVO dummy is significantly related to technological growth (TG) score, indicating that technological progress was faster and larger in new banks than in old banks. This provides an empirical evidence for the contributions of new banks to enhancing the banking technology in a newly opening Turkish market.

Table 5. Multivariate GLS regressions of total factor productivity change indexes[1]

	PG	TG	EG	PEG	SEG
Constant	1.078[***]	0.986[***]	1.078[***]	1.285[***]	0.820[***]
DENOVO	0.033	0.052[*]	-0.046	-0.111[**]	0.020
PER8690	0.057	-0.087[***]	0.130[**]	0.037	0.101[***]
PER9196	-0.006	-0.021	0.048	-0.012	0.066[**]
STATE	-0.028	0.004	-0.069[*]	-0.030	-0.020
FOREIGN	0.026	0.001	0.012	-0.002	0.003
SIZE	-0.007	0.006	0.000	-0.030[***]	0.025[**]
Model					
#	718	714	716	717	717
R^2	0.012	0.013	0.011	0.021	0.035
DW	1.96	1.330	1.701	1.871	1.520

[1]. [*]Significance at 10% confidence level. [**]Significance at 5% confidence level. [***]Significance at 1% confidence level. PG: Total factor productivity growth; TG: Technological growth; EG: Efficiency growth; PEG: Pure efficiency growth; SEG: Scale efficiency growth.

In addition, efficiency seems to have grown faster in the new liberal environment, mainly due to the notable improvement in the performance of old banks. It may be that liberalization and new entries provided some sort of market discipline on old banks, which had to ration their input usage and expand their output production. There appears to be no significant difference between different ownership types, as state and foreign banks do not reveal any superiority over private banks in terms of productivity and efficiency growth. As expected, productivity and efficiency growth scores (PG and EG) manifest significant negative relation with bank size. With relatively large size in the later years, it naturally becomes more challenging for banks to deliver the same high performance.

CONCLUSION

With a relatively small number of banks and high concentration, the Turkish banking market bears the typical characteristics of an oligopolistic market (Denizer, 1997; Akcaoglu, 1998; Isik and Hassan, 2002). In industries with a small number of players, new entrants face direct retaliation by incumbent firms. Retaliation strategies by old banks may take various forms such as capacity expansion, product proliferation, and long-term contracts (Fraser and Rose, 1972; McCall and Peterson, 1977; DeYoung, 2003a,b). Hence, new banks may need a number of years to cope with such predatory assaults from incumbent banks and to become efficient by fully utilizing economies of scale opportunities from an expansion in production levels.

Financial deregulations and liberalizations are usually associated with market entry. About half of the Turkish banks have entered the system in the deregulatory era of the 1980s. This chapter analyzes the efficiency and productivity levels of new banks vis-à-vis those of old banks . We utilize a non-stochastic production frontier approach to assess the productive performance of new banks that were chartered in Turkey in the post-deregulation period (1981-1996). Selecting 1981 as the base year, this chapter provides insight into new bank performance during a deregulated environment. Employing the generalized least regression (GLS) format, we also test the significance of the estimated performance differential between new and old banks after controlling for a number of other independent factors, such as bank size, ownership, origin, and changes in the regulatory and economic environment. Our examination also seeks to uncover scale issues of new banks to determine whether there are significant economies of scale opportunities for new banks from increasing production levels.

Over the sixteen years under study, new banks demonstrated 76% average managerial efficiency (TE), while older banks registered 63%. Managerial performance in new banks was even stronger after excluding scale effects. After controlling for scale related performance, we found that pure managerial efficiency (PTE) averaged 85% for new banks and 79% for old banks. The average scale efficiency (SE) in ten year old or younger new banks was 88% as compared to 81% in old banks. These results suggest that technical inefficiency in both forms of banks result mainly from operating off the efficient frontier (resource management problems) rather than operating away from the optimum scale (production problems). When we tested the significance of the performance differential in a multiple regression setting, we found that differences in managerial efficiencies (TE and PTE) of new and old banks are also statistically strong at the 1% confidence level.

In the next stage, by allowing shifts in the production frontier over time to reflect the changes in the regulatory and economic environment, we calculated the pace of growth in the efficiency and productivity of new and old banks. We found that between 1981 and 1996, productivity (39% versus 7%), technology (5% versus 1%) and efficiency (42% versus 15%) grew faster on average in new banks than in old banks. Scale efficiency improved equally in both forms of banks over the study period, averaging 8% per year. It is evident that the main source of productivity growth in both new and old banks is increased proximity of inefficient banks to the frontier (efficiency growth) rather than outward expansion of the production frontier by leading banks (technological growth). Furthermore, the lion portion of the productivity growth in new banks appears to have occurred in the first five years of their life. The significant negative coefficient of bank size along with the new bank dummy in regressions suggests that new banks demonstrated most of their productivity and efficiency growth when they were small banks. Apparently, the pace of learning is faster for new banks, somewhat supporting the *learning by doing hypothesis* in economics.

Not hampered by a legacy of inefficiency from the past, new banks could operate nearer the efficiency frontier (Canhoto and Dermine, 2003). Most of the old banks in Turkey come from the pre-liberalization period, when they were greatly protected behind thick entry barriers and provided guaranteed earnings with regulated interest rates on deposits. Thus, when liberalization was launched at full speed in the 1980s, they were caught unguarded as a lot of things from interest rate risk to exchange rate risk, from inflation risk to portfolio risk had to be managed. Although more experienced with respect to new banks, old banks' accumulation of knowledge did not mean a lot in a totally new environment. New banks, especially foreign ones, were better equipped with technology and professional personnel. Most of these banks, with strong support from parent companies and handsome compensation packages, hired very successful and professional managers, mostly transferred from leading banks in the country or overseas. Thus, inexperience of new banks was mostly eliminated with strong management and contacts of the owners.

Lack of price competition in the pre-liberalization period had resulted in a mania among old banks to establish large branch networks. When interest rates were liberalized in the 1980s, these excess capacities proved unprofitable and inefficient, which started a downsizing spree among old banks. However, new banks focusing on profitable market niches provided their services mainly from a single outlet or limited branch offices. This business orientation may have resulted in more bank outputs per employee and per dollar invested in capital for new banks. Finally, a country with limited savings and capital, rapidly growing economy, and large government budget deficits, creates sufficient demand and profit opportunities for all types of banks, new or old, unless they become greedy and take excessive risks, as demonstrated in the recent financial crises of Turkey.

ACKNOWLEDGEMENT AND DISCLAIMER

The authors would like to acknowledge insightful comments from M. Kabir Hassan, Iftekhar Hasan, Oscar Varela, Osman Kilic, Dogan Uysal, Savas Alpay, Ali F. Darrat, Larissa Kyj and D.H. Bao. Also special thanks go to the graduate assistants Kristina Boyd and Al-Qumar Atkins for their editorial help. However, all errors are our mere responsibility. The findings, interpretations and conclusions expressed in this chapter are entirely those of the authors and do not necessarily represent the views of the Central Bank of the Republic of Turkey (CBRT) or its staff.

REFERENCES

Aly, H.Y., Grabowski, R., Pasurka, C. and Rangan, N., 1990. Technical, scale, and allocative efficiencies in U.S. banking: An empirical investigation. *Review of Economics and Statistics* 72, 211-218.

Akcaoglu, E., 1998. Financial innovation in Turkish banking, Capital Markets Board of Turkey, Publication Number 127, Ankara, Turkey.

Altunbas, Y., L. Evans and P. Molyneux, 2001. Bank ownership and efficiency, *Journal of Money, Credit and Banking* 33, 926-954.

Arshadi, N. and Lawrence, E., 1987. An empirical investigation of new bank performance. *Journal of Banking and Finance* 11. 33-48.

Atiyas, I., and Ersel, H., 1994. The impact of financial reform: Turkish experience, in Caprio, G., Atiyas, I., and Hanson, J. (Eds.) Financial Reform: *Theory and Experience,* Cambridge University Press, UK.

Barr, R., L. Seiford and T. Siems (1994), Forecasting Bank Failure: *A Non-Parametric Approach, Recherches Economiques de Louvain*, Vol. 60, pp. 411-29.

Berg, S.A., Forsund, F., Jansen, E., 1991. Technical efficiency of Norwegian banks: A nonparametric approach to efficiency measurement. *Journal of Productivity Analysis* 2, 127–142.

Berger A. N. and Humphrey, D.B., 1997. Efficiency of financial institutions: International survey and directions for future research. *European Journal of Operational Research* 98, 175-212.

Berger, A.N., Mester, L.J., 1997. Inside the black box: What explains differences in the efficiencies of financial institutions? *Journal of Banking and Finance* 21, 895-947.

Bhattacharya, A., C.A.K. Lovell and P. Sahay (1997), The Impact of Liberalization on the Productive Efficiency of Indian Commercial Banks, *European Journal of Operational Research*, Vol. 98, pp. 332-345.

Brislin, P. and Santomero, A. M., 1991. De novo banking in the third district. *Federal Reserve Bank of Philadelphia Business Review*, January-February, 3-12.

Canhoto, A. and Dermine, Jean, 2003. A note on banking efficiency in Portugal: New vs. old banks. *Journal of Banking and Finance* 27, 2087-98.

Denizer, C., November 1997. The effects of financial liberalization and new bank entry on market structure and competition in Turkey. World Bank Development Research Group, working paper no.: 1839.

DeYoung, R., and Hasan, I., 1998. The performance of de nova commercial banks: A profit efficiency approach. *Journal of Banking and Finance* 22, 565-87.

DeYoung, R., 2001. Learning-by-doing, scale efficiencies, and financial performance at internet-only banks, FRB Chicago Working Paper No. 2001-06.

DeYoung, R., 2003a. The failure of new entrants in commercial banking markets: A split-population duration analysis, *Review of Financial Economics* 12, 7-33.

DeYoung, R. 2003b. De novo bank exit, Journal of Money, Credit and Banking 35, 711-728.

Evanoff, D.D. and Israilevich, P.R., 1991, 'Product efficiency in banking', Federal Reserve Bank of Chicago Economic Perspectives, 15(1), pp. 11-32.

Färe, R., Grosskopf, S., Norris, M., and Zhang, Z., March 1994. Productivity growth, technical progress, and efficiency change in industrialized countries. *The American Economic Review*, vol.84, no.1, 66-83.

Fraser, D.R., and Rose, P.S., 1972, Bank entry and bank performance. *The Journal of Finance,* vol. 27, no. 1, 65-78.

Geroski, P.A., 1995. What do we know about entry? International Journal of Industrial Organization 13, 421-440.

Hunter, W.C., and Srinivasan, A., 1990. Determinants of de novo bank performance, Federal Reserve Bank of Atlanta Economic Review, 14-25.

Isik, I., 2007. Bank ownership and productivity developments: Evidence from Turkey, *Studies in Economics and Finance* 24, 115-139.

Isik, I. and Hassan, M.K., 2002. Technical, scale and allocative efficiencies of Turkish banking industry, *Journal of Banking and Finance* 26, 719-766.

_____, 2003a. Financial disruption and bank productivity: The 1994 experience of Turkish banks, *Quarterly Review of Economics and Finance* 43, 291-320.

_____, 2003b. Financial deregulation total factor productivity change: An empirical study of Turkish commercial banks, *Journal of Banking and Finance* 27, 1455-1485.

_____, 2003c. Efficiency, ownership and market structure, corporate control and governance in the Turkish banking industry. *Journal of Business*, Finance and Accounting 30, no.9-10:1363-1421.

Isik, I. and Uysal, H., 2009. Bank efficiency and failure: Evidence from Turkey. Working paper. University of Pensylvania, Department of Economics, Philadelphia, PA, USA.

McCall, A.S. and Peterson, M.O., 1977. The impact of de novo commercial bank entry, *Journal of Finance* 32, 1587-1604.

Mester, L.J., 1996. A study of bank efficiency taking into account risk-preferences. *Journal of Banking and Finance* 20, 1025-1045.

Mukherjee, K., Ray, S. C., and Miller, S. M., 2001. Productivity growth in large US commercial banks: The initial post-deregulation experience. *Journal of Banking and Finance* 25, 913-39.

Rose, P.S., July-August 1977. Competition and the new banks. The Canadian Banker and ICB Review 84, 61-66.

Selby, E., Spring 1981. The role of director deposits in new bank growth, *Journal of Bank Research*, 60-61.

Shephard, R.W., 1970. The theory of cost and production functions. Princeton: Princeton University press.

Wheelock, D.C. and Wilson, P.W., 1999. Technical progress, inefficiency, and productivity change in U.S. banking, 1984-1993. Journal of Money, Credit, and Banking 31-2, 212-234.

Yulek, M.A., 1998. Financial liberalization and the real economy: The Turkish experience. Capital Markets Board of Turkey, Publication Number 110, Ankara, Turkey.

In: Regulation and Competition in the Turkish Banking... ISBN: 978-1-61324-990-1
Editors: Tamer Çetin and Fuat Oğuz © 2012 Nova Science Publishers, Inc.

Chapter 7

DEPOSIT INSURANCE AND BANK RESOLUTION IN TURKEY REGULATION AND EXPERIENCE

Ridvan Cabukel and Sanem Frisch***

Savings Deposit Insurance Fund,
Turkey

ABSTRACT

An examination of various financial crises experienced in different parts of the world shows that, among the measures taken in terms of post-crisis restructuring, establishing new deposit insurance schemes and empowering existing ones play a major part in maintaining confidence and stability in financial systems. For example, the financial crisis of the 1930s in the US was the catalyst that led to the establishment of Federal Deposit Insurance Corporation (FDIC), and the savings and loan crisis of 1980s led to increased authority vested in the FDIC to resolve the assets of failed institutions through the Resolution and Trust Corporation (RTC). We observe similar developments in countries including Japan, Korea and Russia after the Asian crisis of 1998. The recent global economic crisis triggered international organizations including the International Association of Deposit Insurers (IADI), the Bank for International Settlements (BIS) and the International Monetary Fund (IMF) to work collaboratively and set internationally accepted best practices for deposit insurance and bank resolution regimes. In Turkey, the Savings Deposit Insurance Fund (SDIF) acquired new mandates such as receivership after the economic crisis of 1994 and became an independent agency with additional tools including the ones for the recovery of bank assets after the banking crisis of 2001. This chapter will provide information about the SDIF's deposit insurance and resolution practices and the legal grounds associated with it.

---

* lrcabukel@gmail.com.

** The views expressed in this chapter are those of the authors and do not necessarily represent the views of, and should not be attributed to the SDIF.

INTRODUCTION

Ideally, Deposit Insurance Systems, one of the major players in the Financial Safety Net (FSN), protect depositors and help maintain financial stability by taking proactive measures based on explicit prudential policies. It is the effectiveness of such policies that instills trust in the financial system, minimizes the risk of failure and dampens the systemic burden if failures occur.

However, deposit insurance systems have historically been predominately implicit, and adoption and design of explicit systems have resulted from economic and/or political pressure (Demirgüç-Kunt, Kane and Laeven, 2006, p. 1). In most cases, financial crises have compelled government authorities to stabilize their financial systems by saving distressed financial institutions and/or paying depositors' claims at significant expense to taxpayers. During these periods, new governmental institutions are often established to apply deposit insurance policies and take part in the resolution activities of distressed financial institutions.

The first developments in the area of deposit insurance started in the U.S. after the great depression. The financial breakdown and bank failures that occurred between 1929 and 1934 pushed the U.S. government to create the Federal Deposit Insurance Corporation (FDIC) in order to increase the stability of the financial system and raise confidence in the public (FDIC, 1998, p. 20-32). Later, as the market experienced new challenges, the corporation's roles and responsibilities were expanded. The post Second World War period brought expanded powers regarding the handling of failing banks (FDIC, 1998, p. 36, 37) and then the Savings and Loan Crisis brought various regulations that increased the corporation's effectiveness in the late 1980s, including increased flexibility to increase premium rates and responsibility for the new Savings Association Insurance Fund (FDIC, 1998, 51). These developments enhanced the internal systems and processes at the FDIC and made it a role model for other countries.

Similarly, other countries expanded the mandates of their deposit insurance authorities after financial crises have occurred. For example, South Korea's deposit insurance fund (KDIC) assumed the role of providing financial support for the troubled financial institutions after experiencing the challenges of the Asian crisis (Jeon, 2009, p. 123).

In the European Union, Directive 1994/19/EC[55] formed the minimum requirements to establish mechanisms to protect small depositors and Directive 2001/24/EC[56] set the framework for winding-up procedures for cross border bank branches in European countries. However, after the recent global financial crisis, the current regulatory framework has proven insufficient to maintain financial stability in European countries. In this context, the European Commission started discussing revisions to the structure of deposit insurance.[57] Moreover, the European Commission and the European Forum of Deposit Insurers (EFDI) have been increasing their policy research efforts with the aim of enhancing the stability of the financial environment (www.efdi.net).

With regard to global efforts, in June 2009, the International Association of Deposit Insurers (IADI) and the Basel Committee on Banking Supervision (BCBS) issued a report

---

[55] For more information, see Directive 1994/19/EC on Deposit Insurance Schemes

[56] For more information, see Directive 2001/24/EC on the Reorganisation and Winding up of Credit Institutions

[57] For more information, see EC's Consultation Document: Review of Directive 94/19/EC on Deposit-Guarantee Schemes (DGS), 2009.

detailing methods to increase resilience in the global financial system entitled "The Core Principles for Effective Deposit Insurance Systems", which was welcomed by the Financial Stability Board (FSB).[58] Then, in December 2010, together with the IMF, the World Bank, the European Commission and EFDI, they developed an assessment methodology to quantify compliance with the core principles laid out in said report. Also, FSB requested that the IADI and the IMF conduct research on extraordinary measures taken regarding deposit insurance in different jurisdictions, and thus the two organizations, with the assistance of EFDI, conducted research to identify jurisdictions that have increased deposit insurance coverage or adopted full depositor/full creditor guarantees after the beginning of the global financial crises. The research showed that 46 jurisdictions adopted some form of enhanced depositor protection (FSB, 2009, p. 1).

In Turkey, the first regulations to protect the depositors and give them priority rights in case of liquidation were enacted in 1933. However, the deposit insurance fund - with the name Savings Deposit Insurance Fund of Turkey (SDIF) - was formed in 1983 as a pay-box[59] system under the umbrella of the Central Bank of Turkey (CBT). Later on, after three banks went bankrupt during the 1994 economic crisis, the SDIF gained the rights to strengthen and restructure the financial structure of the banks when necessary, besides insuring savings deposits. But, as problems in the banking sector continued, in 1999, governance of the SDIF was transferred to the Banking Regulation and Supervision Agency (BRSA) in order for the resolution processes to be executed more effectively. Utilizing a shared Board and staff at the SDIF and the BRSA helped the country achieve efficiency and overcome the 2001 financial crisis.

On the other hand, the need to facilitate and expedite the successful resolution of non-performing assets gave rise to certain amendments in the Banking Law, and in this context, a new, autonomous SDIF Board was appointed in January 2004. During this period of legislative review and onwards, the SDIF gained additional authority to develop policies regarding deposit insurance.

1. INSTITUTIONAL DEVELOPMENT

The institutional focus of the SDIF has evolved according to the economic climate and the associated legal developments in the country. Before 1999, the SDIF had limited personnel to collect ex-ante premiums and perform related operational work. After the enactment of the 1999 Banking Law, the BRSA and the newly hired SDIF personnel dealt with taking-over failed bank shares, purchase and assumption (P&A) applications, deposit sales, mergers, taking care of non-performing assets, inter alia. During this period - and especially after the 2001 crisis - the functions and strategic priorities of the SDIF have evolved to be more proactive, and thus, to apply a risk based approach started to have critical value. Moreover, the transfer of the banks and their problem assets to a government institution brought accountability and transparency issues to the foreground.

---

[58] For more information, see press release regarding FSB inaugural meeting in Basel, 2009, http://www. Financialstabilityboard.org/press/pr_090627.pdf.

[59] A pay-box system is the simplest form of deposit insurance system where the deposit insurer merely has the power to collect basic information to calculate insurance premiums and reimburse depositors in a timely and efficient manner when required to do so.

1.1. Institutional Capacity

The SDIF has improved its institutional capacity for deposit insurance and bank resolutions over time by changing its organizational structure, developing strategic plans, strengthening its financial condition and enhancing human resources policies.

Currently, the deposit insurance and resolution processes in the SDIF can be analyzed in four main groups. The Insurance and Risk Monitoring Department is responsible for the first group that involves setting the policies regarding deposit insurance and monitoring the member banks in terms of their riskiness. This function works in coordination with the Asset Management Department in the context of early warning and resolution preparations. In the resolution process, bringing the failed banks back into the system by P&A or take-over is performed by the Asset Management Department and the liquidations are done by the Liquidation Department. The recovery process is executed by the collective effort of the Collections Department and the Subsidiaries and Real Estate Department. Finance, Legal Matters, Audit, Strategy and Support Services Departments are involved in all processes. The departments and their functions are shown in Figure 1 below.

The Insurance and Risk Monitoring Department, in the context of its risk monitoring function, follows the developments regarding the general economic environment, banking sector and individual banks from various data sources. Call Reports[60] that are utilized collaboratively by the BRSA and the SDIF constitute the major source in this regard. The reports, which are prepared by using the data in Call Reports, are shared with the Asset Management Department for early warning purposes and evaluated in the Financial Risk Committee[61] for Deposit Insurance Fund (DIF) management purposes. Additionally, bank and industry information is evaluated by the SDIF's Board for corporate risk management purposes.

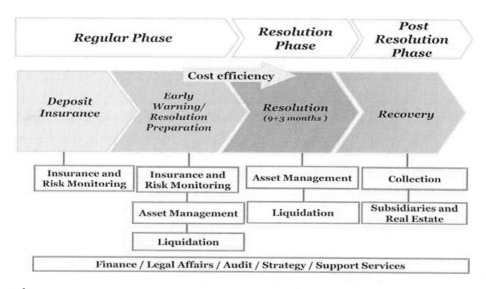

Figure 1.

---

[60] Call Reports are electronic reports that must be filed by all member banks in the system.
[61] SDIF's Financial Risk Commitee consists of supervisors from Insurance and Risk Monitoring, Asset Management and Finance Departments.

The two Strategic Plans prepared for the 2005-2007 and 2008-2010 periods played an important role in the improvement of the SDIF's institutional capacity. Institutional performance indicators and goals were set in these plans, and the major performance indicator was related to the revenue to be derived from the sales of failed bank assets and the repayment of Treasury debt.[62] The goal was to resolve the assets transferred to the SDIF in an efficient manner by selling them for a competitive price.

The major focus of the 2008-2010 Strategic Plan was "promoting financial stability" because of the growing importance of international integration and cross border issues in the banking industry. The strategic goals were given within the contexts of confidence and stability, effective risk management, readiness, efficiency and cooperation. To reach these goals, sub strategic goals were defined for categories like stakeholders, financial matters, operational excellence and learning and growth. Also, a balance score-card system was developed and its results were demonstrated in the SDIF's quarterly and annual reports. Figure 2 below summarizes the 2008-2010 Strategic Plan.

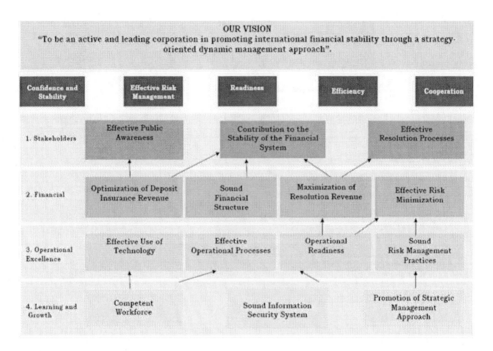

Figure 2.

1.2. Financial Statements

In the post 2001 crisis period, the pay-box deposit insurance system resulted in the SDIF being unprepared for the resolution of many failed banks and their assets, which resulted in being funded by the Treasury on a large scale. The SDIF faced difficulties in developing

---

[62] SDIF's debt to the Treasury arose from the funds it had to obtain in order to pay the deposits of and resolve the banks that failed during the financial turmoils that happened in the country's recent history.

business models and accounting policies for a variety of businesses, which made its financial statements complex to analyze.

During this period, special issue government papers were used to provide liquidity and to takeover shares of failed banks as well as to pay their deposit liabilities. The takeovers necessitated not only the payment of insured deposits but also the claims of various creditors stemming from on and off balance sheet items.

The SDIF sold some banks by using P&A method and performed whole bank sales with loss sharing agreements. The non-performing assets, including the receivables from majority shareholders, were transferred to the SDIF's balance sheet. Table 1 below gives summary balance sheets for 12.31.2007, 12.31.2008 and 12.31.2009.

Table 1.

(Millions of USD)[*]	12.31.2007	12.31.2008	12.31.2009
ASSETS			
Liquid Assets / Securities	3.955	4.428	5.372
Non-Performing Loans	1.752	78	442
Long Term Receivables from Main Activities	11.269	5	5
Assets to be Disposed off	709	563	643
Duty Loss	15.009	313	320
Other Assets	189	67	209
Total Assets	32.883	5.455	6.993
LIABILITIES and EQUITY			
Long Term Loans from the Treasury	45.082	0	0
Interest Expense Accruals and Rediscounts	29.941	0	0
Uncollected Income from Rescheduled Loans	1.586	199	598
Other Liabilities	6.346	2.880	3.089
Total Equity	-50.072	2375	3.305
Total Liabilities and Equity	32.883	5.455	6.993
Off-balance sheet items	171.264	156.830	137.617
Insured deposits	96.373	84.680	92.295

[*] The exchange rates used in conversion are the relevant dates' exchange rates
Source: The SDIF's Annual Reports.

By the end of 2007, the SDIF's asset total was USD 32.8 billion. The duty losses[63] of USD 15 billion that arose from the banks taken over by the SDIF constituted the biggest share of this amount. On the other hand, the SDIF had receivables of USD 11.2 billion because of the sources used for the payment of insured deposits under liquidation. Non-performing loans and assets to be disposed of arose from the receivables, securities and real estate transferred from failed banks to the SDIF.

On the liabilities side, the most outstanding figures were the principal of the Treasury debt, which was USD 45 billion and the interest accrued on this debt, which was USD 33.5

---

[63] Duty Loss is the loss incurred by the SDIF because of the support it provides for its subsidiaries and affiliates. For more information see Principle 270 of the SDIF's Accounting Principles.

billion. However, the principal reflected the nominal values of the government debt instruments that were given to the SDIF; the market values at the origination of the debt were lower. Additionally, the accrued interest was dramatically high since the SDIF defaulted in its payment to the Treasury and was exposed to higher interest rates[64].

The development that led to a major improvement in the SDIF's financial outlook took place in July 2008. A legal arrangement[65] allowed the SDIF to erase its liabilities to the Treasury. However, this arrangement neither terminated the SDIF's rights and powers to pursue and collect receivables stemming from failed banks nor did it require any changes to its business model. It only required the SDIF to repay its debt in line with the rules set by the Treasury. On the other hand, the SDIF may still request additional resources from Treasury for resolution expenses when needed.

The reflection of this development on the SDIF's financial statements has been dramatic. Elimination of the Treasury debt caused the balance sheet to shrink and had a demonstrably positive impact on the bottom line.

1.3. Accountability and Transparency

The SDIF executes its authority with board resolutions and devolution of board power. The functions performed based on this authority are reflected in the activity reports prepared quarterly and annually, and are subject to legislative, executive and judicial audit[66].

The SDIF has the responsibility to inform the Parliament of its annual activities and to answer their written questions. Also, the Government has the power to inspect the SDIF's administrative functions through the auditors of the Prime Ministry. Additionally, although the SDIF Board uses non-judicial power regarding the prosecution of public debt, its decisions can be subject to administrative lawsuits.

The SDIF's financials are also subject to annual audits by Turkish Court of Accounts and external auditors. Turkish Court of Accounts performs its audit process through examination of annual expenses and expenditures. The external audit report is incorporated into the annual activity report. The annual activity report analyzes the activities of the SDIF in the previous year including Board resolutions, regulations and their economic and social implications, and analysis of the SDIF performance.

Related parties may commence public prosecutions or file private lawsuits against the SDIF's Board members and staff. However, Banking Law carries provisions to protect the SDIF employees in connection with their duties. According to this legislation, employees cannot be held personally responsible for such actions, and lawsuits can be filed only against the SDIF. Furthermore, the prosecutions are subject to the permission of the relevant Minister for the Chairman and members of the Board, and the permission of the Chairman for the staff.[67]

---

[64] "Procedures for Collection of Public Receivables" (also known as Law no. 6183) requires applying higher interest rates for defaulted claims. For example, the said rate was around 25% in 2007 whereas the average rate for TL denominated Treasury Bonds was around 18% during the same period.

[65] A temporary article (article 17) incorporated into Law no. 4749 on "Regulating Public Finance and Debt Management"

[66] Legislation regarding SDIF audit takes place in articles 124 & 128 of the Banking Law.

[67] See article 127 of the Banking Law.

2. Deposit Insurance System

The SDIF's policies play a significant role in the Turkish financial system as it protects the rights and interests of the depositors, prevents bank runs - especially during financial turmoil - and helps create an environment conducive to fair competition.

Membership in the Turkish deposit insurance system is mandatory for all deposit and participation banks.[68] As of December 2009, the SDIF has 36 member banks with 9,483 branches and 179.000 employees. Total assets of the member banks have reached USD 550 billion and total deposits are USD 342 billion. Insured deposits are USD 92 billion. The SDIF insures 27 percent of deposits and 92 percent of depositors. Average Capital Adequacy Ratio of member banks is 19 percent with a target ratio of 12 percent.[69]

Four of the 36 member banks are participation banks, which constitute 5% of the industry. They mainly operate according to the Islamic Banking principles that involve profit/loss sharing agreements. After a participation bank failed during the 2001 crisis, an assurance fund was created within the Participation Banks Association of Turkey in order to secure real persons' savings at such banks. By the enactment of the current banking law in 2005, accounts in said banks have also started to be insured by the SDIF. As a result, participation banks have been subject to the same regulations as deposit banks.[70]

2.1. Financial Safety Net

The Turkish FSN is implemented by four government agencies: the CBT, the Treasury, the BRSA and the SDIF. The CBT acts as the lender of last resort and Treasury provides financial resources if needed. While the BRSA develops and implements prudential regulation and risk-focused supervision that govern financial institutions, the SDIF insures depositors and provides for the resolution of failed financial institutions. While on-site examination and off-site monitoring powers are vested in the BRSA, the responsibilities of risk monitoring for premium calculations and resolution preparations, as well as preparing strategic resolution plans are implemented by the SDIF.

Although each player has clearly defined operating authority and discrete responsibilities, the four agencies' actions are synergized to maintain financial stability under a wide range of micro and macro economic conditions. This is demonstrated by a cooperative spirit that is not only codified but also practiced between the agencies, particularly in terms of sharing data and information.[71] Regularly scheduled inter-agency committee meetings[72] are supplemented with ad hoc conversations between various staffs, which creates a collective intelligence on the state of the financial sector and helps insure the synchronization of market intelligence between agencies.

---

[68] See article 63 of the Banking Law.

[69] See interactive monthly bulletins published on BRSA's website www.bddk.org.tr/WebSitesi/English.aspx.

[70] A subcommitee on islamic banking has been established at the IADI and there's ongoing research on principles by which islamic banks are to abide. For additional information, see IADI Research Letter – Update on Islamic Deposit Insurance Issues, 2006, http://www.iadi.org/research_letters/vol1/IADI_ResearchLetter_ Vol1_ Iss3. pdf.

[71] See article 98 of the Banking Law.

[72] See articles 99 and 100 of the Banking Law.

An additional safety net is that agencies by design share a common responsibility of detecting the possibility of systemic risk, which is jointly and severally required by law. To realize this in practice, each entity has the legal authority as well as the moral imperative to demand information pertinent to its area of expertise from another relevant agency or institution. Roles and responsibilities of the Agencies are defined with a Memorandum of Understanding (MOU) based on the Banking Law[73].

Such synergy in the FSN helps early detection and timely intervention. In Turkey, early detection mechanisms are designed through prudential regulation, stress testing, penalty systems, disclosure requirements and call reports. The BRSA requires all banks to disclose audited financial statements with detailed explanations[74] and obtain an external audit report on information technology in line with international practices such as COSO standards regularly.[75] Banks provide daily, weekly and monthly call reports and the BRSA prepares weekly and monthly sector reports from consolidated data.[76]

The BRSA acts proactively by introducing prudent regulations such as setting liquidity requirements and higher levels of capital requirements.[77] The BRSA also performs stress tests with multiple variables for the purposes of supervision and financial stability. These practices instill higher levels of market discipline, transparency and trust in the Turkish banking sector as a whole.

A penalty system is the first line of defense against failure, acting as a deterrent and as a means of timely intervention. The BRSA has legal authority to sanction banks for breaching provisions of regulations such as bookkeeping, record keeping and reporting standards, sufficiency of provisions and loan limits[78]. Generally, banks are highly compliant, but transgressions are detected from time to time, and in 2009, approximately USD 2 million in penalties was collected from various banks.[79] These penalties are a source of income for the deposit insurance fund.[80]

Disclosures are analyzed in conjunction with off-site monitoring and/or on-site examination results, as appropriate. When flags are raised regarding capital adequacy, liquidity compliance, insufficient profitability, etc., the BRSA demands corrective action, including increasing equity capital and liquidation of assets. If a bank fails to implement such actions, the Agency commences rehabilitation measures such as appointing new board members and restricting certain expenses. If compliance remains problematic, the BRSA then imposes restrictive measures that range from temporarily suspending banking activities to forcing the offending bank to merge with a compliant bank.[81]

---

[73] See article 72 of the Banking Law.

[74] For further information see Regulation on the Procedures and Principles for Accounting Practices and Retention of Documents by Banks dated November 1, 2006.

[75] For further information see Regulation on Information Systems Audit to be Made in Banks by Independent Audit Institutions dated January 13, 2010.

[76] See interactive monthly bulletins published on BRSA's website www.bddk.org.tr/WebSitesi/English.aspx.

[77] See articles 45-46 of the Banking Law.

[78] For more details, see articles 146-148 of the Banking Law.

[79] See the SDIF's 2009 annual activitiy report for the revenues of the Fund.

[80] See article 130 of the Banking Law.

[81] For more information about the specific indicators and corrective measures, see articles 67-70 of the Banking Law.

In the unlikely event that a bank remains rouge or if corrective action is insufficient, the BRSA appoints the SDIF as receiver by either revoking the bank's license or transferring the bank to the SDIF. [82]

2.2. Level of Coverage

The SDIF insures deposit accounts of natural persons as long as said deposits occur within Turkey. This protection extends to accounts denominated in foreign currency, gold or other precious metals. [83] The SDIF plans to extend its insurance coverage to deposit accounts of corporations and other legal entities in order to comply with European Union regulations and international best practices.

The insurance coverage is standardized across all banks and its limit is TL 50,000 (approximately USD 33,000 as of December 31, 2009) per person, per bank, including accrued interest.

The SDIF regulation carries exclusions for depositors taking excessive risk and depositors that have a direct relationship with relevant bank(s). Excessive risk taking is measured based on accrued interest, which exceeds the lowest of interest calculated by applying the average interest rate of five largest deposit banks and interest calculated by applying the interest rate announced to the public and declared to the CB by the failed bank. Depositors that have a direct relationship with the relevant bank(s) are defined as relatives of majority shareholders and bank managers of the failed bank(s). [84]

2.3. Risk Based Premium System

Risk based premium systems compel banks to pay premiums according to the risks they cause in the banking system and thus help create a fair financial environment. As stated in international best practices, risk based premium systems should be effective in grouping banks into relevant risk categories, encourage banks to implement stronger risk management practices, meet the funding needs of the deposit insurance system, be structured so that the relevant distinctions are clear and transparent to banks, and be accepted by the FSN players and the banking sector.

The SDIF has been applying a differential premium system since 1992. The first differential premium system had only one risk factor, which was the capital adequacy ratio (CAR). Banks that were able to achieve a CAR of 8% used to pay 25 Bp[85] while the ones that weren't used to pay 26 Bp of their insurable deposits quarterly. After being applied for ten years, in 2003, the system was totally changed in an effort to make it more risk sensitive. It involved a basic premium rate of 12.5 Bp plus add-ons calculated according to five risk

---

[82] See articles 71, 106 & 107 of the Banking Law.

[83] During 1990s, the Turkish Economy was so dollarized that almost 50 percent of deposits were in foreign currency, mainly Dollar, Dutche Mark and Euro. Also, Turkish poeple traditionally invest their savings in gold and thus deposit insurance policy has been extended to cover deposit accounts opened in gold. Currently, 27 percent of deposits are in foreign currency and deposit accounts in gold are less than 1 percent.

[84] For more information see Regulation Regarding Insured Deposits and Participation Funds & Premiums to be Collected by SDIF dated May 5,2008.

[85] 1 Bp = 1/10,000

factors. In 2004, the basic rate was changed to 15 Bp of insured deposits. Table 2 below shows the basics of the said premium system:

Table 2.

RISK FACTORS (%)[86]	Threshold Values	Quarterly Rates (Bp)
THE BASIC PREMIUM RATIO		15
CAR	< 8	5
	≥ 8 and < 12	2
	≥ 12	0
FX Position Ratio	> 20	1
Connected Lending Ratio	> 20	5
NPL Ratio	> 5	1
Free Capital Ratio	≤ 0	1
MAXIMUM ADDITIONAL PREMIUM RATIO		13
MAXIMUM PREMIUM RATIO		28

However, with the enactment of the current Banking Law in October 2005, the authority to determine the insurance premium tariff, premium collection dates, premium collection methods and other aspects were taken from the BRSA Board and handed over to the SDIF Board. The SDIF did not make any changes in the insurance premium tariff within the scope of this regulation and decided to continue implementing the same risk factors and premium rates.

Said premium tariff had gradually lost its efficacy in differentiating premium rates according to risk factors associated with banks. Almost all banks were clustered within a specific interval and paid premiums based on the basic premium rate. As of December 2007, all banks except one had been paying premiums at the basic premium rate. In this respect, the SDIF determined that the premium tariff was not efficient enough in differentiating the banks according to the level of risk associated with them and decided that it would be appropriate to change it.

Within the context of changing the premium tariff, examples in other countries were examined and efforts were exerted towards creating a model compatible with the structure of the Turkish banking sector. In this respect, initially, risk factors were determined and then threshold values and risk weights for these risk factors were analyzed and set. For the implementation of the new tariff, an amendment to the premium regulation was passed in May 2008 with an effective date of January 1, 2009. Same methodology is used for the assessment of premiums for participation banks.

According to the new amendment in the premium regulation, each bank gets a total score between "0" (zero) and "100" (one hundred) calculated according to its score associated with each risk factor mentioned in the "Risk Categories and Score Summaries Table", which is represented by Table 3 below.

---

[86] The definitions of risk factors are provided in Annex I.

Table 3.

RISK FACTORS (%)[87]	Threshold Values	Scores
CAPITAL ADEQUACY		25
Capital Adequacy Ratio		20
Consolidated*	%10-16	I. Group 20
Solo*	%10-16	II. Group 13
Tier 1 Capital	% 8-14	III. Group 0
Asset Capital Multiplier	10-15	5-3-0
ASSET QUALITY		20
Connected Lending Ratio*	%8-15	5-3-0
Non-Performing Assets Ratio*	%1-3	5-3-0
Credit Concentration Ratio	%20-30	5-3-0
Asset Growth Ratio	%15-25	5-3-0
PROFITABILITY		10
Return On Assets	%5-3	5-3-0
Effectiveness Ratio	%50-75	5-3-0
LIQUIDITY		10
Free Capital Ratio*	%80-60	5-3-0
Insured Deposits Ratio	%30-20	5-3-0
OTHER FACTORS		35
Supervisory Rating (CAMELS)	1-2-3-4-5	30-24-16-8-0
Free Float of Bank Shares	%25-10	5-3-0
TOTAL		100

* Factors also used in the previous system.

Based on this total score, the bank falls into one of the four premium categories shown in the "Premium Categories and Premium Rates Table", which is represented by Table 4 below.

Table 4.

Total Score	Premium Category	Premium Rate (per 10.000)
≥ 85	A	11
≥ 70 and < 85	B	13
≥ 50 and < 70	C	15
< 50	D	19

Premium amounts are calculated based on banks' quarterly financial statements. Banks send their declaration forms, which involve their values and scores for the corresponding risk factors, their total scores, their insured deposit amounts and the premium amounts they have to pay in 45 days and make their premium payments within two months following the end of each quarter. A verification process defined at the SDIF crosschecks the declaration forms

---

[87] The definitions of risk factors are provided in Annex II.

with the call reports shared by the SDIF and the BRSA. Also, said declarations are examined by the BRSA in cooperation with banking supervisors.

Insurance premiums are paid in Turkish Lira, Euro and US Dollar with respect to relevant insured deposits. Insurance premiums for the other currencies and precious metals are paid in US Dollars using the official conversion rate of the CBT. The SDIF has collected a premium income of USD 518 million in 2009.[89]

2.4. Deposit Insurance Fund

As of December 31, 2009, the SDIF's Deposit Insurance Fund (DIF), which reflects the funds accumulated as a result of the main activities of the SDIF, totals USD 4.3 billion[90]. The amount of total deposits and insured deposits (including participation funds) at the same date are USD 342.0 billion and USD 92.3 billion respectively. As a result, the "Fund Ratio", defined either as the ratio of the DIF amount to total deposits or as the ratio of the DIF amount to insured deposits, is calculated as 1.34% or 4.98% respectively. There is not a target fund ratio defined in banking regulation. Figure 3 below shows the development of the deposit insurance reserve in years.

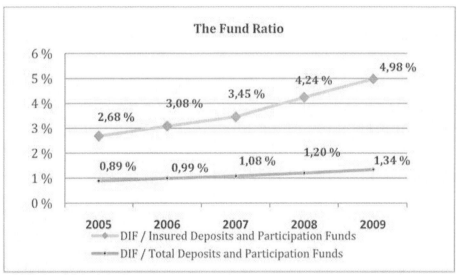

Source: 2009 Annual Activity Report.

Figure 3.

The SDIF has investment and risk management policies for its DIF. As of December 31, 2009, 51 percent of DIF is invested in bank deposits and 49 percent in Treasury Bonds. 30 percent of the investment is in foreign currency, namely Euro and US dollars. The SDIF determines risk limits to manage credit risk, foreign exchange risk, interest rate risk and liquidity risk, and also designs systems and procedures to control its operational risks.

---

[89] For more information on the current premium system, see Regulation Regarding Insured Deposits and Participation Funds & Premiums to be Collected by SDIF dated May 5,2008.
[90] SDIF's current accounting policy doesn't allow accrued interest on Treasury Bonds to be recognized as income. With such adjustment DIF reaches USD 4.6 billion.

In addition to insurance premiums, the SDIF has other income items stated in the Banking Law such as revenues from prescribed assets, revenues from banking system entrance fees, revenues from share transfer fees, and judicial and administrative fines.[91]

Furthermore, the SDIF has means to reach additional resources. It is legally allowed to borrow from the market with the permission of Treasury. Treasury may issue specially structured debt instruments for the SDIF on the basis of jointly agreed terms. Also, the SDIF may ask advance payments for expected premium liabilities of member banks. Advance payments cannot exceed the premium paid in the previous year.[92]

3. RESOLUTION EXPERIENCE

The SDIF gained its receivership and conservatorship mandates after the failure of three banks during the post 1994 crisis period. Since then, it has executed said mandates for 25 banks with USD 43 billion of assets and USD 34 billion of deposits.[93] Size and cost of failures have been remarkably high and created big challenges for the economy as a whole. The situation required new authority to be vested to the SDIF in order to effectuate its resolution functions, which has considerably increased its experience in the relevant field.

This section explains the SDIF's bank resolution process and recovery experience. The major aim of the resolution process is to make the economy regain the values lost during failure as well as to recover the public cost because of bank failures. In terms of recovery, the resources transferred to banks are considered as public claims and thus the SDIF has a special authority to use the Law on the Procedure for the Collection of Public Receivables.[94] Also, Commercial and Economic Integrity (CEI) Sales facilitate the sales of assets and help achieve a competitive environment.

3.1. Bank Resolution Process

There are various types of bank resolution frameworks designed and applied by authorities in different countries. Corporate Insolvency Regimes (CIR) and Special Bank Resolution Regimes (SBRR) constitute the two ends of the continuum. In CIR, countries apply their corporate insolvency framework to banks and deal with insolvent banks as they deal with insolvent non-financial corporations. On the other hand, in SBRR, there are special regimes for cases of bank insolvency. While CIR proceedings take place in courts, SBRR proceedings can be either court based or administrative in nature. However, in jurisdictions where the proceedings are administrative in nature, provision for ex-post judicial review needs to be provided. Most countries chose a hybrid approach between CIR and SBRR (IMF and World Bank, 2009).

Turkey employs a hybrid approach, where execution and bankruptcy law has a majority role in the adjudication of failed banks, with banking law superseding in select aspects of the

---

[91] See Article 130 of the Banking Law.

[92] See Article 131 of the Banking Law.

[93] Exchange rates used in the calculation of assets and deposits are based on the then current exchange rates on the date of each bank's failure.

[94] See Article 132 of the Banking Law.

process. This method preserves certain advantages of judicial reviews while delivering some of the efficiencies that come from administrative proceedings.

The BRSA decides on the fate of an insolvent bank in Turkey. It either decides to revoke the operating permission of a bank or transfers its management and control to the SDIF.[95]

When a bank's operating permission is revoked, the SDIF is appointed as receiver to take necessary actions for the liquidation of the bank[96]. The SDIF first pays the insured deposits and petitions for the bankruptcy of the bank directly on behalf of the insured depositors, and then participates in the bankruptcy estate as privileged creditor and liquidates the bank, with duties and powers of the bankruptcy office, creditors' meeting and bankruptcy authority.

In the case where the BRSA transfers the management and control of a bank to the SDIF, the SDIF has the power to take over the shares of the bank, to make purchase and assumption (P&A) or to ask the BRSA to revoke the license of the bank. In the case where the Fund takes over the shares of the bank, it may restructure the bank or strengthen its financial structure through measures like increasing the capital, purchasing real estates, subsidiaries and other assets or making deposits at the bank. In a P&A situation, the bank's insured deposits as well as its liquid assets or various other assets are transferred to another financial institution. The assets and liabilities that are not transferred are liquidated. The SDIF has a limitation to complete these processes in nine months, which might be extendible by three additional months. On the other hand, the SDIF does not have the authority to establish a bridge bank as stated in international best practices.

Since 1994, the SDIF, as receiver, has paid the insured deposits of five banks and carried out their liquidation processes. One bank went through voluntary liquidation. Among 19 banks that were taken into conservatorship, four were directly sold, six were sold after being merged, one was transferred to a government bank and eight were merged as a "bad bank" after their deposits and some of their assets were sold.[97]

3.2. Recovery Experience

The SDIF has transferred - in historical values - USD 30 billion of resources to the failed banks during the crisis of 2001. As a result of the actions performed to bring said banks back to the financial system, as of December 31, 2009, USD 18.6 billion was recovered and an additional USD 3 billion is expected to be recovered.[98] Such actions include the following:

- Restructuring agreements for receivables from bank majority shareholders
- Sales of non-performing corporate loans
- Discount programs and restructuring agreements for other receivables
- Rescheduling programs for corporate loans

6. The SDIF signs restructuring agreements with majority shareholders for the receivables it assumed from failed banks. As the majority shareholders agree on their

---

[95] See Article 71 of the Banking Law.

[96] Deposit taking institutions are liquidated by SDIF according to the provisions of the Banking Law, whereas Investment and Development Banks are liquidated according to general provisions.

[97] This bank is still under the control of the SDIF and its liquidation and recovery functions are being continued.

[98] See SDIF's 2009 Annual Report.

payables to the SDIF and the repayment schedules, legal proceedings are suspended. The SDIF may accept personal properties of majority shareholders as additional collateral for the restructuring agreement. Restructuring agreements allow majority shareholders to minimize financial stress in their non-banking activities, to repay their debt and to reduce litigation expenses. The facility contributes as well to the continuation of employment and economic activities. With regard to restructuring agreements, four shareholders paid out the full amount of their debt and four shareholders still continue to pay. As of 31.12.2009, the total income from majority shareholders reached USD 6 billion.

7. The SDIF realized two non-performing corporate loan sales. The first sale was a "direct sale" of 281 credit files with a total book value of USD 223 million and generated cash revenue of USD 22.5 million in 2004. The second sale was based on "revenue sharing agreement". It was a sale of 10.812 credit files with a total book value of USD 934 million and 43% revenue sharing, and generated an initial cash payment of USD 161 million in 2005. The SDIF has been the first to perform NPL Sales in Turkey. As a result of said sales, a secondary market for NPLs has been formed and currently there are six asset management companies functioning in this field.

8. The SDIF introduced discount programs for the loans it took over from failed banks in order to encourage and accelerate repayments. Discount programs for corporate loans, consumer loans and credit card receivables helped the SDIF to collect USD 251 million by resolving 42.000 credit files.

9. The SDIF utilized rescheduling programs for corporate loans as well. It settled the amounts of loans with the corresponding creditors and rescheduled the payments based on the debtors' cash flows. Additionally, between 2002 and 2005, The SDIF participated in a special restructuring program for the NPLs of corporate borrowers[99]. The program, called "Istanbul Approach", allowed banks and other financial institutions to restructure the loans due from viable borrowers. Figure 4 below shows the distribution of resolution income as of December 31, 2009.

Distribution of Resolution Income (USD Millions) (As of December 31,2009)	
Recoveries	17.849
Recoveries from Non Performing Loans	14.387
Recoveries from Subsidiaries	679
Recoveries from Real Estate and Other Assets	783
Recoveries from Banks and Liquidated Subsidiaries	2.000
Financial Income	808
TOTAL	18.657

Source: The SDIF's 2009 Annual report.

Figure 4.

---

[99] A new law (no. 4743) was enacted regarding the execution of this program, and under the supervision of the BRSA, a restructuring that involves the whole banking sector has been done. SDIF was involved in this process because of the NPLs that were taken over from the failed banks. For further information see www.tskb.com.

The SDIF has been subject to all sorts of lawsuits that had been filed against failed banks before said banks were taken over as well as new lawsuits filed against it after they were taken over. As of December 31, 2009, 103 attorneys in the SDIF have been following around 80.000 legal files with regard to majority shareholders, defaulted debtors and international arbitration.

On the other hand, the SDIF participates in lawsuits related to failed banks with the goal of repatriating misappropriated funds. In this respect, the SDIF has sought criminal and civil recourse against majority shareholders and managers of failed banks where said parties violated their fiduciary obligations by misappropriating bank resources, engaging in fraudulent accounting practices, and violating banking principles and procedures.

The SDIF also is involved in legal proceedings in international jurisdictions against corporate entities and majority shareholders with standing. As of December 31, 2010, it is collaborating with other government organizations in six international arbitration cases, four of which have been filed against the Republic of Turkey in the International Centre for Settlement of Investment Disputes (ICSID), and two others have been filed in reference to United Nations Commission on International Trade Disputes (UNCITRAL) rules. In addition, there is one lawsuit filed in the European Court of Human Rights (ECHR).

3.3. Special Powers Used in Resolution Process

The SDIF leverages additional powers given by the current Banking Law other than the powers given by the related provisions of the Bankruptcy Law and the Turkish Commercial Code. Such powers enable collection processes to accelerate effective recovery and shorten litigation periods.

Under provisions of the Banking Law, the SDIF is authorized to utilize powers embodied in the Procedure for Collection of Public Receivables (Law no. 6183), to demand payment of receivables and enforce such. These provisions allow the SDIF to seek recourse against majority shareholders and/or managers in cases where fiduciary obligations were violated. For instance, the SDIF's board has the authority to seize assets acquired through misappropriation of a failed bank's resources without a judicial order. This mechanism allows for swifter liquidation when compared to the process provided under general bankruptcy law.

In addition, the SDIF has the right to designate and institute bankruptcy proceedings against the bank whose management and control have been assumed by it in the name of the bank's depositors after paying the insured amounts to the depositors. In the event that a bankruptcy judgment is issued, the SDIF participates in the bankruptcy committee, has priority over all privileged creditors, and liquidates the bank. The SDIF has the duties and powers of the bankruptcy office, creditors' meeting and the bankruptcy administration. In cases where a bankruptcy judgment is not issued for the bank, the voluntary liquidation of the bank is executed through the appointment of liquidators by the SDIF. This process does not require the resolution of the general assembly of the bank and is not subject to all provisions of the Turkish Commercial Code.

The SDIF may file lawsuits against failed banks' senior managers, majority shareholders, auditors and board of directors to recover said banks' losses. First, it may demand repayment of misused bank funds and file a lawsuit against those who fail to do so. Second, it may commence bankruptcy procedures against majority shareholders and auditors when said individuals' actions have a causational role in the bank's failure. Third, it may file lawsuits against failed banks' boards of directors seeking repayment of losses due to their actions in violation of articles of incorporation and the Turkish Commercial Code. In this case, the SDIF Board may take decisions in lieu of the general assembly of the bank.

Lastly, the SDIF may seize shareholder rights (except the right of dividends) and management of those companies of which the failed bank and related parties have operating control. It may also appoint management to those companies on behalf of their general assemblies and may assign liquidators for those companies that do not have any economic value.

3.4. Commercial and Economic Integrity Sales

The SDIF has the power to sell groups of tangible and intangible assets of companies seized in return of public claims for failed banks and its related parties by forming Commercial and Economic Integrities (CEI). [100] This mechanism allows companies to continue their operations without financial stress that might arise from their past liabilities and also from the liabilities of their majority shareholders. Only selected assets of the core business are brought together so that higher market and franchise value can be achieved. This mechanism permits the SDIF to handle the complex businesses and operational structures of conglomerates.

The proceeds of the sales are liquidated under the rules and procedures defined in the Banking Act. They are first used to the pay public debts of companies such as tax debts and social security obligations. Then the SDIF gets its receivables, and the remaining balance is distributed to other creditors.[101]

As of December 31, 2009, the SDIF has realized 38 CEI sales and collected USD 7,450 million. Through CEI sales, companies operating in media, telecom, beverage and other industries have had the opportunity to continue their economic activities with more than 9,000 employees. This method enabled the sale of Turkey's second biggest GSM operator for USD 4.5 billion and the sale of Turkey's biggest media company for USD 1.1 million.

CONCLUSION

Established as a pay-box system 30 years ago, the SDIF's charter has evolved over time to include receivership powers, policy setting authority and risk monitoring responsibility. While it doesn't have the power of supervision, it cooperates with and enters into MOUs with the BRSA and other FSN participants under the authority granted by the Banking Law. Thus, currently, it is considered as more than a pay-box system.

The SDIF played a particularly important role by restructuring the banking system and resolving non-performing assets of failed banks during the 2001 crisis. During this period,

---

[100] In line with the provisions of Law no. 6183 and Banking Law and with the right of the Fund Board to act as full assembly.
[101] See Article 134 of the Banking Law.

banks that had franchise value and could be effective in terms of their credit channels were brought back into the system by P&As and bank sales.

During the institutional development of SDIF, experienced personnel who worked in failed banks and worked effectively during resolutions became its permanent employees. In 2005, provisions similar to those of the BRSA regarding SDIF's administration and personnel were incorporated into the Banking Law. Afterwards, various projects that improved the SDIF's institutional capacity were executed and strategic plans were structured.

After the 2001 crisis, due to non-performing assets and liabilities transferred to the SDIF, its financial statements became quite complex. The cancellation of the debt to the Treasury, which was technically an impossible liability to satisfy, enabled the restructuring of its financial statements.

The SDIF insures real persons' deposits of up to 50,000 TL (approximately USD 30,000), but an amendment to applicable law is required to enable the SDIF to insure the deposits of legal persons. The ultimate aim is the SDIF's compliance with related EU directives within the context of Turkey's program for alignment with the EU. By law, the SDIF is vested with the duty of establishing and executing the risk-based premium system. In this context, in 2008, it evolved the risk-based premium system that was implemented in 1992 into one that has strong theoretical background and is parallel to international practices.

The current risk-based premium system employs credit scoring models, similar to those used in Canada, Malaysia and Taiwan. It takes into account internationally accepted risk indicators as well as risk indicators that are specific to the Turkish Banking sector. It involves threshold values and scores. During its development process, the regulation authority, banks and academicians were consulted and the latest premium model was approved by said parties. By applying this model, the SDIF receives USD 500 million in premium revenue per year. Currently, the DIF has USD 4.3 billion in reserve, which equates to a Fund Ratio of 1.34% when calculated by total deposits and 4.98% when calculated by insured deposits.

The SDIF has increased its experience during the resolution of 25 failed banks and their non-performing assets, and developed policies to increase its effectiveness. The bank resolution process, which is dependent on BRSA's decision, has been legally defined and a special bank resolution regime has been developed to increase the effectiveness of bank resolutions. In addition, the bank liquidation process has been made more efficient by superseding various provisions of the Bankruptcy Law with the Banking Law.

The cost of failed banks to the public has been high, particularly because of the misuse of bank resources by banks' majority shareholders and managers. Receivables due to the misuse of bank resources have been defined as receivables of the Treasury, and the authority (other than Turkish Commercial Code and Bankruptcy law) to collect these receivables has been vested in the SDIF. The SDIF has been given the authority to apply Law no. 6183 to increase the effectiveness in the collection of public receivables.

The SDIF's authority to form Commercial and Economic Integrity Sales is an important tool, as it enables the economy to regain companies that are in financial distress because of the misuse of their parent banks' resources, and allows for a high recovery. This method allows gathering the assets that are required for the continuation of the company's business while keeping its liabilities in receivership. It lets the SDIF provide interested investors with more realistic prices and also mitigates uncertainties related to liabilities.

Going beyond basic compliance with the principles developed by the IADI and BCBS, the SDIF has contributed its practical and functional expertise in risk mitigation to the benefit of the Turkish economy, with policy changes since 2001 having played a particularly significant role in maintaining financial stability in the face of the recent global economic crisis. The agency also contributes to the International community by sharing its experience at IADI conferences and within working groups of the EFDI.

ANNEX I

Definitions for the risk factors are as follows:

CAR (%): The smaller of the two ratios below:

Capital Adequacy Ratio[102] Solo (CAR Solo) (%):

"Equity / (Minimum capital requirement for credit risk, market risk, and operational risk)"

Consolidated Capital Adequacy Ratio (CAR Consolidated) (%):

"(Equity calculated on a consolidated basis) / (Minimum capital requirement for credit risk, market risk and operational risk)"

FX Position Ratio (%):

"Weekly simple arithmetic mean of unconsolidated FX Net Positions (in absolute terms) / Equity"[103]

Connected Lending Ratio (%):

"Loans provided to bank's risk group / Equity"

Non-performing Loans Ratio (%):

"Non-performing loans (net of provisions) / Total loans"

Free Capital Ratio (%):

"(Equity – non-performing loans (net of provisions) - subsidiaries – affiliates – real assets – prepaid expenses and deferred taxes) / Equity"

ANNEX II

Definitions for the risk factors are as follows:

Capital Adequacy Ratio Solo (CAR Solo) (%):

"Equity / (Minimum capital requirement for credit risk, market risk, and operational risk)"

Consolidated Capital Adequacy Ratio (CAR Consolidated) (%):

"(Equity calculated on a consolidated basis) / (Minimum capital requirement for credit risk, market risk and operational risk)"

---

[102] Currently, Basel I standards are applied in Turkey. Additionally, Basic Indicator Approach and Standardized Approach of the Basel II standards are applied in terms of calculating operational risk and the subsequent requirement of capital. For further details, see BRSA's Regulation on Measurement and Evaluation of Capital Adequacy of Banks and Regulation on Equity of Banks dated November 1, 2006.

[103] FX Position Ratio was added to risk factors to restrict banks from holding short FX positions by executing carry trade and taking excessive risks. According to the relevant regulation, the Weekly simple arithmetic mean of the FX net general position (in absolute terms) /Equity standard ratio calculated for business days shall not exceed twenty percent. For more information, see BRSA's Regulation on the Calculation and Implementation of Foreign Currency Net General Position / Equity Standard Ratio by Banks on Consolidated and Non-consolidated Basis dated November 1, 2006.

Tier 1 Capital Adequacy Ratio (Main CAR Solo) (%):
"(Tier 1 capital - Assets to be deducted from capital) / (Minimum capital requirement for credit risk, market risk and operational risk) "
Assets Capital Multiple:
"(Assets + Contingencies + Commitments except derivatives) / Equity"
Connected Lending Ratio (%):
"Loans provided to bank's risk group / Equity"
Non-performing Loans Ratio (%):
"Non-performing loans (net of provisions) / Total loans"
Credit Concentration Ratio (%):
"Total loans launched to 50 biggest customers / Total loans"
Asset Growth Ratio (%):
"($\sum$ (Assets + Contingencies + Commitments except derivatives) / $\sum_t$ (Assets + Contingencies + Commitments except derivatives)) - 1"
Return on Assets (%):
"Net Income / ((Minimum capital requirement for credit risk and market risk) / 2)"
Effectiveness Ratio (%):
"Non-interest bearing expense / (Net interest bearing income + non-interest bearing income)"
Free Capital Ratio (%):
"(Equity – non-performing loans (net of provisions) - subsidiaries – affiliates – real assets – prepaid expenses and deferred taxes) / Equity"
Insured Deposits Ratio (%):
"Insured deposits / Total deposits"
Supervisory Rating (CAMELS):
The CAMELS rating given by the BRSA
Free Float of Bank Shares (%):
"Publicly traded shares / Outstanding shares"

REFERENCES

[1] Demirgüç-Kunt, A., Kane, E. J. and Laeven, L. (2006). Determinants of Deposit Insurance Adoption and Design, *World Bank Policy Research Working Paper, 3849,* p. 1.

[2] FDIC (1998). *A Brief History of Deposit Insurance in the United States.* Washington D.C.: FDIC.

[3] Jeon, B. N. (2009). From the 1997-1998 Asian financial crisis to the 2008-2009 global economic crisis: Lessons from Korea's experience. *East Asia Law Review, Vol. 5,* p. 123.

[4] FSB (2009). Exit from extraordinary financial sector support measures, p. 1.

[5] Annual Report 2008 (2008), *SDIF.* http://www.tmsf.org.tr/index.cfm? fuseaction=public.dsp_menu_contentandmenu_id=61.

[6] Annual Report 2009 (2009), *SDIF.* http:// www. tmsf.org. tr/index.cfm? fuseaction=public.dsp_menu_contentandmenu_id=61.

[7] The SDIF's Quarterly Report, 2009-Q3 (2009) (Turkish). www.tmsf.org.tr.

[8] Banking Law no. 5411 (2005) www.tsmf.org.tr.

[9] AIDI Core Principles for Effective Deposit Insurance Systems (2009). www.iadi.org

[10] Directive 94/19/EC of the European Parliament and of the Council of 30 May 1994 on deposit-guarantee schemes (1994). *Official Journal L 135* , p. 5 – 14.

[11] Directive 2001/24/EC on the Reorganization and Winding up of Credit Institutions (2001). *Official Journal L 125* , p. 5 – 14.

[12] Consultation Document: Review of Directive 94/19/EC on Deposit-Guarantee Schemes (DGS) (2009), *EC Internal Market and Services DG.*

[13] Press Release: Financial Stability Board holds inaugural meeting in Basel, http://www.financialstabilityboard.org/press/pr_090627.pdf.

[14] Procedures for Collection of Public Receivables (Law no. 6183) (1954).

[15] Regulating Public Finance and Debt Management (Law no. 4749) (2008).

[16] IADI Research Letter – Update on Islamic Deposit Insurance Issues, 2006, http://www.iadi.org/research_letters/vol1/IADI_ResearchLetter_Vol1_Iss3.pdf.

[17] Banking Law (Law no. 5411) (2005).

[18] An Overview of the Legal, Institutional and Regulatory Framework for Bank Insolvency (2009), the World Bank and the IMF.

[19] Monthly Interactive Bulletin, *BRSA,* www.bddk.org.tr/WebSitesi/English.aspx.

[20] Regulation on the Procedures and Principles for Accounting Practices and Retention of Documents by Banks (2006), *BRSA.*

[21] Regulation on Information Systems Audit to be Made in Banks by Independent Audit Institutions (2010), *BRSA.*

[22] Regulation Regarding Insured Deposits and Participation Funds and Premiums to be Collected (2008), *SDIF*

[23] Restructuring of Debts to the Financial Sector and Amendments to be made to some Acts (Law no. 4743)(2002)

[24] Regulation on Measurement and Evaluation of Capital Adequacy of Banks and Regulation on Equity of Banks (2001), *BRSA*

[25] Regulation on Equity of Banks (2006), *BRSA*

[26] Regulation on the Calculation and Implementation of Foreign Currency Net General Position / EquityStandard Ratio by Banks on Consolidated and Non-consolidated Basis (2006), *BRSA*

In: Regulation and Competition in the Turkish Banking...   ISBN: 978-1-61324-990-1
Editors: Tamer Çetin and Fuat Oğuz   © 2012 Nova Science Publishers, Inc.

Chapter 8

INTERACTION BETWEEN PAYMENT SERVICES AND CREDIT SERVICES IN CREDIT CARD MARKETS

G. Gulsun Akin,[1] Ahmet Faruk Aysan,[1] Gultekin Gollu,[2] and Levent Yildiran[1]*

[1]Department of Economics, Bogazici University,
Bebek, Istanbul, Turkey
[2]Department of Economics, University of Wisconsin, U. S.

ABSTRACT

Credit card markets are complicated structures where two different services, payment services and credit services, are provided. The Turkish credit card market has recently undergone two important regulations: one on payment services in November 2005 and the other on credit services in June 2006. As these two service markets have externalities on each other, regulating one may have unintended consequences on the other. In this regard, our chapter aims to shed light on the link between these two service markets by investigating the revenues from each of them: the non-interest and interest revenues. Estimating the interest and non-interest revenues of banks simultaneously in a 3SLS framework, we examine the effects of the regulations on payment services and credit services. Our results indicate that the regulations on payment services had no significant impact on banks' revenues, whereas the regulations on credit services affected the interest and non-interest revenues in opposite directions. Reacting to stifled interest revenues, banks shifted their focus toward non-interest revenues. Looking at the results, we suggest careful consideration of the possible effects on all segments of a credit card market when a regulatory action is planned. Moreover, from the response of revenues to changing prices in these two service markets, we infer that the demand in the Turkish credit card market is inelastic.

---

* e-mail: gulsun.akin@boun.edu.tr.

164 G. Gulsun Akin, Ahmet Faruk Aysan, Gultekin Gollu et al.

Keywords: Credit Cards, Regulation, Credit Services, Payment Services, Three Stage Least Squares (3SLS)

JEL classification: G21, G28, O16

1. INTRODUCTION

Credit card markets, which thrive all around the world, entail quite intricate business arrangements whereby two different services, credit services and payment services, are provided, and at least five different parties are involved, namely cardholders, merchants, issuers, acquirers and network providers. In return for the credit services they provide, issuing banks earn interest revenue from revolving cardholders. From their payment services, on the other hand, banks earn non-interest revenue: they collect annual fees from cardholders, merchant discounts from merchants and interchange fees (IF's) from acquirers.[104] Because of their complex nature, bright growth prospects and high profitability that suggests the existence of market failures, credit card markets have undergone important regulations in numerous countries[105], including Turkey.

Upon the complaints contending that the Interbank Card Center (ICC)[106] illegally fixes IF's and thus leads to high merchant discounts, regulations were imposed on the payment services side. The Turkish Competition Authority brought changes upon the formula used by the ICC to determine IF's in November 2005, linking IF's to banks' funding costs and to the operational costs of the ICC. While IF's were about 2.75% in 2004, this rate fell to 1.75% in November 2005, and gradually declined to 0.91% by the end of 2008.[107] On the credit services side, credit card rates were untenably high before 2006, reaching 130% annual effective rates though inflation and short term interest rates were about 15% in the same period. The Credit Cards Law that was enacted in March 2006 mandated the Central Bank to regulate the credit card market. While the monthly credit card rates were about 7 percent by the end of 2005, the Central Bank imposed a cap of 5.75 percent in June 2006, and gradually lowered that cap to 4.39 percent by the end of 2008. Actually, the Central Bank did not only target the credit card rates. Regulations included many other provisions that would restrict banks' interest revenues, like the minimum amount payable, interest fee calculation method, credit card limits, solicitations, etc.

Interest and non-interest revenues of banks are likely to interact, as regulations imposed on one of these two types of services are likely to implicate the other. For instance, after the regulations on credit card rates in Turkey, banks started to charge annual fees to card holders, and although data is unavailable there is anecdotal evidence that they also increased merchant discounts. Being aware of such interactions, in Akin et.al (2011b), to investigate the effects of the aforementioned regulations on banks' overall competitiveness in the Turkish credit card market, we took account of both their interest and non-interest revenues, and analyzed banks'

---

[104] See Akin et.al (2011b), Evans and Schmalense (1999), (2005), Rochet and Tirole (2002), (2003) and the refrences therein for more on how credit card markets operate.

[105] See, e.g., Akin et al (2010), (2011a), Weiner and Wright(2005), Ausubel (1991), Scholnick et al (2008)

[106] ICC is the local network provider in the Turkish credit card market. It was established in 1990 as a partnership of 13 public and private banks to settle the local credit and debit card transactions and to develop rules and standards for the Turkish card payment system.

[107] For more on IF regulations, see Karayol A.H. (2007).

total revenues in a Panzar-Rosse framework. We found that although banks enjoyed considerable market power in the early 2000's, the credit card rate regulation in 2006 significantly suppressed their power. Moreover, contrary to expectations, total revenues of banks from their credit card operations increased after those regulations. Regarding the latter, we conjectured that the rise in quantity demanded for credit after the reduced interest rates might have increased banks' interest revenues. Alternatively, banks' non-interest revenues might have increased due to the rise in the unregulated prices (annual fees and merchant discounts) of their payment services. The estimations in that chapter did not allow testing these two scenarios.

Our objective in this chapter is twofold. First, we want to provide empirical evidence for the interactions between the two revenue types, showing that regulations on one type of service may affect the revenues from the other type. This is important because the complex structure of credit card markets makes it necessary to consider the effects of a regulation on all aspects of the market if unexpected consequences are to be avoided. To our knowledge, no such study has been conducted for credit card markets. Second, we want to discover the source of the rise in banks' total revenues after the credit card rate regulations. This will not only make our previous results more meaningful and precise, but also shed light on the demand elasticities in payment services and credit services markets.

We estimate banks' interest and non-interest revenues simultaneously in a three stage least squares (3SLS) framework, where interactions are allowed for. Our data consists of quarterly credit card revenues and various other variables of individual banks in the Turkish credit card market between the years 2002 and 2008. We start our period from 2002 in order not to deal with the effects of the 2000-2001 banking crises. The data come from various sources, including the Central Bank of Republic of Turkey, the Banks Association of Turkey, and the Banking Regulation and Supervision Agency. Our results indicate that the regulation on payment services had no significant impact on banks' revenues, whereas the regulations on credit services affected banks' interest and non-interest revenues in opposite directions. In response to falling interest revenues, banks shifted their focus toward non-interest revenues. Also, the analysis of revenues and prices reveals that the demand for credit card services is inelastic.

The chapter is presented in the following order: The next section gives a brief account of the Turkish credit card market. The third section explains the data and methodology used in the analysis. The fourth section presents the results, and the last section concludes.

2. THE TURKISH CREDIT CARD MARKET

Credit cards have been used in Turkey since 1968. However, mostly due to the favorable domestic and international macroeconomics conditions, the market expanded drastically in the last decade. The number of credit cards increased from 13.4 million in 2000 to 43 million in 2008.

The average growth rates of total outstanding balances and the total transaction volume in the 2002-2008 period were 53 and 42 percent, respectively. [108] In Figure 1, banks' interest and

---

[108] For a detailed account of the financial markets and particularly of the credit cards markets in Turkey, see Akin et al. (2009) and (2010), respectively.

non-interest revenues, which followed the same trend and almost quadrupled in this period, show that the fastest growth in the market occurred around years 2004 and 2005.[109] Figure 2, which depicts the growth rates of outstanding credit card balances, supports this observation. In the first half of 2000's, which we can call the expansion period, growth rates are very high, peaking in 2004. Afterwards, however, growth slows down and saturation creeps up.

Interest and non-interest revenues, when normalized by the outstanding credit card balances, can be interpreted as the prices charged by banks for their credit and payment services. A close inspection of these prices in Figure 3 offers interesting insights into banks' strategic behavior. During the expansion period, banks kept their prices for payment services low.

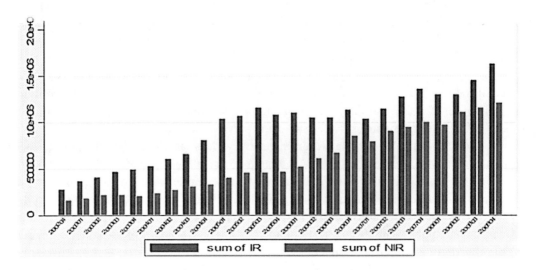

Figure 1. Banks' Interest and Non-Interest Revenues in the Credit Card Market.

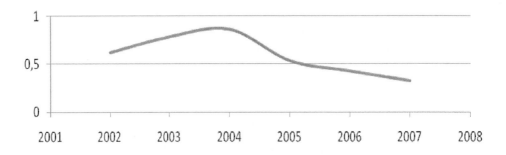

Figure 2. Growth Rates of Outstanding Credit Card Balances.

---

[109] Before 2005, around 65 percent of banks' total revenue came from the interest component. After this period, although the interest component is still more important than the non-interest component, the growth rate of the latter is greater.

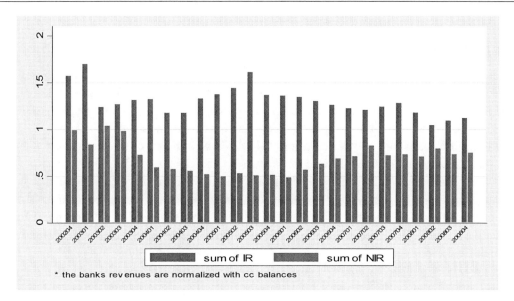

Figure 3. Normalized Interest and Non-Interest Revenues.

Penetration and acquisition were probably the most important concerns for banks in this period. Charging no annual fees and low merchant discounts, banks must have tried to grab market shares as issuers and acquirers. This period is indeed characterized by banks' aggressive marketing strategies and soliciting campaigns. They distributed credit cards on the streets or at universities heedless of prospects' default risks. Given that switching costs are high in credit card markets (Akin et. al 2011a), their strategies may well be justified.

In the second half of 2000's, however, the prices in the payment services are on the rise, while those in the credit services are on the decline. In 2006, when the market had virtually settled, banks were constrained with the credit card rate regulations, and interest revenues were suppressed. As the growth prospects were already low in the nearly saturated market, banks started to increase the unregulated prices of their payment services, so that they could compensate the fall in their interest revenues. Although holding credit cards was normally costless until 2006, all issuers started to collect annual fees from cardholders after 2006. Anecdotal evidence shows that merchant discounts also rose in this period. For instance, one of the leading banks demanded the following merchant discounts from Arçelik retailers for not-on-us transactions: 1.90 % in July 2006, 2% in April 2007 and 2.2 % in October 2007. In a not-on-us transaction, where the acquirer and issuer bank are different, the acquirer pays IF to the issuer. Acquirers normally pass IF's to merchant discounts. As IF's declined in this period, the above rates suggest that merchant discounts considerably rose after 2006.

3. METHODOLOGY AND DATA

The benchmark model employed in this chapter is the following system of equations:

$$\ln(Non\text{-}interest\ revenues)_{it} = \beta_0 + \beta_1 \ln(Interest\ revenues)_{it}$$
$$+ \beta_2\ Interchange\ fee\ regulation\ dummy_t + \beta_3 \ln(Number\ of\ customers)_{it}$$
$$+ \beta_4 Trend_t + \beta_5 Trend\ squared_t + \delta_i + \varepsilon_{it}$$

$$\ln(Interest\ revenues)_{it} = \alpha_0 + \alpha_1\ \ln(Non\text{-}interest\ revenues)_{it}$$
$$+ \alpha_2\ Interest\ rate\ regulation\ dummy_t + \alpha_3\ \ln(Total\ credit\ card\ limits)_{it}$$
$$+ \alpha_4 Trend_t + \alpha_5 Trend\ squared_t + \mu_i + \eta_{it}$$

The method used in this chapter is the three stage least squares method, shortly known as 3SLS. 3SLS method is a combination of two stage least squares (2SLS) and generalized least squares (GLS), used when there is a system of equations in which endogenous variables stand as explanatory variables in other equations. This method consists of three steps. First, using 2SLS, the endogenous variables are estimated. In the next step the estimated structural equations' errors are calculated and using these errors the variance-covariance matrix of disturbance terms in the system is estimated. Lastly, using this estimated matrix GLS is applied to estimate the equation system (Kennedy 1992). This method is used in simultaneous equation systems. It is employed when one or more of the regressors in an equation are thought to be correlated with the error term of any of the equations in the system. This method is preferred given that it is consistent and asymptotically more efficient than 2SLS. As we aim to explore the interaction between the interest and non-interest revenues of banks in the Turkish credit card market, and as these revenue types are possibly the determinants of each other, we prefer to use 3SLS.

The data are collected from the Central Bank of the Republic of Turkey, the Banks Association of Turkey and the Banking Regulation and Supervision Agency. Although there are twenty-two banks in the credit card market, some were eliminated due to missing observations. The data set covers quarterly data of seventeen banks between the last quarters of 2002 and 2008. Moreover, twenty-eight observations were deleted since in those observations banks had very few credit card customers[110][111]. All the nominal values were converted to real values through CPI conversion to get rid of inflationary effects.

The two endogenous variables in the model are *Non-interest revenues* and *Interest revenues*. *Non-interest revenues* are the quarterly deflated non-interest revenues of banks. This item comprises all fee revenues including interchange fees, merchant discounts and annual card fees. *Interest revenues* are the deflated interest revenues of each bank in a given quarter.

As mentioned, instrumental variables are used to correctly estimate the endogenous variables in the model. In choosing the instrumental variables, the aim is to find the ones which are correlated with the instrumented variable but uncorrelated with the other endogenous variable's error term. For each equation, two instruments are used. One variable used to instrument *Non-interest revenues* is *Number of customers*, which is the number of credit card customers of a bank in a given quarter. As the number of customers increases, both the volume of transactions, which should directly affect the amount of merchant discounts and interchange fees obtained from these transactions, and the annual fees collected are expected to increase. This is not a very good instrument since it may be correlated with the error term of the *Interest revenues* equation. For lack of a better one, though, it is used with the idea that *Interest revenues* are actually affected by the number of revolvers and their borrowing amount, which are not necessarily reflected in the number of credit card customers. The other instrument is the *Interchange fee regulation dummy*, a dummy variable

---

[110] The deleted observations had less than 300 customers on average, while the minimum number of customers for the rest of the sample exceeds 30,000.

[111] Including these twenty-eight observations in the estimations does not affect the results significantly.

Interaction between Payment Services and Credit Services ... 169

which takes on the value 1 after the IF regulation (last quarter of 2005), and 0 in the pre-regulation period.

For *Interest revenues* the instrument used is *Total credit card limits*, which is expected to have an immediate effect on the volume of credit card debt and hence interest revenues. The other instrument is the *Interest rate regulation dummy,* which takes on the value 1 for the quarters following the interest rate regulation (third quarter of 2006). The regulation dummies also provide information about the changes in the intercept terms for the regulation period.

In our sample period, during which very favorable macroeconomic conditions prevailed, consumption expenditures, demand for credit, etc., were on the rise all around the globe. *Trend* and *Trend squared* variables are used in order to control for any quadratic effect of such macroeconomic conditions on *Non-interest revenues* and *Interest revenues*. Since we have a cross-sectional time series data set, bank dummy variables are used to capture fixed effects. All the variables used in the estimations except for the dummy variables are in the natural logarithmic form. The descriptive statistics of the variables are given in Table 1 below, and the correlation matrix is presented in Table 2.

4. RESULTS

Table 3 presents the estimation results. They are intriguing as they show that the interaction between the two variables of interest, *Interest revenues* and *Non-interest revenues*, is not symmetrical. Normally, the two revenue types are expected to be highly correlated since both of these bank revenues are highly related with the transaction amount executed by the card holders of the bank. Two major components of banks' non-interest revenues are interchange fees and merchant discounts in the Turkish credit card market, especially up until the interest rate regulation in 2006. Since these two items are collected by banks per transaction, non-interest revenues of banks are expected to increase as the transaction volume increases. Interest incomes are also expected to go up with the transaction volume since the amount of revolving balances is expected to increase with the overall credit card balance. Therefore, both non-interest and interest revenues are expected to move in the same direction. The regression results, however, show that the coefficient of *Interest revenues* in the *Non-interest revenues* equation is negative and significant, whereas the effect of *Non-interest revenues* on *Interest revenues* is positive but not significant.

Table 1. Summary Statistics

	Number of observations	Mean	Standard deviation	Minimum value	Maximum value
Non-interest revenues	274	35,348.19	44,050.87	43.05	222,305.00
Interest revenues	274	57,066.56	65,244.89	0.64	323,827.70
Total credit card limits	274	20,021.91	18,543.18	321.80	74,396.20
Number of customers	274	1,579,804.00	1,479,478.00	31,396.00	6,601,755.00

Note: Non-interest revenues, Interest revenues and Total credit card limits are deflated. Non-interest revenues, Interest Revenues and Total credit card limits are measured in millions of TL.

Table 2. Correlation Coefficients

	Interest revenues	Non-interest revenues	Number of customers
Non-interest revenues	0.6002		
Number of customers	0.7727	0.7639	
Total credit card limits	0.7374	0.6133	0.8669

Note: The variables are in natural logarithmic form. Non-interest revenues, Interest revenues and Total credit card limits are deflated.

The negative effect of *Interest revenues* on *Non-interest revenues* provides evidence for our claim that banks endeavor to increase their non-interest incomes when their interest incomes are reduced.

As banks try to compensate their foregone interest revenues by increasing non-interest revenues, a lower interest income results in a higher non-interest income, making the sign of the coefficient negative. The insignificant coefficient of *Non-interest revenues* in the *Interest revenues* regression indicates that interest incomes are not affected by non- interest incomes in a similar way. Banks' reduced control over their interest revenues after the regulations may be partially responsible for this result.

Table 3. 3SLS Regression Results

	Dependent variable	
	Non-interest revenues	*Interest revenues*
Interest revenues	-0.4564 (-1.83)[*]	
Non-interest revenues		0.3284 (0.83)
Interchange fee regulation dummy	-0.0198 (-0.10)	
Interest rate regulation dummy		-0.6651 (-2.44)[**]
Number of customers	0.6288 (3.61)[***]	
Total credit card limits		0.5704 (3.17)[***]
Trend	0.0884 (1.16)	0.1103 (1.70)[*]
Trend squared	0.0001 (0.03)	-0.0023 (-1.13)
Bank dummies	Included	Included
Constant	5.9796 (2.37)[**]	1.0532 (0.23)
Number of observations	274	

Note: All variables except for dummy variables are in natural logarithmic form. z statistics are in parentheses. [*], [**] and [***] denote significance at 10, 5 and 1 percent, respectively.

In the early periods, banks may have purposely kept non-interest revenue items such as annual card fees and merchant discounts low in order to obtain bigger shares in the rapidly growing market. As these are the prices that the two customer types of the market face directly, curbing them may have been very important in gaining customer bases. In other words, banks may have competed in fees in the pre-regulation period and keep their non-interest incomes low while their interest incomes increased. Though this conjecture about the pre-regulation period is not supported by the estimation, there is one piece of hard evidence from the market: banks did not start charging annual fees until the interest rate regulation in 2006. In the post-regulation period, however, they responded to the reduction in their interest revenues by boosting non-interest revenues. As the market shares were already settled in the saturated market by that time, this was a viable strategy.

The non-dummy instrumental variables in both equations, *Number of customers* and *Total credit card limits*, have significant positive coefficients. Both are consistent with expectations. *Trend* variable signifies the positive effect of macroeconomic conditions on both revenue types. It is significant in the *Interest revenues* equation. Banks issued more credit cards and hence supported higher total limits over time as the market expanded. Even though this is controlled by *Total credit card limits*, *Trend* is still a significant determinant, denoting that in the period covered by the data, people gradually increased their borrowing. In the *Non-interest revenues* variable, on the other hand, *Trend* is only nearly significant. Increasing numbers of credit card customers seem to account for the increase in non-interest incomes over time. *Trend squared* is insignificant in both equations, precluding any quadratic effects.

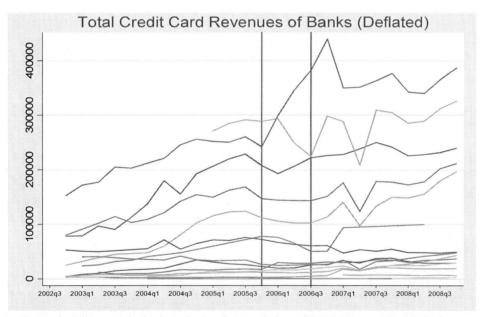

Note: The vertical lines mark the interchange fee regulation of 2005 (quarter 4) and the interest rate regulation of 2006 (quarter 3).

Figure 4. Total Credit Card Revenues of Banks.

The coefficient of the *Interest rate regulation dummy* is significant and negative in the *Interest revenues* regression. This result signifies that the credit card interest rate regulation in 2006 reduced banks' interest incomes in the market, even though these incomes increased in time. Prior research (Akin et.al 2011b) indicates that total credit card revenues of banks mounted after the credit card rate regulation. We proposed two possible explanations for this increase. If the demand for credit card debt was elastic, then the reduced price of borrowing might have escalated the interest income.

Or, banks might have shifted their focus towards unregulated non-interest income sources. The resulting rise in the prices of payment services might have increased the non-interest income, provided that the demand for payment services was inelastic. The regression results show that it is the latter explanation which accounts for the higher credit card revenues of banks after the regulation. These results are supported by the following Figures 4-6, where individual banks' total, interest and non-interest revenues, all deflated by CPI, are depicted. So, we conclude that the demands in both payment services and credit services markets are inelastic.

We also control for bank effects using dummy variables in both sides of the simultaneous equations. These results are not presented in Table 3. Most bank dummy coefficients are not significant in the *Non-interest revenues* regression. The other explanatory variables seem to capture the important variations between banks in explaining non-interest income. On the other hand, it is seen that banks with the highest shares in the credit card market receive higher interest incomes even when we control *Total credit card limits*. An implication of this result may be that the most prominent banks in the credit card market have higher shares of revolving balances.

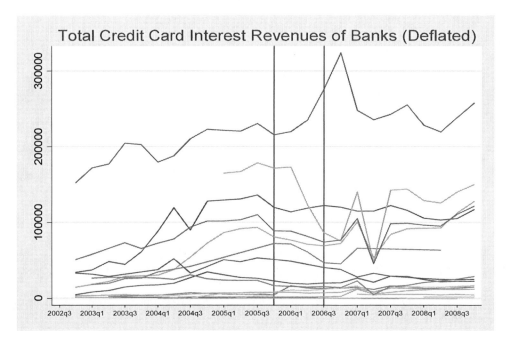

Figure 5. Credit Card Interest Revenues of Banks.

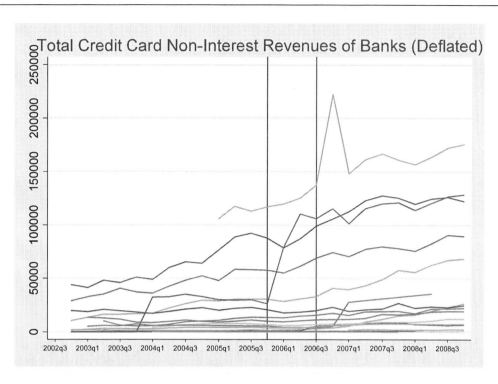

Figure 6. Credit Card Non-Interest Revenues of Banks.

To sum up this section, our analysis provides evidence for the credit card rate regulation's lessening effect on the interest incomes of banks. The credit card interest rate regulation in 2006 reduced the interest revenues of banks in the market, and since some components of the non-interest revenue side were not regulated, banks shifted their focus to the non-interest sources to compensate their lost incomes. The rise in non-interest revenues caused total revenues to increase despite the reduction in interest revenues.

CONCLUSION

Credit card markets are complicated structures which entail two different services and five different parties. As there will surely be externalities in such markets, a regulation designed for a certain aspect of a credit card market will have implications on the other aspects. The Turkish credit card market was recently subjected to two important regulations: one on payment services, and the other on credit services. By analyzing the credit card interest and credit card non-interest revenues of banks, earned from credit and payment services, respectively, in a 3SLS framework, we explore the effects of each of those regulations on the two service markets.

This study is unique to the best of our knowledge, and is important in that it contributes to our understanding of credit card markets by displaying the interaction between the possible revenue sources of banks in the market. Our results indicate that the regulations on payment services did not affect banks' revenues much. The regulations on credit services, however, suppressed banks' interest revenues and caused them to shift their focus towards the unregulated non-interest revenue sources. To compensate their revenue losses, banks reacted by increasing the unregulated prices of their payment services. The consequent rise in banks' non-interest revenues caused their total revenues to rise as well.

Looking at these results, we suggest careful consideration of the possible repercussions of a regulatory action on all segments of a credit card market. Moreover, from the rising prices of payment services and the rise in non-interest revenues, and also from the falling prices of credit services and the fall in interest revenues, we infer that the demands for payment and credit services of credit cards are inelastic.

ACKNOWLEDGEMENT

Authors acknowledge the financial support of the Bogazici University Research Funds (Project # 08C103 and Project #09C105P).

REFERENCES

Akin, G. G., A. F. Aysan, D. Boriçi and L. Yildiran (2011b), "Regulating Payment Services and Credit Services of Credit Cards: Evidence from Turkey", Mimeo, Bogaziçi University.

Akin, G. G., A. F. Aysan, G. I. Kara and L. Yildiran (2011a), "Non-Price Competition In Credit Card Markets Through Bank Level Benefits." Forthcoming in *Contemporary Economic Policy.*

Akin, G. G., A. F. Aysan, G. I. Kara and L. Yildiran (2010), "The Failure of Price Competition in the Turkish Credit Card Market." *Emerging Market Trade and Finance*, Vol.46, pp 23-35.

Akin, G. G., A. F. Aysan, and L. Yildiran (2009), "Transformation of the Turkish Financial Sector in the Aftermath of the 2001 Crisis", Turkish Economy in the Post-Crisis Era: the New Phase of Neo-Liberal Restructuring and Integration to the Global Economy, Z. Onis, and F. Senses (eds.) Routledge, pp. 73-100.

Ausubel, L. M. (1991), "The Failure of Competition in the Credit Card Market." *American Economic Review*, Vol. *31,* pp 50–81.

Evans, D. S. and R. Schmalensee, (1999), "Paying with Plastic: the Digital Revolution in Buying and Borrowing." Cambridge and London : MIT Press.

Evans, D. S. and R. Schmalensee, (2005), "Paying with Plastic.*" 2nd Ed.*, Cambridge, Massachusetts: MIT Press.

Karayol, A. H. (2007), "Kartlı Ödeme Sistemlerinde Rekabet." *Rekabet Kurulu Uzmanlık Tezleri Serisi No:75*

Kennedy, Peter (1996). *"A Guide to Econometrics" The MIT Press.* Cambridge, Massachusetts

Rochet, J. C. and Tirole J. (2002), "Cooperation among Competitors: Some Economics of Payment Card Associations." *Rand Journal of Economics, vol. 33, no. 4 (Winter)*, pp. 549-570.

Rochet, J. C. and Tirole J. (2003b), "Platform Competition in Two-Sided Markets." *Journal of the European Economics Association, vol. 1, 4,*, pp. 990-1209.

Scholnick B., N. Massoud, A. Saunders, S.C. Valverde and F. R. Fernandez, (2008), "The Economics of Credit Cards, Debit Cards And ATMs: A Survey And Some New Evidence." Journal *of Banking and Finance*, Vol.*32, 8,* pp 1468-1483.

Weiner, Stuart E. and Julian Wright (2005) "Interchange Fees in Various Countries: Developments and Determinants", Federal Reserve Bank of Kansas City Working Paper 05-01.

PART III. REGULATION OF FINANCIAL MARKETS IN TURKEY

In: Regulation and Competition in the Turkish Banking…   ISBN: 978-1-61324-990-1
Editors: Tamer Çetin and Fuat Oğuz   © 2012 Nova Science Publishers, Inc.

Chapter 9

TURKISH CAPITAL MARKET REGULATION

Guray Kucukkocaoglu[1]* *and Cemal Kucuksozen*[2]**

[1]Başkent University, Faculty of Economics and Administrative Sciences,
Management Department B219, Bağlıca Kampüsü, 06530,
Ankara – Turkey + 90 (312) 234 10 10 / 1728
[2]Capital Markets Board of Turkey, Board Chairman's Advisor,
Eskişehir Yolu, Ankara

ABSTRACT

The securities market in Turkey is supervised by the Capital Markets Board of Turkey (CMBT). The principal statute governing the securities market is the Capital Market Law No 2499. The subject of this law is to regulate and control the secure, transparent and stable functioning of the capital market and to protect the rights and benefits of investors with the purpose of ensuring an efficient and widespread participation by the public in the development of the economy through investing savings in the securities market. This law contains regulations with respect to company and shareholder disclosure obligations, admission to listing and trading of listed securities, public tender offers and insider dealing, among other things. CMBT monitors compliance with these regulations and aiming to achieve international best practices, and encourage market-integrity through clear and self-enforcing rules of the game while encouraging the game itself. Within the framework of investor protection and moving the capital market forward and to be a major source of medium and long term finance, laws and regulations assist the CMBT to perform its role in maintaining market integrity and meeting fairness and transparency principles. The objective of this chapter is to examine the current developments and their effect on changes in capital market regulations and to provide conceptual understanding and in-depth knowledge of securities laws and the regulatory framework concerning capital markets in Turkey.

---

* gurayk@baskent.edu.tr.
** cemal.kucuksozen@spk.gov.tr

1. INTRODUCTION

The flow of capital to the major emerging market economies is important to the welfare of the global financial markets. Greater financial integration is evident from the sustained rise in both gross capital inflows (ie non-resident purchases of domestic assets) and outflows (ie resident purchases of foreign assets) to and from the emerging market economies. Although the structure of flows has become more stable, capital flows continue to be very volatile and this has major macroeconomic implications for recipient countries. The size and the structure of inflows are heavily conditioned by, and exert a major influence on, the state of development of local financial markets (Muhan, R. 2009).

The benefits and costs of capital market integration and regulation have become a controversial topic of debate among academicians and policymakers. The rapid growth in capital movements around the global capital markets and the needs of capital in emerging market economies have forced to improve these economies' capital markets in order to attract a larger share of global portfolio investment.

Major obstacles facing emerging market economies in their attempt to establish effective and attractive capital markets, Guzman, (1999) identifies three problems that are especially severe in these countries, and considers how the appropriate use of choice of law and choice of forum rules might resolve them. These problems are: the creation of a set of desirable substantive rules and policies; the establishment of a reliable and effective system for the resolution of disputes; and the develeopment of a system to ensure the enforcement of court judgments and arbitral awards.

In keeping up with the global growth and capital movements around the world, regulation of the capital markets and protection of investor's interest in Turkish Capital Markets, is primarily the responsibility of the Capital Markets Board of Turkey (CMBT), which is located in Ankara - Turkey. Ultimately, regulation of the capital markets in Turkey has been designed primarily to give a basis for all participants (residents and non-residents) and in the markets to have confidence in its integrity. CMBT's role under this regulatory environment is to make the market more credible and efficient by establishing and enforcing principles which ensure fairness and trust, and prevent activities of illegal acts which damage investor confidence.

The primary legislation governing the capital markets in Turkey is the Capital Market Law (CML), and the subsidiary regulations made under this law is its regulations, communiqués and decisions. These regulations have been in force since the establishment of CMBT, and many changes have been made by the Capital Markets Board (CMB) where it has been making detailed regulations for organizing the markets and developing capital market instruments and institutions. The objective of the CML is to regulate, supervise and provide for the secure, fair and orderly functioning of the capital markets, while protecting the rights and interests of investors. Capital market instruments, public offerings and sales, issuers, exchanges and other organized markets stipulated in the CML, capital market activities, capital market institutions and the structure of the Capital Markets Board are all subject to the provisions of CML.

The institutional investor sector in Turkish Capital Market is comprised of investment funds, pension funds, investment companies, and real estate investment trusts. In order to increase product variety, long-term investments, and to broaden the institutional investor base, new instruments such as hedge funds, guaranteed and protected funds, funds of funds, exchange traded funds and warrants have been introduced into the market. Moreover, by taking into consideration the needs of the market and European Union (EU) regulations, a new Draft Law on Capital markets, which brings about fundamental changes for the institutional investor market has been prepared. The Turkish financial system has a fragmented regulatory structure. Banking Regulation and Supervision Agency (BRSA) is in charge of the banking system, whereas the Capital Markets Board of Turkey (CMB) is the main regulator of the capital markets. The Undersecretariat of Treasury, on the other hand, oversees the insurance industry (Fıkırkoca et.al. 2010). Major institutions regarding capital markets are briefly introduced in the following sections and a chart is provided on the next page with an illustration of jurisdictions.

2. CAPITAL MARKETS BOARD OF TURKEY

The Capital Markets Board of Turkey (CMB) is the sole regulatory and supervisory authority which aims to regulate and enhance the secure, transparent and stable functioning of the capital markets and seeks to protect the rights and benefits of investors with the purpose of ensuring an efficient and widespread participation by the public in the development of the economy by promoting investment in the securities markets in Turkey. The CMB was established as a self-funding statutory public legal entity with administrative and financial autonomy empowered by the Capital Markets Law (CML) which was enacted in 1981 with the aim of implementing the duties and exercising its authority endowed by this Law. The CMB has an executive board consisting of seven Members/Commissioners, two of whom are the chairman and the deputy chairman. The CMB's headquarters is located in Ankara, and there is also a regional office in Istanbul.

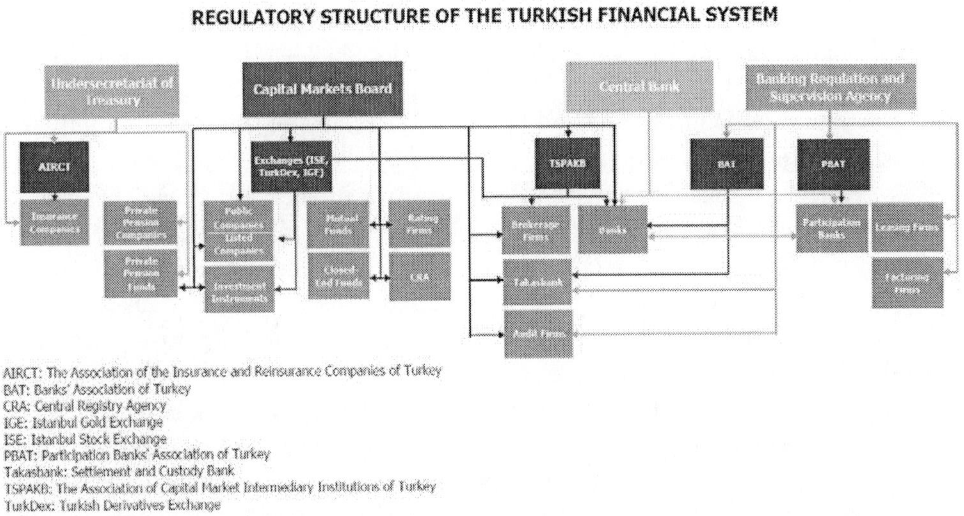

REGULATORY STRUCTURE OF THE TURKISH FINANCIAL SYSTEM

AIRCT: The Association of the Insurance and Reinsurance Companies of Turkey
BAT: Banks' Association of Turkey
CRA: Central Registry Agency
IGE: Istanbul Gold Exchange
ISE: Istanbul Stock Exchange
PBAT: Participation Banks' Association of Turkey
Takasbank: Settlement and Custody Bank
TSPAKB: The Association of Capital Market Intermediary Institutions of Turkey
TurkDex: Turkish Derivatives Exchange

Source: The Association of Capital Market Intermediary Institutions of Turkey, The Structure of the Turkish Capital Markets, 2010.

Figure 1. Regulatory Structure of the Turkish Financial System..

The main duties and authorities of the CMB are as follows (CMBT, 2010):

- To regulate and control the conditions of the issuance, public offering and sale of capital market instruments with respect to the application of this Law;
- To register capital market instruments to be issued or offered to public and to halt the public offering sale of capital market instruments temporarily in case the public interest so requires;
- To determine standard ratios related to financial structures, and the use of resources of capital market institutions subject to the CML in general or by areas of activity or types of institutions, and to regulate the principles and procedures related to the publication of these ratios;
- To determine the principles related to independent auditing operations, including when appropriate with respect to use of electronic media in the capital markets; to determine the conditions for establishment and the working principles of institutions engaged in independent auditing operations with respect to the capital market according to Law No. 3568, dated 1 June 1989 by consulting with the Union of Chambers of Public Accountants of Turkey and to publish lists of those who have such qualifications;
- To reach general and specific decisions to ensure duly and timely enlightment of the public and to determine and issue communiqués about the content, standards and principles for the publication of financial statements, reports and their audit, of prospectuses and circulars issued at the public offering of capital market instruments, and of important information affecting the value of instruments;
- To supervise the activities of the issuers subject to the CML, banks with respect to provisions in paragraph (a) of Article 50 of CML, capital market institutions and stock exchanges and other organized markets for compliance CML, decrees, communiqués of the Board and other legislation related to capital markets by demanding all the necessary information and documents;
- To monitor all kinds of publications, announcements and advertisements related to the capital markets via any means of communication, and to ban those which are determined to be misleading and to inform the related organizations to duly execute what is required;
- To review the financial statements and reports and other documents obtained by the CMB or submitted to it in accordance with the provisions of CML, to request reports also from issuers and internal auditors and independent auditors about matters deemed to be necessary and by evaluating the results obtained, to take the required measures as proven in this Law;
- To determine the principles related to proxy voting in the framework of the general provisions at the general assemblies of publicly held joint stock corporations and to make regulations related to those who collect proxies or acquire shares in an amount enabling them to change the management of such corporations, or the obligation of purchasing other shares and the rights of the partners who are in the minority to sell their shares to persons or a group which has taken over the control;
- To regulate the qualifications and sale and purchase principles of derivative instruments, including futures and options contracts based on economic and financial

indicators, capital market instruments, commodities, precious metals and foreign currency, the supervision of the obligations of those employed at the exchanges and markets where these instruments are traded, and of the rules and principles of activities and of the rules, principles, and guarantees of the clearing and settlement system;

- To regulate agreements for the purchase or sale of capital market instruments with the promise to resell or repurchase; to adopt market transaction rules related to these contracts; and to determine operating rules and principles related to these transactions;
- To determine rules and principles related to borrowing and lending capital market instruments and short selling transactions and, after obtaining the opinions of the Undersecretariat of the Treasury and the Central Bank of the Republic of Turkey, to adopt regulations related to transactions involving margin trading;
- To make necessary regulations within the framework of related legislation with respect to the issuing and public offering of capital market instruments in Turkey by non-residents;
- To regulate and supervise the clearing and custody of capital market instruments and the rating of capital market institutions and capital market instruments;
- To determine the principles of establishment, operation, liquidation and termination of newly established capital market institutions and to supervise them in order to ensure the development of capital markets;
- To perform the examinations requested by the Related Minister; to submit reports to the Related Minister in relation with its activities; to submit proposals to the Related Minister with respect to the amendment of legislation concerning the capital market;
- To establish the qualifications necessary to serve as an expert institution with respect to the appraisal of real estate for the purpose of capital market activities and to publish a list of the institutions that have met these qualifications;
- To determine the rules and principles applicable to persons and organizations engaged in making investment recommendations on the capital market, including in the media and by electronic means;
- To determine the principles for issuing certificates showing the vocational training and vocational adequacy of persons who shall engage in activities on the capital markets and managers and the other employees of capital market institutions and with this objective to establish centers and to determine the principles with respect to the activity;
- To regulate and supervise public offerings and capital market activities and transactions that are made by means of all kinds of electronic communication tools and media and similar tools including internet and pursuant to general rules to provide for and supervise the use of electronic signatures in activities within the scope of the CML;
- To make rules and regulations with respect to the method of collective use of voting rights wholly or partly to select members of the board of directors and of company auditors by the general assemblies of stockholders of publicly held joint stock companies subject to the CML;

- To collaborate in every aspect and to exchange information regarding the capital markets with any equivalent authority.

At present, Turkish capital markets have the ability to compete at international level in terms of instruments, institutions and legal infrastructure and have the privilege to be listed among major financial markets in the world. Some of Turkish capital markets indicators for 2009 and 2010 are given in the Table 1 below.

Table 1. Turkish Capital Markets Indicators

	2009	2010
NUMBER OF CORPORATIONS REGISTERED BY THE CMB	548	566
NUMBER OF CORPORATIONS TRADED ON ISE	322	344
NUMBER OF CORPORATIONS NOT TRADED ON ISE	226	222
MARKET CAPITALIZATION (TL Million)	350,761	472,553
($ Million)	235,966	307,551
NUMBER OF INVESTORS ON THE ISE	1,000,261	1,043,135
NUMBER OF INVESTORS OF MUTUAL FUNDS	2,998,648	3,248,601
NUMBER OF INTERMEDIARY INSTITUTIONS	144	144
-Banks	41	41
-Brokerage Houses	103	103
NUMBER OF MUTUAL FUNDS	393	555
-Number of Domestic Mutual Funds	316	486
-Portfolio Values (TL Million)	29,6	33.2
($ Million)	19,9	21.6
-Number of Foreign Mutual Funds	77	69
-Portfolio Values (TL Million)	58	55
($ Million)	39	35
NUMBER OF PENSION FUNDS	130	140
-Portfolio Values (TL Million)	9,105	12,018
($ Million)	6,126	7,822
NUMBER OF INVESTMENT TRUSTS	33	31
-Portfolio Values (TL Million)	712	750
($ Million)	479	488
NUMBER OF REAL ESTATE INVESTMENT TRUSTS	14	21
-Portfolio Values (TL Million)	4,740	17,246
($ Million)	3,172	11,189
NUMBER OF VENTURE CAPITAL INVESTMENT TRUSTS	2	2
-Portfolio Values (TL Million)	153	187
($ Million)	103	121
NUMBER OF PORTFOLIO MANAGEMENT COMPANIES	23	28
-Values of portfolios under management (TL Million)	40,0	46.9
($ Million)	26,7	30.3
NUMBER OF INDEPENDENT AUDITING FIRMS	95	92
REAL ESTATE APPRAISAL COMPANIES	63	82
RATING INSTITUTIONS	9	9

Source: Capital Markets Board of Turkey – Annual Report 2010.

2.1. Main Legislative Developments in the Turkish Capital Markets

In order to attract investment funds to Turkish capital markets and increase the effectiveness of these rules and regulations, CMBT continually establishes and update these rules, regulations and practices and ensure their functionality. Recent changes in the capital markets law and regulation are discussed below.

2.1.1. Legislation on Securities Issue

CMB has recently taken several initiatives in order to increase the availability and attractiveness of capital markets for the financing needs of firms and to provide new investment instruments for investors. In this context, several communiqués and amendments about the legislation on securities issues were approved recently (CMBT Bulletin, October 2010).

In March 2010 the Communiqué on the Sale and Registration of Bonds with the Board was amended in order to provide more flexibility to issuers on corporate bond issues. The amendment enables all bond issue applications with different interest rate and maturity profiles that will take place during one year to be registered by the CMB at once, issuers can then decide whether or when they will sell the bonds, taking into account market conditions and their financial situation.

With regard to shares, an amendment was made to the Communiqué on Sale and Registration of Shares in April 2010 with the objective of eliminating current problems in practice, facilitating public offers and advancing alignment with the related EU acquis. Accordingly, the minimum public offer rate requirement and mandatory undertaking requirement in the public offers have been abolished; shelf registration system principles have been revised to provide companies that are not traded at a stock exchange to benefit from this system; and the possibility of electronic publication of prospectuses and circulars was provided.

Furthermore, with a decision of the CMB Executive Board in February 2010, prospectus standards for shares and debt securities have been harmonised with the EU Commission Regulation (EC) No 809/2004. Technical guidance on new prospectus standards has also been adopted by the CMB Executive Board.

Finally with an amendment was made to the Communiqué on Sales Methods in the Sales of the Capital Market Instruments in April 2010, issuers were enabled to decide freely on price, sale and distribution principles as long as they explain them in detail in the prospectus. Furthermore the prohibition of share purchase by persons who have the potential to acquire inside information has been abolished, principles on payment methods of share prices were clarified, the provision of cash and non cash incentives to specific investor groups were enabled, the period to make book building has been shortened, and it has been made possible that the prospectus can be signed by the issuer and the consortium leader rather than all the intermediary institutions involved in the offer.

2.1.2. New Communiqué on Foreign Securities and Depository Receipts

The principles regarding registration and sale of foreign capital market instruments and Depository Receipts have been redesigned. Before the new communiqué it was mandatory to make a public offer for foreign securities only through Depository Receipts. Now foreign securities can directly be offered to public as this requirement has been removed. The existing requirement for foreign securities to be offered to public in Turkey, to be listed in a stock exchange in the country they were issued was abolished. Foreign capital market instruments that are not listed in any exchange may now be offered to public in Turkey given that absence of a listing is not due to the need to protect investors (CMBT Bulletin, October 2010).

2.1.3. Market Surveillance and Enforcement

In 2009, CMBT created a Market Surveillance and Enforcement Department for the purpose of both accelerating the action and decision-making processes of the market in response to a shock and also in order to help combat financial fraud and market manipulation. This department will enable a closer monitoring of the markets, and will enable the CMB to act and decide on certain aspects much more efficiently and promptly in response to a sudden shock. The lack of proper and effective market surveillance systems was indeed one of the main reasons for the outbreak of the financial crisis.

Preventing market manipulation was the main focus of the Capital Markets Board, during auditing activities in 2009, according to a report published recently by the Board. More than half of audits conducted by the CMB specialists were related to manipulation attempts. The proportion of audits conducted in 2008 on suspicion of manipulation was 36.2 percent, while the number of audits on suspicion of manipulation in 2009 jumped to 53 percent, with a total of 103 manipulation audits being carried out (CMBT Annual Report, 2009).

On the other hand, the proportion of audits concerning publicly traded companies has dropped. Audits for publicly traded companies ranked second at 19 percent. Most audits of public companies were undertaken to investigate earnings management attempts to avoid tax, a practice known as "income shifting," the report said.

An increase in audits from 2008 to 2009 concerning insider trading was also observed. The proportion of audits concerning insider trading, which constituted 4.6 percent of all audits in 2008, increased to 6.2 percent in 2009.

In 2009 the main part of enforcement activity consists of market manipulation cases, which started heavily on the denouncements of the ISE. The number of manipulation cases informed by the ISE is 82 in 2009 and together with previous years denouncement the total number reaches to 225. Almost half of them have been finalized in 2009.

The number of manipulation cases informed by the ISE is 33 in 2010 and together with previous years denouncement the total number reaches 151. 124 of them have been finalized in 2010. Information about market manipulation cases, which started with the ISE denouncements, is given in the Table 2 below (CMBT Annual Reports, 2009 and 2010).

Table 2. Manipulation Cases

	2008	2009	2010
The number of cases continued from previous year	130	143	118
The number of cases denunciated from the ISE in current year	89	82	33
Total	219	225	151
	2008	**2009**	**2010**
The number of cases resulted in current year	76	107	124
The number of cases transferred to next year	143	118	27
Total	219	225	151

2.1.4. Accounting/Financial Reporting Standards

In order to achieve full disclosure in Turkish capital markets, CMBT has been determined and carried out the accounting/financial reporting standards and formats of financial statements since 1982. The first regulation in this area, other than tax purposes, is done by the CMBT. This regulation has been improved for many years within the framework of international developments and daily requirements. CMBT, depending on the improved requirements to meet the needs, has published new communiqués and continued to work on the standards of financial reporting with quality.

To comply with European Union regulations, The Serial: XI, No: 29 Communiqué was issued in 2008. Through this legislation, listed companies, intermediary institutions and portfolio management companies are obliged to prepare their financial statements in accordance with International Accounting/Financial Reporting Standards. So that, fully compliance with European Union regulations is established regarding financial reporting.

In addition, to ensure identical application in Turkish capital markets, financial statement formats and related explanations are still be determined and published by CMB.

2.1.5. Auditing in Turkish Capital Market

In Turkey, the real activity of auditing is based on the auditing works which are carried out within the framework of capital market law. The first regulation in the area of auditing in Turkey is done by the Capital Market Board (CMB). This regulation has been improved for many years within the framework of daily requirements. CMB, depending on the improved requirements to meet the needs, has published new communiqués and continued to the works of standards on auditing with quality.

Particularly, negative issues which took place in the global markets during years of 2000 have created a hesitating environment about the reliability of information presented on the financial statements. Depending on this, standards prepared with the objective of increasing the effectiveness of the auditing duty in the global and national context were updated and these regulations and developments were tried to be adjusted on timely basis (Guredin, 2007).

In this context, Communiqué on Standards on auditing in Capital Markets (Serial: X, No: 22) which is completely compatible to the International standards on auditing that constitute the final step in the area of auditing, was published by CMB in Official Journal No: 26196 (repeated) at the date of June 12, 2006 and came into force (Kucuksozen, 2008).

The foundation of the auditing regulation for publicly held companies was realized by CMB in 1982 before the legal basis of the accounting profession. The need of auditing of private sector as well as the audit of its financial information that must be publicly available improved following the legal act of profession which came into force in 1989 (Arikan, 2004).

Communiqué Serial: X, No: 22 on the Standards on Auditing in Capital Market is compatible to the International Standards on Auditing, which constitute the final step in the area of auditing and was published by International Auditing and Assurance Standards Board within International Federation of Accountants, as well as it is compatible to the related foreseen directives of the European Union. This communiqué provides the opportunity to solve the problems arising from auditing in the capital market and implement standards which will lead to the realization of auditing needs with quality (CMB, 20.02.2006 Press Call).

3. ISTANBUL STOCK EXCHANGE

Inaugurated at the end of 1985, the Istanbul Stock Exchange (ISE) has been established to provide trading in a wide variety of securities, namely, stocks, exchange traded funds, government bonds, Treasury bills, money market instruments (repo/reverse repo), corporate bonds and foreign securities. The ISE is a public organization whose members are banks and brokerage houses.

In the process of improving and realizing the growth potential of the Turkish capital markets, the ISE sets its functions as to (ISE, 2010):

- Examine the application of the securities to be listed within the framework of the principles stated in the CMB and ISE Regulations, request additional information and documents, evaluate the applications and make a decision,
- Launch the Derivatives Market in compliance with the regulations,
- Open markets for the securities to be traded on the Exchange, determine the types of securities to be traded and disclose information about traded securities on the ISE's Daily Bulletin,
- Determine and disclose the working days and hours for the Exchange markets and disclose them on the ISE's Daily Bulletin,
- Release prices and the trading volumes of the securities traded on the ISE markets at the end of the trading sessions,
- Assure the trading of securities in a reliable and stable environment under free competition and sanction the ISE members violating ISE regulations,
- Take the necessary precautions in line with the rules and regulations in case of extraordinary adverse developments on the Exchange.

3.1. Trading in the ISE

Electronic stock trade system has partially started in ISE on 3rd December 1993 and became fully functional with all stocks tradable on an electronic environment after 21st October 1994. This system has increased transaction speed and amount considerably, but with increased interest of investors at the end of year 1999 and start of year 2000 this increase has reached top levels and the system began to be pressured insistently. ISE management has considered the complaints of brokers of not being able to deliver the orders to the system on time and decided as an intermediate solution step to accept the delivery of orders with diskettes for the first session after 28th April 2000 and for the second session after 13th August 2001 until the start of Express-API system. Before the application of delivery of orders with diskettes, it was observed that accumulated orders of overnights caused high transaction volumes and somedays it was also observed that not all the transactions could be processed. In these days the brokers preferred to differentiate their customers and gave priority to the ones with higher trading volumes and postponed the ones (mostly small investors) with lower volumes. This situation, however, gave rise to high volatilities in the morning hours (Kucukkocaoglu, 2008). After the date 4th April 2002 the order transmission through Express-API system has started and the system has started giving faster responses with no difficulty.

Although, it is observed that this situation has a positive effect on the liquidity in the start of sessions, the returns of ISE market during the day continued to show a W shaped curve, i.e., at the star of the session high, at the middle of session low and at the end of the session high returns (Kucukkocaoglu, 2008).

The finding in the literature that investigates returns during the day is that for most of the cases the stock prices are active at the start and end of sessions. Additional findings by Kucukkocaoglu, show that returns, total transaction volumes, volatilities, buy-sell orders, the price difference between buy and sell orders at the opening and end is significantly higher than the rest of the day. These anomalies are particularly observed in the first 30 minutes of the first session and in the last hour before the closing session leading to difficulties in effective price formation. In order to prevent the opening and closing price anomalies in the ISE, competent authority changed transaction times and closing methods. After this change the result for all stocks implemented single-price auction system is that the new price mechanism has a more effective closing price and it is observed that closing anomalies decreased to low levels (Kucukkocaoglu and Kucuksozen, 2009).

Another issue on price formation and trading in the ISE has been solved by a CMB decision dated July 23, 2010. The Decision is based on detailed research and technical analysis completed by the CMBT specialist and aims at ensuring conditions that will prevent the formation of artificial prices and support efficient price discovery.

According to the Decision, all companies traded on the ISE will be classified into 3 groups (A, B or C). Some trading rules are differentiated based on this classification. For example, Group B and Group C companies cannot be subject to margin trading and short sale.

The Decision defines (CMBT Bulletin, July 2010);

- Group A listed companies as companies that are not listed under Group B or Group C.
- Group B companies as companies that meet following criteria (1) the value of the publicly traded shares is under 10 million TL and the number of shares in circulation is under 10 million or (2) the value of the publicly traded shares is under 45 million TL and percentage of actual shares in circulation is under 5%. Besides; an investment trust is classified as Group B company if its stock price is 1,5 times higher than its NAV per share.
- Group C companies as companies that meet following criteria: (1) companies traded in the Watch List Companies Market or (2) actual number of shares in circulation is under 10 million. Besides, an investment trust is classified as Group C company if its stock price is 2 times higher than its NAV per share (with an exception for investment trusts with a market maker).

3.2. IPO's in the ISE

Companies, which have traditionally used banks for financing, started using more sophisticated financing sources, particularly syndications of financial institutions and from the capital markets, by issuing bonds. Some larger companies (including state corporations) have also listed their shares (by way of initial public offerings, rights issues or secondary floatation) on the Istanbul Stock Exchange (ISE) as a means of raising equity.

In spite of the fact that Turkish capital markets offer a wide range of opportunities for companies such as low-cost financing, institutionalization, domestic and international recognition, providing liquidity to shareholders, and credibility, some major Turkish companies have not yet had recourse to this important facility and are not traded on the Istanbul Stock Exchange (ISE). In order to attract these companies to the capital markets, CMBT and Istanbul Stock Exchange (ISE) initiated an "Initial Public Offering Campaign" in 2008, with the protocol signed with, the Union of Chambers and Commodity Exchanges of Turkey, and the Association of Capital Market Intermediary Institutions of Turkey, to encourage small and medium-sized companies to benefit from the opportunities offered by the capital markets, to facilitate access to the funds they need for growth, to ensure the sustainability of particularly family businesses through public offering, and to contribute to the growth of the Turkish capital markets. The common purpose of this initiative is to uncover the main reasons behind the failure of companies to have recourse to the capital markets, which play a key role in converting savings into investments, to eliminate any hurdles to public offering, to prepare publications and organize meetings that will create awareness about the opportunities offered by the capital markets (Erkan, 2010).

3.3. Disclosure in the ISE

Over the years there have been significant infrastructure investments in the ISE. The stock exchange uses electronic clearing systems and has integrated exchange, custody and back-office functions.

The latest developments in the regulatory framework in the Turkish capital markets had also been encouraging. The Turkish capital markets are transparent and well-regulated. In the recent years, there has been much focus on public disclosure of material events, and within this context, in 2010 the CMBT and ISE introduced the Public Disclosure Platform which is an electronic disclosure system using internet and electronic signature technologies for company disclosures. The system encompassed over 550 companies, including the listed companies, exchange traded funds, intermediary institutions and independent auditors registered with the CMB and allows all users to access current and past notifications of a public companies, to access current announcements and up-to-date general information on an equal and timely basis (ISE Annual Report, 2009).

3.4. Investor Relations Practices in the ISE

Implementation of investor relations practices in the ISE is somewhat recent. Within the context of the Corporate Governance Principles of the Capital Markets Board that have been published in July 2003, all public companies are advised to have an investor relations department.

When investor relations practices in the ISE are analyzed, it is observed that the ISE-30 index companies providing highly competitive and world-class investor relations. However there are over 300 companies traded on the exchange, so the number of companies with good investor relations practices is still very limited. This is evident in the high concentration at the ISE. When the share of top 20 companies in the ISE total trade volume and m-cap are analyzed, the results are quite impressive. The share of top 20 companies is 62% in the trade volume and 70% in the mcap, reflecting a very high concentration (Gungor, 2009)

3.5. New Practices in the ISE

New rules regarding trading party member codes started to be applied on October 8, 2010. According to the new rules, trading party member codes included in inquiries of transactions executed in the Stock Market shall not be displayed, whereas executed transactions shall be sent to the data vendors without buyer and seller information. Trading books including member codes will be available for the ISE members at the end of day T+1.

Order cancellation is now unconditionally allowed in the ISE. Henceforth, orders pending in the Stock Market Trading System may be cancelled one by one, on order basis, in full or in part. This new arrangement however, does not hold for the quotation orders entered for the securities traded with market making method on the Collective Products Market and the Warrants Market. The ISE will charge a fee equal to 0.025 basis points (2.5 millionths) of the TL amount of the cancelled orders (CMBT Bulletin, October 2010).

The first warrant started to be traded on Istanbul Stock Exchange (ISE) on 13 August 2010 after the gong rang. The warrant qualifies as an "intermediary institution warrant". It was issued by Deutsche Bank AG (London) through the intermediary of Deutsche Securities Menkul Değerler A.Ş.

- Warrants are traded on the Warrant Market of ISE, established within the Institutional Products Market (CMBT Bulletin, August 2010).

4. TURKISH DERIVATIVES EXCHANGE

Inaugurated on February 4, 2005, the Turkish Derivatives Exchange Inc. (TurkDEX) is the sole derivatives exchange in Turkey established to provide trading in derivatives instruments. TurkDEX was established in July 2002 as a private entity in accordance with the amendments in the CML (No. 4487).

One of the main objectives of TurkDEX is to develop and provide financial instruments that would help individuals and institutions to effectively manage their risks against price fluctuations. Currently, 10 different derivative instruments, namely; currency futures contracts (cash settled and physically delivered TRY/US$ and TRY/€), interest rate futures contracts (Benchmark Treasuries), equity index futures contracts (TurkDEX-ISE 30 Stock Index and TurkDEX-ISE 100 Stock Index), cotton futures contracts, wheat futures contracts and gold futures contracts are traded on TurkDEX's electronic trading platform (Turkdex, 2010).

5. ISTANBUL GOLD EXCHANGE

The Istanbul Gold Exchange (IGE) officially began its operation on July 26, 1995. The establishment of the IGE became an important step in canalizing gold to financial system, developing gold-based investment instruments and international integration of gold sector in Turkey. After the establishment of the IGE, local gold prices were standardized in conformity with the international prices, imported gold bars were enforced to meet generally accepted standards and fineness, and the system gained a transparent structure (IAB, 2010).

Amendments made in December 1998 to the Decree No. 32 concerning the Protection of the Value of Turkish Currency made trading of silver and platinum possible at the IGE besides gold. The IGE has two types of markets; Precious Metals Market (spot transactions), Precious Metals Lending Market. Futures and Options Market, which was launched on August 15, 1997 at the IGE, was closed on January 31, 2006 and new Futures and Options Market for gold was opened in Turkish Derivatives Exchange on February 1, 2006. Non-standard gold transactions within the Precious Metals Market were launched in October 1999. This enables scrap gold trading in a secure environment by eliminating counter-party risk. It also removes assaying concerns regarding non-standard bullion. In March 2008 trading rules and principles of domestically produced precious metals and non standard precious metals were determined in accordance with Communiqué of Refineries and Standards of Precious Metals dated 18/11/2006. The Precious Metals Lending Market started its operations on March 24, 2000 for the purpose of bringing supply and demand into an organized market, lowering the production costs of the jewelry sector and securitization of gold.

Besides, precious metals buying and selling transactions of gold based Exchange Traded Funds and other funds are done in IGE's Precious Metals Market and their precious metals are stored in the Exchange vault physically (Fıkırkoca et.al. 2010).

Main functions of the IGE are as follows (IAB, 2010):

- To create markets in the Exchange for precious metals that their standards defined by the Treasury,
- To make needed legal regulations and organization for markets will be formed,
- To provide execution of trade under security, stability and free competition in the Exchange and also to apply legal sanctions for members who violate the rules,
- To take necessary measures under powers of legislation given in case of unusual negative developments,
- To create markets for securities based on precious metals and lending transactions,
- To engage in tasks given by the Treasury and Capital Markets Board.

6. TAKASBANK (ISE SETTLEMENT AND CUSTODY BANK)

ISE Settlement and Custody Bank Inc. (Takasbank) is the Central "Clearing and Settlement Institution for the Istanbul Stock Exchange", the "Clearing House for the Turkish Derivatives Exchange" and the "National Numbering Agency of Turkey" authorized by the Capital Markets Board (CMB). Apart from these unique services, Takasbank provides ISE members with money market, securities lending market and banking services including cash credits, and cross-border settlement and custody. Takasbank, established in 1988 as a department within the ISE, originally dealt with the provision of settlement services for securities traded by the members of the ISE. In January 1992, the operations of that department were transferred to an independent company, the ISE Settlement and Custody Inc. which was set up under the ownership of the ISE and its members. This company was transformed into a bank and renamed as Takasbank in 1996 (Fikirkoca, 2010).

Established under the Turkish Banking Law and incorporated as a non-deposit taking investment bank, Takasbank is a specialized bank dedicated to securities services in Turkey.

Rules relating to clearing and settlement are specified by the ISE in accordance with the general rules and regulations of the CMB. Due to Takasbank's status as a bank, the Banking Regulation and Supervision Board also regulates Takasbank.

Main functions of the Takasbank are as follows (Takasbank, 2010):

- Central Clearing and settlement for the organized markets of the ISE,
- Clearing House for Turkish Derivatives Exchange (Turkdex),
- SWIFT integrated Delivery versus Payment (DvP) facility designed to facilitate real-time gross settlement among brokers and custodians for equities in an STP environment,
- Book-entry transactions via online connections provided for all members,
- Takasbank Electronic Transfer System (TETS) – TETS enables brokerage houses to transfer securities (government bonds and treasury bills) and cash in and out of Takasbank electronically in real-time connection with the Central Bank's "Electronic Fund Transfer" (EFT) and "Electronic Securities Transfer" systems,
- Takasbank offers international settlement and custody services to both domestic and foreign institutions on the basis of its overseas securities and cash correspondent accounts.
- Through its correspondent relations with an international settlement and custody institution, Euroclear Bank, and as a SWIFT member, Takasbank is able to offer international securities correspondence services for all securities accepted by Euroclear Bank and for all national markets connected to it.
- Domestic settlement and custody services for foreign institutions; Takasbank offers domestic settlement and custody services to foreign financial institutions . This service covers the settlement transactions of securities in custody, the services related to the transmission of information related to these securities disclosed to public the intermediation for exercising the rights provided by the securities, giving transaction confirmations, delivery of account status and account statements to the customer via SWIFT and services related to foreign currency transactions.
- Cash credit services (securities purchasing loans, spot credits, optional collection before the maturity date, intra day),
- Securities lending market,
- Takasbank Money Market - A market organized by Takasbank where ISE members can lend and borrow Turkish Lira (TL) funds from other ISE members through telephone orders directed to Takasbank or through remote access terminals,
- Associate member of World Federation of Exchanges (WFE). Guarantee Account ISE has established "Guarantee Account" in compliance with Article 34 of "Regulations of the Istanbul Stock Exchange" with an aim to avoid the delays in

settlement of transactions realized on ISE Stock and Bonds and Bills Markets and to protect the counter party unable to collect receivables as a result of the failure of the other party. The funds of the Account are made up of the fines collected from ISE members with late payments and deliveries to settlement. These funds, currently managed by Takasbank, are activated every day providing the initial liquidity to the settlement process. At the end of the settlement, if all the parties fulfill their obligations, the fund is released in full and remunerated in market terms via the Treasury Department of Takasbank. Otherwise, it is used to cover the failure of the buyer against the seller. The coverage is limited to the prevailing value of the Funds. Therefore these funds are actually a temporary liquidity facility for the settlement process. Additionally, for the settlement of transactions realized on the Turkdex, Takasbank's guarantee is limited to the collateral taken from the members of the market for trade, for membership and for the guarantee account. This guarantee account consists of two types of collaterals: Cash and non-cash collaterals. The cash portion of the collateral in TL that is deposited to the guarantee account will be renumerated on best effort basis while the non-cash portion of the collaterals will be evaluated by their prevailing market values at the end of each day.

7. THE CENTRAL REGISTRY AGENCY

Central Registry Agency Inc. (CRA) is the central securities depository for all dematerialised capital market instruments in Turkey. It was established in 2001 as a private entity in line with the amendments in the CML, (Capital Market Law, Article No. 4487).

The incorporation, operation and supervision of CRA are regulated by a Regulation legislated in July 2001, and the "Communiqué on Terms and Conditions Governing Book-entry Registration of Dematerialised Capital Market Instruments" was legislated on 17 December 2002.

CRA is incorporated in the form of a private for-profit company for the purpose of operating in accordance with the law and regulatory provisions.

Main functions of CRA are to (MKK, 2010);

- Registry and custody of dematerialised capital market instruments and rights attached thereon, in electronic form, with respect to issuers, intermediary institutions and right owners,
- Check the integrity and consistency of actual records among member groups. In case of determination of any inconsistency in the records or violation of regulations concerning the dematerialised system, request necessary corrections by members, and inform the CMB accordingly, and implement necessary measures in order to ensure safe and secure operation of the system,
- Ensure confidentiality of records as per the applicable regulatory provisions,
- Act as the securities agent for real-time securities settlement, Takasbank securities lending and borrowing market, and securities collateral management.
- Manage legal operations (i.e. distraint, right of retention, bankruptcy, usufruct) on securities.

- Carry out corporate actions management and provide investor services (general assembly blockages, investor blockages, information on accounts via call center, e-mail, SMS alerts, IVR, e-CAS and er@gon).
- Manage and represent the Investors' Protection Fund (IPF) and conduct all the issues on behalf of the Fund as per the applicable regulatory provisions,
- Implement liquidation procedures of intermediary institutions which are subject to gradual liquidation as per a CMB resolution on behalf of the IPF as per the applicable regulatory provisions,
- Carry out other duties assigned by the CMB according to the capital market legislation and other issues required under the existing regulations.

At the moment CRA provides custody services for the following dematerialised market instruments: equities, ETFs, mutual funds, corporate bonds and commercial papers, and bank bills. Accounts at CRA are opened with respect to issuers and intermediary institutions. However, authorised settlement and custody institutions may open accounts directly at CRA in order to ensure performance of settlement transactions. CRA and its members are subject to supervision and inspection of the CMB.

7.1. New Amendments to the Communiqué on Recordkeeping of Dematerialized Securities

The dematerialized system for equities traded in ISE became effective as of November 28, 2005. Currently, equities traded in ISE are kept under custody at the Central Registry Agency under a system that keeps securities in intermediary accounts divided into individual client sub-accounts, over which clients have direct access and control, thereby providing protection for client assets.

Following the new Communiqué on foreign securities and DRs, which had entered into force in October 2010, the Communiqué Serial: IV, No: 28 on Procedures and Principles with regard to record keeping of dematerialized securities, was also amended in November 2010, with respect especially to foreign instruments. The amendments are summarized below (CMBT Bulletin, November 2010):

- The amendment enables the Central Registry Agency (CRA) to open accounts at foreign custodian institutions under principles and procedures it will determine.
- It was previously determined that dematerialized capital market instruments including government debt instruments would be kept under investor accounts. With the amendment, the CMB was authorized to determine cases where a capital market instrument should be kept under the account of the intermediary, depending on the instruments' nature or the nature of a transaction on such an instrument.
- With regard to foreign securities issued in accordance with the new Communiqué on
- foreign securities and DRs, the CMB will be authorized to determine different conditions from those already specified in relation to notifications to be made to the CRA.

- Furthermore it will no longer be mandatory to deposit foreign securities that are issued and sold within Turkey in the Central Registry Agency, where such securities are already deposited at a custodian in accordance with the rules and regulations of the related foreign country.

8. ASSOCIATION OF CAPITAL MARKET INTERMEDIARY INSTITUTIONS OF TURKEY (TSPAKB)

The Association of Capital Market Intermediary Institutions of Turkey (TSPAKB) has been established as a self-regulatory organization in March 2001. The objective of the TSPAKB is to perform the duties assigned by the Law and this Statute for the purpose of providing development of the capital market and the intermediary activities, providing the operation the TSPAKB members in solidarity, and in due diligence and discipline required by the capital market, protecting the economic benefits of the members, preventing unfair competition and to inform the members on professional subjects. All the brokerage firms and banks that are authorized for capital market operations are supposed to become a member of the TSPAKB. As of April 2010, 41 banks and 103 brokerage houses are members (Fıkırkoca et.al. 2010).

The Duties and Functions of the TSPAKB are as follows (TSPAKB, 2010);

a. To conduct research and organize training programs to contribute to the development of the capital market and intermediation activities.
b. To establish professional rules and regulations to provide that activities performed by the TSPAKB members are fair and honest, to provide business ethics, to facilitate the solidarity among the TSPAKB members, to safeguard the prudent and disciplined conduct of business by its members
c. To take and inform CMB of necessary measures to prevent unfair competition.
d. To cooperate with relevant organizations in order to give disciplinary penalties specified in the Statute.
e. To monitor professional, administrative and legal regulations and inform members on this subject.
f. To strengthen professional solidarity among intermediary institutions.
g. To assist in the resolution of disputes arising from operations excluding exchange transactions among its members or between its members and investors, to establish arbitrator lists for this purpose and to provide arbitration services under the Code of Legal Procedures by appointing arbitrator(s) if agreed by the parties.
h. To notify CMB its proposals on principles related to commissions and fees to be charged to its members in consideration of services rendered to customers.
i. To evaluate complaints against its members and inform CMB on the results.
j. To establish, enforce and supervise regulations on subjects assigned to it by the legislation or specified by CMB.
k. To cooperate with corresponding organizations in international capital markets.

l. To participate in national and international financial, economic and professional institutions, organizations and partnerships and/or to acquire shareholding therein on subjects related to its objectives.

TSPAKB shall be obliged to comply with the Law, the Statute, regulations, communiqués, resolutions of CMB and the related legislation in its resolutions and regulations. If any action contrary to the legislation in force is noticed, CMB may request the TSPAKB to cancel or modify the regulation established.

9. OTHER CAPITAL MARKET INSTITUTIONS

Other capital market institutions refer to the institutions whose establishment and principles of operation are determined by the CMB including:
- Intermediary institutions dealing with futures transactions,
- Portfolio safekeeping companies,
- Audit firms,
- Rating Agencies,
- Investment consultancy and portfolio management,
- Asset management companies,
- Venture capital investment companies,
- Venture capital mutual funds,

CONCLUSION

The existence of a strong regulatory framework is essential to the creation of a credible capital market which is attractive to both investors seeking to find a legitimate place to invest their money, and issuers seeking to attract capital to support legitimate businesses. The existence of credible rules must be supported by a vigorous enforcement program which has the ability to respond to misconduct in the market, and sanctions which will ensure the credibility of the market is maintained and deter the unscrupulous from abusing the market in dishonest and fraudulent schemes (Watson, 2010).

The Turkish capital markets offer a wide array of opportunities for equity investors. Istanbul Stock Exchange, which is relatively transparent, well regulated, and highly liquid, has been witnessing increased level of foreign investment on a continuous basis. The market already has a strong technological infrastructure with electronic clearing systems and integrated exchange and custody functions. CMBT monitors compliance with regulations and aiming to achieve international best practices, and encourage market -integrity through clear and self-enforcing rules of the game while encouraging the game itself. Within the framework of investor protection and moving the capital market forward to be a major source of medium and long term finance, laws and regulations assist the CMBT to perform its role in maintaining market integrity and meeting fairness and transparency principles. TurkDEX is developing and providing financial instruments that would help individuals and institutions to effectively manage their risks against price fluctuations. Istanbul Gold Exchange is canalizing gold to financial system, developing gold-based investment instruments and international integration of gold sector in Turkey. ISE Settlement and Custody Bank is setting rules relating to clearing and settlement are specified by the ISE in accordance with the general rules and regulations of the CMB. The Central Registry Agency is checking the integrity and consistency of actual records among member groups. In case of determination of any inconsistency in the records or violation of regulations concerning the dematerialised system, request necessary corrections by members, and inform the CMB accordingly, and implement necessary measures in order to ensure safe and secure operation of the system, and provides custody services for the following dematerialised market instruments: equities, ETFs, mutual funds, corporate bonds and commercial papers, and bank bills. The Association of Capital Market Intermediary Institutions of Turkey is conducting research and organize training programs to contribute to the development of the capital market and intermediation activities, establishing professional rules and regulations to provide that activities performed by the Association members are fair and honest, to provide business ethics, to facilitate the solidarity among the Association members, to safeguard the prudent and disciplined conduct of business by its members.

All of these increasing efforts by these regulators and agencies aiming to enhance the existing corporate governance and investor relations practices in a risk-focused effort to achieve further transparency and supervision in the markets make Turkish capital markets more appealing for further investments while supporting Turkey's endeavor to realize its full potential as a significant capital markets player in the world (Gungor, 2008).

REFERENCES

Arikan, Yahya, (2004), "Dünden Bugüne Türkiye'de Muhasebecilik ve İSMMMO Tarihi", ISMMM Yayınları, Istanbul - Turkey.

CMBT, (2010), Capital Markets Board of Turkey, www.cmb.gov.tr

CMBT Bulletin, (October 2010), "Main Legislative Developments", *Bulletin of the Capital Markets Board of Turkey,* Ankara, Turkey.

CMBT Bulletin, (July 2010), "New Trading Rules", *Bulletin of the Capital Markets Board of Turkey*, Ankara, Turkey.

CMBT Bulletin, (August 2010), "Amendments to Investment Fund Regulations", *Bulletin of the Capital Markets Board of Turkey*, Ankara, Turkey.

CMBT Bulletin, (November 2010), "Amendments to the Regulation of Recordkeeping", *Bulletin of the Capital Markets Board of Turkey*, Ankara, Turkey.

CMBT Annual Report, (2009), *"Capital Markets Board of Turkey Annual Report 2009"*, Ankara - Turkey.

CMBT Annual Report, (2010), *"Capital Markets Board of Turkey Annual Report 2010"*, Ankara - Turkey.

Erkan, H., (2010), *"See you at the Initial Public Offering Campaign: Bursa Summit"*, http://www.ipoturkeysummit.com/anasayfa.aspx

Fıkırkoca, E., Budak, A., Altas, G., *"The Structure of the Turkish Capital Markets 2010"*, TSPAKB Publication No. 47, Istanbul -Turkey.

Gungor, F., (2008), "*Uncovering unique investment opportunities in the Turkish equity market*", Funds World Turkey 2008, White Paper.

Gungor, F., (2009), "*Turkish Capital Markets and Istanbul Stock Exchange: An Attractive Investment Case*", Funds World Turkey 2009, White Paper.

Guredin, E., (2007), "*Denetim ve Güvence Hizmetleri*", Arıkan Basım Yayım Dağıtım, Ltd. Şti., 11. Baskı, Istanbul - Turkey.

Guzman, A.T. (1999), "Capital Market Regulation in Developing Countries: A Proposal", *Virginia Journal of International Law*, Vol. 39, 607-645.

IAB, (2010), Istanbul Altın Borsası – Istanbul Gold Exchange, www.iab.gov.tr.

ISE, (2010), Istanbul Menkul Kıymetler Borsası - Istanbul Stock Exchange, www.ise.org.

ISE Annual Report, (2009), "*Istanbul Stock Exchange Annual Report 2009*", Istanbul - Turkey.

Kucukkocaoglu, G., (2008), "Intraday Stock Returns and Close End Price Manipulation in the Istanbul Stock Exchange", *Frontiers in Finance and Economics*, Volume 5, No.1.

Kucukkocaoglu, G., Kucuksozen, C., (2009), "Açılış Seansı Uygulamasının İMKB'nin Mikroyapısı Üzerine Etkileri", *Standard – Ekonomik ve Teknik Dergi*, Sayı 564, Yıl.48.

Kucuksozen, C., (2008), "*The Devolopment of Auditing in Turkey and Audit Application in Turkish Capital Markets*", 12th World Congress of Accounting Historians, July 20-24, 2008, Istanbul - Turkey.

MKK, (2010), Merkezi Kayıt Kuruluşu - Central Registry Agency Inc., www.mkk.com.tr

Muhan, R., (2009), "*Capital Flows and Emerging Market Economies*", Committee on the Global Financial System CGFS Papers No 33, Bank for International Settlements, Switzerland.

Takasbank, (2010), İMKB Takas ve Saklama Bankası A.Ş. - ISE Settlement and Custody Bank Inc., www.takasbank.com.tr

Turkdex, (2010), Vadeli İşlemler ve Opsiyon Borsası A.Ş. – Turkish Derivatives Exchange, www.turkdex.org.tr

TSPAKB, (2010), Türkiye Sermaye Piyasası Aracı Kuruluşları Birliği – The Association of Capital Market Intermediary Institutions of Turkey, www.tspakb.org.tr

Watson, M.J., (2010). "*The Regulation of Capital Markets-Market Manipulation and Insider Trading*", British Columbia Securities Commission – Working Paper.

In: Regulation and Competition in the Turkish Banking...   ISBN: 978-1-61324-990-1
Editors: Tamer Çetin and Fuat Oğuz   © 2012 Nova Science Publishers, Inc.

Chapter 10

EFFICIENCY AND PRODUCTIVITY OF THE BROKERAGE HOUSES IN TURKEY

Necmiddin Bağdadioğlu[1], Mehmet Reşit Dinçer[2] and Ahmet Burçin Yereli[1]

[1]Hacettepe University, Department of Public Finance, Ankara, Turkey
[2]Turkish Court of Accounts, Ankara, Turkey

ABSTRACT

This chapter calculates the efficiency and productivity of 63 Brokerage Houses operating in Turkey by applying the well known methodology of Data Envelopment Analysis to the most recent data available covering the period between 2000 and 2008. The findings clearly depict the adverse impacts of both the domestic financial crisis of 2001 and the global financial crisis of 2008 on the Turkish Brokerage Sector as very low efficiency scores and declining productivity. The main sources of inefficiency and poor productivity during the period, however, appear to be originated from managerial incompetency at individual brokerage houses level, and dominance of banks at the financial sector level.

Keywords: Financial sector; Brokerage house; Technical efficiency; Data envelopment analysis; Productivity; Malmquist index

INTRODUCTION

The intermediary activities through institutions play important role in facilitating transactions in free market economies. Brokerage houses (BHs) carry out this intermediary role in financial sector in various ways, for instance, by bringing together those with excess and shortage of funds, managing risks, providing advisory services for investors, and reducing cost of participation for their clients in financial sectors (Allen and Santomero, 1996). Today, due to the development of internet technology and increasing usage of internet, the forms and types of intermediary activities have changed in financial sector dramatically, but the need for intermediary institutions has not lessened. The Turkish transformation into a free market economy initiated in 1980 was commenced in financial sector, including reoperationalizing the BHs first established in the 1860s. Since then the BHs have played important roles in the development of Turkish financial sector, but their efficiency and productivity have rarely been investigated empirically.

This chapter aims to contribute to this limited literature by examining the efficiency and productivity of 63 BHs in Turkey by applying the well establish methodology of the Data Envelopment Analysis (DEA) on the most recent data available covering the period between 2000 and 2008. This also provides an valuable opportunity to observe the state of BHs after one of the worst internal financial crisis hit the Turkish economy in 2001 (Akyüz and Boratav, 2002) and just before the global financial crisis of 2008 (Crotty, 2009) started to show its full impact on the Turkish economy.

Accordingly, this chapter is organized under three main sections. The following section briefly accounts for the development of BHs in Turkey. The third section reviews the previous literature and introduces the methodology of DEA. The fourth section presents the data and findings. The chapter ends with an assessment of the findings.

1. DEVELOPMENT OF BROKERAGE HOUSES IN TURKEY

The early development of Turkish BHs is well accounted for in Fertekligil (1993), and thus, this section accommodates information from that study as required. The origin of BHs and stock exchange in Turkey dates back to the era of increasing debt of Ottoman Empire after the Crimean War in 1854. The issue of equity to cover the debt facilitated the emergence of equity market dominated by the Galata bankers in Istanbul. The Galata bankers formed a union in 1864, which together with the lender countries played a key role in the establishment of the first stock exchange called the Dersaadet in 1866. However, not until the accouncement of by-law of 19 November 1873, the legal and institutional requirements completed, a commissioner appointed, and at last, the Dersaadet Stock Exchange gained its legal status. The by-law of 1873 arranged the transactions in stock exchange to be carried out by three intermediary groups, namely, stockbrokers, agents, and cobers.

In principle the design of intermediary activities in the Dersaadet Stock Exchange during the Ottoman time was inspired from the old Frence system. Accordingly, the stockbroker resembled to the agent de change and the agent to the remisier. Both the stockbrokers and the agents were allowed to operate only on behalf of their clients, while the cobers, like in the London Stock Exchange, were granted with the right of transaction of bonds only under their names. Later, the by-law of 1906 allowed the stockbrokers to operate under their own name, as well.

In any case, the main component of the intermediary system was the stockbrokers since the members of other groups were not permitted to make transaction directly with their clients, for that they needed the stockbrokers. Later on, another group called the subscribers were added to the system, which consisted of three subgroups, namely, banks, corporations, and bankers.

Table 1. Intermediary Institutions during the Ottoman Era

Institution Type	Number
Stockbroker	46
Cober	19
Agent	30
Banker	27
Money agent	50

Source: Fertekligil (1993: 34).

The by-law of 1885 introduced the money agents as another intermediary group enpowered with the right to operate in market activities, but they were not mentioned about in the by-law of 1906. Table 1 shows the type and number of these groups before the Republic of Turkey was established in 1923.

In 22 August 1923, the Council of Ministers announced an additional by-law involving important changes in the rules and regulations governing the stock exchange in Turkey. The name of stockbroker changed to agent, and the intermediaries divided into two main groups as principal and voluntary. The agents, bankers and cobers included in the former group, and they were required to be Turkish by nationality. Besides, unlike the Ottoman time, the books were made compulsory to be kept in Turkish.

The Stock and Foreign Exchange Law (No: 1447) announced in 30 May 1929 redefined the exchange activities, participants and intermediary system in Turkey. Accordingly, while the agents were regarded as the principal members of stock exchange by this law, the cobers, bankers and money agents were regarded as registered members. The principal members were permitted to process the orders of their clients directly or indirectly. However, the cobers were allowed to do dealings only under their own names. Later, a new dealer called coulissiers was introduced to work as intermediary between the money agents and the investors. Finally, the banks were given the right to forward the orders of their clients to the agents.

At the beginning of 1960s, a view emerged that the Law No: 1447 of 1929 was not sufficient enough to provide diversified saving options to match the economic development achieved during 30 years of its implementation. This view was intensified during the early years of 1970s as the improvement in the Turkish economy strengthened private campanies, leading them to pay high dividends to their shareholders. Some campanies were even considering to offer their shares to public. However, the economic collapse due to the rapidly rising oil prices of 1970s, accompanied with political instability, killed this spirit and led many clients to keep their savings as deposit in banks. Thus, the planned changes for the capital market institutions were postponed, and the emergence of modern intermediary institutions had to wait a little longer (Manavgat, 1991).

Meanwhile, in 24 January 1980 the economic stabilization reform was introduced in Turkey (Arıcanlı and Rodrik, 1990). As an extention of the reform the banks were given the right to issue deposit certificates and to determine their own interest rates for credits and deposits freely in 01 July 1980. However, the banks' unwillingness to rise the interest rates, led the bankers to seize the opportunity by giving deceptive advertisements, presenting themselves as reliable intermediaries and collecting deposits at very high interest rates. The bankers were legally allowed to collect deposits and to sell bank issued certicifates, but they were not subject to the tight regulation and rigorous monitoring the banks were facing. Their tax obligations were not as heavy as of the banks, either. These conditions led to a dramatical and uncontrolled increase in the number of bankers and their deposits. This period, as often recalled as the era of bankermania, lasted less than two years, but created substantial financial losses as the depositors realized that they would not be able to receive either the money they deposited or the high interest promised.

The government responded to this case by announcing the long waited Capital Market Law (No: 2499) in 28 July 1981, which as mentioned before was under preparation for almost 20 years since 1960. This was followed by the Capital Market Activities and Capital Market Institutions Law (No: 3794) announced in 29 April 1992 amending the Law No: 2499. The fifth section of the Law No: 3794 redefined the scope, market activities, establishment conditions of intermediary institutions, and fundementally changed the intermediary system implemented since the Ottoman time. The new definition of intermediary institution given in the amended law was very much in line with the definition used in the United States of America which broadly covered the scope of operations of brokers, dealers, underwriters and investment banking (Ünal, 1997). The Law No: 3794 divided the intermediary institutions principally into two groups in Turkey, namely, BHs and banks. Since then these two intermediary groups have been handling public offerings, commercial transactions between sellers and buyers, repo and reverse repo, investment consultancy, and portfolio management in the Turkish financial sector.

After the terrible financial consequences of the aforementioned era of bankermania, the establishment of a new BH was made subject to very strict conditions by the Law No: 3794. By the words of the Law, to qualify for intermediary financial activities, the BH must be established as a joint stock company in compliance with the provisions of the Law No: 3794, its capital must be in the form of registered shares, fully paid and not to be less than the amount determined by the Capital Market Board, and its founders must not have been subject to any legal prosecution due to bankruptcy or other infamous offence. In any case, the establishment of BH was conditional on the approval of Capital Market Board.

Before proceeding with the efficiency and productivity measurment of BHs it might be useful to summarize their activities in the stock exchange market and the fixed-income security market, which involved bonds issued by private sector or government, and Treasury bills, during the period of 2000-2008. As seen from Table 2, the transaction volume of securities handled by the BHs declined sharply (almost 50%) after the financial crisis of 2001. The activities started to pick up in 2004, exceeding the transaction volume of 2000 only in 2005 and 2006. Then, the transaction volume of securities decreased dramatiacally as the global financial crisis started to show its full impact on the Turkish economy in 2007 and 2008.

According to the data derived from the annual capital market reports published by The Association of Capital Market Intermediary Institutions of Turkey (TSPAKB), 28 private BHs with total assets exceeding $5 Million realized about half of the securities transactions in 2001 and 2002. This continued until the market share of bank-owned BHs started to pick up in 2003. Then, the market share of 37 bank-owned BHs gradually increased to 57% in 2004, to %59,3 in 2006, 61,1% in 2007, but contracted sharply by 25% reducing to 54% as the global financial crisis started to effect the Turkish financial sector in 2008.

Efficiency and Productivity of the Brokerage Houses in Turkey

Table 2. Transaction Volume of Securities ($ Billion)

2000	362.7
2001	160.7
2002	141.5
2003	200.3
2004	295.5
2005	403.5
2006	459.3
2007	602
2008	523

Source: Compiled from the annual reports of Turkish Capital Market published by the TSPAKB.

The number of listed companies and their share of public offerings also effected the transaction volume in the stock exchange. As seen in Table 3, compared to 2000, the initial public offerings and the volume of transactions decreased remarkably after the 2001 financial crisis. The number and volume of public offerings started to pick up only after 2004, reaching to $3.400 Million in 2007 before reducinging to $1.900 Million in 2008, reflecting the impact of global financial crisis.

Table 3. Public Offerings and Number of Companies

Initial Public Offerings		Number of Transacted Company	Volume of Transactions ($Million)
2000	35	315	2.800
2001	1	310	0.2
2002	4	288	56
2003	2	285	11
2004	12	297	483
2005	11	306	1.790
2006	19	321	949
2007	11	327	3.400
2008	3	326	1.900

Source: Compiled from capital market reports published by the TSPAKB.

Table 4. Fixed-income Securities Market Transaction Volume ($ Million)

2000	499
2001	403
2002	317
2003	428
2004	665
2005	709
2006	744
2007	863
2008	803

Source: Compiled from capital market reports published by the TSPAKB.

206   Necmiddin Bağdadioğlu, Mehmet Reşit Dinçer and Ahmet Burçin Yereli

The transactions in the fixed-income security market shown in Table 4 were dominated by government bonds and Treasury bills. In fact, since 1994 only two private companies issued bonds which was in 2006. During the period of 2000-2008 only 20% of transactions in the fixed-income security market was undertaken by BHs. The remaining 80% was realized by banks. Between 2000 and 2005, all fixed-income securities were issued by public sector. Only after 2006, the private sector started to issue bonds, but the volume of transaction remained small. The banks handled transactions always had the largest portion in this market since 2002.

The number of BHs by ownership type is shown in Table 5. As seen in Table 5, the number of BHs was decreasing since the permission for establishment of new BH was not permitted after the 2001 financial crisis. The share of foreign ownership gradually increased during the period, particularly after 2005, while the new Banking Law (No: 5411) was published in compliance with the accession requirement to the European Union (Bakir and Onis, 2010). Some of the bank-owned BHs were transferred to the Savings Deposits Insurance Fund (SDIF) in 2001. However, as of 2007, there was no BH left under the ownership of SDIF. The private, bank-owned, and foreign BHs dominated the sector.

Table 5. Brokerage Houses by Ownership

	2001	2002	2003	2004	2005	2006	2007	2008
Private	95	98	97	91	86	77	69	67
Foreign	5	9	9	9	6	18	26	27
Public	4	4	4	4	4	4	4	4
SDIF	19	8	7	8	5	1	0	0
Total	123	119	117	112	101	100	99	98
Brokerage houses	49	38	38	37	33	30	31	31
Bank-owned brokerage houses	74	81	79	75	68	70	68	67
Total	123	119	117	112	101	100	99	98

Source: Compiled from capital market reports published by the TSPAKB.

Table 6. Number of Brokerage Houses by Type of Certificate of Activity

	2001	2002	2003	2004	2005	2006	2007	2008
Exchange intermediary	123	119	117	112	101	100	99	98
Repo/Reverse repo	119	74	72	68	67	64	63	59
Credit-based security	98	99	99	97	98	97	96	97
Public offerings	81	68	64	61	59	60	61	55
Portfolio management	64	61	59	54	57	58	59	52
Investment consultancy	62	65	54	51	57	55	59	59
Derivative transaction	29	5	5	5	42	46	63	68

Source: Compiled from capital market reports published by the TSPAKB.

The BHs were required to obtain certificate for each type of activity in financial sector. As seen in Table 6, in terms of type of activity the exchange intermediary, repo/reverse repo, and credit-based security dealings were the main activities performed by the BHs between 2001 and 2008.

The BHs performed their activities by either their head quarter or their branch, liaison office and agency established in connection with banks. Table 7 shows the number of branches, liaison officies and agencies of BHs. During the period the number of liaison officies decreased, while the number of agencies increased, suggesting that the BHs were performing their activities largely through their branches and agencies. The basic drive behind this preference might be to utilize from the large number of bank branches and their network. By this way they were cutting their personnel usage, as well. Accordingly, the number of employees gradually decreased during the period from 8336 in 2000 to 5102 in 2008. 30% of labor force become unemployed between 2000 and 2004. The decreasing trend started in 2001 slowed down in 2005. However, due to the global financial crisis the employee number, which was around 5900 in 2005, dropped to 5100 in 2008. In 2000, there were 58 BHs operating through branch, 41 through agent and 35 through liaison office, while in 2008 only 37 BHs were operating through branch, 23 through agent and only 21 through liaison office, respectively.

Table 7. Number of Branches, Liaison Offices, and Agencies

	2000	2001	2002	2003	2004	2005	2006	2007	2008
Branch	211	219	293	227	224	234	246	231	185
Liaison office	88	88	96	73	63	69	64	52	44
Agency	3412	3948	3813	3688	4450	4406	4514	4775	5664
Total	3711	4255	4152	3988	4741	4709	4824	5058	5893

Source: Compiled from capital market reports published by the TSPAKB.

Table 8. Income and Expenditure of Brokerage Houses (Thousand YTL)

Year[*]	Income	Expenditure
2000	463.473	368.833
2001	545.453	452.559
2002	467.089	469.746
2003	535.397	471.528
2004	425.639	358.276
2005	922.303	619.801
2006	856.581	684.533
2007	1.082.200	779.700
2008	861.400	788.700

Source: Compiled from capital market reports published by the TSPAKB.
[*] In 2004 inflation accounting was implemented, thus only the data of 90 BHs are accounted for in Table 8.

The income of BHs consisted of commissions they receive in return to their intermediary services in sells/buys of securities, public offerings, portfolio managements, credit-based and other related activities. Their expenses involved of expenditures on personnel, operating, salling, and costs of custody services. The largest portion of expenditures were on personnel plus operating activities, together making 80% of total expenditures (see Table 8). As seen in Table 8, perhaps as a result of the global financial crisis of 2001, only in 2002 the expenditures slightly exceeded the income of BHs. After 2005, the gap between income and expenditure started to increase in favor of income, reflecting the increase in concentration of BHs on their main activities, and thus, rise in their commission income.

Last but not least, the equity capital of BHs showed a considerable improvement during the period, as well, increasing their financial strength as seen in Table 9. The equity capital of BHs increased more than 6,5 folds from 325281 Thousand YTL in 2000 to 2149000 Thousand YTL in 2008.

Table 9. Equity Capital of Brokerage Houses (Thousand YTL)

2000	325.281
2001	573.903
2002	719.647
2003	895.570
2004	810.180
2005	1.500.862
2006	1.499.548
2007	1.941.700
2008	2.149.000

Source: Compiled from capital market reports published by the TSPAKB.

Nevertheless, despite the significance of BHs in the Turkish financial sector their efficiency and productivity have not been examined thoroughly. For this the following section reviews the previous efficiency and productivity studies of BHs and introduces the methodology of DEA frequently applied to examine the efficiency and productivity of BHs.

2. PREVIOUS STUDIES AND METHODOLOGY

The examination of efficiency and productivity of BHs is not as popular as of those financial institutions operating in banking and insurance sectors (Liao *et al.* 2010). Likewise, compared to the empirical examinations of institutions operating in banking sector (Atan 2003, Atan and Çatalbaş 2005, Öncü and Aktaş 2007, Denizer *et al.* 2007, Özgür 2008, Borluk 2008, Aydın *et al.* 2009) and insurance sector (Bülbül and Akhisar 2005, Kılıçkaplan and Baştürk 2005, Turgutlu *et al.* 2005), there are few studies investigating the efficiency and/or productivity of BHs in Turkey, namely, by Gündüz *et al.* 2001, Karacabey 2003, Aslantaş 2004, and Aktaş and Kargın 2007, respectively.

Unlike our study in this chapter, all these studies on the Turkish BHs relied on fairly old data. Evidently, Gündüz *et al.* (2001) used data for 1997 and 1998 to analyse the efficiency of 11 BHs, which were holding the largest portion of assets in the Turkish securities sector (60%). Only two BHs in 1997 and four in 1998 were found relatively more efficient in terms of getting commissions with regard to services they provided considering their equity capital and general operating expenditures. Karacabey (2003) used data for 2002 to investigate the efficiency of 116 BHs. Of those, only four BHs were found efficient in converting their inputs (personnel number, branch number, and capital) into outputs (account number and transaction number). Aslantaş (2004) used data coincided with the previous studies for the period of 1999-2002 to examine the efficiency of 90 BHs. The results signified widespread inefficiencies among BHs. In this study, for the efficiency calculation, personnel number, financial capital and equity capital were used as inputs, while commission earnings and transaction volume of stock were used as outputs. Finally, in a more recent study, Aktaş and Kargın (2007) used the data set for the period of 2000-2005 and found a declining trend in efficiency of BHs possibly due to the increasing investment on internet technologies. The efficiency and productivity calculations were carried out by using equity capital and operating expenses as inputs and transaction volume of stock and commissions as outputs.

These studies employed the DEA methodology for the efficiency calculation of BHs. This was partly because of the difficulties in finding complete set of dynamic panel data about activities of BHs. Besides by using the DEA methodology, it was possible to lessen the difficulties of accommodating multiple-input and multiple-output nature of activities of BHs. Indeed, one of the alternative efficiency measurement techniques, the financial ratio analysis enables to examine efficiency only partially, while the stronger alternative, the stochastic frontier analysis necessitates an arbitrary choice of dependent variable for the estimation of efficiency frontier under a predefined functional form and distributional assumptions for error term. In that sense, the DEA methodology is more suitable since it does not need to specify any functional form to fit data or any particular assumption about distributional behavior of components of error term (Seiford, 1996).

In a nutshall, the DEA calculates the efficiency of a Decision Making Unit (DMU) as was called by Charnes *et al.* (1978) relative to a frontier consisted of efficient DMUs. The distance from the efficiency frontier shows the rate of inefficiency as well as the potential of the same DMU to join the peer of efficient DMUs. Charnes *et al.* (1978) initiated the DEA methodology upon the foundation laid by Farrell (1957) who defined (in Charness *et al.*'s term) a DMU as technically efficient when produces maximum amount of output with given set of inputs, and as price efficient when uses inputs at optimal proportion given their respective prices. Farrell (1957) defined the combination of these two efficiency components as overall efficiency.

Farrell's (1978) efficiency measurement generalized by Charness *et al.* (1978) to include multiple-output productions, and later extended by several others, as reviewed by Cooper *et al.* (2006), to accommodate various options of efficiency measurement under different technologies, such as, constant returns to scale (CRS) or variable returns to scale (VRS). For instance, the efficiency frontier can be calculated as input-based, aiming to assess the ability of a particular DMU (in our case, BH) to produce the same outputs by using fewer inputs, or as output-based, targeting to identify a BH producing more of outputs by the same amount of inputs.

The empirical studies reviewed at the beginning of this section assume that the production approach rather than intermediary approach characterizes the activities of BHs. The intermediary approach is regarded as more suitable for efficiency measurement of banks, which concentrate on intermediation between fund suppliers and fund demanders, while the main focus of BHs is assumed to increase transaction volume and commission income.

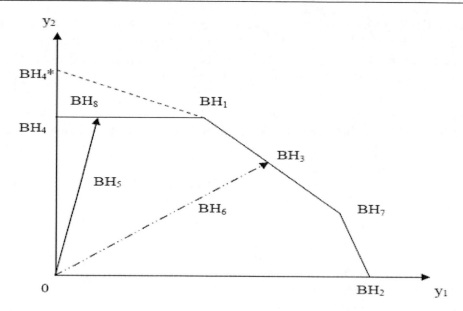

Figure 1. Output-based DEA.

Thus, the focus of explanation in this section is henceforth on output-based efficiency calculation. Besides, as the data used in this chapter did not involve price variables, the calculation is directed for technical efficiency.

The construction of output-based technical efficiency frontier can be explained graphically, assuming BHs providing two services (y_1 and y_2) by consuming only one input (x). As shown in Figure 1, the technical efficiency frontier is constructed by the efficient BHs, namely, BH_4, BH_1, BH_7, and BH_2. Those BHs laying inside the technical efficiency frontier, namely, BH_5 and BH_6, are regarded as inefficient. The distance from the efficiency frontier shows the extent of technical inefficiency. For instance, the technical inefficiency of BH_6 is given by the ratio of BH_6/BH_3, which corresponds to a value between 0 and 1, when the upper boundary of efficiency is set at 1. Accordingly, $1-(BH_6/BH_3)$ gives the extent of technical inefficiency, or, the potential of BH_6 to become efficient.

Two issues require attention in Figure 1. Firstly, notice that BH_6's projection point BH_3 at the efficiency frontier is a fictitious BH consisted of a combination of BH_1 and Bh_7. Secondly, the projection point of BH_5 on the efficiency frontier, that is BH_8, is actually not technically efficient, since BH_8 can still produce more of y_1 without consuming more of x. This indicates the presence of output slack in the case of BH_8 in output y_1. To avoid regarding BH_8 as efficient while there is such an output slack, an very small number is included in actual calculation of technical efficiency, which shifts the efficiency facet upward in Figure 1 from BH_4 to BH_4^*.

Following Coelli (1996: 23) the corresponding DEA model of output-based technical efficiency can be defined as follows:

$$\max_{\phi,\lambda} \phi, \tag{1}$$

Subject to

$$-\phi \mathbf{y}_i + \mathbf{Y}\lambda \geq 0,$$

$$\mathbf{x}_i - \mathbf{X}\lambda \geq 0,$$

$$\lambda_j \geq 0,$$

In this model, the BH under examination is regarded as technically efficient only when $\phi =1$ and there is no slack in either inputs or outputs. The slack in outputs and inputs shows the potential of further increase in outputs and decrease in inputs, respectively. If there is no slack, ϕ-1 shows the proportional increase in outputs that could be achieved by the BH to become efficient. The model compares each BH under evaluation with those of BHs which use at least the same amount of inputs to produce at least the same amount of outputs. The $\lambda_j \geq 0$ gives the reference set of BHs with similar level of activities that the inefficient BH could imitate to reach the efficiency frontier. $1/\phi$ gives output-based technical efficiency score, which takes a value between zero and one.

Technical efficiency scores under different production technologies can be explained by the help of CRS and VRS frontiers depicted in Figure 2. Under the CRS technology, where an increase in inputs of a BH create a proportionate increase in outputs, the technical efficiency scores are the same no matter in which direction (input-based or output-based) the efficiency calculation is carried out. The CRS technology reflects the production along with the line passing through $0BH_2$ in Figure 2. However, the direction of efficiency calculation matters under the VRS technology, which is made of BH_1, BH_2 and BH_3 in Figure 2. The VRS reflects that production technology might show increasing returns to scale (IRS) or decreasing returns to scale (DRS) (Cooper *et al.* 2000).

Under the VRS, the frontier envelops data points tighter than under the CRS. Accordingly, while only BH_2 is efficient under the CRS, the number of efficient BHs rise under the VRS. BH_1, BH_2 and BH_3 are efficient under the VRS, but not efficient under the CRS. BH_4 is inefficient under both frontiers. The output-based technical efficiency score of BH4 is given by $0O_1/0O_2$ under the VRS, while it is given by $0O_1/0O_3$ under the CRS. Clearly, $(0O_1/0O_3)<(0O_1/0O_2)$. The CRS signifies optimal scale of operation. The deviation from the optimal scale of operation can be calculated by $(0O_1/0O_3)/(0O_1/0O_2)$, which reflects the scale efficiency (SE). Then, the total technical efficiency (TTE) of BH_4 can be expressed as multiplication of these two efficiency components: pure technical efficiency (PTE) represented by TE_{VRS}, and the SE. That is, $(TTE)=(PTE)x(SE)$, where $(0O_1/0O_3)=(0O_1/0O_2)x(0O_2/0 O_3)$.

The output-based technical efficiency score under the VRS can be calculated simply by adding another constraint to (1) as $N1'\lambda =1$.

A practical way of identifying the type of production technology is by floating another frontier called the non-increasing returns to scale (NIRS) by changing the VRS constraint to $N1'\lambda \leq 1$ in (1). In Figure 2, the NIRS frontier is represented by the discontinious line $0BH_2BH_3$. The comparison of the frontiers helps to identify the type of technology. The production technology is characterized by IRS when $TE_{NIRS} \neq TE_{VRS} = TE_{CRS}$, by CRS when $TE_{NIRS} = TE_{VRS} = TE_{CRS}$, and by DRS when $TE_{NIRS} = TE_{VRS} \neq TE_{CRS}$, respectively (Fare *et al.* 1989).

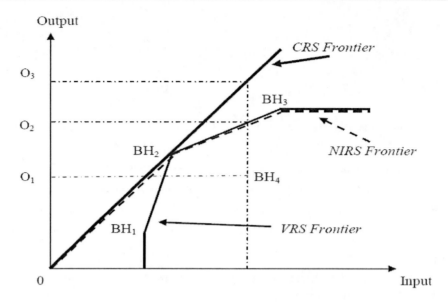

Figure 2. Efficiency Frontier Under Different Production Technologies.

This DEA approach explined so far enables to observe static efficiency of each BH. To investigate dynamic efficiency of each BH, the MI of total factor productivity (TFP) growth developed by Fare *et al.* (1994) is employed. Based on Farrell's (1957) work, the output-based MI is an output distance function characterising the production technology, searching for a maximum proportional expansion of output vector when input vector is given. The MI calculates the productivity change of each BH between two adjacent time periods by estimating the ratio of distance functions of BH from the frontier. The decomposition of TFP growth into two components enables to observe changes in technical efficiency and shifts in technology over time. The former is a measurement of catching-up with best practice frontier, while the latter is a measure of technological improvement.

Following Fare *et al.* (1994), the output-based TFP change (TFPCH) between time period *t* and *t+1* can be expressed as the geometric mean of two MI as follows:

$$M_o^{t,t+1}(y^t, y^{t+1}, x^t, x^{t+1}) = \left[\frac{D_o^t(y^{t+1}, x^{t+1})}{D_o^t(y^t, x^t)} \frac{D_o^{t+1}(y^{t+1}, x^{t+1})}{D_o^{t+1}(y^t, x^t)} \right]^{\frac{1}{2}} \quad (2)$$

where the productivity of production point (y^{t+1}, x^{t+1}) is compared with the production point (y^t, x^t). A value greater than 1 signifies a positive TFPCH in period *t+1*, while a value less than 1 indicates performance deterioration over time.

The output-based TFPCH can be decomposed further into two components to examine efficiency improvement and technological progress of BHs separately as follows:

$$M_o^{t,t+1}(y^t, y^{t+1}, x^t, x^{t+1}) = \frac{D_o^{t+1}(y^{t+1}, x^{t+1})}{D_o^t(y^t, x^t)} \left[\frac{D_o^t(y^t, x^t)}{D_o^{t+1}(y^t, x^t)} \frac{D_o^t(y^{t+1}, x^{t+1})}{D_o^{t+1}(y^{t+1}, x^{t+1})} \right]^{\frac{1}{2}}$$

$$(3)$$

where the term outside the brackets measures the change in the output-based technical efficiency (EFFCH) between periods t and $t+1$. The EFFCH calculates efficiency change as the ratio of technical efficiency in period t to the technical efficiency in period $t+1$. It shows whether production is getting closer to or drifting away from the efficiency frontier. The EFFCH index gets a value greater than, equal to, or less than 1 depending on whether the BH achieves efficiency increase, no efficiency change, or efficiency decrease, respectively. The term within brackets measures the change in production technology (TECHCH) as geometric mean of two ratios of distance functions. The TECHCH measures the shift in technology between year t and $t+1$. It shows whether or not technical advancement occurred at the input-output combination in our case in BH sector. A value greater than 1 signifies technological advancement, while a value of less than 1 indicates a decline in performance. Consequently, TFPCH =(EFFCH)x(TECHCH).

Four separate DEA based linear programming problems need to be solved to calculate the required output distance functions for each BH. The models with the assumption of CRS technology is as follows (Fare *et al.* 1994):

$$\max_{\phi,\lambda} \phi = \left[D_o^t(y^t, x^t) \right]^{-1}$$
$$st \quad -\phi y_i^t + Y^t \lambda \geq 0,$$
$$x_i^t - X^t \lambda \geq 0,$$
$$\lambda \geq 0$$

$$(4)$$

$$\max_{\phi,\lambda} \phi = \left[D_o^{t+1}(y^{t+1}, x^{t+1}) \right]^{-1}$$
$$st \quad -\phi y_i^{t+1} + Y^{t+1} \lambda \geq 0,$$
$$x_i^{t+1} - X^{t+1} \lambda \geq 0,$$
$$\lambda \geq 0$$

$$(5)$$

$$\max_{\phi,\lambda} \phi = \left[D_o^t(y^t, x^{+1t}) \right]^{-1}$$
$$st \quad -\phi y_i^{t+1} + Y^t \lambda \geq 0,$$
$$x_i^{t+1} - X^t \lambda \geq 0,$$
$$\lambda \geq 0$$

$$(6)$$

$$\max_{\phi,\lambda} \phi = \left[D_o^{t+1}(y^t, x^t) \right]^{-1}$$

$$st \quad -\phi y_i^t + Y^{t+1} \lambda \geq 0,$$

$$x_i^t - X^{t+1} \lambda \geq 0,$$

$$\lambda \geq 0 \tag{7}$$

Both the EFFCH and the TECHCH can be calculated to account for VRS by adding to each model another constraint as $\sum_{i=1}^{N} \lambda_i^t = 1$. The output–based measure of SE can also be calculated as the ratio of a distance function for VRS technology to that of CRS technology as follows:

$$S_o^t(y^t, x^t) = \frac{D_o^t(y^t, x^t | VRS)}{D_o^t(y^t, x^t | CRS)} \tag{8}$$

The EFFCH component could be decomposed further into pure efficiency change (PECH) and scale efficiency change (SECH). The SECH shows how close a BH is to the most productive scale size. A BH is regarded as scale inefficient if it not operating at the most productive scale size (Banker, 1984).

Based of explanation given so far, the efficiency and productivity of BHs are calculated and evaluated in the next section.

3. DATA AND FINDINGS

The calculation of efficiency and productivity of BHs is carried out using annual data published by the TSPAKB covering the period between 2000 and 2008 for 63 BHs. All BHs are required to be member of the TSPAKB, which was established as public institution by the Law No: 4487 in 1999. The variables commonly used in the literature, reviewed in the previous section, are included in efficiency and productivity calculation of the Turkish BHs. The personnal number, the branch number, the operating expenses and the equity capital of BH are used as inputs, while the volume of transaction in the equity securities market, the volume of transaction in the fixed-income securities market and operating income are employed as outputs. All variables are measured in the New Turkish Lira, except number of personnel and branch of BHs.

Table 10 presents the number and share of the BHs included in efficiency and productivity analysis compared with the whole sector involving all BHs operated in a particular year. The comparison is focused on the transaction volume in the equity securities market and the fixed-income securities market as well as the equity capital and personnel number. The sample used for the calculation is fairly representitive of the brokerage sector since the sample average covers 64% of the transactions in the equity securities market and about 75% of transactions in the fixed-income security market, equity capital and personnel employed during the period of 2000-2008, respectively.

Table 10. Comparison of the Sample of Brokerage Houses with the Brokerage Sector (Million YTL)

		2000	2001	2002	2003	2004[*]	2005	2006	2007	2008
Transaction volume in equity security market	Sector	222	186	213	293	417	540	650	776	665
	Sample	131	113	144	206	244	380	464	532	303
	Share of sample (%)	59	61	68	70	59	70	71	69	46
Transaction volume in fixed-income security market	Sector	305	467	468	639	950	949	1065	1126	1227
	Sample	223	326	311	420	513	650	983	1019	1201
	Share of sample (%)	73	70	66	66	54	68	92	90	98
Equity capital	Sector	325	574	720	895	810	1500	1499	1941	2149
	Sample	214	371	494	627	737	1122	1187	1561	1721
	Share of sample (%)	66	65	69	70	91	75	79	80	80
Personnel number	Sector	8336	7156	6626	6035	5906	5916	5896	5861	5102
	Sample	5058	4913	4800	4460	3979	4593	4695	4562	4212
	Share of sample (%)	61	69	72	74	67	78	80	78	83

[*] In 2004, the sample includes only 59 BHs due to missing data.

The code, title, and ownership type of BHs are given in Table 11. Of 63 BHs, 43 are domestic private, 11 are domestic private bank-owned, 6 are foreign private bank-owned and 3 are public bank-owned.

The efficiency and productivity analysis are carried out by using the DEAP software (Version 2.1) developed by Coelli (1996). Recall that by definition the BHs achieving larger transaction volume in equity securities market and fixed-income securities market, and earning higher operating income with their given number of personnel and branch, operating expenses and equity capital is regarded as technically efficient. An inefficient BH indicates the presence of similar BH(s) with higher production level under given inputs.

Table 12 shows the average efficiency scores of BHs on yearly basis. The small drop in average TTE from 79% in 2000 to 72% in 2001 can be interpreted as the impact of the financial crisis experienced in 2001. The TTE did not reached of its level in 2000 until 2003. Then, it stayed fairly stable until the global financial crisis of 2008, while it droped to 80%. The quite high average SE scores signifies that the scale inefficiency was not the major problem of BHs during the period. The main problem appears to be originating from managerial incompetency reflected by the relatively lower average PTE scores of BHs during the period.

As seen in Table 13, the number of BHs with unit score of TTE and SE range between 17 and 24 BHs with a percentage ranging between 27% and 38%, respectively. The lowest efficiency score and percentage belong to 2001. In terms of PTE, however, the number and percentage of efficient BHs are slightly higher ranging between 29 and 39 making 47% and 62% of BHs, respectively.

Table 11. Type of Brokerage House

Code	Brokerage House	Ownership Type
1	ACAR YATIRIM MENKUL DEĞERLER A.Ş.	Domestic Private
2	AKDENİZ MENKUL DEĞERLER TİCARETİ A.Ş.	Domestic Private
5	ATA YATIRIM MENKUL KIYMETLER A.Ş.	Domestic Private
6	ATAONLİNE MENKUL KIYMETLER A.Ş.	Domestic Private
7	AYBORSA MENKUL DEĞERLER TİCARETİ A.Ş	Domestic Private
8	BAHAR MENKUL DEĞERLER TİCARETİ A.Ş.	Domestic Private
9	BAŞKENT MENKUL DEĞERLER A.Ş.	Domestic Private
11	CENSA MENKUL DEĞERLER A.Ş.	Domestic Private
12	ÇAĞDAŞ MENKUL DEĞERLER A.Ş.	Domestic Private
13	DEHA MENKUL KIYMETLER A.Ş.	Domestic Private
14	DELTA MENKUL DEĞERLER A.Ş.	Domestic Private
16	DÜNYA MENKUL DEĞERLER A.Ş.	Domestic Private
17	ECZACIBAŞI MENKUL DEĞERLER A.Ş.	Domestic Private
18	EGEMEN MENKUL KIYMETLER A.Ş.	Domestic Private
19	EKİNCİLER YATIRIM MENKUL DEĞERLER A.Ş.	Domestic Private
20	ENTEZ MENKUL DEĞERLER TİCARETİ A.Ş.	Domestic Private
21	ETİ YATIRIM A.Ş.	Domestic Private
22	EVGİN MENKUL DEĞERLER TİCARET A.Ş.	Domestic Private
26	GEDİK YATIRIM MENKUL DEĞERLER A.Ş.	Domestic Private
27	GFC GENERAL FİNANS MENKUL DEĞERLER A.Ş.	Domestic Private
28	GLOBAL MENKUL DEĞERLER A.Ş.	Domestic Private
29	GÜNEY MENKUL DEĞERLER TİCARETİ A.Ş.	Domestic Private
30	GÜVEN MENKUL DEĞERLER A.Ş.	Domestic Private
31	HAK MENKUL KIYMETLER A.Ş.	Domestic Private
33	HEDEF MENKUL DEĞERLER A.Ş.	Domestic Private
35	İNFO YATIRIM A.Ş.	Domestic Private
38	MARBAŞ MENKUL DEĞERLER A.Ş.	Domestic Private
39	MEKSA YATIRIM MENKUL DEĞERLER A.Ş.	Domestic Private
40	MERKEZ MENKUL DEĞERLER A.Ş.	Domestic Private
42	OYAK YATIRIM MENKUL DEĞERLER A.Ş.	Domestic Private
43	ÖNCÜ MENKUL DEĞERLER A.Ş.	Domestic Private
44	ÖNER MENKUL KIYMETLER A.Ş.	Domestic Private
45	PAY MENKUL DEĞERLER A.Ş.	Domestic Private
46	POLEN MENKUL DEĞERLER A.Ş.	Domestic Private
47	PRİM MENKUL DEĞERLER A.Ş.	Domestic Private
48	SANKO MENKUL DEĞERLER A.Ş.	Domestic Private
49	SAYILGAN MENKUL DEĞERLER TİCARETİ A.Ş.	Domestic Private
50	SOYMEN MENKUL KIYMETLER A.Ş.	Domestic Private
51	STRATEJİ MENKUL DEĞERLER A.Ş.	Domestic Private
53	TACİRLER MENKUL DEĞERLER A.Ş.	Domestic Private
57	TOROS MENKUL KIYMETLER TİCARET A.Ş.	Domestic Private
58	ULUS MENKUL DEĞERLER A.Ş.	Domestic Private
59	ÜNİVERSAL MENKUL DEĞERLER A.Ş.	Domestic Private
3	ALTERNATİF YATIRIM A.Ş.	Domestic Private Bank-owned
4	ANADOLU YATIRIM MENKUL KIYMETLER A.Ş.	Domestic Private Bank-owned
10	CAMİŞ MENKUL DEĞERLER A.Ş.	Domestic Private Bank-owned
25	GARANTİ YATIRIM MENKUL KIYMETLER A.Ş.	Domestic Private Bank-owned
36	İŞ YATIRIM MENKUL DEĞERLER A.Ş.	Domestic Private Bank-owned
41	NUROL MENKUL KIYMETLER A.Ş.	Domestic Private Bank-owned
52	ŞEKER YATIRIM MENKUL DEĞERLER A.Ş.	Domestic Private Bank-owned
54	TEB YATIRIM MENKUL DEĞERLER A.Ş.	Domestic Private Bank-owned
55	TEKSTİL MENKUL DEĞERLER A.Ş.	Domestic Private Bank-owned
60	VAKIF YATIRIM MENKUL DEĞERLER A.Ş.	Domestic Private Bank-owned
62	YATIRIM FİNANSMAN MENKUL DEĞERLER A.Ş.	Domestic Private Bank-owned
15	DENİZ YATIRIM MENKUL KIYMETLER A.Ş.	Foreign Private Bank-owned
23	FİNANS YATIRIM MENKUL DEĞERLER A.Ş.	Foreign Private Bank-owned

Code	Brokerage House	Ownership Type
24	FORTİS YATIRIM MENKUL DEĞERLER A.Ş.	Foreign Private Bank-owned
34	HSBC YATIRIM MENKUL DEĞERLER A.Ş.	Foreign Private Bank-owned
56	TİCARET YATIRIM MENKUL DEĞERLER A.Ş.	Foreign Private Bank-owned
61	YAPI KREDİ YATIRIM MENKUL DEĞERLER A.Ş.	Foreign Private Bank-owned
32	HALK YATIRIM MENKUL DEĞERLER A.Ş.	Public Bank-owned
37	KALKINMA YATIRIM MENKUL DEĞERLER A.Ş.	Public Bank-owned
63	ZİRAAT YATIRIM MENKUL DEĞERLER A.Ş.	Public Bank-owned

Table 12. Average Efficiency Scores of Brokerage Houses[112]

	Total Technical Efficiency (TTE)	Pure Technical Efficiency (PTE)	Scale Efficiency (SE)
2000	0.790	0.855	0.930
2001	0.718	0.803	0.904
2002	0.755	0.859	0.873
2003	0.816	0.877	0.929
2004	0.790	0.871	0.911
2005	0.796	0.889	0.900
2006	0.792	0.886	0.886
2007	0.835	0.913	0.906
2008	0.797	0.877	0.909

At the beginning of period in 2000, of 63 BHs, 32 were technically inefficient due to operating at the IRS portion of the efficiency frontier, while 10 were technically inefficient due to operating at the DRS portion of the efficiency frontier, respectively. However, at the end of the period in 2008, only 27 BHs were inefficient due to operating with the IRS and 15 were inefficient due to operating with the DRS. Those of BHs identified as inefficient due to opereting at the IRS (DRS) portion of the efficiency frontier can became efficient by increasing (decreasing) their activities accordingly to their corresponding peers.

Table 13. Efficiency of Brokerage Houses[*] by Number and Percentage

Year	Total Technical Efficiency (TTE)		Pure technical Efficiency (PTE)		Scale Efficiency (SE)	
	Number of Efficient BH	%	Number of Efficient BH	%	Number of Efficient BH	%
2000	21	33	31	49	22	35
2001	17	27	30	47	17	27
2002	20	32	38	60	20	32
2003	24	38	33	52	26	41
2004	18	30	29	49	23	39
2005	19	30	30	47	22	35
2006	24	38	36	57	24	38
2007	24	38	39	62	24	38
2008	21	33	36	57	24	38

[*] Recall that in 2004 only 59 instead of 63 brokerage houses were included in efficiency calculations.

---

[112] The individual efficiency scores of each BH for each year are not shown in this chapter due to page restriction. However, they are available from the authors on request.

218 Necmiddin Bağdadioğlu, Mehmet Reşit Dinçer and Ahmet Burçin Yereli

Table 14. Reference Set for Inefficient Brokerage Houses in 2008

Inefficient Brokerage House	Reference Brokerage Houses
AYBORSA MENKUL DEĞERLER TİCARETİ A.Ş. (DP)	8 (DP), 11(DP), 16(DP), 38(DP)
BAŞKENT MENKUL DEĞERLER A.Ş. (DP)	5(DP), 8(DP), 22(DP), 33(DP)
DELTA MENKUL DEĞERLER A.Ş. (DP)	6(DP), 21(DP), 35(DP), 51(DP)
EGEMEN MENKUL KIYMETLER A.Ş. (DP)	2(DP), 6(DP), 11(DP), 33(DP)
EKİNCİLER YATIRIM MENKUL DEĞERLER A.Ş. (DP)	6(DP), 15(FPB), 17(DP), 23(FPB), 41(DPB), 61(FPB)
ENTEZ MENKUL DEĞERLER TİCARETİ A.Ş. (DP)	6(DP), 8(DP), 21(DP), 38(DP)
GEDİK YATIRIM MENKUL DEĞERLER A.Ş. (DP)	4(DPB), 5(DP), 15(FPB), 42(DP)
GÜNEY MENKUL DEĞERLER TİCARETİ A.Ş. (DP)	4(DPB), 6(DP), 8(DP), 11(DP), 40(DP)
GÜVEN MENKUL DEĞERLER A.Ş. (DP)	2(DP), 8(DP), 16(DP), 35(DP), 38(DP)
ÖNER MENKUL KIYMETLER A.Ş. (DP)	2(DP), 11(DP), 38(DP), 35(DP)
PAY MENKUL DEĞERLER A.Ş. (DP)	2(DP), 8(DP), 21(DP), 38(DP)
POLEN MENKUL DEĞERLER A.Ş. (DP)	4(DPB), 40(DP), 41(DPB), 49(DP)
PRİM MENKUL DEĞERLER A.Ş. (DP)	6(DP), 8(DP), 11(DP), 38(DP)
SANKO MENKUL DEĞERLER A.Ş. (DP)	2(DP), 22(DP), 35(DP), 37(PB), 51(DP)
SOYMEN MENKUL KIYMETLER A.Ş. (DP)	4(DPB), 6(DP), 8(DP), 21(DP), 38(DP)
TACİRLER MENKUL DEĞERLER A.Ş. (DP)	4(DPB), 5(DP), 15(FPB)
TOROS MENKUL KIYMETLER TİCARET A.Ş. (DP)	6(DP), 11(DP), 33(DP)
ULUS MENKUL DEĞERLER A.Ş. (DP)	2(DP), 11(DP), 38(DP), 35(DP)
ÜNİVERSAL MENKUL DEĞERLER A.Ş. (DP)	2(DP), 12(DP)
ALTERNATİF YATIRIM A.Ş. (DPB)	16(DP), 23(FPB), 35(DP), 61(FPB)
CAMİŞ MENKUL DEĞERLER A.Ş. (DPB)	8(DP), 11(DP), 23(FPB), 49(DP), 61(FPB)
GARANTİ YATIRIM MENKUL KIYMETLER A.Ş. (DPB)	4(DPB), 15(FPB), 34(FPB), 54(DPB)
ŞEKER YATIRIM MENKUL DEĞERLER A.Ş. (DPB)	23(FPB), 33(DP), 34(FPB), 41(DPB)
TEKSTİL MENKUL DEĞERLER A.Ş. (DPB)	4(DPB), 33(DP), 41(DPB)
VAKIF YATIRIM MENKUL DEĞERLER A.Ş. (DPB)	34(FPB), 49(DP), 61(FPB)
FORTİS YATIRIM MENKUL DEĞERLER A.Ş. (FPB)	4(DPB), 34(FPB), 56(FPB)
ZIRAAT YATIRIM MENKUL DEĞERLER A.Ş. (FPB)	21(DP), 34(FPB), 61(FPB)

* DP: Domestic Private; DPB: Domestic Private Bank-owned; FPB: Foreign Private Bank-owned; PB: Public Bank-owned.

Table 15. Adjustment Requirement of ZIRAAT YATIRIM MENKUL DEĞERLER A.Ş.

Efficiency Score: 0.708
Scale Efficiency: 0.884 (DRS)

	Current Level	Targeted Level (slack included)
Transaction Volume in Equity Securities Market	5 282 883	10 329 799
Transaction Volume in Fixed-income Securities Market	45 565 769 101	45 567 769 101
Operating Income	7 232 646	10 217 469
Equity Capital	48 755 419	48 755 419
Operating Expenditure	11 254 571	11 254 571
Branch Number	446	200
Personel Number	99	32

Reference Brokerage Houses (Lambda):
HSBC YATIRIM A.Ş. (0.580); ETI YATIRIM A.Ş. (0.404); YAPI KREDI Yatırım Menkul Değerler A.Ş. (0.016)

Table 16. Results of Malmquist Index of Total Factor Productivity Change

Periods	TFPCH	EFFCH	TECHCH	PECH	SECH
2000-2001	0.609	0.737	0.827	0.957	0.770
2001-2002	1.075	1.276	0.842	1.040	1.227
2002-2003	1.212	1.144	1.059	1.037	1.103
2003-2004	1.005	0.953	1.055	0.993	0.960
2004-2005	1.148	1.016	1.130	1.011	1.005
2005-2006	0.985	0.973	1.013	1.005	0.968
2006-2007	1.141	1.074	1.062	1.031	1.041
2007-2008	0.018	0.963	0.018	0.977	0.985
Average	0.606	1.006	0.602	1.006	1.000

Of 21 technically efficient BHs in 2000, 12 were bank-owned, while 9 were domestic privately-owned BHs. However, the number of bank-owned efficient BHs droped to 7, and the number of efficient privately-owned domestic BHs increased to 14 at the end of the period. Since 20 of 63 BHs were bank-owned (see Table 11), 57% of bank-owned BHs was efficient in 2000, while this percentage reduced to 33% in 2008.

The presence of an inefficient BH suggests the presence of at least one efficient BH that can be imitated to become efficient.

The second column of Table 14 shows the respective efficient peer of BHs for each inefficient BH under the VRS, since the managerial incompetency was identified as slightly more responsible from average total technical inefficiency in Table 13. Notice that the reference set of in efficient domestic BHs was usually made of efficient domestic BHs, suggesting the similarities of their activities.

Table 15 exemplifies how an inefficient BH, for instance, ZIRAAT YATIRIM MENKUL DEĞERLER A.Ş. in 2008, can be efficient by adjustment of its inputs and outputs. ZIRAAT YATIRIM MENKUL DEĞERLER A.Ş. can adjust its activities according to the projections shaped of combination of activities of ETI YATIRIM A.Ş., HSBC YATIRIM A.Ş. and YAPI KREDİ MENKUL DEĞERLER A.Ş. The second column in Table 15 shows the current level of activities of ZIRAAT YATIRIM MENKUL DEĞERLER A.Ş., while the third column presents the targets that ZIRAAT YATIRIM MENKUL DEĞERLER A.Ş. should reach to become efficient.

Recall that the TFPCH consists of four components, namely, EFFCH, TECHCH, PECH, and SECH. The TFPCH and its components for the period of 2000-2008 are given in Table 16.

The average TFPCH index is very low (0.606), indicating that BHs registered negative productivity growth during the period in Turkey. This seems to be derived from poor technological improvement during the period represented by very low average TECHCH score of 0.602. That is, the production frontier did not shift up between 2000 and 2008.

The average values of other components of TFPCH index, namely, EFFCH, TECHCH, PECH and SECH, were around unity, suggesting that BHs were just catching up with the best practice production frontier. The adverse impacts of internal financial crisis of 2001 and the global financial crisis of 2008 manifested itself by the low value of TFPCH index 0.60 and very low TFPCH index of 0.018, respectively. The individual performance of BHs are given in Table 17.

Table 17. Malmquist Index of Total Factor Productivity for Individual Brokerage Houses

BH	TFPCH	EFFCH	TECHCH	PECH	SECH
58	0.772	1.620	0.477	1.000	1.620
59	0.741	1.020	0.727	1.031	0.989
12	0.733	1.047	0.701	1.000	1.047
2	0.721	1.103	0.653	1.071	1.031
13	0.710	1.037	0.685	1.066	0.974
21	0.700	1.000	0.700	1.000	1.000
6	0.687	1.088	0.631	1.000	1.088
5	0.686	1.026	0.668	1.026	1.000
8	0.671	1.059	0.634	1.000	1.059
17	0.669	1.040	0.643	1.040	1.000
35	0.662	1.000	0.662	1.000	1.000
7	0.657	1.097	0.599	1.096	1.001
53	0.648	1.052	0.616	0.995	1.057
43	0.643	1.074	0.598	1.072	1.002
44	0.633	1.050	0.603	1.000	1.050
1	0.625	1.016	0.615	1.022	0.994
19	0.614	0.972	0.631	0.973	0.999
50	0.612	1.044	0.586	1.079	0.967
28	0.609	1.000	0.609	1.000	1.000
40	0.608	1.051	0.579	1.060	0.992
14	0.597	1.011	0.591	1.000	1.011
9	0.592	0.962	0.615	1.018	0.945
46	0.591	0.981	0.602	1.026	0.957
22	0.588	1.000	0.588	1.000	1.000
30	0.582	1.034	0.563	0.969	1.067
33	0.581	0.990	0.588	1.000	0.990
38	0.579	0.963	0.602	1.000	0.963
29	0.574	0.990	0.580	1.009	0.981
47	0.569	0.994	0.572	0.989	1.005
20	0.564	0.949	0.595	1.008	0.942
49	0.560	0.953	0.588	1.000	0.953
39	0.550	1.064	0.517	1.000	1.064
45	0.550	1.002	0.549	1.000	1.002
42	0.544	1.000	0.544	1.000	1.000
48	0.541	0.953	0.568	1.000	0.953
31	0.539	0.929	0.580	1.091	0.851
26	0.537	0.971	0.553	0.988	0.983
11	0.535	0.987	0.542	1.000	0.987
27	0.529	0.981	0.539	1.010	0.972
18	0.528	0.925	0.571	1.000	0.925
16	0.515	1.066	0.484	1.000	1.066
57	0.507	0.994	0.510	1.000	0.994
51	0.479	0.925	0.517	0.928	0.997
60	0.705	0.968	0.728	0.970	0.998

BH	TFPCH	EFFCH	TECHCH	PECH	SECH
36	0.684	1.005	0.681	1.000	1.005
52	0.652	1.000	0.652	1.000	1.000
10	0.648	0.951	0.681	0.967	0.984
3	0.631	0.957	0.659	0.960	0.997
4	0.611	1.029	0.593	1.029	1.000
62	0.594	0.977	0.608	1.000	0.977
55	0.574	0.975	0.589	1.000	0.975
41	0.571	1.055	0.541	1.051	1.003
54	0.523	0.932	0.561	0.960	0.971
25	0.501	0.922	0.544	0.939	0.982
61	0.739	1.000	0.739	1.000	1.000
24	0.732	1.019	0.718	1.010	1.009
34	0.661	0.989	0.668	1.000	0.989
15	0.600	1.027	0.584	1.026	1.000
56	0.559	0.928	0.602	0.946	0.981
23	0.499	1.000	0.499	1.000	1.000
32	0.634	0.979	0.647	1.000	0.979
63	0.623	0.943	0.661	0.949	0.994
37	0.548	0.899	0.609	1.047	0.858
Average	0.606	1.006	0.602	1.006	1.000

Overall, the EFFCH and the SECH components of the TFPCH index were considerably higher than the TECHCH, indicating that the BH sector did not experience innovation or technological progress in the past nine years. Of 63 BHS, 34 BHs had the EFFCH score 1 or higher, signifying their success in catching up with the best practice production frontier in the BHs sector over time.

CONCLUSION

Due to lack of data, the efficiency and productivity calculations of this chapter did not involve any indicators of service quality or client satisfaction. This leads one to interpret the findings with caution. Nevertheless, the following assertions are in place.

The Turkish financial sector is at the development stage, and thus, it has not got the capital market depth, the investor base or the diversified instruments that are usually encountered in relatively more advanced countries. The Derivatives Exchange established in 2005 has not reached the foreseen transaction volume, either. According to the Banking Regulation and Supervision Agency, as of November 2009, the equity capital and the total assets of 48 banks operated in Turkey were 108 Billion TL and 804 Billion TL, respectively. In contrast, in the same year according to the TSPAKB, the equity capital and the total assets of around 100 BHs operating in Turkey were only around 2.5 Billion TL and 5 Billion TL, respectively. This may be seen as a reflection of trust felt towards banks in Turkey. Evidently, the largest portion of activities in the fixed-income securities market is still handled by banks. The large investment funds are managed by bank-owned portfolio companies. However, this does not necessarily mean that all bank-owned BHs were more efficient. There were many bank-owned BHs with low efficiency scores during the period.

In addition to the domination of banks, the increasing usage of technological facilities intensified competition in the Turkish BH sector. That led the BHs to put more efforts to operate more efficiently. Perhaps due to these reasons, 18 BHs voluntarely stoped their operations in 2009. Five of them were included in our sample, namely, AKDENIZ MENKUL KIYMETLER AŞ, GFC GENERAL FINANS MENKUL KIYMETLER AŞ, HEDEF MENKUL KIYMETLER AŞ, KALKINMA YATIRIM MENKUL KIYMETLER AŞ, and NUROL MENKUL KIYMETLER AŞ. Except NUROL MENKUL KIYMETLER AŞ, they were not operating efficiently during the period.

In any case, there are many financial instruments available that companies in Turkey can use to obtain funds, such as, through issuing bills, bonds, asset-backed securities, commercial papers. However, due to the quite high borrowing requirements of public sector, and the interest and tax advantages provided to the publicly issued equity and bonds, the funds tend to go to domestic government bonds. Thus, the equity securities and the publicly issued equity and bond dominate the capital market, and the companies do not prefer to go for obtaining funds through public offerings. Evidently, according to the Istanbul Stock Exchange (ISE), amongst the largest 1000 industrial companies listed by the Istanbul Commerce Chamber in 2008, only 126 companies were quoted in the ISE. This shows how few companies were open to public in Turkey. Lastly, the dominance of banks in the financial sector appears to be one of the main obstacles before the emergence of strong and efficient BHs in Turkey, which is a prerequisite for reliable BH sector.

REFERENCES

Aktaş, H. and Kargın, M. (2007) "Aracı Kurumların Etkinlik Analizi," *İktisat işletme ve Finans*, 22: 97-117.

Akyüz, Y. and Boratav, K. (2002) "The Making of the Turkish Crisis," UNCTAD, Cenevre. http://www.bagimsizsosyalbilimciler.org/yazilar/AkyuzBoratav.htm

Allen, F. and Santomero, A. M. (1996) "The Theory of Financial Intermediation," Financial Institutions Center, University of Pennsylvania, The Whorton School.

Arıcanlı, T. and Rodrik, D. (1990) *The Political Economy of Turkey: Dept, Adjustment and Sustainability*. New York: St. Martin's Press.

Aslantaş, Ş. (2004) *Türk Sermaye Piyasasında Aracı Kurumların Piyasa Yapısı ve Etkinlik Analizi*, Marmara Üniversitesi, Bankacılık Ve Sigortacılık Enstitüsü, Doktora Tezi.

Atan, M. (2003) "Türkiyede Bankacılık Sektöründe Veri Zarflama Analizi ile Bilançoya Dayalı Mali Etkinlik ve Verimlilik Analizi," *Ekonomik Yaklaşım*, 48(14): 71-86.

Atan, M. and Çatalbaş, G. (2005) "Bankacılıkta Etkinlik ve Sermaye Yapısının Bankaların Etkinliğine Etkisi," *VII. Ulusal Ekonometri ve İstatistik Sempozyumu*, 26-27 Mayıs, 2005, İstanbul.

Aydin, N., Yalama, A. and Sayim, M. (2009) "Banking Efficiency in Developing Economy: empirical evidence from Turkey," *Journal of Money, Investment and Banking*, 8: 49-70.

Bakir, C. and Onis Z. (2010) "The Regulatory State and Turkish Banking Reforms in the Age of Post-Washington Consensus," *Development and Change* 41(1): 77-106.

Banker, R. D. (1984) "Estimating Most Productive Scale Size using Data Envelopment Analysis," *European Journal of Operational Research*, 17: 35-44.

Borluk, S. (2008) *Kriz Sonrası Bankacılık Sektörü Etkinlik Analizi*, MPM Yayınları No: 702, Ankara.

Bülbül, S. and Akhisar, İ. (2005) Türk Sigorta Şirketlerinin Etkinliğinin Veri Zarflama Analizi ile Araştırılması, *VII Ulusal Ekonometri ve İstatistik Sempozyumu*, 26-27 Mayıs 2005, İstanbul.

Charnes, A. Cooper,W. W. Rhodes, E. (1978) "Measuring The Efficiency of Decision Making Units", European Journal of Operational Research, 2: 429-444.

Coelli, T. (1996) "A Guide to DEAP Version 2.1: A Data Envelopment Analysis Program," Centre for Efficiency and Productivity Analysis Working Papers.

Cooper, W. W., Seiford, L. M. and Tone, K. (2000) *Data Envelopment Analysis: A Comprehensive Text with Models, Applications, References and DEA-Solver Software*, Kluwer Academic Publishers, Boston.

Cooper, W. W., Seiford, L. M. and Tone, K. (2006) *Introduction to Data Envelopment Analysis and Its Uses*, Springer, New York.

Crotty, J. (2009) "Structural Causes of the Global Financial Crisis: A Critical Assessment of the 'New Financial Architecture'," *Cambridge Journal of Economics*, 33 (4): 563-580. *doi: 10.1093/cje/bep023.*

Denizer, C., Dinc, M. and Tarimcilar, M. (2007) "Financial Liberalization and Banking Efficiency: evidence from Turkey," *Journal of Productivity Analysis*, 3: 177-195.

Fare, R., Grosskopf, S., Lindgren, B., and Roos, P. (1989) "Productivity Development in Swedish Hospitals: A Malmquist Output Index Approach", Discussion paper No. 89-3, Southern Illinois University.

Fare, R., Grosskopf, S., Norris, M., Zhang, Z. (1994) "Productivity Growth, Technical Progress and Efficiency Change in Industrial Countries", *American Economic Review*, 84: 66-83.

Farrell, M. J. (1957) "The Measurement of Productive Efficiency," *Journal of the Royal Statistical Society*, 120: 253-290.

Fertekligil, A. (1993) *Türkiye'de Borsa'nın Tarihçesi*, İMKB Yayınları, İstanbul.

Gündüz, L., Yilmaz, C. and Yılmaz, M. K. (2001) "Türkiye'de Aracı Kurumların Performans Analizi(1995-1998), Kantitatif Bir Değerlendirme," *Bahçeşehir Üniversitesi Ekonomi ve Yönetim Bilimleri Dergisi*, 1(3): 38-53.

Karacabey, A. (2003) *Türkiye'de Sermaye Piyasasının Mali Sistemler İçerisindeki Yeri, Sorunları ve Geleceği*, Sermaye Piyasası Kurulu, Ankara.

Kılıçkaplan, İ. S. and Baştürk, F. (2005) "Tobit Modeli Kullanılarak Türk Sigorta Sektöründe Etkinlik Değişiminin Ölçülmesi," *Mevzuat Dergisi*, 8(88): 654-73.

Liao, C-S., Yang, C-H. and Liu, D. (2010) "Efficiency, Productivity and Ownership Structure for Securities Firms in Taiwan," *Journal of Money, Investment and Banking*, 14: 46-58.

Manavgat, Ç. (1991) *Sermaye Piyasasında Aracı Kurumlar*, Banka ve Ticaret Hukuku Araştırma Enstitüsü, Ankara.

Öncü, S. and Aktaş, R. (2007) "Yeniden Yapılandırma Döneminde Türk Bankacılık Sektöründe Verimlilik Değişimi," *Celal Bayar Üniversitesi İİBF Yönetim ve Ekonomi Dergisi*,14(1): 247-266.

Özgür, E. (2008) "Kamu Bankalarının Finansal Etkinliği," *Afyon Kocatepe Üniversitesi Sosyal Bilimler Dergisi*, X(3): 247-260.

Seiford, L.M. (1996) "Data Envelopment Analysis: The Evolution of the State of the Art (1978–1995)," *Journal of Productivity Analysis*, 7, 99-137.

Turgutlu, E., Kök, R. and Kasman A. (2005) "Türk Sigorta Şirketlerinde Etkinlik: Deterministik ve Şans Kısıtlı Veri Zarflama Analizi," *İktisat, İşletme ve Finans*, 251: 85-102.

Ünal, Ö. K. (1997) *Aracı Kurumlar*, Yaklaşım Yayınları, İstanbul.

In: Regulation and Competition in the Turkish Banking...
Editors: Tamer Çetin and Fuat Oğuz

ISBN: 978-1-61324-990-1
© 2012 Nova Science Publishers, Inc.

Chapter 11

INSTITUTIONAL INVESTORS IN TURKEY

Ayhan Algüner[*]
Baskent University, Faculty of Economics
and Administrative Sciences,
06810, Ankara, Turkey

ABSTRACT

Securities mutual funds, pension mutual funds, life insurance companies, real estate investment trusts, venture capital investment trusts, securities investment trusts are the types of institutional investors that have operations in Turkey. Mutual funds are established in the form of open-end investment companies in Turkey. They do not have any legal entity. They are operated in terms of the rules stated in the internal statute of the fund, which includes general terms about management of the fund, custody of the assets, valuation principles and conditions of investing in the fund. The ratio of the investment funds' portfolio size to GDP is an indicator of the development level of the institutional investor base in that country. Although the ratio of the investment funds to GDP in Turkey has increased through the years, it is considered to be low when compared with other countries. There are two major classes of mutual funds in Turkey; fixed income and equity. Fixed income funds are the leading group, constituting 2/3 of total assets. Equity mutual funds represent only 2.5% of total assets. On the other hand, the private pension system that was introduced towards the end of 2003 has been growing exponentially. It is required to make the investment fund legislation coherent with European Union Directives and to provide the integration of European fund market and Turkish funds. Investment trusts are closed-end investment companies managing portfolios composed of capital market instruments, gold and other precious metals. Three types of investment trusts operate in Turkey, namely; Securities Investment Trusts, Real Estate Investment Trusts and Venture Capital Investment Trusts. As of the end of 2009, 48% of Istanbul Stock Exchange companies' shares which are open to public are in the custody accounts of foreign institutional investors at The ISE Settlement and Custody Bank Inc.

---

[*] E-mail address: alguner@baskent.edu.tr.

Introduction

One of the most important developments observed in financial markets in the recent years is the phenomenon of savings' institutionalization as a result of the growth in the pension funds, life insurance companies and investment funds. This situation emerged from the management of the savings by professional portfolio managers, instead of individual investors' direct investment on securities or bank deposits.

In developing countries such as Turkey, the most important factors in the provision of stable growth and financial development are to supply the required capital accumulation and to direct it to the investment correctly. In order to increase the saving tendency of the household, to provide the funds which will finance the investments at a low cost and a high amount, and to distribute these funds in an effective and efficient way, the related country should have a developed capital market. The effectiveness and the development level of the capital market, on the other hand, is highly determined by the development of the institutional investors and the wideness of the institutional investment base at that market.

In order to perceive the institutional investors' affecting capability on the markets, it would be appropriate to analyze some figures in the world. According to the statistics of the international investment funds industry, which was prepared by ICI (Investment Company Institute) depending on the data from 45 countries, the size of world investment funds is 22 trillion US dollars as of 2009 (Table 1.1). In the world ranking, the USA ranks the first with an investment fund size of nearly $11 trillion. Turkey ranks the 30th as for investment funds. According to the statistics for the third quarter of the year 2009, which was published by EFAMA (European Fund and Asset Management Association) as for the European funds, the size of investment funds in Europe has risen to 6.84 trillion Euros.[113]

An important part of institutional investor base in Turkey is comprised of investment funds (Table 1.2). Despite the rapid development observed in the investment funds in the recent years, it is observed that the size of institutional investors in Turkey is still at very low levels in international comparisons. The ratio of the investment funds' portfolio size to GDP is the indicator of the development level of the institutional investor base in that country.

According to the data obtained by ICI, the investment funds' portfolio size in Turkey is $20 billion, which is 3.2% of the national income.

Table 1. Investment Funds (09/2009)

	Investment Funds (Billion $)	Investment Funds Share	Investment Funds/GDP
1.USA	10,832	48.4%	76%
2. Luxembourg	2,239	10.0%	4814%
3. France	1,851	8.3%	70%
6. Brazil	742	3.3%	50%
30. Turkey	20	0.1%	3%
Total	22,376	100%	

Source: Investment Company Institute, www.ici.org.

---

[113] Source: European Fund and Asset Management Association, www.efama.org

Table 2. Institutional Investments (Million $) (at the Year-end)

	2001	2004	2008	09.2010	Share
Equity Mutual Funds	394	554	365	761	3%
Fixed Income Mutual Funds	2,894	15,996	15,253	18,581	63%
Pension Funds	-	112	4.193	7.311	25%
Exchange Traded Funds	-	-	128	135	0.5%
Investment Trusts	89	215	152	362	1%
Real Estate Investment Trusts	600	611	776	2.071	7%
Venture Capital Companies	3	5	27	105	0.4%
Total	3,963	17,492	20,895	29,326	
Institutional Investors/GDP	2.70%	7.00%	3.3%	4.5%	

Source: The Association of Capital Market Intermediary Institutions of Turkey (TSPAKB), Capital Market Factsheet, www.tspakb.org.tr.

Table 3. Breakdown of Savings (Billion $) (03/2010)

	Total	Share of Domestic Investors	Share of Foreign Investors
Deposits	329	76%	10%
Fixed Income	69	11%	25%
Equities	90	7%	65%
Mutual Funds	26	6%	-
Total	513	82%	18%

Source: TSPAKB (2010a).

When the investment preferences of domestic investors in Turkey are examined, it is seen that these investors mainly invest their savings in deposits. The primary investment preference of foreign investors, on the other hand, is equities. Only 6% of the total savings is invested on investment funds (Table 1.3).

Institutional investors can be distinguished from each other in terms of the relationships attached to the contracts between the assets owners and the assets managers. It is observed that the liabilities of the sides to each other or the rules determining the risk-return distribution lead to differences among the institutional investors. Pension mutual funds, life insurance companies, real estate investment trusts, venture capital investment trusts, securities investment trusts, securities mutual funds are the types of institutional investors that have operations also in Turkey.

1. COLLECTIVE INVESTMENT INSTITUTIONS IN TURKEY

Investing on financial markets requires knowledge and competence. Besides, as the individual savings can not often reach sufficient amounts, an effective diversification can not be conducted and risks are encountered due to the reasons such as the lack of knowledge on capital markets and inability to reach the knowledge at due time. Depending on this, collective investment institutions, which gather the individual investors' savings in an investment pool and manage these investments in accordance with the professional management and portfolio diversification, have been established.

When the country applications are considered, collective investment institutions can be classified in four groups (Okat, 2000):

- Collective investment institutions which are based on contracts (such as the investment funds in Turkey),
- Collective investment institutions which are established according to trust law (such as the unit trusts in Anglo-Saxon countries, whose samples do not exist in Turkey),
- Collective investment institutions which are open-end investment companies or which are companies with variable capital (such as the mutual funds in the USA),
- Collective investment institutions which are closed-end investment companies or which are companies with fixed capital (such as the investment trusts in Turkey).

According to this classification, types of collective investment institutions in some countries are displayed on the Table 1.4.

Collective investment institutions in Turkey are called investment trust when they are established as a distinct and independent legal personality as for their legal structure and they are named as investment fund when they are established by another community in the framework of a contract. While they are similar to each other as for their aims and economic functions, they differ from each other in their working styles and the service they offer to investors.

Table 4. Types of Collective Investment Institutions in Some Countries

Type of collective investment institution (CII)	The USA	England	Luxembourg	Turkey
CIIs which are open-end and which are established according to trust law	yes (Unit Investment Trust)	yes (Unit Trust)	no	no
CIIs which are open-end and which are established according to law of contract	no	no	yes (Collective Investment Fund)	yes (investment funds)
CIIs which are open end and which are established as companies	yes (Open-end Investment Company or Mutual Fund)	yes (Open-end Investment Company)	yes (Investment Company with Variable Capital)	no
CIIs which are closed-end and which are established as companies	yes (Closed-end Investment Company)	yes (Investment Trust)	yes (Investment Company with Fixed Capital)	yes (Investment Trust)

Source: Okat (2000).

1.1. Investment Funds in Turkey

Mutual funds are defined as the collections of assets which have been established with the money to be collected from the public in return for participation certificates with the purpose of managing portfolios on capital market instruments, gold and precious metal on the account of the holders of these certificates.

In Capital Markets Board's communiqués on investment funds[114], the principles for investment funds are determined as the distribution of risk, fiduciary ownership, professional management and protection of the fund's assets.

The principle for the distribution of risk enables investment funds to distribute the risk with an extent that the individuals can not manage with their own opportunities. This principle is realized through the diversification of the instruments which are included in the portfolio.

In the principle of fiduciary ownership, the fund manager faithfully possesses the fund assets. Owners of the savings leave some of the transactions to the ownership of the fiduciary in return for a participation certificate. This devolution is carried out by means of a fiduciary contract (fund contract) (Bastı, 2000). The manager becomes the owner of the money which s/he receives in return for the participation certificate and in the framework of the contract. However, s/he has to use this money within the framework of the contract.

The principle of professional management refers to the management of the portfolio by qualified persons and in accordance with the present conditions. The manager has to follow the progress in the markets and take positions accordingly. Some management principles and portfolio restrictions related to this principle are included in the Communiqués on the Principles of Investment Funds, issued by Capital Markets Board, which manages the securities investment funds in Turkey. Separately guarding the profit of each fund which the manager is in charge of, complying with objective data and documents in the decisions about purchasing and sale concerning the fund portfolio and complying with the investment principles determined by the contract, not purchasing entities for the fund portfolio that are over the current price and not selling entities from the fund portfolio for a price that is below the current one are some of these principles. Besides, some restrictions such as unattainability of investing more than 10% of the portfolio values of the investment funds to a single security of a trust, restraint for an investment fund to possess more than 20% of the capital or the whole voting rights in any trust at its own, unattainability of including equities, bonds and other debt instruments which belong to the founder or the manager into the fund portfolio are included in the Communiqués (Kılıç, 2002).

The principle for the protection of the fund's assets brings the fund's assets into safety and the assets of the fund which does not have a community are considered seperately from the assets of the founder. Besides, the assets of the fund can not be put in pledge, given as warranty, or confiscated by the third party.

Mutual fund founders are restricted to banks, insurance companies, non-bank intermediaries, unemployment funds and pension funds.

---

[114] Capital Markets Board of Turkey (CMB), Communiqué on principles regarding mutual funds, serial : VII, no: 10.

Table 5. Investment Funds/GDP

	2005	09/2009
Brazil	34%	50%
South Africa	27%	36%
South Korea	25%	34%
Poland	6%	5%
Turkey	5%	3%
Argentina	2%	1%

Source: Investment Company Institute, www.ici.org.

The ratio of the investment funds' portfolio size to GDP is an indicator of the development level of the institutional investor base in that country. Although the ratio of the investment funds to GDP in Turkey has increased through the years, it is considered to be low when compared with other countries. For example, the ratio of investment funds to national income in some countries such as South Korea and South Africa is over 30% (Table 1.5). Despite showing a steady increase through the years in Turkey, this ratio, which was 1.6% in 2000, reached only 3% in the year 2009.

Investment funds can be established in two types. 25% of the portfolios of type A investment funds is made up of the equities of Turkish companies at least in monthly average base. There is not such a restriction for type B investment funds. These two main groups are divided into 17 sub-main groups of funds depending on the financial instruments in their portfolio. These are Bills and Bonds, Equity, Sector, Affiliate Companies, Group, Foreign Securities, Gold, Other Precious Metals, Variable, Balanced/Mixed, Index, Liquid, Fund of, Private, Protected, Guaranteed and Hedge funds (CMB, 2010c).

368 items of funds have been operating in Turkey as of May, 2010. Among these funds, variable fund with 61 items and liquid fund with 52 items are the most common ones (CMB, 2010a). As for the portfolio size, liquid funds having a share of 76% are well ahead of the other funds. The main reason for this is the fact that liquid funds, which invest in short term instruments, can be purchased and sold without loss of days and that they are considered as alternatives to other short term investment tools, especially an alternative to repos.

The total value of the investment funds, the first of which was founded in 1987, reached $19.9 billion at the end of the year 2009 (Table 1.6). While the portfolio value of type A funds is $706 million as of the end of the year 2009 (a share of 4% of the total), the portfolio value of type B funds is $19.2 million (a share of 96% of the total).

When the portfolio compositions of type A investment funds are considered, it is seen that the weight was on Treasury Bills and Government Bonds during the initial years (1994-1998) but the portfolios changed into a structure in which equities prevail in there recent years (1999-2003). As of the year 2009, the share of equities in total portfolio increased to 62%. The most important reason for this development is the fact that it is legally obligatory to include Turkish companies' equities in the type A investment funds at least with a proportion of 25%.

In the portfolio of type B investment funds, on the other hand, this composition has a structure in which repos and public debt instruments prevail. This structure reveals that type B investment funds are composed mainly of liquid values and therefore economic units prefer to remain liquid in the recent years.

Table 6. Historical Consolidated Portfolio Structure of Mutual Funds

Year	Number of Funds	Net Asset Value (Mil. $)	Number of Investors	S %	GB %	RR %	MM %	FS %	Other %
A TYPE MUTUAL FUNDS									
1995	-	73	-	36.2	63.7	0.0	0.0	0.0	0.0
2000	-	775	-	45.7	11.3	42.7	0.0	0.1	0.1
2009	114	706	191,565	62.8	20.6	16.3	0.2	0.1	0.0
05.2010	114	790	211,079	62.2	19.5	17.3	0.8	0.1	0.1
B TYPE MUTUAL FUNDS									
1995	-	435	-	0.4	95.7		0.0	3.8	0.2
2000	-	2,113	-	0.2	13.2	86.4	0.0	0.2	0.0
2009	202	19,214	2,807,083	0.5	32.4	60.2	5.3	0.1	1.4
05.2010	254	18,241	3,122,239	0.5	28.0	62.1	7.2	0.3	1.8
ALL MUTUAL FUNDS									
1995	-	508	-	5.5	91.0	0.0	0.0	3.3	0.1
2000	-	2,888	-	12.4	12.7	74.6	0.0	0.2	0.1
2009	316	19,920	2,998,648	2.7	32.0	58.7	5.1	0.1	1.4
05.2010	368	19,031	3,333,318	3.0	27.7	60.3	7.0	0.3	1.7

S % : Proportion of Stock in the portfolio.
GB % : Public debt instruments in the portfolio.
RR % : Proportion of Reverse Repo in the Portfolio.
MM % : Proportion of Money Market Instruments in the Portfolio.
FS % : Proportion of Foreign Securities in the Portfolio.
Source: CMB (2010a, 2010b).

When the two types of funds are evaluated together, it is seen that as of 2009 60% of the portfolios is composed of reverse repo, 28% of the portfolios is treasury bill and government bonds, and only 3% of them is stocks.

Management prices in Turkish fund industry are 2.5-3.5% in average and they do not include any other cost items such as commissions for admission and leaving. In this way, they are almost at the same level with the USA and EU fund industry.

Comparison of Investment Fund Legislation in Turkey with the EU Legislation

It is required to make the investment fund legislation coherent with European Union Directives[115] (UCITS- Undertakings for Collective Investment in Transferable Securities) and to provide the integration of European fund market and Turkish funds.

In case of the lack of sufficient and appropriate control mechanisms, the conflicts which arise between personal interests of the investors (principals) and the managers of the collective investment institutions (attorneys) may cause a decrease in the investor's trust for

---

[115] http://ec.europa.eu/internal_market/investment/ucits_directive_en.htm.

the collective investment institution (CII) as an investment alternative by causing the investor's interests to experience losses (Yeşilürdü, 2010).

In CIIs the concept of corporate governance is defined as the system which ensures the provision of keeping investor's profits in the forefront during the fund organization and procedures, which prevents the conflicts of interests, which provides a field of application for the concepts of justice, ability to account for things, transparency and responsibility.

According to European Union Directives on collective investment institution, which is known as UCITS, founding and managing the collective investment institutions by "fund management companies" is a fundamental principle. In Turkish legislation, on the other hand, a distinct investment fund management company is not specified; banks, insurance companies, intermediary institutions, pension funds and some employee funds which are legally authorized are determined as founders.

The privilege of being a fund's founder, which is given to banks and intermediary institutions by the current legislation, does not improve competition, and does not motivate the founders of the funds to give due importance to the profits of the investors and to take precautions to prevent conflicts of interests. It will not be realistic to expect that the fund committee members, who have other duties and responsibilities in the fund's founder banks and intermediary institutions, whose main field of activity is not "to found and govern funds", would be able to keep the profits of the fund's shareholders in the forefront or would have the whole authority which will set and apply the required mechanisms to prevent conflicts of interest during the fund organization and procedures.

In the fifth article of UCITS Directives, the functions of portfolio management and custody have been separated from each other; the custody institution has undertaken the duty of supervision as well as custody of the fund assets and has become responsible to both investor and management company. Besides, in the tenth article of the directives, the management company and the institution conducting the custody service have been obliged to operate independently from each other and only in accordance with the interests of the shareholders.

Fund assets in Turkey are kept in custody in Istanbul Stock Exchange Settlement and Custody Bank, Inc., but this custody is conducted in accordance with the principle of disunity of fund assets. Therefore, it does not include a supervision function as a part of the responsibilities envisaged by UCITS Directives.

Making the investment fund legislation in Turkey coherent with EU legislation, and providing the sector with competition through enabling the establishment of fund management companies, whose main field of activity is "to establish and manage funds", will be an important stride as for the development of the investment fund sector.

It is also required to remove the classification which is denominated as type A and type B and which is applied in the classification of investment funds, and to provide a fund structuring in the EU standards (UCITS) (Gordon, 2008). In the current classification, investment funds are mainly divided into two as A and B according to the share of the values in their portfolios. Later these two groups are denominated among themselves again according to the shares which the values have to include in the portfolio. For example, the funds which have to include public sector securities with a proportion of at least 51% in their portfolio are called B type bills and bonds fund. Investment funds which have these portfolio restrictions and which include long term bills in their portfolios are classified in the same group with all funds which have a short-medium term portfolio structure. Therefore, it becomes possible to compare the returns of the funds whose risks are completely different from each other due to duration and which therefore need to be evaluated differently.

In addition to this, it is also necessary to organize all collective investment instruments with a separate law, like it is in Individual Pension Savings and Investment System, to enable the foundation of investment funds which are sold with foreign currency, and to carry out the regulations related to complex derivatives and real estate investment funds.

Pension Funds

In every developed or developing country, a big or small crisis about social security is experienced. The reasons for the crisis are not the same for every country. In this context, the developed countries and the developing countries more or less differ from each other. In developed countries, as a result of the concept of social state, the rapid increase in the salaries and payments, aging of the population, decrease of births, continuous and high level of unemployment, and increase in the costs of health services dragged social security systems into crisis by increasing the financing burden of these systems. In developing countries, on the other hand, the economic sources allocated to social security are insufficient. As a result, an improvement could not be performed in this field (Ege, 2002).

The crisis which developed countries as well as under-developed and developing countries experience in their social security systems led to a need for restructuring in social security system, and this initiated a tendency towards the application of pension mutual funds rather than public social security programs.

Today, it is observed that some countries have privatized their social security system by means of private pension funds while some countries, such as Turkey, kept public social security system and preferred to tend to pension mutual funds in order to support the current system.

In Turkey, besides public social security institutions, there are also public institutions' or private companies' employee funds, which have a foundation status, and private insurance companies, which offer pension insurance to individuals and various institutions.

In the public social security system, which covers 82%[116] of the country population, problems are encountered due to some applications such as the failure in collecting the premiums, illegal working, incompetence in investing the savings professionally, early retirement, which are contrary to insurance principles.

In Table 1.7, budget transfers carried out in order to finance the deficits of social security institutions in Turkey are displayed. The system, which is experiencing the problem of financing deficit, is unable to lead the funds to the capital market.

Table 7. Budget Transfers to Social Security Institution

Year	Budget Transfers (Billion $)	Shares of Budget Transfers In GDP
2008	17.4	2.9%
2009	19.8	3.1%

Source: Republic of Turkey Social Security Institution, http://www.sgk.gov.tr/wps/portal /Anasayfa/ Istatistikler.

---

[116] Source: Republic of Turkey Social Security Institution, www.sgk.gov.tr

On October 07, 2001 the law no. 4632 on Individual Pension Savings and Investment System came into effect as a part of the social security reform in Turkey and with the aim of forming private pension programs, which are complementary to the public social security system. Besides, through the regulations perfomed, tax incentives have been brought about in the processes of admission to Individual Pension Savings and Investment System, directing the contributions for investment in pension investment funds, or regaining the savings obtained from these funds as collected money or wages.

- With the implementation of the Individual Pension Savings and Investment System;
- Providing a saving which is equal to 5-10% of the gross national product,
- Expanding the content of social security and contributing to the increase of the welfare of participants by providing them with an additional income in their retirement,
- Creating additional resources for the real sector to use; and in this way realizing a stable growth by means of providing an increase of production and employment,
- Contributing to the improvement and specialization of markets by providing money markets and capital markets with new resources; and in this way facilitating the money borrowing opportunities of public and private sectors, are aimed (CMB, 2004).
- Main features of Individual Pension Savings and Investment System can be classified as follows (CMB, 2010d):
- System will operate in accordance with the principle of willingness and will be open to participation of every segment.
- Savings will be invested on the pension investment funds which will be formed in the framework of the legislation of capital market board.
- Pension companies will establish pension investment funds which have a combination of at least 3 different types of risks and returns, and this will enable the individuals to make investment choices that are suitable to their risk and return expectations.[117]
- Pension investment funds will be led to investment in the framework of the professional portfolio management principles by portfolio management companies, which are dependent on capital markets board. It will be possible to transfer the savings to another pension investment fund or pension company at the end of a minimum period.
- Assets of the pension investment fund will be kept in custody separately from the assets of the pension company, and in a central custody institution which will be authorized by Capital Markets Board.

In Table 1.8, the information related to pension mutual funds in Turkey is presented. According to statistical data, since the system came into effect, fund diversification, asset value of pension mutual funds and the number of participants have displayed a trend of rapid increase, the number of participants have reached 2 million people, and the asset value of funds have reached $6 billion.

Institutional Investors in Turkey

Table 8. Data of Pension Mutual Funds (at the Year-end)

	2004	2006	2009
Number of Pension Mutual Funds	68	102	130
Total Number of Participants	15,245	1,073,650	1,978,335
Total Net Asset Value of Pension Mutual Funds (Million $)	219	1,984	6,126

Source: Pension Monitoring Centre (2009), www.cmb.gov.tr.

Table 9. Consolidated Data of Pension Mutual Funds as of December 31, 2009

Average Term Days	S%	GB%	RR%	FS%	Other%
332	10.01	68.68	15.26	0.32	5.73

S % : Proportion of Stock in the portfolio.
GB % : Public debt instruments in the portfolio.
RR % : Proportion of Reverse Repo in the Portfolio.
FS % : Proportion of Foreign Securities in the Portfolio.
Source: Pension Monitoring Centre (2009).

The average term which is 57 days for investment funds is 332 days for pension mutual funds.[118] The proportion of stocks which is only 2.7% in investment fund portfolios rises to 10% in pension mutual funds (Table 1.9).

Life Insurance Companies

The funds gathered by life insurance companies can not be evaluated effectively in the financial system or capital markets. Life insurance companies in Turkey encounter some restrictions in their legislations especially in terms of investment fields. Besides, these insurance companies do not have an active role as institutional investors in financial markets due to the reasons such as the fact that they operate with high agency costs and they do not receive professional portfolio governing service while governing the funds. Similarly, as the resources gathered in insurance sector are rather limited, the resources transferred to capital markets are caused to be limited as well.

When compared with life insurances, Individual Pension Savings and Investment Systems in Turkey, provide their participants with more tax advantages at the participation share payments to be made to the system and at the payments to be made when the retirement right is gained.

In Table 1.10, distribution of the securities in the portfolio of insurance sector as of the end of 2009 is given. According to this, the share of the stocks has remained at only 18% while the public borrowing tools have a share of 74%.

---

[117] Capital Markets Board of Turkey (CMB), Implementing regulation on the principles applicable to the establishment and operations of pension investment funds.

[118] Source: Pension Monitoring Centre, www.egm.org.tr.

Table 10. Investment Portfolio of Insurance Sector

	Government Bills, Notes	Stocks	Others	Fixed Assets
2009	%74	%18	%1	%7

Total Investments $7.27 billion.

Source: The Undersecretariat Turkish Treasury, http://www.treasury.gov.tr.

Exchange Traded Funds

Exchange Traded Funds (ETFs) are investment funds which base on an index; aim to reflect the performance of the index, on which they base, to investors and whose shares go into transactions in stock exchanges.

The first exchange traded fund was enforced to Turkish Capital Markets in January, 2005. The number of the exchange traded funds which were exported and went into transactions in Istanbul Stock Exchange (ISE) between January 2005 and May 2010 reached 10.[119]

ETFs are formed by means of identically reproducing the content of the index on which the equities in the fund base.[120] They identically replicate the performance of the index on which they base. At the same time, they combine the equities' features such as high liquidity opportunity and competence of being easily purchased and sold with the investment funds' features such as risk distribution, competence to enable investors to benefit from the returns of the markets in which they invest.

When we look at the advantages of the ETFs as for the investors;

Exchange Traded Funds can be purchased and sold in the same way with the equities during the performance hours on the days when Istanbul Stock Exchange is open for transactions. Transactions are carried out through directives given from any intermediary institution having the authority to intervene at ISE, which is similar to the way it is with equities.

ETFs are the products which have the lowest cost of transaction all over the world. When compared to the investment funds, they provide the investors with the opportunity of investment with a rather low cost. Individual and institutional (domestic/ foreign) investors only pay the transaction commission which the intermediary institutions collect in the transactions they perform within the ETFs at ISE.

Portfolio compositions, having an indicator quality, of the indexes which ETFs pursue are revealed every transaction day. Investors can daily and easily follow which assets their ETFs are composed of.

In Turkey, as of the end of 2009, the market value of the funds is $128 million (ISE, 2010).

Hedge Funds

In Turkey, founding and operating hedge funds under name of free investment funds have recently been allowed. Free investment funds, contrary to their samples in other countries, take place in the registration of the board and are bound to the regulations of the board. For

---

[119] Source: Istanbul Stock Exchange, www.ise.org.

[120] Capital Markets Board of Turkey (CMB), Communiqué on principles regarding exchange traded funds, serial: VII, no: 23.

example, in order to take the shares of the funds to the registration of the board, they need to form an internal control system which also includes the risk management systems concerning the management of the funds. Besides, it is seen that the proportion of leverage in the internal legislation of the current free investment funds, which have been allowed to be founded, is determined as 5 times maximal (Iskender, 2009).

Investment funds in Turkey only have a long position while free investment funds can take short positions.

Another feature that differs free funds from traditional investment funds is that they can be invested by persons who are defined as qualified investors, like it is generally seen in the samples all over the world. Qualified investor, in summary, is defined by Capital Markets Board as real or legal persons, except for various institutions or institutional investors defined in the legislation[121], who have Turkish and/ or foreign currency and capital market instruments of at least 1 million Turkish Liras.

Investment funds in Turkey have liquidity. Free funds, on the other hand, allow purchasing and selling on the dates determined in their internal legislations; they usually do not have daily liquidities.

Portfolio Management Companies

A portfolio management company is a corporation which has received a certificate of authority from Capital Markets Board by fulfilling the conditions determined in Capital Markets Legislation in order to conduct specifically portfolio management activities. Within the context of Capital Markets Legislation, portfolio management activity is defined as the management, by procuration, of the portfolios which are composed of capital markets instruments, money market instruments and transactions, forward transactions and options, cash items, foreign currency, deposits and other assets and transactions approved by the board according to the risk-return choice to be determined by the investor or the portfolio manager within the framework of the portfolio management contract to be made with the clients (CMB, 2004). Portfolio management companies in Turkey are not allowed to act as founders of funds.

According to the data revealed by CMB, as of the end of 2009, 23 portfolio management companies have been furnishing services. Within the managed portfolio, the proportion of the individual investors' portfolio size is 2% while the proportion is 98% for institutional investors (investment funds, investment trusts, pension funds and insurance companies) (Table 1.11).

Table 11. Portfolio Management (Million $) (03/2010)

	Portfolio Size Managed By Brokerage Firms	Portfolio Size Managed By Portfolio Management Companies
Individual	227	547
Institutional	2,498	26,538
Total	2,725	27,080

Source: CMB (2010a).

---

[121] Capital Markets Board of Turkey (CMB), Communiqué serial: VII, no: 29.

Public Offer and Institutional Investors

In the public offers realized in Turkey, allocations are conducted for various groups. Main allocation groups which are encountered in almost every offer are Employees of Companies and/ or Groups, Domestic Institutional Investors and Foreign Institutional Investors.

In the public offers realized in Turkey, domestic institutional investors can demand for shares provided that they put out the cost at the maximum price range of the public offer at the time of the demand. Foreign institutional investors, on the other hand, can convey their demand to the intermediary institution with various amounts and at various prices provided that it is within the price range (Karayel, 2008). In this case, they are able to be involved in determining the concluding price. Besides, among foreign institutional investors, distribution is usually carried out in accordance with the way issuer approves. While the demands of some investors are completely satisfied, the demands of the others may not be satisfied at all. In this way, an opportunity of creating a difference between the long term institutional investors who will keep the share for a long time and the institutional investors who pursue a short term profit and purchase with this aim, emerges in favor of the previously mentioned investor. Depending on these reasons, it is observed that in the public offers realized in the recent years, foreign institutional investors are provided with allocations by reserving a maximum level of share which will also comply with the legal restrictions mentioned above.

When the denominator which has to be allocated to individual investors is taken into consideration, the allocation made for domestic institutional investors in public offers can be at very low levels. Domestic institutional investors in Turkey can participate in public offers within the allocation group of 2-5% which is reserved for them, and they do not have any determinant effects on the prices. The amount of the share they receive after the distribution usually constitutes a rather minor amount when compared with their portfolio size. Therefore, a short time after the beginning of the transactions at stock exchange, decisions for selling are made.

1.2. Investment Trusts in Turkey

Investment trusts are capital markets institutions which are established in the form of joint-stock corporations in order to operate the portfolio of gold and other precious metals which go into transactions in national and international stock exchanges by means of capital markets means or in organized markets excluding stock exchange.[122] Differences between investment trusts and investment funds can be classified as follows;

- While investment trusts are established in the form of joint-stock corporations and they have a legal personality, investment funds do not have a distinct legal personality. Investment fund is an asset which is established by a legal personality in the framework of a contract (CMB, 2010e).

---

[122] Capital Markets Board of Turkey (CMB), Communiqué on principles regarding investment companies, serial: VI, no: 4.

- While investment funds can only be established by banks, intermediary institutions, insurance companies, or pension funds, this restriction is not valid for the founders of investment trusts.
- While the participation certificates for investment funds are given by the founders of the funds, investment trust equities are only received through the directives given to intermediary institutions which are authorized to make transactions in the stock exchange. Participation certificates for investment funds can be turned into money by selling them back to the fund, but investment trust equities can not be sold back to the investment trust; they can only be sold at stock exchange.

Investment funds can not distribute the profit, but investment trusts can distribute the profit like other companies.

As for the investment funds, dividing the net asset value of the fund by the number of the current shares gives the price of item participation certificate. However, as the equities go into transaction at stock exchange in investment trusts, the price of these bills are formed according to the demand and supply in stock exchange.

Risk distribution and professional management principles, which are valid for investment funds, are also valid for investment trusts. Securities which are included in trusts portfolio according to the principle for the protection of funds assets, have to be kept in custody separately from the founding partners and portfolio managers (at the ISE Settlement and Custody Bank Inc.).

Investment trusts can invest in foreign and Turkish, private and public debt instruments and equities, futures and options, and gold and other precious metals. Investment trusts can be established in two different types as A and B, like it is in investment funds. Investment trusts which invest at least 25% of their portfolio value on the equities of the trusts established in Turkey are called type A whereas the other investment trusts are named as type B.

In Turkish capital markets, 33 items of type A investment trust, which have a market value of $337 million and a portfolio value of $479 million, have been operating as of the end of 2009. 35.2% of the portfolios are made up of equities, 37.6% is made up of government bonds and treasury bills, and 22.0% is made up of reverse repo transactions (Table 1.12).

Table 12. Historical Consolidated Portfolio Structure of Investment Trusts

Year	Number of Trusts	Net Asset Value (Mil. $)	Market Capitalization (Mil. $)	S %	GB %	RR %	MM %	FS %	Other %
1998	17	66	46	50.5	14.5	34.6	-	-	0.5
2005	26	364	337	53.4	31.5	12.6	2.5	-	0.0
2009	33	479	337	35.2	37.6	26.2	0.1	0.2	0.7
05.2010	33	444	325	31.6	44.7	22.0	0.3	0.2	1.3

S % : Proportion of Stocks in the Portfolio.
GB % : Proportion of Public Debt Instruments in the Portfolio.
RR % : Proportion of Reverse Repo in the Portfolio.
MM % : Proportion of Money Market Instruments in the Portfolio.
FS % : Proportion of Foreign Securities in the Portfolio.
Source: CMB (2010a, 2010b).

Market prices of the most of securities investment trusts are transacted with a discount in comparison to their actual values. As of the end of 2009, the discount proportion in the sector is 30% on average. With the aim of decreasing this discount, some legal regulations which will enable investment trusts to purchase their shares from the markets within the principles to be determined by Capital Markets Board are tried to be carried out.

Real Estate Investment Trusts

Real Estate Investment trusts are closed-end investment companies managing portfolios composed of real estates, real estate based projects and capital market instruments based on real estates.[123]

The aim of Real Estate Investment Trusts is to invest in real estates with high potentials of returns and real estate based projects, to provide rental incomes from the real estates in their portfolios, and to reach a high income of real estates by means of the incomes from rentals, purchases and sales. An investor who becomes a partner by means of purchasing the equity of a real estate investment trust benefits from the real estates with high returns indirectly. The trust which provides a profit from the purchase and sale of the real estate in its portfolio distributes this profit to its partners as dividend at the end of the year and distributes the income from the real estate to its partners (CMB, 2010f).

The legal regulation concerning the Real Estate Investment Trusts (REITs) in Turkey was prepared by Capital Markets Board (CMB) in 1995. The first REIT was established in 1996 and REITs started to go into transactions in Istanbul Stock Exchange (ISE) after 1997.

REIT returns in Turkey have been variable due to the high inflation and economic crisis. Although REIT companies determine their prices as for their actual values in public offers, in the following periods they start to effect transactions at discount. Although the sector effected some bonus transactions in 1997, in the following years it continuously effected discount transactions. Whereas a tendency to decrease, which resulted in a discount of 70%, was observed in the sector between 1999 and 2002, through the revival in the construction sector in 2003-2004 the discount rate decreased, and it started to effect bonus transactions with the admission of mortgage law in 2005.

Table 13. Historical Consolidated Portfolio Structure of REITs

Year	Number of Trusts	Net Asset Value (Mil. $)	Market Capitalization (Mil. $)	R %	RP %	GB %	RR %	MM %	Other %
1998	5	433	120	84.7	10.7	2.7	1.9	0.0	0.0
2005	9	1,645	1,856	84.9	0.0	0.0	0.0	14.7	0.4
2009	14	3,172	1,920	69.5	17.4	4.4	0.0	0.0	8.6
03.2010	14	3,089	2,226	68.6	18.3	4.2	0.0	0.0	8.8

R % : Proportion of Real Estates in the Portfolio.
RP % : Proportion of Real Estate Projects in the Portfolio.
GB % : Proportion of Public Debt Instruments in the Portfolio.
RR % : Proportion of Reverse Repo in the Portfolio.
MM % : Proportion of Money Market Instruments in the Portfolio.

---

[123] Capital Markets Board of Turkey (CMB), Communiqué on principles regarding real estate investment companies, serial: VI, no: 11.

Source: CMB (2010a, 2010b).

The discount rate in REITs, which are among the companies foreign investors first abandoned in Turkey due to the mortgage crisis emerging from the USA, was 40% at the end of March, 2008 while it was recorded as 61% at the end of 2009. 13 of the 14 companies effect transactions with values which are rather below their book value.

In Turkey as of the end of 2009, 14 real estate investment trusts, which have a total portfolio value of $3.172 billion and a market value of $1.92 billion, have been operating. 69.5% of the portfolios of these trusts, which are listed in ISE, are composed of buildings and lands. 17.4% of them consist of real estate based projects (Table 13).

Venture Capital Investment Trusts

Venture capital investment trust (VCIT) is defined as a joint-stock corporation which is denoted as "risk capital investment trust" in the Law[124] and which directs its capitals basically to venture capital investments.

VCITs are a form of collective investment institutions, directing issued capital toward venture capital investments which are defined as long-term fund transfers, through investing in capital market instruments issued in primary markets by the entrepreneur companies already established or to be established, with the aim of obtaining capital or interest gains. VCITs may purchase stocks and borrowing instruments issued by the entrepreneur. They can also invest in other venture capital investment trusts. (CMB, 2010g).

In Turkey as of the end of 2009, two venture capital investment trusts, which have a portfolio value of $104.5 million and a market value of $55 million, have been operating. 53.6% of the portfolio of these trusts is composed of venture capital investments (Table 14).

Table 14. Historical Consolidated Portfolio Structure of VCITs

Year	Number of Trusts	Net Asset Value (Mil. $)	Market Capitalization (Mil. $)	VCI %	GB %	MM %	RR %	Other %
2000	1	5	4	54.2	0.0	0.0	45.8	0.0
2005	2	83	69	48.4	0.0	0.0	0.0	51.6
2009	2	103	55	40.8	19.0	0.0	0.0	40.2
03.2010	2	102	107	53.6	8.4	0.0	0.1	38.0

VCI % : Proportion of Venture Capital Investments in the Portfolio.
GB % : Proportion of Public Debt Instruments in the Portfolio.
MM % : Proportion of Money Market Instruments in the Portfolio.
RR % : Proportion of Reverse Repo in the Portfolio.
Source: CMB (2010a, 2010b).

1.3. The Situation of Investment Funds and Trusts in View of Various Tax Laws

Securities investment trusts and securities investment funds can only perform "portfolio management" activities and obtain securities portfolio returns from these activities according to Capital Markets Legislation.

---

[124] Capital Markets Board of Turkey (CMB), Communiqué regarding the principles about venture capital investment companies, serial: VI, no: 15.

According to the Article 2 of Corporate Tax Law, these funds and trusts, which are defined as "payer of corporate tax", are excluded from corporate tax according to the article 5 of the same law due to their fields of operation (Kumuşoğlu and Bingöl, 2008).

Securities investment trusts and securities investment funds do not apply any withholding taxes on yearly earnings within the framework of Income Tax Law. In other words, these trusts and funds collect the incomes they receive, such as deposit rate, repos rate, profits from the purchasing and sales of securities, without withholding.

Incomes from the purchasing and sales during the transfer of equities of the investment trusts' shareholders are subject to income tax withholding with a proportion of 10% according to the same article. Like it is in investment trusts, the drawback of the investment funds' participation certificates to the fund are also subject to income tax withholding with a proportion of 10%. However, the income from the purchasing and sales of the participation certificates of the investment funds, 51% of whose portfolios are composed of equities going into transactions in Istanbul Stock Exchange (ISE), are excluded from this income tax withholding.

Before 2009, the incomes of the foreign funds which the portfolio management companies in Turkey manage all over the world were subject to corporate tax. This situation was leading to a disadvantage causing foreign funds to abstain from establishing the management center in Turkey.

According to the tax incentive, imposed through the Law No. 5838 in 2009, the returns of the funds which are managed in other countries by international portfolio management companies to be established in Turkey through the authorization from Capital Markets Board will not be subject to taxes in Turkey. In this way, it is aimed to encourage the management of the foreign funds' portfolios from Turkey.

2. FOREIGN INSTITUTIONAL INVESTORS IN TURKEY

Foreign investors in a country's capital markets are of great importance in both expanding the investor base and providing new capital flows. Another importance, on the other hand, is the fact that the existence and the weight of foreign investors are considered to be an indicator of the reliability of that country's capital markets.

In the portfolio capital movements, which are observed to be realized from developed countries to developing countries in 2000s, while the low return rates of the markets in developed countries acted as stimulating factors for the capital to move out of the country, the high return rates and the portfolio diversification opportunities provided for the investors in developing countries acted as attractive power.

It seen that in Turkey a liberal foreign currency regime is being applied. In addition to Turkish Lira's being completely convertible, since 1989 a policy which allows the purchase and selling of securities freely by foreign individual and institutional investors at Istanbul Stock Exchange (ISE) has been followed. With the decree No. 32, which was issued in 1989, Turkish equities and bonds markets became open for foreign investors without any restrictions about taking the capital and profits to abroad.

Institutional Investors in Turkey

Table 15. Foreign Investors in Istanbul Stock Exchange

Year	Share in Total Equity Portfolios	Share in Trading Volume	Average Holding Days
2003	51%	9%	213
2007	72%	24%	275
2009	67%	14%	322

Source: ISE (2010), TSPAKB (2010b).

Foreign investors have a significant share at ISE equities market. As of the end of 2009, 67% of ISE companies' shares which are open to public are in the custody accounts of foreign investors at The ISE Settlement and Custody Bank Inc. (Table 15). In the total for 2003, the share of the foreign investors' custody balance in the total was 51%. While the share of the foreign investors in trading volume was 9% in the year 2003, it reached 14% at the end of the year 2009.

The data related to foreign investors' average investment terms are given in Table 1.15. According to this, in the year 2009, foreign investors changed their portfolios every 322 days on average. It is seen that foreign investors' average investment terms have shortened since 2003. Besides, the average investment term of domestic investors is about one month. As a result, it is perceived that the foreign investors have an effect on the capital market, which increases the stability.

Between 1999-2009, ISE equity market experienced a net foreign capital inflow of $22.3 billion. It is observed that foreign investors remained in the market and increased their portfolio investments despite the high amounts of arising losses during the financial crisis encountered in Turkey in 2000 and 2001 and the global financial crisis the effects of which started to be experienced in 2007. During these 10 years, domestic investors regularly obtained more returns than the foreign investors or their losses remained relatively less (Table 16).

Table 16. Foreign and Domestic Investors in the Equity Market

Year	Net Equity Investments (Million $)		Portfolio Return	
	For. Investors	Dom. Investors	For. Investors	Dom. Investors
1999	1,034	-925	224%	267%
2000	-461	4,900	-50%	-21%
2001	518	-508	-29%	-41%
2002	49	183	-39%	-24%
2003	1,097	-997	97%	101%
2004	2,277	-1,061	44%	62%
2005	6,727	-3,829	48%	72%
2006	2,129	-483	-2%	12%
2007	8,524	-3,272	61%	61%
2008	-1,794	4,253	-59%	-58%
2009	2,256	-1,985	90%	123%

Source: TSPAKB (2010b).

In Table 17, individual clients include real persons; corporations include corporations, limited companies, legal persons -such as foundations, cooperatives- and the intermediary institution's own portfolio transactions. Institutional investors are investment funds, investment trusts, and insurance companies. The distribution of the trading volume of various investment instruments in the client basis, as of March 2010, is given in Table 17.

The weight of domestic equity investors, which has a proportion of 86.3%, is clearly seen in the trading volume. The proportion of the domestic institutional investors in this figure is 8.3%. Almost all of the trading volumes of foreign investors are realized by corporations and institutional investors.

Domestic institutional investors have a proportion of 58.3% in Treasury bill trading volume. This proportion is 83.5% as for repos. In the futures stock exchange, on the other hand, the trading volume of foreign institutional investors is higher than that of domestic investors.

Table 17. Investor Breakdown of Trading Volume (03/2010)

	Equity Trading Volume	T-Bills Trading Volume	Repo Trading Volume	Futures Trading Volume
Domestic Investors	86.3%	92.8%	99.5%	89.5%
Dom. Individuals	69.0%	7.0%	10.6%	74.8%
Dom. Corporations	9.0%	27.4%	5.4%	12.1%
Dom. Institutionals	8.3%	58.3%	83.5%	2.5%
Foreign Investors	13.7%	7.2%	0.5%	10.5%
For. Individuals	0.2%	0.1%	0.3%	0.3%
For. Corporations	9.8%	7.1%	0.1%	4.5%
For. Institutionals	3.7%	0.0%	0.1%	5.7%

Source: TSPAKB (2010c).

Table 18. Investor Breakdown of Equity Ownership as of December 31, 2009

	Equity Ownership (mn. $)	Share
Domestic Investors	27,292	32.7%
Dom. Individuals	16,476	19.7%
Dom. Corporations	7,886	9.4%
Dom. Institutionals	1,115	1.3%
Dom. Other	1,776	2.1%
Foreign Investors	56,274	67.3%
For. Individuals	296	0.4%
For. Corporations	15,913	19.0%
For. Institutionals	40,057	47.9%
For. Other	8	0.0%
Total	83,566	100%

Source: TSPAKB (2010a),

The Central Registry Agency, www.mkk.com.tr.

In Table 18, legal persons refer to corporations and limited companies. The category "other" includes institutions such as foundations, cooperatives, etc. The share of foreign investors in total equity portfolio size is 67%. The proportion of foreign funds is 48%. Domestic funds, on the other hand, include only 1% of the total equities in their portfolios.

CONCLUSION

Despite the rapid development observed in the investment funds in the recent years, it is observed that the size of institutional investors in Turkey is still at very low levels in international comparisons. When the investment preferences of domestic investors in Turkey are examined, it is seen that these investors mainly invest their savings in deposits. Making the investment fund legislation in Turkey coherent with EU legislation, and providing the sector with competition through enabling the establishment of fund management companies, whose main field of activity is "to establish and manage funds", will be an important stride as for the development of the investment fund sector.

REFERENCES

Bastı, E., 2000. Türkiye Sermaye Piyasasında Menkul Kıymet Yatırım Fonları: Problemleri ve Çözüm Önerileri. *İktisat İşletme ve Finans.* 167, 84-94.

Capital Markets Board of Turkey (CMB), 2004. *Annual Report* 2003.

Capital Markets Board of Turkey (CMB), 2010a. *Annual Report* 2009.

Capital Markets Board of Turkey (CMB), 2010b. *Turkish Capital Markets Monthly Bulletin-June* 2010.

Capital Markets Board of Turkey (CMB), 2010c. *Investor Guide for Investment Funds.*

Capital Markets Board of Turkey (CMB), 2010d. *Investor Guide for Individual Pension Savings and Investment System.*

Capital Markets Board of Turkey (CMB), 2010e. *Investor Guide for Securities Investment Trusts.*

Capital Markets Board of Turkey (CMB), 2010f. *Investor Guide for Real Estate Investment Trusts.*

Capital Markets Board of Turkey (CMB), 2010g. *Investor Guide for Venture Capital Investment Trusts.*

Ege, İ., 2002. Dünyada Özel Emeklilik Sistemleri ve Bireysel Emeklilik Tasarruf ve Yatırım Sistemi Kanununa Eleştirel Bir Bakış. *İktisat İşletme ve Finans.* 196, 81-91.

Gordon, D., 2008. Yatırım fonlarında sınıflandırma ve derecelendirme. *Kurumsal Yatırımcı.* 2, 34-36.

Istanbul Stock Exchange (ISE), 2010. *Annual Factbook* 2009.

Iskender, C., *2009. Kurumsal Yatırımcılar Üzerine Genel Bir Değerlendirme.* Kurumsal Yatırımcı. 1, 6-11.

Karayel, Y., 2008. Halka arzlarda kurumsal yatırımcılar. *Kurumsal Yatırımcı.* 4,10-11.

Kılıç, S., 2002. Türkiye'deki Yatırım Fonlarının Performanslarının Değerlendirilmesi, İMKB Yayınları, İstanbul.

Kumuşoğlu C., Bingöl M., 2008. Yatırım Ortaklıklarının Çeşitli Vergi Kanunları Karşısındaki Durumu. *Kurumsal Yatırımcı.* 3, 38-41.

Okat, Y.Ö., 2000. Kollektif Yatırım Modellerine İlişkin AT ve Ülkemiz Düzenlemelerinin Karşılaştrılması ve Yeni Bir Kollektif Yatırım Modeli Olarak Değişken Sermayeli Yatırım Ortaklıkları. SPK Yeterlilik Etüdü, Ankara.

Pension Monitoring Centre, 2010. *Individual Pension System Progress Report* 2009.

The Association of Capital Market Intermediary Institutions of Turkey (TSPAKB), 2010a. *Turkish Brokarage Industry 2009 Annual Review.*

The Association of Capital Market Intermediary Institutions of Turkey (TSPAKB), 2010b. *Turkish Capital Market Report 2009.*

The Association of Capital Market Intermediary Institutions of Turkey (TSPAKB), 2010c. *Sermaye Piyasasında Gündem.* 95, 7-10.

Yeşilürdü, T., 2010. Yatırım fonlarında kurumsal yönetim: fund governance kavramı. *Kurumsal Yatırımcı.* 1, 12-15.

LEGAL FRAMEWORK

Capital Markets Board of Turkey (CMB), Communiqué on principles regarding investment companies, serial: VI, no: 4.

Capital Markets Board of Turkey (CMB), Communiqué regarding the principles about venture capital investment companies, serial: VI, no: 15.

Capital Markets Board of Turkey (CMB), Communiqué on principles regarding real estate investment companies, serial: VI, no: 11.

Capital Markets Board of Turkey (CMB), Communiqué on principles regarding mutual funds, serial: VII, no: 10.

Capital Markets Board of Turkey (CMB), Implementing regulation on the principles applicable to the establishment and operations of pension investment funds.

Capital Markets Board of Turkey (CMB), Communiqué on principles regarding exchange traded funds, serial: VII, no: 23.

NAME INDEX

A

Ausubel, L. M., 164, 174

E

Evans, D. S., 138, 164, 174

F

Fernandez, F. R., 175

K

Karayol, A. H., 164, 174

M

Massoud, N., 175

O

Onis, Z., 17, 31, 174, 206, 222

R

Rochet, J. C., 99, 100, 118, 164, 174, 175

S

Saunders, A., 175
Schmalensee, R., 174
Scholnick, B., 164, 175

T

Tirole, J., 164, 174, 175

V

Valverde, S. C., 175

W

Weiner, S.E., 164, 175
Wright, J., 164, 175

SUBJECT INDEX

A

Adverse selection, 122

B

Bank resolution, viii, 12, 141, 144, 154, 159
Banking Regulation, 4, 9, 10, 50, 153
Budget deficit, 17, 19, 23, 27, 53, 54, 58, 75, 95, 137

C

Capital Market, 183, 196, 222, 226, 243
Central Bank, 129
Collective investment institutions, 228, 241
Competition, 4, vii, 3, 6, 9, 11, 17, 18, 20, 41, 50, 54, 57, 64, 68, 81, 83, 94, 95, 96, 97, 98, 99, 100, 101, 115, 117, 122, 125, 137, 138, 148, 188, 192, 196, 222, 232, 245
Concentration, 10, 11, 66, 70, 81, 93, 94, 99, 100, 101, 102, 103, 104, 106, 108, 109, 111, 112, 113, 115, 116, 117, 132, 136, 191, 208
Consumer protection, 6, 50
Coverage, 143, 150, 194
Credit card market, ix, 12, 163, 164, 165, 167, 168, 169, 172, 173, 174
Credit Services, ix, 163, 173

D

Deregulation, viii, 10, 11, 16, 50, 121, 122, 125, 130, 136, 139
Derivative Instruments, 67, 73, 182, 191
Differential Premium System, 150
Duty losses, 20, 53, 57, 60, 97, 146

E

Economic Crisis, 143
Efficiency, 128, 130, 134, 138, 210
Entry performance, 124
Equity capital, 149, 208, 214, 215, 221
Exchange rate, 16, 18, 19, 20, 23, 53, 55, 56, 57, 58, 66, 67, 68, 78, 81, 137, 146, 154

Exchange traded funds, 188, 190, 236, 246

F

Financial and Operational Restructuring, 60
Financial discipline, 57, 58
Financial Liberalization, 53, 95, 130, 138
Financial market, vii, 3, 4, 10, 12, 49, 59, 70, 73, 94, 95, 117, 165, 180, 184, 226, 227, 235
Floating rate, 57, 58, 60, 67
Foreign investors, 227

G

Global Financial Crisis, 79, 142
Government deficit, 15, 26, 28, 30

H

Hedge funds, 181

I

Inflation targeting, 20, 23, 58
Institutional investors, 10, 238
Institutions, vii, viii, 3, 4, 8, 15, 34, 36, 37, 49, 50, 59, 61, 65, 67, 70, 73, 75, 82, 83, 94, 95, 97, 98, 122, 123, 124, 130, 135, 138, 141, 142, 148, 155, 156, 180, 181, 182, 183, 184, 185, 187, 189, 190, 191, 193, 194, 195, 196, 197, 201, 203, 204, 208, 228, 231, 232, 233, 236, 237, 238, 239, 241, 245
Interchange Fees, 168
Interest Rates, 16, 19, 53, 67, 69, 77, 203
International Financial Institutions, 15
Investment funds, 180, 230, 232, 234, 236, 237, 239, 242, 244
Investment trusts, x, 13, 225, 227, 237, 239, 241, 242, 244

L

Liberalization, 4, 16, 134
Life insurance companies, x, 13, 225, 227

Liquidity, 19, 24, 49, 52, 55, 56, 57, 62, 64, 67, 69, 73, 76, 77, 79, 80, 81, 98, 146, 149, 153, 189, 190, 194, 236, 237

M

Market Power, 101
Market structure, viii, 3, 8, 10, 11, 93, 94, 97, 99, 101, 104, 106, 108, 117, 138, 139
Merchant Discounts, 164, 167
Monetary policy, 23, 52, 55, 57, 58, 95, 97
Moral hazard, 3, 6, 50, 54, 117
Mutual funds, x, 13, 195, 197, 198, 225, 227, 229, 246

P

Payment Services, 164, 167, 173
Pension funds, 180, 226, 239
Portfolio management companies, 234
Price stability, 57, 58, 97
Privatization, 9, 16, 18, 23, 55, 57, 60, 135
Productivity, viii, ix, 10, 11, 13, 18, 34, 38, 121, 123, 124, 125, 126, 127, 128, 130, 132, 133, 134, 135, 136, 137, 139, 201, 202, 204, 208, 209, 212, 214, 215, 219, 221
Property rights, vii, 6, 10, 16, 18, 33, 34, 35, 37, 38, 44
Public Debt, 9, 18, 20, 23, 29, 74, 147, 158, 230, 239
Public finance, 27, 29, 55, 57, 59

R

Real estate investment trusts, x, 13, 225, 227, 241
Regulatory commitment, 7, 8, 9
Regulatory state, 10, 11
Rent seeking, 3, 44
Repatriation of Capital, 75
Restructuring, viii, 9, 11, 12, 20, 23, 24, 49, 51, 55, 56, 59, 60, 62, 63, 64, 68, 77, 78, 81, 93, 94, 97, 98, 117, 125, 141, 155, 156, 158, 159, 233
Risk Management, 50, 54, 55, 56, 59, 69, 70, 71, 72, 77, 79, 81, 83, 96, 97, 144, 145, 150, 153, 237
Risk premium, 53

S

Saving, 142, 203, 226, 234
Stabilization Program, 55
State banks, 20, 23, 53, 56, 57, 60, 61, 63, 96, 97, 134, 135
Strategic Plan, 144, 159
Structural Reforms, 19

T

Transformation, vii, 3, 10, 11, 15, 16, 17, 21, 30, 51, 58, 93, 106, 202
Twin Crises, 51

U

Uncertainty, 57, 64, 76, 105

V

Venture capital investment trusts, x, 13, 225, 227, 241